DUBLIN
TENEMENT
LIFE

AN ORAL HISTORY

By the same author

Georgian Dublin: Ireland's Imperilled Architectural Heritage
Dublin's Vanishing Craftsmen
Stoneybatter: Dublin's Inner Urban Village
Dublin Street Life and Lore: An Oral History
Dublin Pub Life and Lore: An Oral History

DUBLIN TENEMENT LIFE

AN ORAL HISTORY

Kevin C. Kearns

GILL & MACMILLAN

Gill & Macmillan Ltd
Goldenbridge
Dublin 8
with associated companies throughout the world
© Kevin C. Kearns 1994

0 7171 2468 1

First published in hardback 1994

This paperback edition first published 1996

Printed by ColourBooks Ltd, Dublin

A catalogue record for this book is available from the British Library.

5 4

For my sister, Happy, and brother, Joe

Dublin Tenements

These were the homes of those who pushed aside
The broken children of a sweeter race:
These are the cast-off garments of their pride
Because of whom a thousand heroes died:
Alien and sinister, these hold their place.

The light has died upon the pavements grey,
From shattered window and from blackened door
Where, in a sunny, heartless yesterday
Silken and jewelled beauty was at play,
Stare out the hopeless faces of the poor.

Oh, dark inheritors, who hither came,
The flotsam of that splendid brazen sea,
For taint on this your heirship ours the blame,
The shame that clouds your beauty is our shame,
On us and on our children it shall be.

You punish us with gifts. We brought defeat,
And stained with folly any grace we gave.
Our bauble gift that frothed upon the street
In artful silks and laces, you repeat
In foam of lovely childhood, wave on wave.

That surges all about the grimy walls,
That frolics round the doorways' evil gloom:
If heaven can smile above these ruined halls,
The light that crowns this shining wave recalls
The heaven that gave to Eden flowers their bloom.

Ah, must the story of our time record
The buds we mired and trampled in the sod?
Are these grey dwellings, shutting out the Lord,
The fairest nursery we could afford
For such bright blossoms of the Tree of God?

Susan L. Mitchell, in K. F. Purdon, *Dinny of the Doorstep*, (Dublin: Talbot Press, circa 1920)

"The history of a tenement house, fully told, might be as interesting as a passage in a novel and its gradual degradation shewn to be as terrible a tragedy."

Report of the Royal Sanitary Commission, 1880

"Dubliners are wont to describe their City affectionately as 'An old lady'. When visitors admire her outer garment—the broad streets, the old 18th century houses, Fitzwilliam Square and St Stephen's Green—they smile complacently and feel proud. Lift the hem of her outer silken garment, however, and you will find suppurating ulcers covered by stinking rags, for Dublin has the foulest slums of any town in Europe. Into these 'quaint old eighteenth century houses' the people are herded and live in conditions of horror."

Letter written by Dr Robert Collis to the editor of The *Irish Press*, 3 October 1936

Contents

ACKNOWLEDGMENTS   xiii

INTRODUCTION   1

1. HISTORY AND EVOLUTION OF THE TENEMENT SLUM PROBLEM   6
   Physical Deterioration   8
   Profiteering Landlords and Powerless Tenants   10
   Overcrowding, Sanitation, and Illness   12
   Social Stigmas and Stereotypes   14
   The Press and Public Enlightenment   17
   Housing Reform and Slum Clearance   20
   Oral History and Tenement Folklore   22

2. SOCIAL LIFE IN THE TENEMENT COMMUNITIES   25
   Community Spirit and Gregarious Nature   25
   The Home Setting   27
   Economic Struggle   29
   Securing Food and Clothing   32
   Health, Sickness, and Treatments   35
   Entertainment and Street Life   39
   Religion and Morals   43
   Courting, Marriage, and Childbirth   46
   The Role of Men, Mothers, and Grannies   49
   Drinking, Gambling, Prostitution, and Animal Gangs   51
   Death, Superstitions, and Wakes   57

3. ORAL TESTIMONY: THE MONTO AND DOCKLAND   61

4. ORAL TESTIMONY: THE LIBERTIES   93

5. ORAL TESTIMONY: THE NORTHSIDE   155

6. FOUR TENEMENT TALES   184
   Mary Doolan of Francis Street   184
   Noel Hughes of North King Street   192
   Mary Corbally of Corporation Street   202
   May Hanaphy of Golden Lane   210

NOTES   221

BIBLIOGRAPHY   226

INDEX   232

Acknowledgments

From the outset, the research for this book proved to be a great challenge. Tracking down surviving tenement dwellers from the early days of this century required some resourceful detective work. This could not have been accomplished without the generous assistance of many individuals scattered throughout the old neighbourhoods of inner Dublin. The entire process of field research, oral history taping, transcribing, and writing took three years. Gratitude is extended to the following persons for their invaluable contributions to this book: Mick Rafferty; John Gallagher; fellow writer Mairin Johnston; Bernie Pierce of the Lourdes Centre for old folks; Paula Howard, librarian for the Gilbert Collection at the Pearse Street Library; and Michael Rush, director of the North Inner City Folklore Project. I owe special thanks to good friend and research assistant Kim McCulloch for tireless effort in the quest to find and tape record survivors of the bygone tenement days. Appreciation is also extended to the American Philosophical Society and the University of Northern Colorado Research and Publications Committee for their grant support. Particular acknowledgment is due to the National Geographic Society for its support and financial funding for this project.

Introduction

In 1805 the Reverend James Whitelaw in his *Essay on the Population of Dublin* recorded with alarm that the insidious seeds of tenement dwellings were taking root across the cityscape. Drawing upon his visitations to rooms which were like "styes", he graphically wrote:

"I have frequently surprised from ten to fifteen persons in a room not fifteen feet square, stretched on a wad of filthy straw, swarming with vermin, and without covering, save the wretched rags that constitute their wearing apparel . . . a degree of filth and stench inconceivable, except by such as have visited those scenes of wretchedness."[1]

For nearly 150 years the squalid tenement rows stood conspicuously throughout Dublin as a physical blight, political scandal, and moral outrage. Indeed, they were proclaimed "Ireland's most pitiable and heart-breaking tragedy".[2] By the 1930s Dublin's dilapidated tenements were deemed the "worst slums in Europe".[3]

The decline of Georgian Dublin from elegant abodes of the aristocracy to "human piggeries" is one of Dublin's saddest sagas. Myriad historical events contributed to the process of degeneration. A major factor was the Act of Union in 1801 and the dissolution of the Irish Parliament which triggered a mass exodus of wealthy and prominent citizens. The departing gentry left their grand domiciles to be managed by agents as property values began a precipitous decline. Resplendent Georgian houses purchased for £8,000 in 1791 were sold for a paltry £500 in the 1840s. At mid-century when Ireland was in the cruel grip of the Great Hunger the spacious structures fell increasingly into the hands of the "profiteering landlords" who gradually came to rule the dark Dublin slums. The downtrodden masses carried out what has been aptly termed the "colonisation" of the brick Georgian terraces.[4] Rack-renting landlords viewed their properties as little more than cattle sheds to be packed with humanity. As the "respectable" classes fled to the suburbs in the second half of the nineteenth century entire districts fell into tenement "slumdom". In 1900 there were over six thousand tenement houses in Dublin and one-third of the entire population lived in these "foul rookeries".[5] By 1938 there were still 6,307 tenements in the

1

capital occupied by 111,950 persons.[6] A paradoxical scene was fashioned in which the impoverished families were huddled together thick as cockroaches amidst bestial squalor in the same ornate chambers where upper-crust society had once dressed in silken finery, dined lavishly, and danced the minuet in carefree manner.

The living conditions of many tenement dwellers were hellish. Their buildings were decayed, dangerous, and sometimes collapsed, killing occupants. Conditions of overcrowding were appalling. Some tenement areas had 800 people to the acre, as many as a hundred persons in one house, and fifteen to twenty family members in a single tiny room. A primitive toilet and water tap in the rear yard had to serve all the inhabitants of a house. Amid such suffocating humanity and lack of sanitation it is small wonder that the tenements were condemned as "multitudinous fever nests and death traps".[7] In 1898 an investigative article in *The Daily Nation* revealed that twice as many people died of tuberculosis in Dublin as in London and the Irish capital had the highest overall death rate of any city in the United Kingdom.[8] In 1904 Sir Charles Cameron, Chief Health Inspector of Dublin, published his shocking report on *How the Poor Live* in which he documented the hunger, malnutrition, disease, congestion, and lack of clothing suffered by the lower classes. Many, he noted, literally subsisted on bread and tea in rooms that were "fetid haunts of horror".[9] By the dawn of the twentieth century the tenements were accepted as a "traditional feature" of Dublin.[10] As one distressed observer commented, "Irish folk have come, through long use, to regard Dublin slums as something normal, inevitable."[11]

Dublin's slums existed well into the late 1940s, a powerful indictment of government neglect and ineptitude. As one of the most contentious issues in Irish society for many generations, the tenement problem had become a "standard topic" of examination by Royal Commissions, Corporation surveys, Health Congresses, and other inquiry boards.[12] While the documents issued by these groups contained information and statistics on the tenements they were essentially sterile, clinical reports based on observational conclusions, quite devoid of "humanistic" insights to the daily life, struggle, and emotions of the dwellers themselves.

Joseph O'Brien in his book *Dear, Dirty Dublin* explores the tenement problem early in the 1900s and laments:

> "What little we know of the domestic arrangements of their inhabitants comes down to us second-hand from the witnesses of their misfortune in reports that were often coloured by moral outrage and human sympathy to stir the social conscience, yet still suggestive of the grim realities."[13]

He reasons that while the literary Dublin of Joyce and Yeats has been much admired and glorified, the "nether world of the tenement . . . one that evokes harsher images" has been largely ignored because it was "a disgrace to civilisation".[14] While writers such as Sean O'Casey and James Plunkett depicted fragments of tenement life in fictionalised form, academic scholars were notably negligent. Professor F. H. A. Aalen of Trinity College notes with regret that the social life of the tenement folk has been "almost totally neglected by historians and geographers".[15]

Simply put, there exists no first-hand authentic chronicle of Dublin tenement life as experienced by one-third of the city's population during the first half of this century. In terms of social history this is a regrettable omission because the tenement dwellers had a distinct social milieu, possessed a unique ethos, and developed a remarkably cohesive community rich and complex in its customs, traditions, neighbouring patterns, survival strategies, and urban folklore. However, as anthropologist Messenger explains, we cannot learn about these innate features of tenement life from official reports because they are based on information and impressions "filtered through the minds of out-siders looking in". To reconstruct historical reality we must seek to record the personal "missing portions of the picture of life" within a social community.[16] In the case of Dublin's tenement enclaves what is conspicuously missing from the historical scene is credible verbal testimony about daily life patterns by those who were looking out from behind the grim brick walls.

Only through the oral historical method can we reliably capture life experiences of tenement folk. This means seeking out and tape-recording original oral testimony from the survivors of the tenements, those born and reared in the dingy rooms nearly three-quarters of a century ago. Collectively, they comprise an invaluable repository of oral social history and urban lore which should be preserved for future generations. Most are now "old-timers" between sixty and ninety years of age, a vanishing breed of Dubliner from the hard days early in the century. Yet their memories remain remarkably vivid for, as Kelly avows, the "people who lived in them, those who survived, will never forget them . . . for you never forget the feeling of a tenement . . . never quite get the smell of a tenement out of your nostrils."[17] As pioneering oral historian Thompson explains, by gathering oral evidence from these "under-classes, the defeated" we truly democratise history by recording the experiences and perspectives of the urban poor themselves.[18] Their oral accounts constitute an important supplement to the sketchy and superficial written records of external investigative groups.

In recent years a new genre of memoirs about Dublin in the "rare ould times" has appeared. Some of these works, such as Mairin Johnston's *Around the Banks of Pimlico* are excellent in their accuracy. Many, however, are tainted by what has been criticised as a "blinding nostalgia" in which the author endeavours to "sanitise the past" by describing life as it should have been.[19] The historic realities of glaring poverty and human suffering are too often con-veniently omitted. By contrast, the avowed purpose of this book is to create an authentic and wholly original chronicle of Dublin tenement community life based on the oral histories of the last surviving dwellers.

To be sure, the oral accounts by the many individuals featured in this book are not sanitised or rosily sentimentalised reminiscences—but the hard truths. As seventy-five year old Mary Doolan of the Liberties so bluntly puts it, "They weren't the good old days, they were *brutal* days." This was confirmed back in 1936 during her childhood by an article in the *Irish Press* declaring that "in the slums the ancient code of survival of the fittest holds true."[20] Hers was indeed a hard world of unemployment, hunger, evictions, illness, heavy drinking, abusive husbands, street brawling, animal gangs and prostitution. Yet, in dramatic contrast to this stereotypically dark and dismal image of tenement life there also existed a marvellously vibrant, close-knit social community in which the poor indisputably found great security and happiness. It is principally the story of this facet of Dublin tenement life which has never been adequately told.

Paddy Casey, a policeman on the roughest northside beat half a century ago, recalls that tenement dwellers were *"extraordinarily happy* for people who were so savagely poor", an observation often made by outsiders. This seemingly incongruous human condition is explained by the closeness and security the poor found in their tightly-knit community. Family ties were strong and neighbours unfailingly looked after one another. It was a custom in the tenements that people cared for those around them—feeding the hungry, sharing fuel and clothing, nursing the sick, comforting the dying, waking the dead, and taking in orphans. Women were especially known for their kindness and self-sacrificing acts of generosity. Says eighty-three year old Moore Street dealer Lizzy Byrne, "Oh, their hearts were as big as themselves." Another salient trait of the poor was their deep pride and dignity. Commonly they rejected assistance from outside sources even when their need was dire. When times were hardest they always found solace in their religion and community.

In his 1918 book entitled *Dublin Types*, Sidney Davies not only praised this close "communal life" of the tenement population but marvelled at the "unruffled cheerfulness and good humour" of the poor, despite their daily hardships.[21] The exuberant social life of the tenements was widely renowned and the people famed for their raw wit, rousing hooleys, and spirited wakes which became a part of Dublin's urban folklore. And the cobblestoned streets were always alive and teeming with children playing games and delighting in acts of devilment, while shawled women clustered at doorways animatedly chatting and sharing delicious gossip. Men enjoyed great camaraderie with their pub mates, played cards beneath gas lamps, and held "toss schools" down hidden lanes. Always a major feature of social life was impromptu singing and dancing, be it at a doorfront or out in the street. The scene was enlivened by a colourful cast of local characters, balladeers, and buffoons. In the truest sense, the tenement streets were a grandiose stage upon which all sundried sort of human drama was enacted. The cry of a good "ruggy-up" between bellicose women street dealers or sodden pub mates would bring all humanity streaming from the tenements to watch the free show. Never, the people swear, was there a dull moment in the tenements.

Elizabeth "Bluebell" Murphy, now seventy-six years of age, was born and reared in the notorious Monto district. She knew well all the agonies and joys of tenement life but what she remembers most profoundly is that a person was *never alone and neglected.* Within the tenement community everyone felt loved and cared for—secure. Now living in an inner-city flat on the northside and feeling lonely and estranged from the outside world she quietly confides:

> "It was a hard life . . . but I wish I was back in the tenement again. We were all one family, all close. We all helped one another. If I had a tenement house now I'd go back and live in it . . . yes, I would."

This is not mere nostalgia but a genuine longing for the communal security she knew earlier in life. This same sentiment is often expressed by her peers.

In seeking to capture the true heart and spirit of the old tenement community the individuals whose oral histories are featured in this book were allowed to tell the tales in their own inimitable manner. No novelist could contrive the purity and poignancy of their vernacular. While lengthy narratives were condensed and organised for literary cohesion, their words and expressions remain unchanged. If their testimonies are sometimes tragic and emotionally wrenching they are also inspiring, humorous, joyful. The astonishing range of personal life experiences shared by these individuals creates a rich human mosaic of the bygone tenement world. In essence, this book is their collective story—an oral historical chronicle of struggle, survival, and a splendid triumph of the human spirit.

1

History and Evolution of the Tenement Slum Problem

*"Like most Irish questions the slum evil has a long history behind it.
It is a legacy of alien rule. It is the fruit of generations of neglect
and civic blindness."*

Irish Press, *1 October 1936*

The origin of tenements in Dublin may be traced back as far as the sixteenth century when the population probably did not exceed sixty thousand. Gilbert's *Calendar of Ancient Records of Dublin* makes reference to a law in 1556 stating that "none shall divide the dwelling-houses of this City into sundry rooms for their private gain without the warrant of the Mayor and six Aldermen."[1] This clearly suggests that civic authorities were already experiencing problems with tenement houses. In 1798 a house-to-house census conducted by the Reverend James Whitelaw and his assistants confirmed that tenement dwellings were well established in the city. His report revealed that two-thirds of the city's population of 172,000 were of the "lower class", most of whom lived in "truly wretched habitations . . . crowded together to a degree distressing to humanity".[2] He commonly found thirty to fifty individuals living in a single house and in Braithwaite Street he personally counted 108 inhabitants in one tenement.

While Dublin was noted for its slums well before the nineteenth century, the tenement process was greatly accelerated after the Act of Union in 1801. Directly following the dissolution of the Irish Parliament there occurred a mass exodus of prominent citizens who had occupied the stately and spacious Georgian houses. The terraces and squares of Georgian mansions were built largely for the Anglo-Irish gentry during the reign of monarchs from George I to George IV (1714–1830).[3] They were two-to five-storey brick structures splendidly ornamented with ornate plasterwork ceilings, marble fireplaces, mahogany woodwork, and elegant doorways and fanlights. They represented a glorious period of architectural achievement and social life in Dublin but when the aristocracy departed they left behind their grand homes to be managed by agents. Property values plummeted dramatically. Resplendent Georgian abodes purchased for £8,000 in 1791 sold for £2,500 a mere decade later and by 1849 could be bought for a paltry £500.[4]

During the great famine and its aftermath Dublin became the principal urban catch-basin for the desperate masses fleeing the rural districts. Between 1841 and 1900 the population of Ireland declined but that of Dublin increased from 236,000 to 290,000. Consequently, during the second half of the nineteenth century competition for housing among the city's expanding poor was intense. The conspicuously spacious Georgian houses abandoned by their original owners provided the logical solution for the city's lower classes who were simply seeking "an enclosed space to sleep in and shelter their bodies from the elements".[5] Once the grand domiciles had depreciated sufficiently in value they were grabbed up by what the Irish Press aptly called the "despotic and merciless" slum landlords.[6]

Under this new breed of rentier the houses of the nobility were put to dramatically new use. The expansive quarters were crudely converted into multiple single-room dwellings and crammed full with poor families. A typical Georgian house could hold from fifty to eighty persons. As the burgeoning poor class systematically "colonised" the Georgian rows their "social superiors moved to more commodious dwellings with pleasanter surroundings" in the suburbs.[7] As Aalen explains, the "retreat of the wealthy and advance of the poor fed upon one another" leading to a progressive segregation between the tenement slums and surrounding respectable residential areas.[8] Within the inner-city there were surviving "pockets of gentility" around the Georgian Squares and adjacent streets. But the remaining middle and upper classes feared the encroachment of the lower social elements as the "decay spread block by block and street by street . . . whole terraces lapsed into tenements."[9] Even the most formerly fashionable residences fell victim. Henrietta Street, known as Primate's Hill in the eighteenth century because of the number of Church of Ireland bishops who resided there, still retained its prestige in the 1840s but by the 1870s had degenerated into common tenement houses. Similarly, Dominick Street, still predominantly middle-class in the 1860s, had fallen into sordid slumdom only twenty years later. In 1889 an article in The Irish Builder described this degeneration:

"The history and fate of thousands of fine old well-built private mansions in Dublin is a chequered and sad one—for go where you will, either north and south of this city, streets of houses will be found now occupied as tenements. The evil is yearly enlarging and there are large districts now possible of being mapped out where this tenement property has become long blocks and lines of rookeries and chronic fever-nests. The evil has grown so gigantic that the Corporation are powerless to grapple with it in its entirety."[10]

By the close of the century Dublin's tenement districts had deteriorated into what were known as "slumlands". Certain sections of the city were especially noted for their squalor. The slums along Church Street, Beresford Street, Cumberland Street, Railway Street, Gardiner Street, Corporation Street and on Mary's Lane and Cole's Lane were particularly appalling. The worst tenement slums around the Liberties were on the Coombe and on Francis Street, Cork Street, Chamber Street, and Kevin Street. These slumlands "in their most hideous forms hovering on the very edge of respectable life" were perceived by the higher classes as a malevolent cancer threatening to engulf all of inner-Dublin unless somehow thwarted.[11] Indeed, by 1900 fully one-third of Dublin's population, some 21,747 families, lived in single-room dwellings in 6,196 tenements, many condemned by the Corporation as "unfit for human habitation."[12] Dublin had a higher proportion of poor than any other city in the British Isles as the rows of dilapidated tenement houses had become a "traditional feature" of the urban landscape.[13]

PHYSICAL DETERIORATION

"Slums are to be found, large and small, dotting the city like so many ugly plague marks."
The Daily Nation, *5 September 1898*

It was during the second half of the nineteenth century that the tenement houses suffered their greatest deterioration and decay.[14] Since Dublin nestles in the basin of a river estuary, the air above the city was naturally trapped in the polluted mist of sulphuric acid formed from the high sulphur content of the soft bituminous coal burned at that time. The honeycomb pattern of the lofty Georgian terraces proved a magnet for catching and retaining the acid-laden polluted smoke, mists, and rain which charred and corroded the brick exteriors. Exterior slates, roof-fastenings, lead sheathings, and guttering also yielded to acidified rain. Moisture penetrated brickwork, weakening parapets, pock-marking walls, and eventually entering timber supports. Houses were also attacked from within. Deeply excavated basements drew ground water and, added to the existing warm, moist air from normal cooking and laundering activities, this created an atmosphere of extreme dampness which penetrated roof timbers, floor-boards, wall foundations and led to dry rot and woodwork infestation. To combat such physical decay was highly expensive and only the remaining wealthy residents of Georgian houses were able to retain their property in prime form. Tenement landlords had neither the financial resources nor the will to do so.

The rapacious process of tenementation itself ravaged the interiors of buildings. Converting a large Georgian home into partitioned rooms for perhaps a dozen families meant drastically altering interior frame-works and stripping away fittings. During hard winters desperate tenants would tear out floor-boards and banisters for firewood. Succeeding generations of slum dwellers each took their toll on the property. By 1900 the tenement houses, then mostly between 100 and 150 years old, typically suffered from corroded brickwork, leaky roofs, sagging ceilings, rotting floor-boards and woodwork, cracked walls, crumbling fireplaces, broken windows, rickety staircases—general decay within and without.

Tenements were also highly dangerous. The multiple families in each house had to do their cooking and heating on an open grate with coal, wood and turf. The flying sparks and burning embers created a high fire risk. It was proclaimed by knowledgeable authorities that "practically all slum dwellings are fire-traps," a constant concern to parents.[15] Tenement fires were all too common. Also, the arthritic, brittle brick buildings could collapse without warning. In fact, many of the houses were so structurally feeble that it was feared that any efforts to make repairs or install water pipes might cause their downfall. One on-site inspection revealed that the situation was so precarious that "a wall might fall if you were hammering a nail to hang a picture."[16] Several tragic tenement collapses occurred early in the century. In 1902 a three-storey tenement on Townsend Street suddenly gave away and "buried two families" who inhabited rooms in the upper portion.[17] On Cumberland Street in 1909 another house toppled to the ground killing one man. The most publicised case was that of two rotten tenement houses on Church Street which completely collapsed in 1913 with an "awful suddenness", killing seven persons and injuring several others.[18] This loss of life shocked Dubliners and generated public outcry for an investigation focusing on the Dublin Corporation which was responsible for the safety of tenement-ridden Dublin and whose inspectors had recently examined the two houses. As *The Irish Times* acerbically put it:

> "In spite of all the inspecting work of the Corporation's officers, the two houses were allowed to stand until they gave magic proof of their dangerous character by killing seven people. We shall never be safe from the tenement slums of Dublin until they became an evil memory. Abolition is the only cure."[19]

Profiteering Landlords and Powerless Tenants

"Never in the history of the slums have the worst landlords had a gayer time."

T. W. Dillon, Studies, 1945

Historical events created the tenements but it was the profiteering landlords who actually operated the tenement housing system. The Georgian buildings were purchased by a "new race of speculating landlords" who lorded over the poor like tyrants.[20] They held the power to set rates, define occupancy terms, and evict tenants. Fear of the landlords gripped many tenement dwellers throughout their lives. As Dillon found, "Most of the tenants contrive by hook or by crook, by semi-starvation, to pay the rent at all costs rather than fall into the power of these ruthless men."[21] To cross one's landlord was to invite harsh retribution and possible expulsion into the cold, cobblestoned street. In 1899 there were about three hundred evictions granted every week in the police courts and countless more unrecorded, illegal evictions. Manipulative landlords also carried out what was termed "rent slavery" by coercing the poorest tenants into cleaning yards and toilets, collecting rents, and performing other unpleasant tasks for them.[22] Throughout the entire tenement period the exploitative landlords were perceived as villains. Even the Reverend Whitelaw nearly two centuries ago saw landlords as the "greatest brutes in the stye . . . money-grabbing wretches who live in affluence in a distant part of the city".[23]

Landlords were notorious not only for their rack-renting practices but also blatant neglect of basic maintenance and repairs of their properties. Leaking roofs, clogged toilets, broken water taps, and dangerous stairways were ignored. Tenants were reluctant to complain about conditions and request repairs for fear of having their rent raised. The Dublin Corporation failed, generation after generation, to force negligent landlords to improve their properties, arguing that the legal complexities of the landlords' ownership system along with subletting practices were so great that it was difficult to assign blame and responsibility to any particular party. It was also noted that many landlords of the worst tenements were themselves "almost paupers" and had no funds to spend on maintenance.[24] But the most persuasive rationale regularly forwarded by the Corporation was that if they carried out the laws condemning and closing dilapidated tenement houses it would lead to large-scale homelessness.

In 1901 an uncommonly critical article in *The Irish Builder* cited the "greed of the owners who extract the last farthing from their unfortunate and demoralised tenants", demanding that the personal identity of all Dublin landlords be made public:

"These speculative middlemen, a curse to society, are generally entirely lost to any sense of responsibility and seeking only to continually evade their liabilities under the law. It would surprise many people not intimately acquainted with the tenement system in Dublin were the names of these owners made public, for many there would be found figuring in the list who are looked upon as eminently useful citizens and leaders of public opinion . . . every tenement house should, like a vehicle plying for hire, bear in some prominent portion a notice setting forth the name and address of its owner, who would be directly responsible."[25]

The threat of such public disclosure was gravely unsettling to many landlords who had carefully kept their identity concealed. These tenement owners were to be found in every stratum of society. The majority probably belonged to the class of small businessmen but there had long been strong suspicion that many tenements were owned by prominent businessmen and even politicians. The 1913 Dublin Housing Inquiry finally confirmed that members of the Corporation itself, as well as five Aldermen and eleven Councillors, were tenement owners.[26] In a later powerful exposé of landlord rack-renting and other abuses the *Irish Press* revealed that the slum dweller "cannot himself take any effective measures" to compel the landlord to act responsibly since "between the landlord and the tenant stand, buffer-like, the Sanitation Officers and the Corporation administration."[27] Since only the Corporation could enforce laws pertaining to tenement properties tenants were utterly powerless to improve their living environment. The Dublin Corporation itself was clearly identified as one of the most egregious landlords in the city:

"And let it not be forgotten that Dublin Corporation is one of the biggest, if not the biggest, slum landlords in Dublin. It is difficult for the Corporation effectively to give itself notice to comply with its own by-laws. It would be Gilbertian if it were not tragic!"[28]

Occasionally, tenement property was so conspicuously dangerous that landlords were actually ordered to act in correcting the condition. For example, in 1899 a landlord who owned horrifying tenements in Cole's Lane was forced by law to put them in a "civilised condition".[29] The summons showed that the dwellings had virtually no sanitary facilities and a staircase only twenty-five inches wide with no hand rails or lighting. But if a few landlords were made to improve their properties the vast majority went their merry way free from government interference. In response to a newspaper article critical of his ilk, one Dublin landlord defiantly wrote, "If you wish to do the people good, teach them to be content with what the Almighty sends them."[30] Such insensitivity to the suffering of tenants explains why the landlords, as a class, were so feared and despised by the poor. However, it should be noted that the oral testimony of tenement dwellers confirms that some landlords were decent and kind-hearted men.

OVERCROWDING, SANITATION, AND ILLNESS

"In the homes of the very poor the seeds of infective diseases are nursed as it were in a hothouse."

Sir Charles Cameron, Reminiscences, *1913*

The greatest threat to health and life did not come from building collapse or fire but from the sickness and disease which were so prevalent among the tenement population. Owing to the deadly combination of overcrowding, poor diet, and lack of sanitation, illnesses ran rampant as the tenements were declared "multitudinous fever nests and death traps". Indeed, by the end of the nineteenth century Dublin had the highest infant mortality level and general death rate of any city in the United Kingdom.

Appalling overcrowding set the stage for maladies of all sorts. Dublin's overall density of 38.5 persons per acre was nearly twice that of the twenty largest cities in Great Britain. In Dublin's four most congested wards the density statistics were astonishingly high: Inns Quay 103; Rotunda 113; Mountjoy 127; and Wood Quay 138.[31] In the worst tenement localities there were 800 people to the acre and as many as a hundred occupants in a single house. Here it was common to find fifteen to twenty persons in one room and eight sleeping in a bed. Some rooms were found to be less than six feet by four and labelled "styes" and "coffins" by witnesses.[32]

One shocked investigator, upon seeing how this "flotsam of humanity" was herded like beasts into pens, declared that "Even homelessness is preferable to some of these wretched abodes in which they live."[33] In 1897 the Chairman of the Sanitary Commission went so far as to proclaim that "They are not fit for animals to live in, much less human beings."[34] In actuality, the existing By-Laws affecting buildings under the Public Health Acts of 1878 and 1890 guaranteed that Irish animals have a generous amount of space, fresh air and water far greater than that provided to the majority of tenement dwellers. For example, it was decreed that "Every shed for horses or horned cattle shall assure each animal therein standing space of not less than six feet by three and a half feet."[35] Paradoxically, tenement families were "herded together" far more tightly than livestock and with less healthy breathing space and water rights.

Combined with the human congestion was a dreadful lack of sanitation. Tenements typically had a single primitive toilet and water tap in the rear yard for use by the hordes of tenants. The "dark, evil smelling, disgusting" privies were abominable and hazardous to health.[36] Some were no more than holes ten to fifteen feet in the ground surrounded by a crude hut and with no means of flushing-out or cleaning. Every family also had its "slop" bucket for night-time use which had to be discreetly disposed of each morning and it was common to find human excreta scattered about the yards and hallway passages. Privies and ashpits sometimes became infested with typhoid germs and yards were regularly flooded with stagnant water and waste creating an environment in which flies, insects, and vermin thrived. Sewer slugs and "clocks" (cockroaches) were so numerous that mothers often filled bottles with them to take to local Health Officers as evidence of what they had to contend with each day. Multiple layers of decomposing wallpaper provided a perfect sanctuary for colonies of insects while rats as big as cats nested in rotting floor-boards and roamed freely at night, even entering beds of nursing mothers and their infants, drawn by the scent of milk.

In 1936 there were an estimated 1,600 families living in dark, damp basements where seepage from sewer pipes commonly emitted poisonous gases. Basement tenancy was regarded as the lowest and most dangerous form of tenement life. Here the poorest of the poor resided in what were often no more than subterranean caves. One doctor visiting such a dwelling found it so dark that he could not even see across the room at noon time. Upon examining the children he found a condition in their eyes which "resembled miners who work in the dark".[37] Inspectors and newspaper reporters confronted with the filth, foul air, human stench, and vermin sometimes became physically ill. Wrote one such distressed reporter for *The Daily Nation* in 1898:

> "I had seen many disagreeable sights in my slumming experiences but none so disgusting as the inhabitants of this horrible den of filth, reeking with every sort of abominable odour . . . a picture of squalor and misery such as, I trust, I shall never be compelled to gaze upon again."[38]

Part of the problem, it was argued, was that the Dublin Corporation had a staff of only thirty Sanitary Officers to visit the homes of 32,000 families in the city. Furthermore, there were but four lady Sanitary Officers whose duty it was to advise tenement women about keeping their rooms, children, clothes, and bedding clean. Even when Sanitary Officers dispensed advice there was little that most mothers could do to improve their home sanitary conditions. Some women were so ashamed of their setting that they declined to invite the local priest in to consecrate their home. Thus, their impoverished condition deprived them of even this small religious comfort.

The most prevalent illnesses afflicting the poor were tuberculosis, diphtheria, smallpox, typhoid, pneumonia, whooping cough, respiratory ailments, rheumatic arthritis, and diarrhoeal diseases. Contagious diseases naturally spread like wildfire amid such congestion. Tuberculosis sometimes wiped out entire families. Sickness and premature death were an accepted part of life in the tenements. In fact, most families suffered the loss of one or more children before they reached the age of six. Many people simply lacked the strength to resist sickness. As Cameron explained, poor diet and malnutrition "lay the foundation for future delicacy of their constitution and renders them less liable to resist attacks of disease".[39] The basic diet consisted of bread, tea, oatmeal, cocoa, potatoes, cabbage, herrings, and parings off cheap pieces of meat for stews and soups. Meals provided little real nourishment and were sometimes barely sufficient to maintain life itself. By the 1930s it was determined that over the generations there had developed within the general tenement population a form of congenital debility which weakened their natural resistance to sickness.[40] The general death rate in the inner-city was double that of the outside neighbourhoods, thus applying to the dark tenements the old proverb that "where the sun does not go, the doctor goes."

Children, naturally, were the most helpless victims. In the 1920s the infant mortality rate (death of infants under age one) was 116 per thousand, a figure five times higher than among the children of the healthy suburbs.[41] About 20 per cent of all deaths in the inner-city occurred among those less than a year old and nearly all of these were among the poorer classes. Even those infants who did survive their first year faced an ongoing struggle to sustain life amid their unhealthy surroundings. An article in the *Irish Press* which described the "slaughter of the innocents in those germ-soaked dens and rookeries" elicited great public compassion:

> "The hereditary tenement waif's chances of survival to manhood or womanhood are so slight . . . the little ones, flecked with a beauty of their own, which gives a deeper tinge of pathos to their unhappy plight, die like flowers in a blight when they are stricken by disease which is always laying in wait for them."[42]

In 1932 there was a highly publicised case in which a tenement mother submitted a photograph of her eight-month old baby in an *Irish Independent* newspaper baby competition and won a prize. Her baby was admired by the judges for her "cherubic countenance and strong healthy body" and deemed one of "Dublin's loveliest babies".[43] Four years later it was found that the same child had been reduced to a "frail little wraith of humanity that walked apathetically by her (mother's) side . . . as the four years of slum life had wilted this flower of the tenements beyond recognition".[44]

SOCIAL STIGMAS AND STEREOTYPES

*"Do the slums make the slum people,
or the slum people make the slums?"*

P. *Cowan,* Report on Dublin Housing, *1918*

During the Victorian period and well into the twentieth century this vexing question was central to the debate over the tenement slums. Many Victorian social reformers believed that it was an inherent moral indolence that caused the poor to live in such "uncivilised" conditions. As a consequence, tenement dwellers were often negatively stigmatised and stereotyped as an inferior class.

In the minds of the higher classes the squalid slums were a "natural habitat" for the poor. Even the well-intentioned Reverend Whitelaw recorded in 1798 that he found the poor "apparently at ease and perfectly assimilated to their habitations . . . filth and stench seem congenial to their nature."[45] Such notions that the plight of the poor was attributable to fate or their own indolent character were comforting since they assuaged the conscience of the upper classes and freed them from guilt and responsibility. In 1907 a Miss Roney, writing in the *Journal of Social and Statistical Inquiry Society of Ireland*, reminded her readers that Darwin linked the moral qualities of people directly to their environment, and thus asserted:

"A class will exist in the crowded poor districts, indifferent to insalubrity, harmonising with their surroundings, and sunk in ignorance. Even when change means improvement this class abhors it . . . they prefer the old insanitary rookeries to the modern comforts of block dwellings."[46]

The lower classes inhabiting the tenements were regarded by some as a sort of curious social species to be examined by their superiors. One Dublin Housing Inquiry report determined that "Dublin slum-dwellers must be studied on the spot by those who have a sympathetic interest in them."[47] In Victorian society it actually became fashionable for upper-crust "do-gooders" to visit slum families in their fetid rooms so that they could later issue pious and compassionate pronouncements about what they had observed. One such woman, identified as "Elizabeth, Countess of Fingal" from Earlsfort Mansions, decided to visit a nearby tenement house and wrote "I went to see an old woman . . . I saw a tiny room and a bed I would not like my dog to lie on."[48] Similarly, in 1898 Mrs Tolerton, Secretary of the Philanthropic Reform Association, felt it her Christian duty to observe the poor in their own quarters. In a piece entitled "The Views of a Dublin Lady" she wrote of having witnessed "indescribably filthy conditions and the suffering of children" and expressed a "deep concern" and hope for betterment of their condition.[49] Such sympathetic platitudes were typically offered by outsiders whose hasty visitations were superficial and wholly detached from the realities of daily life of the inhabitants upon whom they intruded.

In the 1890s some ladies from Alexandra College, upon being encouraged to undertake "useful work" in addition to their academic studies, decided to carry out a social experiment in which they purchased several tenement houses, put them in good order, and let them out to families so that they could observe first-hand the social behaviour of the poor. In what surely must have been a curious clash of cultures, it was recorded with pride that the college women "stood by the rocking horse and gave rides to the small children" in raggedy garb while others tried to teach the boys and girls how to play various games. In one experiment where dolls were given to the little girls it led to a display of social behaviour which unsettled some of the ladies of Alexandra:

"Little girls sat by the fire rapturously nursing the dolls, while their brothers more often gave the dolls very rough treatment. One urchin was seen to snatch a doll from his sister, and after threatening it to 'remember now that I'm your husband', then proceeded to enforce his marital rights by knocking its head violently and repeatedly against the door post."[50]

Surely the most fascinating and incongruous visit by an outsider to the Dublin slums was that in 1885 of the Prince of Wales, afterwards King Edward VII, who came to Dublin in his capacity of Chairman of the Commission relating to the dwellings of the working classes. Charles Cameron, Chief Health Officer of Dublin, suggested that since the Prince had already seen the impressive model artisans' dwellings for the working classes he also "ought to see some of the wretched dwellings in which the poor lived".[51] Although members of his entourage initially felt that it might not be safe for the Prince to visit such blighted slums it was finally agreed that he would do so, but strictly *incognito*. At eleven one morning the Prince, accompanied by the Princess of Wales and the Duke of Clarence, left Dublin Castle in a plain carriage and proceeded to one of the worst slums in nearby Golden Lane. As Cameron recorded in his autobiography it was a remarkable event:

"I knew that the Prince, if recognised, would be well received, for the poorer classes in Dublin have generous instincts and would respect any visitor who with kind intentions would come amongst them. Just as we stopped at a large tenement house a woman discharged into the channel course a quantity of water in which cabbage had been boiling and which contained fragments of leaves. In getting out of the carriage the Duke of Clarence unfortunately stepped into this fluid, slipped, and fell. He was much startled and his coat and one glove were soiled. It soon leaked out that the Prince of Wales was in Golden Lane and an immense crowd assembled within a few minutes. I never witnessed greater enthusiasm than was exhibited by those poor denizens of the slum. Many of them shook hands with the Prince and all cheered loudly. One ragged boy familiarly took the Prince by the arm and inquired what he was looking for. The Prince took all this, including the Duke's contretemps, with great good humour, and in visiting the rooms he left something behind which delighted its recipients."[52]

Apart from the occasional visitations by authorities and dignitaries, the upper classes had little personal exposure to the poor. There existed a social segregation between the tenement dwellers and other social classes even when they were in close proximity to one another. The only knowledge many Dubliners had of the poor was based on an occasional glimpse down a disreputable street from a safe distance. Slum dwellers largely kept to the security of their home neighbourhoods while outside classes seldom entered the dark tenement terraces. The resulting lack of social contact is verified by Jimmy McLoughlin who grew up in the worst slums on Marlborough Place:

"Actually, I think my house was the nearest tenement to Nelson's Pillar, so we were near a better area. But we never played on O'Connell Street . . . it wasn't *our* world. I'd no visualisation about the outside world."

This separation of social worlds was especially conspicuous in the heart of the city where the worst slums and most fashionable streets were often in striking juxtaposition to one another. Noting the dramatic contrast between dilapidated Gardiner Street and Dominick Street, and thriving nearby O'Connell Street in the 1930s, Eamon Donnelly, TD, declared:

> "To pass through O'Connell Street at night with all its brilliant lights and picture houses going full swing, one would scarcely think that only some yards away the slaughter of the innocents was going on."[53]

This lack of contact between the classes both created and reinforced negative stereotypes of the poor in the slums. Self-appointed critics condemned them for their intemperance, vulgar language, and sordid surroundings. Tenement folk were sometimes called "beasts" and "savages".[54] One angry resident of Mountjoy Square expressed his displeasure with unsavoury neighbours in an open letter to *The Daily Nation*:

> "I suppose filth and vice generally herd together. Hideous screams and shouts of drunken men and women who occupy rooms in the street I refer to (Grenville Street) are by no means uncommon sounds which reach our ears on the west side of the square. Saturday nights are particularly fruitful in this respect. By some of the occupants of the square the street is usually described as 'Hell Street'. Bad language, drunken rows, stone throwing, and filthy practices are characteristics of Grenville Street."[55]

Such loathsome testimony was grasped by critics of the poor to validate their contention that the lower classes represented a "degeneration of racial stock", a favourite topic of the time.[56] They reasoned that the Dublin "slummers" were genetically inferior and should be purged on "both moral and sanitary grounds to free the locality from such an objectionable class".[57] One man, claiming that slum dwellers were probably born into original sin and thus a menace to respectable society, unabashedly contended that "sterilisation seems the obvious and immediate method" to rid society of their threat.[58]

THE PRESS AND PUBLIC ENLIGHTENMENT

"In truth, it is not want of inquiry that can be complained of, but rather want of action, of driving power of the determination at any cost to abolish an evil."

Irish Press, *2 October 1936*

No problem in Irish urban history, it was declared, had been "subjected to such thorough examination during the last century and a half" as that of the tenement slums.[59] From Reverend Whitelaw's 1805 *Essay on the Population of Dublin* through the multitude of Royal Commission investigations and

Housing Inquiry reports, volumes of words were produced about the tenements over a span of nearly one hundred and fifty years—and yet they
proved to be little more than dead documents stacked on dusty shelves:

> "What did any of the commissions succeed in doing to mitigate the
> tenement dwellers plight? Their findings were interred in library vaults
> as monuments to an era of colossal neglect, ineptitude and want of
> public spirit."[60]

Ultimately, it was the newspapers which best succeeded in enlightening the
public, stirring their social conscience, and generating an outcry for eradication
of the tenements. In 1898 *The Daily Nation* published a series of provocative
articles on the "terrors of life" in the tenemented "human piggeries" which
elicited widespread public concern and compassion.[61] Then in 1913 when the
two tenement houses collapsed on Church Street all of the Dublin newspapers
covered the tragedy and began to focus blame on the government itself for
neglect of duty. Tenement slums were no longer merely regarded as a problem
but declared a "scandal . . . a crime of the first magnitude . . . a government with even a moderate sense of duty would not have left it unremedied for
so long."[62] It was indisputably the 1936 *Irish Press* series of articles generally
entitled "Dublin's Slum Evil" which most strongly mobilised public opinion in
favour of drastic government action to finally "abolish the slums to their last
tentacles".[63] The series ran for nearly three weeks, daily devoting several full
pages to articles with such emotive titles as: "Massacre of the Innocents";
"Tentacles of Slum Monster are Far-Reaching in City"; "Take Us Out Of This
Terrible Place"; "Slum Landlordism Exacts a Huge Tax from Human
Anguish"; "War on the Slums".

Two features of the series particularly stirred the emotions of readers: the
graphic photographs of tenement families and their personal quotations
about the horrors of slum life. Upper-class Dubliners settled comfortably in
their suburban homes were visually confronted by pathetically gaunt, staring
faces of their poor brethren who expressed in the most simple, poignant
words their daily sufferings. For many, the tenement slums suddenly became a
stark reality rather than merely a comfortable abstraction.

Readers responded to the compelling newspaper coverage of the tenement
slums by sending in their solutions which ranged from the practical to the
quixotic. The concept of eradicating the tenement rows and transplanting
dwellers from the "dark and dismal plague-ridden slums to God Almighty's
fair fields and sunshine" was popular.[64] One reader suggested that a city of
wooden huts be built in Phoenix Park for the poor where at least they could
enjoy open space and fresh air. Another thought that the Dublin Corporation
should buy 250 acres and build 500 cottages in the countryside where each
slum family could have a half acre on which to grow potatoes and vegetables.
After reading of the horrors of slum life in the newspaper, one man decided to
visit a tenement house and was so appalled at the sight of a family of eight all
sleeping in one shabby bed that he wrote emotionally:

"If there is not a place in Dublin for this family but the fetid cave in which they now exist, it would be a mercy to throw them out into the streets or let them live as wild animals in the mountains, for wild animals have healthy air to breathe, anyway."[65]

In one particularly forceful article the *Irish Press* exhorted the people and government to "wage war" upon the evil slums and smite them from the cityscape, motivating one reader to write in with his novel solution:

"When the fine summer weather comes I would want all the residents of the Dublin slums put under canvas on the plains of Kildare, the verdant slopes of the Dublin mountains and seaside resorts of the North Dublin coast. When all the slum dwellers would be removed I would mobilise the engineering section of the Army, the Artillery and the Air Force to have the slums blown sky high."[66]

When slum clearance finally began and tenement families were actually transplanted to new Corporation dwellings on the fringes of Dublin there was naturally great social interest in the results. The *Irish Press* assigned one of its reporters to follow the progress of one tenement family moved from the Coombe to a new Corporation house in Crumlin which had two bedrooms, lavatory, pantry, and a kitchen larger than the whole single room they had had in the slums for the nine of them. His report described the transformation as almost miraculous:

"After moving for weeks in the shadows of Dublin's tenements, a visit to Crumlin where many a slum dweller has been mercifully transplanted, gives an impression of ascending from some fetid, subterranean sewer into the blithesome sunlight of a spring morning. Up here, in this airy wind-swept, sun-bathed plateau, far from the squalor that palled their earlier times, there is being written for those reprieved slum denizens a chapter in what might well be titled 'Paradise Regained'. Here are flowers instead of cluttered garbage and debris; song birds instead of stifling effluvium of open drains; the robustious laughter of happy, healthy children instead of the querulous moaning of ailing little ones; hope instead of despair."[67]

Apart from providing an intimately human dimension to the tenement problem—which was much needed—the *Irish Press* convincingly documented "how much worse the slum conditions are today than they were three generations ago".[68] It was no longer easy for Dubliners to ignore the fact that they indeed had the worst slums in Europe.[69] These revelations had a very sobering effect on both private citizens and public figures and generated fresh social-economic discussion about how to realistically solve the problem. A wide array of public officials, businessmen, clergy, doctors, society figures and others joined the fray and openly condemned the tenements as a "deadly menace . . . a disgrace to a Christian country".[70] Sir John O'Connell, one of the major sociological figures of his time, expressed the general public sentiment when he issued a powerful indictment of civic neglect and issued a clarion call for *immediate* "national government intervention".[71] It was, he declared, the "most solemn duty" which the government owes the citizens of Dublin to clear the slums and eradicate poverty once and for all.

By the late 1930s the public was far better informed about the causal relationships between the poor and their tenement environment. Archaic, simplistic notions that the lower classes were somehow to blame for their own misery were being dispelled. Social workers began working directly with the poor while sociologists and others conducted objective inquiry into the background complexities of poverty and published their findings. An enlightened Dublin public came to realise that it was both a moral and practical responsibility to assist the poor and provide decent housing. There seemed to emerge a collective public will to end the tenement slum shame at any cost and for the benefit of Dubliners of all classes. The 1938 *Report on Slum Clearance* reflected this enlightened perspective:

> "Men and women became convinced that Providence had not made the poor to be the means for rich persons to grow richer still, and that there could be no true civilisation unless all the citizens were treated as human beings and given the opportunity of satisfying their essential human needs. Men need houses in which they may rest, sleep, pass their leisure and rear their families. Social reformers turned their energies toward improving houses in which the poor were to live because they saw that the slum was the cause of much evil, physical and moral. We must, as a civilised and Christian community, do our utmost, in the name of commonsense, justice and Christian charity, to provide proper dwellings for our own poor."[72]

HOUSING REFORM AND SLUM CLEARANCE

In historical retrospect, the government's blatant failure to provide decent housing for the poor seems indefensible. As historian Daly correctly notes, this lack of political will to solve the housing problem of the urban lower class stands in striking contrast to the attention given to social and economic problems in rural Ireland.[73] This was due in part to an indifference, even bias against, Irish cities—particularly Anglo-Irish Dublin—based on the long-held belief that they reflected British rule and values rather than native Irish identity.[74] Similarly, even the Roman Catholic clergy expressed little sympathy toward the urban poor and their housing plight compared with the energies they devoted to rural affairs and land questions. This benign neglect generation after generation resulted in the progressive decay of inner-Dublin.

During the last quarter of the nineteenth century the Dublin Corporation did patch up some dilapidated Georgian houses but there was no effort to provide new housing for the poor. During this period the Dublin Artisans'

Dwellings Company was the only substantial private builder of new housing for the working classes. Between the 1870s and 1900 they constructed separate dwellings in the form of block flats, cottages and small houses for about three thousand families but these were made available only to well paid tradesmen and skilled workers who could afford them.[75] It was also stipulated that these houses be given to carefully selected families of high moral character, cleanliness and respectability—which excluded most tenement dwellers in the eyes of the selection authorities.

By 1914 the *Dublin Housing Inquiry Report* determined that the tenement housing situation was so desperate that a real solution was needed without delay. But World War I, followed by the War of Independence, delayed any such efforts to clear the slums. Even self-government brought no dramatic improvement. The 1924 Housing Act encouraged private investment in housing but the result was new middle-class housing on the city outskirts while housing conditions of the poor in the inner-city actually worsened. Only with the creation of the 1931 Housing Bill and the 1932 Housing Act did attention focus on financing slum clearance schemes and the provision of local authority housing for the lower-income classes. For the first time local authorities were empowered to deal directly with the slum problem in a systematic way. Unfit properties could be officially condemned and acquired compulsorily to be renovated or demolished. Most important was the stipulation that tenants of unfit houses had to be provided with alternative accommodation by local authorities. As a consequence, during the thirties tenements began to be torn down along such streets as Cumberland Street, Townsend Street, Mercer Street and Greek Street and new schemes of flats erected on the cleared sites. By 1938 some seven thousand four hundred new dwellings had been completed to re-house tenement dwellers.

During the 1940s and 1950s the gargantuan task of slum clearance gained momentum as the Corporation concentrated on building four- and five-storey blocks of flats scattered across the city centre. Additionally, new housing projects were developed on the periphery at such sites as Crumlin, Cabra, Ballyfermot, Donnycarney, Inchicore, Glasnevin and Marino. But the urgency to provide cheap housing for the lower classes from the tenements led to the creation of typically sterile, dreary housing blocks devoid of social life and sense of community. Though the occupants finally had decent sanitation, basic amenities, and privacy, many felt depressed over being uprooted from their old neighbourhoods and transplanted in a lonely alien setting. Although most of the tenements were eradicated by the end of the 1950s some dwellers remained in their surviving Georgian houses into the 1970s, especially on the neglected northside of the city around North Great George's Street and Mountjoy Square. These tattered relics stood out on the modern cityscape as grim reminders of nearly two centuries of tortured tenement life in the heart of the city.

ORAL HISTORY AND TENEMENT FOLKLORE

"Oral history provides a people's history . . . it charts the history of the unknown people who have not before been considered important, people who do not figure in documents and records."

John D. Brewer, The Royal Irish Constabulary: An Oral History, *1990*

History has traditionally been concerned principally with great political and military events and powerful leaders. Life experiences of the ordinary working classes and of the poor were simply not regarded as worth recording for the archives. With the advent of oral history in the 1940s scholars began focusing some attention on the lives and work of common people, generally in the rural setting. By the 1960s American pioneering oral historians were collecting oral narratives from *city* folk such as merchants, tradesmen, factory workers, dockers, and labour unionists. There was also an emerging interest in the everyday life of ordinary families in traditional urban neighbourhoods. As a consequence, a new genre of literature has appeared which historians and folklorists term "urban folklore".

Simply put, oral history is a data collection technique which can be applied to any topic that is "within the living memory" of people.[76] However, it is especially important to collect oral testimony from the "small number of survivors whose life experiences will be lost to future generations once they pass from the scene".[77] For this reason, oral historians are increasingly gathering information from the likes of vanishing craftsmen, tradesmen and immigrants in older urban neighbourhoods. Furthermore, as Thompson explains, by recording the life experiences and struggles of urban poor classes, whom he calls the "underprivileged and defeated", we truly *democratise* history by understanding poverty itself.[78] This is what Morrisey terms "grass roots" history, proudly asserting that the new breed of oral historians are a fresh vanguard of scholars practising their craft in the "real world".[79]

In Ireland oral history and folklore are still strongly associated with rural life and customs. People do not ordinarily think of the city as a repository of old customs, traditions and folkways as they do of the countryside and village. Actually, Dublin is fertile ground for the extraction of oral urban lore because of its surviving inner-city neighbourhoods and large elderly population. In recent years the concept of collecting Dublin's folklore via the oral historical method has gained both credibility and support. In part, this is due to *Comhairle Bhéaloideas Éireann* (The Folklore Council of Ireland) which came to recognise the "similarity between the traditional customs and social attitudes of Gaeltacht people and those of native Dubliners".[80] Coincidentally, in the early 1980s Professor Seamus Ó'Catháin, lamenting that "ordinary people have been largely written out of history" in the city, launched the Dublin Folklore Project in which students were dispatched to collect the recollections of elderly residents.[81] A few years later the North Inner-City Folklore Project

was initiated with modest government financial support to record the life experiences of dockers, seamen, midwives, tradesmen as well as ordinary labourers
and housewives. Similarly, authors Sheehan and Walsh in their book *The Heart
of the City* draw heavily upon what they label "Dublin folklore" from the 1920s
and 1930s.[82]

In Dublin there is surely no more "real world" oral history to be gathered
than that of the tenement community folk who were seen as the very "salt of
the earth". As cultural enclaves, the tenement slum communities had their
own life-ways which were as distinctive as those to be found in a Gaeltacht
village or Appalachian town. Tenement dwellers had their own social milieu,
forged a unique ethos, and developed a remarkably cohesive community rich
and complex in its customs, traditions, neighbouring patterns, survival strategies and urban folklore. Tenement life-ways focused on family unity, seeking
employment, securing food and clothing, home childbirth, illness and home
cures, courting and marriage, religion, improvised entertainment and hooleys,
death and wakes. Daily tenement life also demanded coping with the hard
realities of personal conflict, alcoholism, wife abuse, animal gangs, prostitution,
and suicide.

But the many official investigative reports on tenements by various commissions do not tell us of such personal parts of life in the Dublin slums. As
Thompson affirms, these intimate life experiences of the poor were previously
"secret areas" before the use of oral history recording techniques.[83] Most of the
individuals whose oral histories are featured in this book are between sixty and
ninety years of age. Their collective memory is an invaluable repository of
urban folklore from the early part of this century. As survivors now in old age,
they value the opportunity to reflect on their tenement days. Indeed, it seems
to give their life a sense of worth and meaning. Too often, their children and
grandchildren have no interest in hearing about the impoverished past. Some
even prefer to disclaim their tenement roots. For others, however, it has
become a sort of badge of pride to now proclaim that their people originally
came from the old Liberties or Gloucester Diamond.

Women were especially willing to share life's most personal trials and tribula-
tions. One of the most powerful and recurrent themes emerging from the oral
narratives in this book—from both men and women—is that of the indispensable, often "saintly", role of mothers and grannies in holding the very fabric
of tenement family life together. This is valuable testimony because, as Professor Ó'Catháin contends, ordinary women in Dublin's poorer inner-city
neighbourhoods have received virtually no attention by historians.[84] The struggling, self-sacrificing women of the old Dublin tenement slums surely fit the
mould of what one historian has rightfully called the "lost heroines" in society.[85]

Taping sessions ordinarily lasted from two to three hours. Some individuals
were re-visited and tape-recorded a second time to expand on original
narratives or clarify dangling themes. With few exceptions, interviews were
conducted in the person's home or local pub, the natural setting in which they
felt most comfortable. Oral historians are keenly aware that the empathy factor

is important in the interviewer-respondent relationship. This is especially true when probing such delicate human subjects as family conflict, religion, alcoholism, morality, physical abuse, and death. Success depends on the bond of trust between the two parties.

Quite often the process of extracting painful memories from tenement dwellers was an emotionally wrenching one. Yet, expressing past pain and sorrows was clearly a cathartic experience for some older individuals. One woman, relating through bitter tears the savage beatings she suffered at her husband's hands, appeared visibly relieved when at the end she confessed "Now I've never told that to anyone before in all my life . . . not my children, not even the priest." Though sadness is still visible as they recount life's struggles, their eyes express delight when reliving childhood games, a mother's lap, or a Christmas dinner in the old tenement room. More than anything else, they speak wistfully about the tenement community and the security they knew earlier in life. Only through their first-hand verbal accounts can we learn of that rich community life. In reading their oral narratives one is perhaps most profoundly struck by the deep pride and dignity they exude, despite their impoverished background. They are truly the last survivors of the bygone tenement era. As a vanishing breed there is an urgency in the task to record their oral histories for future generations.

"We cannot, alas, interview tombstones."[86]

2

Social Life in the Tenement Communities

COMMUNITY SPIRIT AND GREGARIOUS NATURE

"Unfathomable is the goodness of the poor to one another."
K. F. Purdon, Dinny of the Doorstep, 1920

"It is only among the very unfortunate that you find the warm hearts that are almost essential . . . otherwise life in the crowded tenements would be a torment. The very poor have acquired an understanding and feeling that even show in their eyes. However shabby, thin and prematurely aged those very poor women may be, they have so often wonderful bright grey eyes—eyes full of humour and general friendliness."

Olivia Robertson, Dublin Phoenix, 1957

In the 1920s and 1930s, the period during which most of the individuals featured in this book spent their childhood, there were over one hundred thousand tenement dwellers in Dublin. This massive population was concentrated in close-knit communities around the Liberties, dockland, and northside. Tenement communities could be identified by general locality or, more specifically, along the lines of particular neighbourhoods or streets where local identities and loyalties could be nearly as strong as family blood ties.

Dublin's tenement communities were always noted for their strong community spirit and tradition of sharing and caring for one another. There existed a communal system of mutual dependency in which neighbours routinely shared food, clothing, fuel, cared for the sick, consoled the suffering, assisted evictees, took in orphans, and waked the dead. The old, the infirm, the blind, the insane, the dispossessed—*all* were part of the community. Even the dossers, or "knockabouts", who would sleep rough in the tenement hallways would be given a cup of tea and a crust of bread by the tenants. It was a sort of unwritten moral code of the tenements that neighbours look after one another in times of need. Father Michael Reidy worked among the poor a half century ago and remembers their "tremendous resilience and spirit . . . they *helped* one another, they were great neighbours." As many of the old crowd like to put it, it was simply their "nature" to be caring and charitable in those times. Whenever hardship or suffering struck an individual or family, neighbours rallied to the rescue. "It was a *community*," reveals Nellie Cassidy, "everybody knew everybody else. If *one* was in sorrow we were *all* in sorrow." As a result of this communal spirit, the poor of the tenements were never alone in their misery but surrounded by those who genuinely cared about them. This was one of the greatest comforts and securities of tenement life.

Apart from their communal cohesion, tenement folk were widely renowned for their gregarious nature and wonderful, earthy wit. To many outsiders, it seemed incongruous that amidst such dire poverty the tenement dwellers seemed so happily contented. Observers often wrote with a sense of wonderment about this "incurably optimistic and happy-go-lucky" nature of the Dublin "slummers".[1] Sidney Davies, writing about *Dublin Types* in the first quarter of the century, marvelled at the "great numbers of Dubliners who are actually on the starvation line who move about with unruffled cheerfulness and good humour."[2] This sense of contentment with their lot in life, O'Brien concludes, is a major reason why the poor never "revolted" against their deprived conditions.[3] The daily intimacy of extended family, friends, local pubs, shops, and Church provided deep emotional and psychological security. Equally important, the tenement world was constantly aswirl with social interaction and animated street life. Streets were teeming with hordes of children, tuggers, balladeers, shouting traders, crowds of corner men, local characters, and women clustered at doorways or hanging out windows chatting away with neighbours. Simply put, there was never a dull moment in the tenements and the people indeed seemed quite content where they were, as affirmed in a 1936 article in the *Irish Press*:

> "These people who have lived there all their lives, they have no fault to find with the neighbourhood. All their friends live around. They would not live at the other side of the city if they were paid to do so."[4]

There were no grand ambitions to escape the slums to move up to middle-class status because, as the poor philosophically accepted, "We were all in the same boat." Even when they were exposed to the better-off classes along Dublin's shopping streets they felt no resentment or envy. Guard Paddy Casey reflects on the life of the poor he knew so well around the bustling northside:

> "They were *extraordinarily happy* for people who were so savagely poor. They had a great community spirit and a code of honour among themselves. They knew that their place was on the bottom of the ladder and they didn't seem to have any great ambitions to go up to the middle class . . . they were quite happy to stay. They loved this thing, particularly the women, sitting on the steps of the tenements there on a summer's day chatting and the children running around. They *liked* that. That was the extraordinary thing, they were *fulfilled*."

The Home Setting

Early in this century a single, small tenement room was "home sweet home" to nearly one-third of all Dubliners. The setting was confined and congested since most families had between six and twelve children and some had twenty or more. All family activities had to be conducted within the one small space—cooking, eating, bathing, dressing, sleeping, relaxing. The whole cycle of life from births to weddings to wakes was played out in the same tiny room the poor called "home".

In the 1930s the typical room rent was between three and six shillings per week. Basement quarters were the lowest form of habitation. Other rooms were designated by names such as top front, top back, two-pair front, two-pair back, front drawing room, back drawing room, and front and back parlours. Rooms with two windows were much valued and families having two rooms were regarded as very fortunate. Rooms were typically spartan in appearance. Furniture usually consisted of a few chairs, stools or wooden boxes, a dresser or sideboard, one or two beds made of iron or brass, straw mattresses for the floor, and a wooden tea chest for coal. Beside the open fireplace with metal grill were a water bucket, cooking kettle, and metal washing vat. On the mantle board stood religious statues, candles, a paraffin oil lamp, and assorted small artefacts. Walls held religious pictures, family photos and perhaps a calendar. The setting could be embellished by nice lace curtains, a window flower box, and a singing bird in a cage which added a bit of colour and cheer to the otherwise drab atmosphere.

Privacy was virtually unknown. For bathing and dressing purposes rooms had to be divided by sheets hung on a clothes line. Or the husband and sons might be sent out into the hallway to give the females some private time. Slop buckets were discreetly placed in a corner or out in the hallway at night. Eighty-one year old Maggie Murray recalls coping with the hardships of life in her one-room tenement in Queen's Terrace:

> "Eight families in my tenement with one toilet in the rear yard. But during the night in the winter you couldn't *dream* of going down. So a slop bucket was kept in the corner of the room and we put an old curtain around it. Six of us slept in one bed. We had no bedclothes, we had coats over us at night time. We had no handles on our cups . . . broken cups . . . broken everything."

Lighting was provided by paraffin oil lamps and candles and all heating and cooking were done over the open fire using coal, wood or turf. During hard winters some desperate families had to resort to pulling up floorboards, tearing out banisters, or extracting wood setts from the streets for firewood. To keep out the cold, newspapers were stuffed into door and window spaces and children slept with their clothes on.

For family bathing, water had to be hauled up from the tap in the rear yard in buckets and heated over the fire. Hot water was then poured into a galvanised vat about three feet long in which children and even adults could sit and bathe with a cake of Sunlight soap. Three or four children could be scrubbed clean before the water would have to be changed. If finances permitted, one could spend a few pence to go to the *real* baths at the Iveagh or Tara Street public baths but this was always considered a luxury. During the warm summer months children could go for a "swim bath" in the canal or river Liffey.

Laundering the clothing and sheets for a large family was sheer drudgery for women. Monday was generally wash day but many mothers had to carry out the task more than once a week. Margaret Byrne dreaded Mondays in her Thomas Street tenement since the room was entirely given over to the laundering process:

"My mother used to do her washing and you *hated* Monday because everything was getting done in the one room. There was the washing board and she stood over the big vat of washing and bring the water to a boil and she had a big stick and she'd beat the clothes down and they were *snow white*. And she'd iron them then. She had two irons, they were heavy, and you'd put them into the fire. And the sweat used to be *pouring* off her it was so hot. On Monday she'd be in terrible bad form . . . she was *so tired* and so weary."

To dry, sheets and garments then had to be hung on lines strung out the windows of the tenements giving the appearance of "flags of distress".[5]

Apart from having to bathe family members and wash their clothing and bedding, women were also responsible for scrubbing their wooden floor as well as the outside stairs and hallway. In many of the early inquiry commission reports on tenements it was alleged that the tenants lived happily in filthy hovels and made little or no effort to keep their dwellings clean. In 1889 an article in *The Irish Builder* expressed this perception:

"Stairs are seldom washed down and, if washed weekly by some arrangement made between the tenement occupiers, it is done in a slovenly or perfunctory way."[6]

Even O'Brien claims that "there were no effective arrangements for regulating the cleaning of halls, lobbies, and stairs".[7]

Here we find a striking example of oral history testimony clearly refuting the written record since *all* of the tenement dwellers featured in this book, as well as those who daily worked among them, strongly confirm that the vast majority of tenement women took the greatest pride in the cleanliness of their room and hallway—it was a matter of *respectability*. Indeed, one of the most common sights was that of women kneeling down on a rag cloth with bucket, brush, and cake of black soap scrubbing down the floors and stairways with perspiration flowing off their brows. It was actually a long-established custom in the tenement houses that women arranged a weekly schedule for washing hallways and stairs. And, as Lily Foy recounts, in the Liberties women would never waste a good vat of water:

"I remember my granny washing clothes but that big vat of water was never thrown out. That water would be taken by a neighbour next door and they'd wash their clothes in it. And then they'd take that water and start at the top of the tenement house and scrub down the stairs. One woman would do her flight and another hers. And the floors would be like *milk*—you could eat your dinner off the stairs in the tenements. They were poor but they were very clean."

Publican John O'Dwyer, a young barman at the local pub on York Street back in the war years, concurs that the women of the tenements were noted for the enormous pride they took in keeping their tiny rooms clean:

"I remember going to a house on York Street where there was twenty-four families in it—I'm not joking. I don't know how some of them existed at all. Only *one* toilet in the yard and they used to carry water up to the top floor. But they kept their little rooms magnificent and the staircases outside were always immaculate. Oh, great pride."

Keeping a safe roof over her family's head was a mother's prime concern. Fear of eviction haunted every family since tenants could be ejected for reasons completely beyond their control. Most commonly, eviction occurred when a person fell behind in their rental payments or could not afford to pay a raised fee imposed upon them. However, even long-time occupants could be summarily put out into the street simply because the landlord decided to convert their ground-level room into a huckster shop for his profit. Since most tenement families lived financially on a week-to-week basis, barely surviving, it was always possible that, due to some crisis, they could fall behind in their payments and find themselves at the mercy of their landlord. Many landlords had tough agents such as ex-policemen collecting rents for them. Most of the landlords Una Shaw knew around Gardiner Street were mercenary types:

"Most landlords kept their houses just one jump ahead of the law. They were very old houses and falling apart at the seams and they just did the *minimum* of what they had to do. And then if they did any repairs the rent went up! So people didn't complain. Once you'd see the furniture out in front of the house you'd know there was an eviction. You'd see them outside and there wasn't much the neighbours could do . . . take the children in and look after them, feed them, but they couldn't help with money."

ECONOMIC STRUGGLE

Life in the tenements was a constant struggle for financial survival. Most of the poor had minimal literacy, no job skills, and had to seek manual labour on a casual, sporadic basis. Steady employment was unknown to most. Employers sometimes discriminated against tenement dwellers claiming that they were not as healthy, honest, and reliable as people from the country or other parts of Dublin. As a consequence, they had to scour around for whatever work they could find. Some men were fortunate enough to secure factory work and those employed by such firms as Guinness's, Jameson's (Whiskey), or Jacob's (Biscuits) were much envied. But the vast majority of men had to toil in the building and construction trade, on road work, or as carters, draymen, porters, dockers, scrap collectors, drovers, car parkers, and other assorted odd-jobs. If their young sons managed to get a job around age fourteen as a messenger boy or newsboy it was an important added financial contribution to the family.

With the men so often unemployed the financial burden for providing basic needs fell upon the women. Women typically found work in local small factories (shirt, shoe, sacks, rosary, etc.) or as domestics, washer-women, charwomen, tuggers, sewing, and street traders. Others walked miles out into the countryside for the day to pick potatoes and cabbage for farmers. Women street traders hawking fish, fruit, flowers, vegetables, and second-hand clothing were especially conspicuous early in the century when their husbands were unable to find work. For thousands of tenement families these women were the sole financial providers. Ellen Preston, whose family goes back more than a century in street trading, raised her family of twelve children from her work on Henry Street:

> "Oh, there was loads of street traders. All had large families. Times were very hard then, it was very, very poor. I started selling when I was about twelve. Then I got married when I was nineteen and the chil-dren started coming along and I was selling fruit and flowers off me pram. The men, there was no work for them and the women traders, they *had* to go out, they held the families together. Every day I pushed me pram, *every day*. Some days were miserable with the rain beating off me. If you got five shillings from the pram in them days that'd get you loads of bread and butter and milk. You were just making ends meet . . . but we reared our families."

Wives usually managed the family's meagre funds. Always put aside first were the necessary shillings for room rent, food, and fuel—the basics for survival. In times of dire need one could turn to the local relieving officer but, as Paddy Mooney knew, this was only of small help:

> "You had to resort to the relieving officer and you went and begged to get maybe a few shillings from him. I don't think they were trained in *any* way. It was at his discretion whether you got anything or not and you could be turned away."

The St Vincent de Paul Society and the Sick and Indigent Roomkeepers' Society also assisted the poor by providing food, clothing, shoes, bedding, fuel and other necessities. But for reasons of pride many mothers and fathers were reluctant to accept charity. Jimmy McLoughlin saw what a demeaning and emotionally painful experience it was for his mother, a charwoman, when she had to ask the "Vincent men" to visit their tenement room in Marlborough Place:

"I remember my mother crying when she'd be asking to give us money for food. It was a thing she didn't want to do. We always had men—you called them the 'gentry'—and they went into your home to examine your conditions before they'd give you anything. They'd come in and sit down and ask 'why are you asking for help?' They always had this upper-class attitude, snobbish . . . I remember my mother often crying."

When money was short, women habitually trekked down the street to the local pawnbroker. Pawnshops—known then as the "people's bank"—became an institution in Dublin's tenement districts. In 1870 there were seventy-six pawnshops in the city and in the 1930s there were still nearly fifty prospering. As one researcher notes in the *Dublin Historical Record*, without the pawnbroker the "already precarious life of the poor would have been even more unstable".[8] Cameron put it more bluntly—"They must starve if they have nothing which would be taken in pawn."[9] For countless thousands of tenement families their local pawnbroker, referred to as "me uncle", was indispensable to survival. Virtually any item could be pawned for at least a few precious shillings—old tattered suits, shoes, bedding, pictures, wedding rings, statues, irons, even sods of turf and bricks wrapped in brown paper parcels which were never opened. For the most part, pawnbrokers were decent men who treated their customers with friendliness and dignity and pawn days were actually social occasions for the women queued up outside chatting away. As eighty-three year old Chrissie Hawkins reveals, weekly visits to the pawn were one of the most enduring customs of tenement life:

"I was never out of the pawn office . . . *never* out of them. Monday was the big day cause we used to have to pay our debts on a Monday and back on a Saturday to release things out of it. And it was always *packed*. Years ago you'd pawn anything. I used to take my father's photograph. Oh, in a lovely frame, just carried it through the streets. I didn't care if anybody knew it was me father! And I pawned me wedding ring the day after being married. And I got a half crown and that went for me breakfast."

When a few pounds, rather than mere shillings, were desperately needed a person could always turn to the notorious money-lenders who abounded in tenement areas. As a group, they gained the reputation as exploitative but, in retrospect, most tenement dwellers feel that they were simply a "necessary evil" of the times. And clear distinctions are made between types of money-lenders. The local "Jewmen" (the term always used by the tenement population but not in any derogatory manner) who loaned money were seen as shrewd but fair. Conversely, those tenement families who went into the money-lending "racket" among their neighbours tended to be tough and ruthless, often resorting to physical pressure to collect debts. Some were both despised and feared within the community. Mary Corbally, one of fifteen children in her family and later the mother of twenty children herself, saw money-lenders as a necessary part of life around Corporation Street back in the Hungry Thirties:

"Oh, my mother had a Jewman, we couldn't do without them. They were a necessity of life. In them days your first loan off a Jewman would be two or three pounds and you paid it back at a half a crown a week—and you paid five shillings to the pound. You could go twenty, thirty, forty weeks giving that two five shillings and you *still* owed the two pounds! Now the money-lenders, they were the *worst*. The money-lenders were local, they were your own neighbours. Some of them if you didn't pay them you'd get a hammering off them."

Part of managing the family's budget was to save for special occasions such as First Holy Communion, Confirmation, weddings, and Christmas. It was up to the resourcefulness of wives to save and safely stash away a few bob at a time so that husbands would not be tempted to spend it on tobacco, drink or gambling. Such money was hidden behind chimney bricks, beneath wooden floorboards, sewn into mattresses, and dropped down the posts of bedsteads. It could also be deposited in one of the local penny banks which literally accepted ha'pennies and pennies from savers. But back in the days before credit unions and other institutional savings schemes, the most popular means by which tenement women saved money for Christmas was the "didley club". Putting in a few pennies or shillings each week assured mothers that, come Christmas, they would have enough money for the pudding, dinner, and a few simple gifts for the children. Mary Doolan divulges how the "old didleys" around Francis Street worked:

"My mother was always in the didley. My aunt run one. It was for *saving* the money, before credit unions. A didley starts with a ha'penny a week, to a penny, to three, and all up, to about five shillings—from January to December. My aunt would keep the money the whole year around and you wouldn't get it till Christmas. She *wouldn't give* it to you early. She'd have little bags of money and it'd keep going up and at Christmas they'd all get their few pounds. And you might give her two shillings back from the goodness of your heart for running it and bookkeeping the year around."

SECURING FOOD AND CLOTHING

"Half the population of Dublin are clothed in the cast-off clothes of the other half."
Charles A. Cameron, Reminiscences, *1913*

Next to keeping a roof over her family's head a mother's chief concern was securing food and clothing. Most families had barely enough food for physical survival but an insufficient diet for full health. Many were seriously malnourished and real hunger was known. Peggy Pigott, a teacher at Rutland Street school for forty years, could see the hunger in the faces of her children when they arrived in the morning:

"The diet and nutrition, it was hopeless. Some would have tea and bread and maybe porridge. But a lot of them would come without anything in their tummies in the morning because they were so poor."

The basic diet of Dublin's poor was deficient in essential nutrients and caloric levels. For breakfast it consisted, in some combination, of tea, cocoa, bread, margarine, jam, and porridge. For dinner it was mostly stews and soups made from cheap meat scraps, or "parings", which were very fatty. Women would buy sheep's heads, cattle heads, rabbits, fish heads and, combined with potatoes, onions, carrots and other vegetables, make a pot of stew or soup sufficient to feed their family. Also popular were pig's feet, pig's cheeks, herrings, winkles, cockles, and even eels. The major meal was Sunday dinner when perhaps there might be a coddle, corned beef and cabbage, or a bit of bacon. Puddings, pies and tarts were seldom served. It was always the rule that the father and eldest sons, particularly if they were employed, received the lion's share of whatever food was available. Mothers, because they wanted to make sure their children were decently fed, often got the least nourishment by choice. Margaret Byrne is not ashamed to admit that as a child there were days when she knew real hunger:

"Some days we didn't really have a meal, maybe just bread and butter. On a bad day she'd (mother) get a half dozen of eggs and that'd have to do for the father, mother and four children. A boiled egg for dinner—and that would be it!"

Mothers had strategies for converting their few shillings into the maximum amount of food. Buying butcher's scraps and inferior meat parings which were about to spoil was a common practice. And children were regularly sent down to the local bakery to buy stale bread. Most tenement neighbourhoods also had a charitable stew house or soup kitchen to which the people could turn when food was especially scarce. To save their pride, mothers often dispatched their children on such food missions. As a lad, Jimmy McLoughlin never minded helping his mother to bring home food for the family table:

"There was a bakery on North Earl Street and my mother'd give me a pillow cloth and a shilling and I'd go down and ask for stale bread and he'd throw in four or five loaves. And I remember going to the stew house in Sean McDermott Street. You'd bring a big galvanised pot with you and ask them to fill the pot up and you'd bring it home in the pram. Oh, it'd be warm and by the time you got back you might have spilled *half* of it."

When food was brought home it had to be protected against spoilage. Perishables such as milk, margarine, and buttermilk were placed in a bucket of cool water and put in a shaded corner. Tea, oatmeal, bread, sugar and the like had to be sealed in biscuit tins to keep out the bugs and mice. Pieces of gauze were used to cover any exposed foods to keep off the swarms of flies. Because food could not be preserved, mothers had to do their meal shopping virtually every day.

For clothing, tenement dwellers dressed in the discarded garments of the better classes. Men and women ordinarily had a respectable second-hand outfit for Sunday Mass. Children, however, were "all raggedy", recalls Peggy Pigott, "shoes very bad and they cut a Player's Cigarette box and put that on the soles." Many children had no shoes at all and ran barefooted through the rough cobblestoned streets during the dead of winter. Boys and girls typically dressed in ill-fitting scavenged garments that appeared ludicrously small or oversized. New clothes were unknown to most children. The principal source of clothing for the poor were the second-hand markets such as Cole's Lane, Cumberland Street, and the Daisy and Iveagh markets. The clothing, heaped in mounds up to six feet high, was mostly brought in by tuggers. In Dublin there was a veritable army of tuggers, mostly women, who would daily trek miles out to the suburbs pushing their wicker basket on wheels. They would knock on the doors of the well-to-do and ask for clothing, footwear, and anything else of possible value. At day's end their "booty" was sold to women dealers at the markets. Dealers then washed the garments, patched them up, and polished footwear for re-sale. To the more privileged classes these second-hand markets were no more than a tawdry "rag fair . . . rags offered for sale hardly worth picking up as derelict".[10] But to the poor of the tenements there was no shame in wearing used clothing since everyone had to do the same. Actually, there was a tremendous variety of clothing and many pieces were in excellent condition. Absolutely *anything* could be found—shawls, skirts, blouses, suits, trousers, hats, scarves, gloves, coats, footwear, and even christening gowns and Confirmation and First Communion outfits. Poor families were completely outfitted from the market stalls. Ida Lahiffe, who inherited her stall at the Iveagh Market from her father, fondly describes the frenetic, halcyon days when she was a child:

> "It was great here in the old days. The market would be packed, about seventy or eighty dealers in here. Every stall was full. There was great variety, mostly clothing and footwear. Clothes used to be disinfected outside, the Corporation did that. Ah, you'd hear a lot of people coming in here saying, 'Oh, I reared me family out of here.' The Iveagh, it has an awful lot of historical significance . . . it got people through the hard times."

There were, however, those families too poor even to afford a few shillings for the basics of dress. In response, the Herald Boot Fund was established to provide footwear for the barefoot urchins so pathetically in evidence around Dublin's streets. One could also apply for what was known as "police clothing". Usually, only the poorest of the poor would wear these garments since they carried a readily identifiable stamp of "P. C." and a social stigma as well. Mary Doolan accepted police clothing but found it a demeaning experience:

> "Police clothing, I got them myself. They'd be inhuman. You went to a stable for them, an old stable where horses used to be. You should have seen the filth in the stable! They'd look at them (children) and say, 'here, that'll fit him' and hand it out to you. An old shirt and jumper . . . *horrible dirt*. You wouldn't want to put them on, but you *had* to. And there'd be a little stamp on the shirt and jumper and all the kids would know that you got them off the police and they'd jeer you."

HEALTH, SICKNESS, AND TREATMENTS

> *"Thousands of children today face premature death through disease in overcrowded tenement houses. From the moment of their birth they have to face conditions which are fatal to healthy frames or to a happy existence . . . they cannot escape from their squalid surroundings . . . they cannot avoid their fate."*

Irish Press, *1936*

The reputation of the tenements as "multitudinous fever nests and death traps" was, tragically, well deserved. As early as 1880 the Royal Sanitary Commission documented that severe overcrowding, lack of sanitation, poor diet, damp and cold conditions, and foul air all conspired against the health of tenement dwellers. This was dramatically confirmed by the end of the century when Dublin recorded the highest death rate of any city in the United Kingdom. Twice as many people died of tuberculosis in Dublin as in London. Equally alarming was the high rate of infant mortality. About 20 per cent of all deaths in the city occurred among those less than a year old, nearly all from the poorer classes. By the 1930s mortality among the children of the poor was five times greater than among the well-to-do. "The most important determinant of children's health", concludes historian Mary Daly, "was social class."[11] As the *Irish Press* so aptly put it, 'what price for these defenceless little Christians to pay for the accident of birth which brought them into the world of Gloucester Street or Dominick Street rather than that of the salubrious suburbs."[12]

The tenement population was threatened by a host of illnesses—tuberculosis, diphtheria, pneumonia, smallpox, typhoid, whooping cough, rheumatoid arthritis, respiratory problems, diarrhoeal diseases, and various infections. The susceptibility of the poor to sickness and disease was clearly due in great part to their malnourished and physically unhealthy condition from birth. In the 1930s it was found that, next to pneumonia, "congenital debility" ranked highest in the causes of Dublin's infant mortality. It was concluded that this was the "result of the iron law of heredity . . . slum children are born with an inherited physical weakness that makes them an easy prey to all forms of disease".[13] Local chemists from the old days, like Patrick O'Leary of Thomas Street, confirm this diagnosis:

> "A lot of their illnesses were born of the fact that they weren't properly nourished. It would be hereditary because their father and mother had lived on tea and bread and margarine. They'd be pale and red eyes and much more liable to infection because they hadn't the where-with-all to *resist* it."

Apart from serious illness, people were made miserable by scabies, lice, rashes, skin sores, chilblains, stone bruises and other assorted maladies. These problems usually resulted from lack of sanitation and hygiene. The environment was littered with slaughter houses and piggeries while horses, cattle and sheep were always being driven down the streets. Animal dung was splattered in cobblestone crevices and bugs, vermin and rats infested every tenement house. Chemist Con Foley knew that around his shop on Parnell Street in the 1930s the beasts and flies were "potent germ carriers" and a serious health hazard to tenement dwellers who were sometimes called by outsiders the "great unwashed". He saw tragic cases where barefoot lads would get gangrene when they cut their foot and walked in horse manure . . . "Some of them lost limbs like that."

Visiting Englishmen frequently noted in their writings that the poor of Dublin were often stunted in growth and appeared "deformed and mis-shapen".[14] Una Shaw explains that around Gardiner Street these characteristics were readily observable but little understood at the time:

> "Looking back on it now and seeing the children of today, they were so *undersized* and very thin. Their little legs were like matchsticks. And a lot of children in those days suffered rickets and were bow-legged. We thought they were born that way but they weren't, it was malnutrition, they hadn't the vitamins."

When illness struck, a person could go to their local dispensary doctor. But it was a far more common custom in the tenements to head directly to the neighbourhood chemist who was also a long-time friend and confidant in whom they had the greatest faith. Dependence upon the local chemist was so great that many people seldom, if ever, saw a doctor or dentist. A few chemists in the Liberties were so important in the lives of the people that they have become legendary figures in the folklore of the community. Seventy-three year old Mickey Guy tells of the medical care around the Liberties:

> "You never seen doctors. You could go to a chemist and even if your throat was cut he'd give you a cure for it! He'd put a dressing on it. Daddy Nagle was in Meath Street and Mr Mushatt was in Francis Street—they were the *masterpieces*, they were, for a bad chest, bad back . . . from north, south, east and west people'd come for them. Now the

only dentist in my time was a man named Mr Carey. It was a half a crown and he'd put his *knee* up on you and he'd pull. Oh, he'd pull the head off you! One man died of some infection after that."

One of the reasons people had such great faith in the curing powers of their chemist was because he concocted his own old-fashioned remedies in the rear compounding room. His lotions, potions, and tablets were thought to be the purest medicines. "People *really believed* in them, *swore* by them", attests Paddy Mooney, "no matter *what* was wrong." No one was more famous than Harry Mushatt and his brother who served the people of the Liberties for nearly a half century from their tiny shop on Francis Street. Harry tells what it was like behind the counter of his shop back in the thirties:

"We made our own medicines in the shop. My brother and I made up forty-four different preparations, from skin ointments, psoriasis ointments, foot pastes, stomach bottles, skin cremes, tablets for kidneys, headaches, neuralgia . . . *all* different things. Oh, there was a bond of trust and they'd come into the shop and it would be *packed out*. Tenement people, if one wasn't feeling well or met with an accident, 'Go to Mushatt's!', they'd say. They came from *all over* Dublin."

It was also a custom among tenement folk to rely upon home cures. Old-fashioned home remedies were carefully handed down from generation to generation and the oral testimonies in this book are replete with examples of their success. Some of the more common ones were putting tallow and a brown paper vest on a child's chest for a cold, placing mustard behind the ear for a toothache, using goose grease for rheumatism, or boiling the back of a ray fish and washing the legs of a "knocker-kneed" child with the water. Home cures were especially important when standard medical treatments failed. Despite a doctor's negative prognosis, mothers never gave up on an ill child. Una Shaw marvelled at how mothers around Summerhill and Gardiner Street would almost miraculously nurse ill children back to health, often to the astonishment of medical experts:

"See, doctors would have given up on a child. They'd say, 'she's very ill, she won't live another week.' But the mother would *never give up* on a child. It was home cures they'd use, they relied on home cures. I often wondered was it just their *faith* that was in it. They'd *really believe* that it was doing some good and they'd (children) start to pull around and get better and start to fight what was bothering them—and they'd get all right."

The health of the mothers themselves, who usually 'slaved' from morning till night, was always a concern to O'Leary. He knew well that the loss of a mother's health was always a devastating blow to the family. Many laboured on bravely even though their health was visibly very poor. He was sympathetic to their plight and made up special medications to treat their stress and fatigue and give them strength:

"They were generally run-down, *always* under stress. The husband might be going from one job to another and then being unemployed and starting to drink and she having one child after another and they were living in the one room. She never got a *rest* from it. Never got a rest from the stress and strain. They were *run-down!* We sold tablets for nervous strain and I'd give them an iron and vitamin tonic."

When a person fell seriously ill they were commonly cared for at home by family and friends. This often meant the risk of infecting those around them with the same sickness. But back then illness and death were accepted as facts of daily life. Every family, it seemed, lost loved ones prematurely and a wake was being held somewhere in the neighbourhood nearly every week. The loss of infants and children was especially prevalent. For May Hanaphy, born in 1908 in Golden Lane, the loss of young pals and siblings was all too commonplace:

"There were nine of us children but four lost to diphtheria. Nearly every child in Dublin at that time contracted the dreaded diphtheria. Nearly every family lost their first children at six or seven years old. There was a lot of deaths and we didn't understand *why*, *how* they died or what happened to them. We just knew 'oh, so-and-so is dead, and she's twelve.'"

Tuberculosis, then known as "consumption", was the scourge of the tenements. The rate of tuberculosis in Dublin's slums was far higher than in any other part of the British Isles. Every family feared the disease since there was no defence against it. Though everyone was at risk, TB struck particularly hard in certain neighbourhoods. From his butcher's shop window on North King Street, John Morgan looked directly across to a solid row of dark brick tenements:

"Some of those tenement houses were called 'coffin boxes'—it was *reeking* with TB. And the *finest* of the young lads and girls going in there and in about twelve months they were gone! It was terrible."

The threat of TB became an accepted part of tenement life. While the disease took a deadly toll in certain families, neighbours directly next door might be providentially spared. There was no logic or justice in its selection of victims. At the very least, everyone lost friends, if not family members, to TB. Paddy Mooney, who lost several childhood chums, reflects upon the attitudes toward consumption at the time:

"Oh, TB took and awful lot of life. But it was a sort of *accepted* thing. You know, you'd say 'that family has TB' and you didn't throw up your hands in holy terror. But what struck me was the way some families were wiped out. I remember Brigid, ah, she was a lovely looking girl she was, about fifteen years of age when she died. But then her brother, he was coughing up blood and he says to me, 'I don't have TB, not at all.' But he *did* have it and, of course, he died of it. Families just *wiped* out."

As an adult many years later, Paddy was undergoing a routine medical examination when his doctor queried, "When did you have TB?" to which he replied, "I never had TB". "By God, you did," attested his doctor, "your lungs are all scarred." Paddy had never known that he was one of the fortunate survivors.

ENTERTAINMENT AND STREET LIFE

"The life of the poor people in Dublin is made bearable, at times even delightful, by their own vivid imagination. They are loquacious, fiercely interested in their neighbours, in the things they see in the street . . . the latest scandal, the latest good story. In the free pageant of the streets the poor take a delight which many of their jaded superiors can neither guess at nor imagine. A funeral, a scuffle with a policeman, a crowd, a group of well-dressed important people, the look of the shopfronts in Grafton Street—all such things brighten the lives of the very poor."

Sidney Davies, Dublin Types, *1918*

For the congested tenement population the streets were social centres, recreational areas, and a grandiose stage upon which all sundried sorts of human drama were enacted out in the open for all to witness. A runaway horse, feuding women traders, a ruggy-up between drunken men, a strolling balladeer, an organ grinder, or a herd of cattle and drovers all provided great excitement and entertainment. The smallest incident offered welcome diversion from the hardships of tenement life. "The poor classes", it was observed, "dramatise every minute event of their daily lives in such a way as to lend a natural excitement and glamour to even the hardest and most squalid forms of existence."[15]

Life in a one-room tenement was confined, stressful, often very frustrating. The open-air streets allowed freedom and spontaneity of human expression. Here the children could frolic about, releasing energy, men could gather to chat or gamble, and women to commiserate in private around doorways. Streets were natural outlets for human emotions and energies. Civic authorities even conceded that it was far healthier for children to be out in the fresh air than in their fetid, disease-ridden tenements. In his 1920 novel about the tenements entitled *Dinny of the Doorstep*, K. F. Purdon explains the allure of the streets:

"One room in which to exist; to sleep and wake, to wash and dress, to cook and eat . . . never to get away from the others, never to have any privacy . . . add dirt, bad ventilation and worse smells and then you will understand why children spend so much of their waking life in the streets . . . there they cluster, thin, ragged and barefoot, yet cheery withal."[16]

Streets were alive with children scampering about, swinging on lamp-posts, skipping rope, playing relieve-io and other animated games. Girls played house with discarded boxes, boards and bricks, made dolls out of scrap wood and paper, and played shop with broken pieces of cups and plates. Sheer devilment kept many a lad occupied. A popular prank was taunting cranky characters or tormenting old folks for the sake of a good chase. The children would then dash through the maze of tenement "trigging" (tricking) halls, in front doorways and out into rear yards and over walls to safety. When nabbed, however, a good thrashing might be the penalty. Scutting the back of moving horse vehicles was a more serious matter for mischievous lads. One could incur the wrath of the driver and get a sharp lash with his whip, or, worse, slip beneath the heavy wheels and lose a limb. Playing soccer in the streets was another favourite activity. Often the football was no more than a roll of paper or wadded old sock. However, street soccer was prohibited by law and Guards (from the Irish Gardai, official name for the Irish police) were supposed to patrol around and halt violations. As eighty year old Tommy Maher declares, around the Liberties most Guards were "decent coppers" who turned a blind eye, but you could be caught and fined:

> "You could play football in the streets but if you were caught you were summonsed. Take you to Children's Court and might be fined a half crown. The Guards would be on a bike and maybe give you a smack, let you off with a caution . . . they *knew* you had to play in the street cause we'd *nowhere else* to play!"

In the summer-time children had greater freedom to roam from their home quarters. Swimming in the canal or catching pinkeens with a penny net were popular pastimes. A sojourn in Phoenix Park with a sandwich and bottle of milk was a grand day. Even more special were outings to Sandymount and other seaside spots. Families commonly walked out, spent the full day at play and gathering cockles, and returned home exhausted but satisfied. "We all came back filthy dirty and cut legs," says Chrissie O'Hare, "but we all had something to *talk about*." Taking the tram to one's destination made the adventure even more exciting. Children in the Liberties habitually headed for the green countryside on sunny summer days. A half century ago Dublin was a small city, and just beyond the urban fringe a natural wonderland was to be found. John Gallagher tells of the exhilaration felt by tenement lads when they made a day's trip to the countryside:

> "You were living in a *slum* which was dirty but twenty minutes walking would take you to the country—from the Coombe up to Dolphin's Barn—and you had lovely green fields and little rivers and you could pick berries and go robbing orchards. That was a great thing . . . a great sense of adventure."

Attending a matinee at the local picture house was another much anticipated event. Children scavenged about for jam jars, stout bottles, and other scrap items which could be converted into a few pennies for the picture show. They could also earn a couple of bob collecting buckets of food scraps for local pig raisers. Even when such financial endeavours failed, they had ingenious schemes for sneaking into the cinema to see a rousing western cowboy film or a serial mystery thriller. During periods of bad weather and at night-time children congregated in tenement hallways to play make-believe games or tell ghost stories by the light of a single candle. Older children who were gifted at telling tall tales were always welcome companions.

Men from the tenements, most of whom were unemployed or had sporadic jobs, filled their time by mixing with mates in a daily routine. When money was available the local pub was the centre of their social life. When empty pockets prevailed, many habitually clustered outside their pub chatting away, passing around single cigarettes for a few shared puffs, and hopefully awaiting a mate who might invite them in for a jar. Street gambling also helped to pass the time. This could take the form of a large toss school with dozens of men and heavy betting or merely a handful of mates sitting on the kerb beneath the gas-lamp playing cards for buttons or matchsticks. During the daytime men also gravitated toward the cattle and horse markets, the docks, and the fruit and vegetable markets where there was always much activity and lively conversation. Many men also liked to take a daily walk with a few friends out to the suburbs or seaside. Walking was an interesting and therapeutic exercise for tenement dwellers forced to live such a confined domestic life. In the evenings men would gather around corners and became known as the "corner boys" of the tenements. Here they would converse, argue, boast, play-act, or harmoniously sing some of the great old ballads, much to the delight of neighbouring tenants who found it an enjoyable free show.

Though the women's day was filled with work from early morning until nearly midnight, they, too, needed their moments of freedom and socialisation. Their social activity revolved around attending Mass, rosary sessions, and conversing with neighbours. "Mothers could sit and chat, that's all they had," maintains eighty-three year old Mary Chaney, "and they used to go to the rosary *every* night and might stand at the corner and have a chat before they'd go in." Most of their spare time was spent huddled around the front tenement steps talking amiably with neighbours while watching the children play in the street. Some women would enhance this experience by discreetly sipping a bit of gill from a concealed jug or taking puffs from a Woodbine cigarette or clay pipe easily hidden from view beneath their shawls. The only holiday they had was a Church-sponsored outing or seaside trip with their children. But these modest breaks from their daily drudgery helped to revitalise their spirits.

Another favourite pastime of both young adults and courting couples was strolling around the city centre's fashionable streets. Along such thoroughfares as O'Connell Street, Grafton Street, and Henry Street the crowds and shopfronts were always intriguing. Naturally, around Christmas and Easter the show was more glamorous. Here the tenement poor found themselves in direct contact with the privileged classes, actually rubbing shoulders with the "nobs" while peering into Cleary's window. While class distinctions were readily visible, there was no jealousy or resentment. In fact, the swankier the crowd and more elegant their attire, the more fascinated were the tenement folk. As a young woman in the 1920s Mary Chaney and her pals delighted in strolling around the bright lights of Dublin town:

> "We'd walk all about, all around town. Grafton Street was real posh and we used to go up and look at all the styles of the nobs, people that was in the money. You'd feel that you were shabby with all the style and grandeur coming down and they used to be in carriages then . . . but we never used to mind them."

Two events were guaranteed to engage the attention of people of all ages—hooleys and ruggy-ups. Hooleys were a regular feature of tenement life. It was customary that on Saturday and Sunday evenings families and neighbours would gather around the front steps and corners with some individuals sure to bring along a melodion, fiddle, tin whistle, spoons or other instruments to strike up a bit of a tune. This always encouraged those gathered around to join in with a song or spirited jig. Before long the crowd was expanded and a full-fledged hooley was underway. When porter and pig's feet were brought along the mood of merriment was heightened. Observers hanging out of their tenement windows enjoyed the event as much as the participants.

No event in the tenements elicited such high excitement and drama as a fierce ruggy-up in the open street for all to witness—it was the grandest free show in all Dublin. Rows were common between drunken men, bellicose women street dealers, and even feuding families. Sometimes even fathers and their sons would take to the street to have a go at one another to settle long-simmering disputes. In the old days fights were fair fisticuffs and the custom was to shake hands and share a pint when the matter was settled. However, when brawls erupted between trading families, tinker (traveller) clans, or animal gangs, weapons of all sorts were brandished. Whatever the nature of the battle royal, it was certain that an enthusiastic crowd would gather around to see the spectacle. May Hanaphy, now eighty-six, always had a ringside perch from her tenement window along Golden Lane:

> "Our lane was called the 'four corners of hell' because the drink was so terrible and there was rows on the street. There was always fighting. Maybe a family feud between the Connorses and the Ellises, they were dealers. They'd all drink in the pub over there and there was about seven or eight in each family and they'd fall out and come out in the street and fight there with hatchets and hammers and big sticks and they'd *kill* each other. On a Saturday night it'd be murder. *Murder!* You'd run around saying 'ruggy-up! ruggy-up!' and we'd all gather around. Always fighting . . . it was great."

RELIGION AND MORALS

"In speaking of slum life in Dublin, it would be absurd not to mention the influence which more than any other keeps alive in the hearts of the poor the spirit of hope—the Catholic Church. I suppose in few cities in the whole world is the majority of the population as poor, and at the same time as devout, as it is in Dublin. The chapels are thronged with humble people who find consolation there for all the agonies of daily life. Their religion is ever present with them."

Sidney Davies, Dublin Types, *1918*

Without their deep and abiding faith one would have to wonder how the tenement poor could have survived their lot in life. Religion was the central core of their daily existence. Even the most barren tenement rooms always had the ubiquitous oil lamp with red shade burning in front of a statue of the Sacred Heart which "kept flickering hope just barely alive".[17] The most devastating heartbreaks and sorrows could be explained in comforting terms as "God's will". "Religion was their total anchor," vouches Patrick O'Leary, "They had a faith that was beyond all reason . . . a *rock*. Nothing affected it." Surely, God had no more devoted children than the tenement poor of Dublin.

During the Depression of the 1930s the threat of communism was taken seriously by many in Irish society. The tenement slums, it was reasoned, were fertile ground for the seeds of both communism and atheism. Such alien ideologies, however, were eschewed by the devoutly religious tenement population. In 1936 Dr J. P. Brennan, Vice-Chairman of the Irish Christian Front, declared thankfully that "Communism has been knocking at their doors incessantly and perseveringly, only to be repulsed with scorn."[18] Another leading religious figure of his day, Archdeacon Kelleher, praised tenement dwellers for their religious values and high moral character, explaining that communism had been repelled because of the "fundamental Christian virtues of faith, charity and humility which are to be found in greater degree among the poor classes than amongst any others".[19]

The tenement population did indeed have a reputation for being honest and law-abiding. Robberies, vandalism, muggings, and sexual crimes were virtually unknown. Tenement doors were left unlocked, even open, and people walked the streets at all hours without fear of violation. "They had a code of honour among themselves and were extremely religious," affirms Guard Paddy Casey. Most robberies he detected at that time were those of the desperately poor breaking into their own penny gas metres to extract money for food. Rape was "non-existent" in his early years and he regarded fighting among individuals as at least "civilised" in its bare-fist form. Local ruffians were usually tamed within the community by family members or neighbours—all in the public interest.

Religion was especially important to women who depended upon it for refuge and solitude. It has been said, with much truth, that men had their local pub while women had their parish church. "My mother had no social life apart from the home and church," intones Jimmy McLoughlin. In a world of physical hardship, financial struggle, illness, and alcoholism, tenement women bore the greatest burdens. When times were roughest they instinctively turned to their religion for comfort. For many, the local church provided the only private and peaceful moments in their life. Una Shaw admired their unshakeable faith and ability to accept the most heartbreaking tragedy as part of God's plan:

> "An awful lot of infant mortality in those days, the child just didn't survive. But they accepted it all . . . 'oh, it's God's will.' It *wasn't* God's will, but that's the way they'd say it. Religion was their mainstay. If everything else was gone, if you'd nothing else, *that* was never going to change. That was the only thing they had when they were down and out. Just even to sit in a quiet church can take an awful lot off your mind."

There was great respect for the clergy and the local priest was nearly as infallible as the Pope in the minds of parishioners. When approaching a priest along a pathway it was obligatory to reverentially step aside and bow or curtsy with a "God bless you, Father." Priests, however, were often viewed with as much fear as respect. "You were *afraid* of the clergy, they were above you," confides John Gallagher, "the parish priest, he was like God." Most men remember with painful vividness the hell-fire sermons directed at them during their annual retreats. Like some terrible tyrant perched on his lofty pulpit above the cowering masses, the priest in bellowing tone would deliver sobering warnings about drink, gambling, sexual promiscuity, and the impending day of judgement. Noel Hughes recalls seeing burly men tremble with fear as if they were lads being scolded by a parent:

> "All the poor men out working hard all day long in hail, rain, and snow and the Missioner would get up on the pulpit and say, 'You're all *damned to hell*.' He had people *terrified*. You know, if you committed any sin . . . 'you're damned to hell.' Any type of sex was a terrible thing. You had a priest called Father Crosbie and he used to go up the laneway with a stick and any courting couples he'd see he'd hit them with the stick. Oh, he was a terrible man altogether for frightening people."

Sexual morality was a most vexing matter back in the days before reliable sex education was available. For the most part, the subject was taboo, seldom discussed even between parents and children. Young girls consequently often "got into trouble" through sheer ignorance. And adultery, even in those God-fearing times, was quite common. In the vernacular of the tenements an unfaithful husband would have a "fancy woman", or the wife a "fancy man". But women always paid the heaviest price for indiscretion. In fact, even within marriage sexual activity posed a traumatic problem for women. Many wives desperately wanted to limit the number of children they had for survival's sake. But according to the dictates of the Church for a woman to refuse her husband's sexual advances was a sin—even if she already had more children than she could adequately feed and clothe. These women today candidly reveal the anguish they felt when confessing to their priest that they had not complied with their husband's wishes. In the confessional, disclosed Mary Doolan, women were often chastised rather than consoled by the priest:

> "If you went into Confession, if you said that you wouldn't have sex with your husband—but we didn't call it 'sex' in them days—you wouldn't get absolution. You'd be put out! They'd tell you to *'get out!* I'm *not* giving you absolution.'"

Within the tenement community harsh judgment was reserved for unwed mothers. Premarital pregnancy was regarded as high scandal and a moral blight upon the girl's family. When possible, it was covered up and the girl conveniently sent away in time to spare the family's reputation—though suspicions always lingered. More often, the truth became known and was the talk of the neighbourhood. Paddy Mooney contends that such pregnancies were more common than one might imagine at that time:

> "There was a hell of a lot of women made pregnant, had babies. These babies were either handed over to adoption agencies or if they were kept the girl was subjected to all kinds of pressure within the household for her sins. She'd get a dog's life. Many were *thrown out.* Fathers used to go mad . . . yeah, the *disgrace.*"

A dispossessed daughter was sometimes taken in by sympathetic relatives or moved away to England. More commonly, however, she was placed in a convent during her term of pregnancy, sequestered from all normal social life. It was a harsh prison-like existence in which she had to toil all the day at washing, scrubbing and cooking. It was a form of banishment which at the time seemed appropriate for her "crime". In retrospect, most tenement dwellers see it as a cruel, unjustified punishment. "They were *innocent*," asserts Mickey Guy, "the girl was always the victim."

Pregnancy among young, unwed girls in the tenements was indeed due in large part to their innocence and ignorance of sexual matters. Nonetheless, most victims were ostracised by family and socially stigmatised by the community. In the absence of protective social agencies at that time, many girls despaired and turned to prostitution to survive. Others, tragically, met an even worse fate—suicide. Within tenement society suicide was an almost unmentionable act. Even today it is a topic most individuals discuss with some discomfort. However, May Hanaphy, now nearing age ninety and having witnessed the tragedy of young girls taking their lives out of a feeling of estrangement from family, community, and Church, feels that the historical record should be accurate on this sensitive subject:

> "There was innocence then . . . and fear as well as innocence. See, unfortunately the mothers told the girls nothing. *Nothing!* You had to learn it yourself when you were fourteen, fifteen . . . you know, when

you had your period and that. You *had* to learn then. But you'd be afraid to ask your mother, or ashamed. And girls did become pregnant. Oh, you were never kept once you became pregnant. It created girls being put out of their homes. A woman often went on the streets if the fella didn't want you. Some of them went into prostitution. And some of them drowned themselves. Out of despair. And the Church had no sympathy in those days. Oh, *many* a girl took her own life. Oh, the Church, she's a good mother, but she's a *hard* mother."

COURTING, MARRIAGE, AND CHILDBIRTH

"If anyone was getting married the whole parish nearly could be brought down. It would be in the room. Oh, my wedding went on for a week, people coming and going. In a tenement all the tenants could be down and dancing in the street and melodions. And you were lucky if you got a washing board for a wedding present, or a kettle."

Mary Chaney, Age 85

Flirtation between tenement children began around the age of twelve, usually during street games. If a young girl "fancied a fella" she would boldly snatch his cap and dash off hoping to be pursued. During teenage years contact between boys and girls took place mostly within the group settings. But by age eighteen or thereabouts "marriage was their highest ambition," claims Peggy Pigott. It was around this time that young women liked to go "clicking" in pairs. Clicking was an acceptable practice whereby respectable young women would stroll together along fashionable Dublin streets ostensibly window-viewing but in reality hoping to meet decent lads. When May Hanaphy and one of her pals went clicking back in the 1920s it was a perfectly proper way to meet a prospective husband:

"Oh, clicking then was very popular. See, that's how flirting went on. That's how many a girl got her husband, going out at night time. Oh, you'd go out for that purpose at that time. We'd go clicking along mostly O'Connell Street or maybe down Henry Street, you know, slow walking . . . strolling, and two fellas'd come along and say 'there's two mots.'"

It was expected that the women behave decorously and let the men initiate conversation. If an interest developed the woman would agree to meet the young man again in a public place to get further acquainted. Only after several such meetings would she accompany him to the pictures. When romantic interest bloomed a courting couple customarily strolled together with arms discreetly linked, went to local dances and the cinema, and visited Phoenix Park. When time came for physical intimacy they might find a bit of privacy down a secluded lane or some hidden spot in the park. But most couples found the greatest privacy in their own tenement hallway. Stephen Mooney regarded it as the ideal tryst for young couples:

"For intimacy people went into the tenements, on the stairs, the halls. See, there was landings on the tenements and there was niches in the hallways. Anyone passing the hall would look down and couldn't see you. And the advantage lies with you if you wanted to do anything at the foot of the stairs . . . you could hear the sound of anyone opening their door. It'd give you sufficient warning to hop out in the yard. And no lights in the halls and no shadows. You could actually be in the hall and people could go up and down and pass you by and they wouldn't even see you! It was so *pitch* dark. It was great for courting."

Weddings were always a major event in the tenement community. Women especially enjoyed the occasion since it afforded them a break from the routine of housework to socialise, sing, and maybe have a glass of porter. "Oh, for a woman a wake or a wedding, that was a holiday on the Riviera!" exclaims Noel Hughes. Wedding celebrations were held in the tenement room once beds had been removed to the hallway landing. Apart from a wedding cake there was usually a ham, corned beef and cabbage, potatoes and a big bowl of jelly for the wedding party. Sometimes just sandwiches had to suffice. But beer and whiskey were always brought over from the local pub. Music and dancing were part of the merriment as friends and neighbours drifted in and out of the scene. Usually the festivities spilled out into the street for all to enjoy. A lively wedding could last from a few days to a full week. Mary Doolan remembers the girlish innocence of young brides in those times.

"The girl and fella got married and come out of Francis Street Chapel and the girl would go and they'd play skipping rope. Oh, you'd see them out skipping . . . they were after being married but skipping rope! And a few coppers in a brown paper bag was threw out to the kids. Ha'pennies and pennies. The groom would throw that out to the kids. It was called the 'grushie'. Ah, they'd kill one another for it."

A young couple had to find a tenement room of their own in which to start out life together. Very few could afford a honeymoon and when one was taken it was usually to nearby Arklow or Wicklow for a few days. Most couples simply walked down the street to their new room and settled in together. By tradition, the bride was confined to her new quarters for the first few days and was not seen by anyone except perhaps her visiting parents. "Oh, the bride daren't go outside for three days," confirms Mary Waldron, "it was a *custom*."

Most brides entered married life with an incredible naïveté about sexual relations. They looked forward to motherhood but had scant knowledge of exactly how it was achieved. "The mothers were as *innocent* as a child unborn," confides Mary Chaney, "we were nineteen and twenty and didn't know the facts of life even when getting married . . . and we paid for our (in)experi-ence." Indeed, many women today reflecting on their innocence and fear say that they felt like they went "like lambs to the slaughter" on their wedding night. For most it was a traumatic emotional experience. It was common for women to become pregnant right after marriage and have a succession of children almost year after year. Six to twelve children was the norm and some women had as many as twenty-four. Explains Mary Waldron, "They just got married and had their family and that was it! Women daren't say 'no' to their husbands." Women were not only uninformed about the mechanics of the sex act but ignorant about the process of childbirth, as Lily Foy testifies:

> "There was no such thing as sex before marriage. Girls got married and didn't even know where babies came from—you were found under a head of cabbage! This is no joke. They'd say they come out of their navel or something. I reckon that a lot of girls when they got married were frightened and it was a terrible experience for them."

Women usually gave birth in the tenement room with the assistance of a midwife or handywoman. Midwives had to be medically certified, officially "on call" at certain hours, keep a record of the birth, and usually received a modest fee. Handywomen, however, were simply older, experienced women who had had a "batch" of children themselves and rendered their services to other women throughout the tenements. They had no formal training or certification. A few shillings or a baby Power's Whiskey was payment enough for most. Some handywomen became legendary figures for "bringing home" literally hundreds of children. A handywoman lit the fire, put on pots of water, arranged the bed with newspapers, guided the mother through birth, cared for the newborn baby, and looked after the mother for the following nine days until she had regained her strength. As Mary O'Neill from Chamber Street tells it, a good handywoman was like a mother hen:

> "I had eight children. We had a woman called 'Ma' Lakey, she was a handywoman. She brought home about eighty or ninety children up where I lived. She'd get the hot water and have the newspapers, the *Herald* or the *Mail*, for the bed. But you had to bring the baby into the world yourself. No pain killers. She'd stand beside you and hold you down, tell you what to do and the baby'd be born. And the mother'd get a bowl of gruel. She'd look after that baby and do your washing for you and look after you for the whole nine days. And dare you get out of bed—she *would not* let you."

Following childbirth the mother had to be "churched" which involved going to the church, kneeling before the priest with a candle, and being blessed. The belief was that sexual intercourse had tarnished a woman's purity in the eyes of God. "Years ago you were likened to a beast in the field after having the baby," alleges Elizabeth "Bluebell" Murphy, "then by churching you were brought *back* to the Church—purified!" Until a mother was redeemed through churching she was not allowed to "take up a knife and cut bread" or prepare food for the family in any manner, as if there might be some sort of contamination. Few women at the time questioned the moral logic of the ritual but a half century later many, like Mary Doolan, express an unmistakable resentment:

> "The way it was, you were like a fallen women. Truthfully. You were tainted unless you got this candle and (renounced) the Devil and all his

works. It made you into a Catholic again . . . see, you weren't a Catholic. I thought I was a dirty woman cause I had the child . . . it was a *living disgrace*, that was the belief. *Stupid!*"

THE ROLE OF MEN, MOTHERS, AND GRANNIES

"The mothers, they were heroines because there was a lot of problem with men and alcoholism and the thirties was a time of depression. They just struggled on day after day in conditions of just living in the one room and washing, cleaning, cooking. It was the mother that would keep the family together. They had tremendous resilience and spirit, strength of character. And grannies were tremendous people because of the maturity and wisdom which was beyond what the others had and they had a very steadying influence on the family."

Father Michael Reidy, Age 76

One of the most enduring stereotypes of the old Dublin tenement family is that of the intemperate father, saintly mother, and feisty, dependable granny. Such facile characterisations may be traced back two centuries to Reverend Whitelaw's observations that men were mostly feckless creatures while women were hard-working and self-sacrificing. Similar imagery has appeared in the literature of the tenements. In *Dinny of the Doorstep* Purdon depicts men as "frowsy, idle, drunken, often vicious".[20] Conversely, in James Stephens' classic work *The Charwoman's Daughter* the tenement mother was revered for her saintly manner and heroic struggle to provide for her family.[21] Interestingly, the oral evidence culled from a variety of tenement dwellers tends to generally confirm these classical characterisations.

In tenement society men clearly held a dominant position while wives were expected to be obediently subservient to their needs. Men always had plenty of time to spend with mates at the local pub or bookies since the responsibility of rearing a family and maintaining the household fell upon the woman. A mother was expected to care for the children, prepare meals, do the shopping, wash, clean, iron, budget the money, go to the pawn, deal with the relieving officer and St Vincent de Paul Society men, and settle family disputes. Many mothers had to manage all these responsibilities in *addition* to working in a factory or as a charwoman, washerwoman or domestic. And, as Una Shaw often witnessed, when the husband squandered the family's money on drink or gambling it was always left to the mother to somehow provide, even if it meant trekking miles out to the countryside to do a day's hard labour picking potatoes or vegetables, or haggling with the pawnbroker or money-lender to get a few shillings for food:

"Mothers held the families together. The women were the mainstay, they were *everything*. They were mother, father, counsellor, doctor . . .

everything. Women were the providers. The fathers seemed to be *invisible*. Men in those days drank more than they do today and they'd go and collect assistance and might just pop off over to the pub and come back with half of it gone. And she had to manage on the rest. There's women in this parish and I'm quite sure they're saints in Heaven for the life they had."

Multiple childbirth, poor diet, the strain of work, and financial worry took a visible toll on women. "She'd sacrifice and maybe get no meal at all," recalls John Gallagher, "that's how a lot of them would be in their thirties and having a lot of children and be really old." The sight of relatively young women who appeared haggard stands out in the minds of many people to this day. As Noel Hughes observed around North King Street, "Women, I often seen them worn and torn at a young age. A woman looked fifty years of age when she was only twenty-eight or thirty." Husbands, however, seemed to have little or no responsibility at home. Some would mend the family's shoes or make minor repairs in the tenement room, but little else. Even as a young girl, Mary Doolan disapproved of men's privileged status and the double standard between husbands and wives:

"The men had no responsibility. The men was the *men*. Men made sure they were kings. Everything had to be done for them. You wouldn't have a word to say—or they'd bang you with the leg of the chair! My poor mother had no life, *never* had a holiday and she'd thirteen children. She used to go to the Christian Mother's Club and they got a cup of tea and a biscuit, and the rosary. And she *lived* for that every Tuesday. She was a *living saint.*"

Many women also had to endure a life of physical maltreatment at the hands of an abusive husband. This problem was widely recognised at the time but seldom discussed publicly. A husband's brutality to his wife and sometimes to his children was largely attributable to drink, frustration over unemployment, and the strain of life in a single tenement room. A husband would straggle home from the pub in a sodden state and the ensuing row with his wife would turn violent. Con Foley recognised the signs of wife abuse when the women would come into his chemist shop on Parnell Street:

"There were some awful sights. The women would often come in and you'd see them with black eyes and obviously they'd been beaten. You know, he'd been drinking. They had so little food that a few drinks could upset them very easily. And there was a great expression then, a threat to the fellow, 'hit me now with the child in me arms!' That was highly melodramatic."

Despite habitual physical abuse from her husband, a woman had no safe sanctuary in those days. Separation was simply not condoned, either by Church or society. As terrible as a situation might be, the wife was expected to endure the abuse and remain with her family. According to Mary Waldron, when young wives entered marriage they were well aware that the commitment was for life, whether for good or ill:

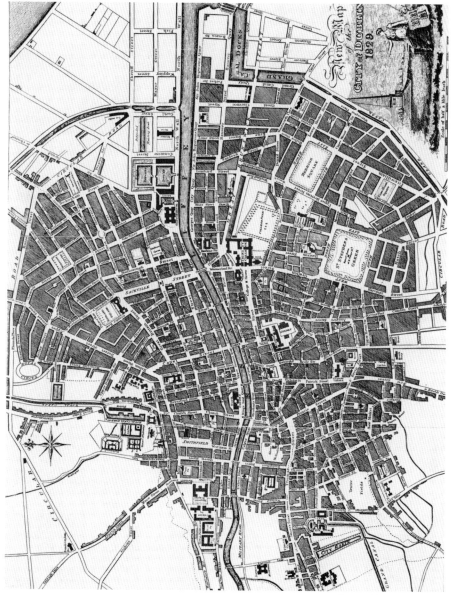

1 Map of the City of Dublin in 1829 before the elegant Georgian terraces and squares fell victim to tenement dwellings.

2 Malton's sketch of Georgian buildings in Rutland (now Parnell) Square when they were still occupied by the Anglo–Irish aristocracy.

3 Tenement dwellers standing on waste ground at North Cumberland Street. (RSAI)

4 Chancery Lane families—some tenements held eighty to one hundred occupants. (RSAI)

5 Henrietta Place tenements. (RSAI)

6 Only a few blocks away from the "slaughter of the innocents" in the tenements was prosperous, bustling O'Connell Street. (National Library of Ireland)

7 Tenement children sometimes ventured into fashionable Earl Street. Note the shabbily dressed barefooted lad in centre compared with the well-to-do children at right. Circa 1910. (Chandler Collection)

8 Fashionable Grafton Street was the domain of the wealthy "nobs" but tenement folk delighted in window browsing and watching the crowds.

9 A tenement street in the Liberties near St Patrick's Cathedral showing tenement shops on the ground level with wares hung outside. Circa 1900.

10 Cross-Stick Alley, a backwater lane off Meath Street, acquired its name in 1758.

11 The dreaded Black and Tans bullied tenement dwellers during the curfew days.

12 Some men found employment as street sweepers.

13 Young lads often got jobs as delivery boys. (Chandler Collection)

14 In Power's Court a Lipton's Tea cart draws a small crowd.

15 Solitary figure in Aungier Place.

16 Thousands of tenement men found manual work on the docks. Coal and timber were big imports.

17 Dockers and carters made just enough to feed their families. (Chandler Collection)

18 Church Street tenements.

19 Patrick Street scene. (Chandler Collection)

20 Bull Alley in the Liberties, circa 1890. (Chandler Collection)

21 New Row in the Liberties. Note pole line with clothes drying.

22 Ragged street buskers were a part of tenement life. (Chandler Collection)

"He was your husband and when you married him you had to do what he *told* you. Like it or lump it! Or you'd get a few punches. That was always battered into you from your *own* parents when you'd be getting married—'don't forget that you're making your bed and you've *got to lie in it!*' That was the way it went years ago."

When a row between husband and wife turned violent, outsiders rarely intervened. It was a custom in the tenements not to interfere in the marital problems of neighbours. Relatives had the right to try and mediate but they, too, usually tried to avoid direct involvement. In the case of brutal beatings a neighbour might dispatch a policeman to the room but it was rare that he arrested the husband and took him to gaol. Normally, the policeman would just sit the couple down in their room and try to reason with them as emotions calmed. Even when a violent husband was apprehended and appeared in court the wife would almost never testify against him. As Guard Paddy Casey found, the wife would more likely tell the judge, "He was drunk last night, Your Honour, he's OK today."

Grannies played a powerful role in supporting mothers and controlling hard husbands. Quite often she was the strongest and most respected member of the extended family. Because of her experience and wisdom she was always relied upon during times of crisis. She could be the most forceful person in settling family disputes, combating abusive husbands, taming wayward children, and warding off eviction threats. "The granny was the matriarch," explains teacher Pigott, "she minded the children and told everybody what to do. That was her role. She was very powerful and *much loved*." Stories of flinty old grannies coming to the rescue of family or neighbours during troubled times are part of tenement lore. Lily Foy's granny, who lived to be ninety-six, was indisputably one of the most loved and legendary grannies in the Liberties early in the century:

"My grandmother was the boss, she was the head of the whole family. She always went to people who were having their babies or if their children were sick they'd run for my granny, or for people that were dead, she'd lay them out. Or if there was any trouble they'd come for her. The men at that time were very hard on their wives. They'd drink a lot and come home and beat some of them up. I saw men not only hitting but kicking their wives. My granny, if they were hitting their wives she'd go in and say, 'This'll stop! You're not going to kick you wife and children while I'm alive.' She feared no one. I remember there was a man hitting his wife and my granny ran up to him and I saw her giving him a punch as good as any man gave a punch. But he wouldn't raise his hand to her cause he *respected* her."

DRINKING, GAMBLING, PROSTITUTION, AND ANIMAL GANGS

Tenement communities had their "underworld" elements. The higher classes commonly cited the excessive drinking, gambling, prostitution, and gang warfare as evidence of moral degeneration within the lower social order. Tenement folk, however, regarded these activities as "unfortunate" rather than "evil" realities of life in the impoverished slums. An examination from *within* the tenement community reveals that these practices were sociologically understandable and socially tolerated under the circumstances of the time. In fact, drunkards and prostitutes were more often treated with sympathy than condemnation and animal gangs were sometimes hailed as heroes for their defence of the downtrodden.

Excessive drinking was always one of the most conspicuous problems among the tenement population. By the 1870s public drunkenness had become so prevalent that the Select Committee of the House of Lords on Intemperance undertook to examine the problem. The population of Dublin at that time was 337,000 and there were 1006 public houses, 310 spirit grocers, 137 beer dealers, and 209 unlicensed drinking houses known as "shebeens".[22] As one frustrated magistrate proclaimed, "Dublin is saturated with drink, it is flooded with drink . . . every third or fourth house deals in drink."[23] Indeed, in 1877 Marlborough Street alone had sixteen public houses and an untold number of shebeens. Most of the shebeens were in tenement rooms where the illicit operator would mark the place with a piece of turf or an oil bottle in the window as an identification sign for customers. Scouts were posted outside in the street to give warning when police might appear so that the evidence could be quickly removed from the site.

The smell of Guinness's brewing process was so strong in the nostrils of tenement dwellers in the Liberties that it might be argued that they were, in a sense, addicted to drink from birth. Actually, porter was often given to infants and children in the belief that it was good for treating worms and sort of sterilised their insides. Even Cameron noted in 1904 that it was "not unusual to see a mother giving a sup of the porter to her infant".[24] However they may have acquired the habit, most men drank heartily and many over-indulged, leading to deprivation at home and abuse of wife and children. Though many Victorian social reformers lambasted the lower classes for their displays of drunkenness and rowdy behaviour, Cameron and other enlightened observers sought to understand their misery and need for drink and took a more sympathetic view:

> "The workman is blamed for visiting the public house, but it is to him what the club is to the rich man. His home is rarely comfortable and in the winter the bright light, the warm fire, and the gaiety of the public house are difficult to resist."[25]

In 1877 the Select Committee on Sale of Intoxicating Liquors on Sunday (Ireland) investigated the causes and effects of drink among the poor. Dozens of impassioned witnesses were called to testify to the evils of drink and to offer suggestions for reform. But many of those who testified were sympathetic to the fact that in the congested tenement environment, fraught with hardship and stress, the public drinking house offered men their only refuge from boredom and despair—it was viewed as a "safety-valve" offering emotional and psychological relief from the pressures of poverty. As one witness affirmed with great feeling:

"Thousands upon thousands of the multitudes in this city live and die in places whence a humane sportsman would be ashamed to whistle forth his spaniels. Surely it is in vain that I, or such as I, should bid them, steeped in squalor and besieged by disease, joyless, hopeless, Godless, not seek the light and warmth of the gin-palace, and the oblivion, however temporary and baneful, they can purchase therein."[26]

There is no doubt that the gloom of single-room tenement life drove men to drink in the local public house. Drink and camaraderie lifted their spirits and allowed them to forget—at least temporarily—their problems. Growing up in the Coombe, John Gallagher understood why so many men spent the better part of their lives in pubs—"There was a lot of drunkenness. It was a form of escape cause you lived in a terrible tenement and to *get out*, to get into a pub, that was a different world . . . like a little club . . . *escapism*." Back then, drink was cheaper than food and many men relied upon it for their daily sustenance. Publican John O'Dwyer worked in his early days behind the bar of some pubs in the poorest tenement districts around York Street and the docks and was always troubled to see men addicted to drink at the expense of their health:

"They had *nothing*. They *lived for pints*. Drink was the main diet. It was food . . . they used to call the pint the 'liquid food'. From the time people were born, up till the end, the centre of life was all in the pub at that time. A lot of people they never went home until the pub closed."

Many men would gladly pawn their soul for that last pint of porter and the tenements so reeked with booze that it was thought of as a natural smell of the Dublin slums.

From early childhood, gambling provided innocent diversion for young lads hanging around the streets. "You started at about six," remembers Stephen Mooney, "pitching up to the wall with your pennies, then you graduated to how to play cards. Oh, it passed the time." Gambling was usually conducted down alleys, in tenement hallways, or on street corners. It was a common sight to see children enjoying their penny toss while down the street a group of men might be engaged in a card game to pass the day away, betting only buttons or cigarettes. Many men, however, took their gambling seriously, squandering their meagre wages in card games or at the toss school. Jimmy McLoughlin remembers as a boy watching the men around his neighbourhood form a circle to hold a toss school, hoping that if the crowd were suddenly dispersed by a police raid there might be a few forsaken coins left on the ground for scavenging:

"They'd come from all over the city for toss schools in those days. They'd toss the pennies and some people'd lose their wages. One man would keep

nix on the corner of Talbot Street and one man on the corner of Marlborough Street to see were the police coming. Oh, he'd give a whistle and
they'd know! The money would be taken up and they'd scatter. And then
we'd all run around to see if any money was left. See, often they wouldn't
get a chance and there'd be money left and you'd get a few coppers."

Police were always on the watch for high-stakes toss schools which would
draw a large crowd of men, some of whom would fritter away their family's
rent and food money. Organised police raids were carried out to break up the
most notorious toss schools which caused wives to complain when their
husbands lost their wages. Back in the 1930s when policeman Senan Finucane
was walking his beat in the Liberties he encountered some big-time jackpots:

"We'd lots of complaints about the toss schools where people would
lose all their wages. Women would complain. And a row often started
at a toss school. Now a big toss school, there may be sixty or seventy
people and often there'd be a hundred pounds or two hundred pounds
on the ground—*a lot of money*. The place would be full of silver, half
crowns. Oh, I often saw *buckets* of money. So emotions were high. So
we'd raid with a force of maybe ten or twelve Guards and they may
have a lookout and then we could go in plain clothes."

Some tenement areas were known as red-light districts, famed for their
brothels. Apart from the notorious Monto district around Montgomery Street,
numerous brothels—or "kip houses" as they were then known—were found
around North King Street, Bolton Street, the dock area, and at boarding
houses such as "Lynch's Den" in the Liberties. Many prostitutes who lived in
the tenements also plied their trade on O'Connell Street and Grafton Street
and around St Stephen's Green where well-to-do gentlemen abounded. In
fact, "A custom grew in O'Connell Street whereby one side of the street was
reserved for 'respectable' people and the other side for prostitutes."[27] While
prostitutes were not regarded as respectable by Dublin's genteel society, within
the tenement community they were accepted, treated with compassion, and
the majority were genuinely well liked.

Young women were driven into prostitution through desperation—it was
a last resort. The majority were country girls who came to Dublin and fell
upon hard times. Many had worked as domestics in the homes of the
wealthy but were made pregnant by the master of the house or a son and then
conveniently expelled. Since they could not return to their families and there
was no social agency to assist them, they turned to the streets. City girls suffered
similar scenarios. Oral testimony of the times confirms that virtually all prostitutes were helpless victims of circumstances beyond their control. Tenement
dwellers understood their plight and accepted them as "unfortunate girls"
deserving of simple kindness. By all accounts, the girls were typically young,
attractive, and renowned for their generosity, especially to slum children. "They
were very decent, very kind, the wives'd even say 'hello' to them and be friendly
enough," recalls eighty-five year old Billy Dunleavy. As a young child growing

up on Corporation Street in the 1920s, Mary Corbally lived in the midst of brothels and prostitutes and remembers the girls with a certain fondness:

"I don't feel any shame in coming from the Monto, but the reputation was there cause of the girls. In them years they was called 'unfortunate girls'. We never heard the word 'whores', never heard 'prostitute'. Very rarely you'd hear of a brothel, it was a 'kip' and the madams we called them kip-keepers. But the girls were very good, they were generous. They were very fond of kids. If you went for a message for them you'd get thruppence or sixpence. If they seen a kid running around in his bare feet they'd bring him into Brett's and buy him a pair of runners . . . the girls were generous."

The madams, several of whom became legendary figures in tenement folk-lore, were Dublin women. They were tough, shrewd businesswomen who ruled their roost in a strict maternal manner. They clothed their girls, housed them, and took a hefty percentage of their earnings. Many of the kip houses also illegally sold drink which made it easier to part a man from his money. Billy Dunleavy was impressed with the array of customers drawn to the Monto brothels: "Oh, men'd come in cars and all, officers in the Army and business-men . . . all *big-shots*." The rougher kip houses employed burly bouncers or, as Dunleavy put it, "whore's bullies we called them." Many a gentleman awoke out on the street the next morning missing his wallet.

Several madams became quite wealthy, wore expensive jewellery, owned cars, and even sent their children off to prestigious schools abroad. Some were possessive of their girls to the point of keeping them virtually house-bound for periods. Timmy "Duckegg" Kirwan, an old docker from Foley Street, likes to brag that "I knew all the madams in the Monto" as a child and befriended many of the girls. He delights in recounting how as a young lad he would deliberately walk beneath the windows of certain kip houses where the prostitutes would be "roaring out the windows and they'd let down a can with a string on it and money'd be in the can to get cigarettes and matches or get them a gargle at the pub." After fetching their needs, which were lifted up to them in their cans, he was rewarded with a few bob.

The most famous madam around the northside was Dolly Fawcett who ran the Cozy Kitchen on North King Street and the Cafe Continental in Bolton Street, both known widely as prostitute pick-up places. Noel Hughes lived virtually next door to the Cozy Kitchen and watched with rapt curiosity as sailors off the ships beat a direct path to her doors. "The whole of Dublin knew about it," he gushes, "Oh, the police raided it a lot of times . . . but they got backhands." Dolly finally closed her doors to business in the 1950s but she lives on in the oral history of the northside.

Mention of the notorious "animal gangs" which ran rampant throughout the slums in the 1930s and 1940s evokes vivid memories in the minds of every tenement dweller. Back in the forties, Professor T. W. Dillon in his study of the Dublin slums explained the sociological pattern in which poor men from the tenements who had "no chance of employment" would commonly "drift into street corner gangs".[28] Within their own group gang members found support and a sense of identity. Gangs ordinarily organised along street lines and some of the toughest were associated with Ash Street, Gardiner Street, Foley Street, and Corporation Street. Most gangs had about thirty hard-core members who ranged in age from their early twenties to mid-forties. Some gangs had their own identifiable cap or shirt for a feeling of unity. Local lore has it that they were christened "animal" gangs because of their vicious animalistic behaviour in street brawls as they wielded all sorts of barbaric weapons.

The general rule was that gangs never violate their own neighbourhood but fight only with rivals from other areas. Bloody clashes between northside and southside gangs often entertained locals but horrified outside society. Basically, they brawled for the sheer excitement of it, usually after drink, and loyally defended their turf against intruders. While it was great street theatre for the neighbourhood folk it was a major problem for the police. A few policemen, most notably the legendary Jim "Lugs" Brannigan, earned their reputation in great part by battling bare-fisted against gang members. One of the most famous and ferocious battles royal between rival northside and southside gangs took place at Baldoyle. John-Joe Kennedy, who served three years imprisonment for his participation in the brawl as a member of the Liberties gang, relives the scene as if it were only yesterday:

"We battled the northside all the time. We used to have to go over in gangs. They used to carry blades in the beaks of their caps and take it off and give you a crack across the face with it. Oh, very dangerous! And you heard about Baldoyle? There was only twenty of us—against the whole of the northside. Oh, everything was involved, knives, walking-sticks, bits of lead pipe, knuckledusters, a French bayonet. There was killing . . . two stabbed. Oh, we all had weapons. People running everywhere. I was twenty, didn't know any better . . . we were drunk. And we all done imprisonment for that row."

A few animal gangs deteriorated into criminal activities and preyed upon their own local population by mercenary money-lending or outright extortion of shop-owners. Paddy Mooney cites the example of a gang around his home ground of Pimlico who were "savage bullies involved in racketeering". They terrorised shop-owners and threatened to burn their property if they didn't receive protection money. When a group of angry residents of Marrowbone Lane formed a vigilante group to protect their neighbourhood from the menacing gang, Paddy's brother, Stephen, personally witnessed the bloodshed in the street:

"Just ordinary folks who just banded themselves together and they went to war with the animal gang. Oh, yeah, men and *women* from Marrowbone Lane against this animal gang and the two gangs *battered* one another with chains, razors, knives . . . had bayonets and everything. There was over fifty (participants). Oh, I *seen* it."

The Marrowbone Lane group repelled the threatening gang and took control over their home territory.

By contrast, there are accounts of local animal gangs who fought to defend the rights and welfare of their own neighbourhoods. For example, in cases where families were being physically evicted by outside authorities the neighbourhood gang would drive off the intruders by force and guard the tenement of the threatened evictees. And in times of dire hardship, such as a dock strike in which local men were laid off and their families without wages, food, and fuel, the animal gang might secure the necessities of life for them. As a docker, Timmy Kirwan knew a few bad strikes in his early years and regarded the local animal gang as bona fide heroes:

"They were *Robin Hoods* in the neighbourhood! We were on strike on the docks one time and we'd no food or nothing. So they went in and robbed a butcher's shop and took two cows off the hook and cut the cow up in pieces and delivered it to all the people at night-time. And another fella broke into a bakery and took bread and brought it to the people . . . they'd get a bit of stuff and give it to the people. We used to call them 'Robin Hoods'."

DEATH, SUPERSTITIONS, AND WAKES

Some of the richest folklore from the old tenements pertains to death, super-stitions, and wakes. People truly believed in the banshee, ghosts, haunted houses, the devil, and exorcisms. Such mysterious lore surrounding the dark tenements added a measure of intrigue and excitement to life. And these mystical beliefs did not, in their minds, contradict the traditional Catholic tenets. Ghost story telling was a part of every tenement child's early education. Beliefs and superstitions about the supernatural were passed down from gene-ration to generation via the oral tradition and, as John Gallagher notes, gifted story-tellers who could hold listeners spellbound were held in high esteem:

"You'd have some natural story-tellers in the tenement houses, some people that'd be able to tell great stories and they'd be well known for it, sitting around the fire at night or with a candle . . . that's how the banshee became known."

Perhaps because death was so much a part of life in the tenements it occupied an important place in the human psyche. There were many supersti-tions relating to death. "Cockroaches coming out of the fireplace or on the wall, a picture falling, they were all warnings of death," intones John-Joe Kennedy, "Oh, they *all* believed in it." There were numerous accounts of sightings of the ghosts of deceased persons and of the devil himself. Detailed and corroborated eyewitness accounts of ghosts in the tenement houses were taken seriously. It was not regarded as sacrilegious to believe in such phenomena. As a young child growing up on Cook Street, Nancy Cullen learned about superstitions through story-telling sessions in her tenement hallway:

> "We used to go up there on a winter's evening and we'd bring a candle and sit on the stairs and tell haunted stories. Everyone heard the banshee, at one time or another. They'd say, 'Oh, I heard the banshee last night, there's going to be a death'—and *surely* there would be! Or somebody'd say, 'I heard three knocks,' that was a sign of death. Or a black dog symbolised the devil. Those were superstitions. And there was a house next to ours and it always had the name of being a haunted house . . . *always*."

Belief in the banshee seems to have been as common in the tenements as it was among country folk in the Gaeltacht. "The banshee followed most families around here," swears Kennedy, "when you used to hear the banshee crying—and we used to hear it regular—well, you always heard of a death the next morning." Tales of the banshee were passed down from grandparents to grandchildren. Descriptions of the banshee's physical appearance and frightening wail were vividly recounted. Virtually everyone from the tenements claims to have heard her cry but only about a third attest to having actually seen her. When sighted, she was dressed in black, usually perched on a wall, window sill, roof, or chimney stack, and combing her straggly grey hair. Mary Corbally depicts the banshee so often seen around Corporation Street:

> "The banshee was always filthy dirty and these long old clothes on her. She had long grey hair, not washed or combed, kind of dirty grey . . . wild. And she had a wrinkled face and a big hook nose—like a dirty witch. You used to say that if you met the banshee she'd throw her comb at you and if the comb struck you you'd die. Oh, we took that seriously."

To many, the cry of the banshee was even more alarming than her appearance. At first, it was often mistaken for the howl of a cat or dog. But the wailing tone was said to be quite distinctive, a sort of "unearthly" haunting sound which resonated throughout the brick corridors of the tenements. When heard, windows would fly open and people peered out. At age eighty, Mary Waldron still remembers it as a sound no human would ever forget:

> "Oh, I *heard* the banshee . . . oh, God. I was living on Cumberland Street. Now I always heard cats crying and dogs howling and this was different. It went through you, it really did. And you got cold. It was really shocking. I'm telling you, if you heard it you wouldn't like to hear it again . . . it was *unmerciful*."

When death came it was greeted with varying emotions. The loss of infants and children was always tragic. So, too, was the death of a mother at childbirth. But when older adults died it was seen as natural, though very sad for the immediate family. It was the custom in the tenements that the deceased be waked at home surrounded by family and friends. Local handywomen prepared the body to be laid out on the bed. A collection was taken among neighbours and shopkeepers to pay for the porter, sandwiches, snuff and perhaps tobacco, cigarettes and clay pipes. Attending wakes was one of the great social occasions in the tenement community. It was, in fact, a form of entertainment replete with games, pranks, story telling and boozing. Wakes could be transformed into grand hooleys. "Going to wakes was a way of life," opines Paddy Mooney. As Mary Doolan avows, a really good wake "would go on for nearly a *week*, smoking clay pipes and drinking stout". However, in the warm summer months Noel Hughes divulges that after a few days "between the smell of the corpse and the smell of the paraffin oil there was a sickening smell all the time."

Not only did family and friends relish a good wake but "moochers" were inevitably lured by the free drink, food, and fun of it all. Certain men in every neighbourhood were noted for their habit of looking up death notices in the paper and attending almost every wake—even when they didn't know the deceased. To John-Joe Kennedy it was fair play:

"There used to be great sport at wakes. We used to look up in the paper to see where the deaths were! Take up the paper and say, 'Ah, there's a wake at such a place, why don't we go.' You'd go to the wake, just sit down, and you were there for the night. You'd get a bottle of stout and snuff and in some places a chug of tobacco and whatever would be going. Wakes was great."

Upon arriving at the wake, moochers would always pretend to have known the deceased. Some would let forth with a sorrowful lamentation, "Oh, I knew him *well*"—only to be curtly informed that it was a woman laid out on the bed. Some impostors would be ejected for their boldness but others were tolerated, especially if they told a good tale or could contribute to the crack and chat.

Women especially enjoyed wakes because it was one of the only occasions when they could take a break from their domestic duties to socialise for a time and perhaps indulge in a bit of drink. Women unabashedly looked forward to wakes as a form of "holiday" from their daily work routine. It was often said that wakes and weddings provided tenement women with their greatest social enjoyment. Following the wake, the funeral was a "last fling" as the funeral party always congregated at a nearby pub directly after the burial. Nellie Cassidy recalls what it meant to the womenfolk around City Quay:

"Oh, the women'd be looking forward to it. They used to be buried and everyone stood around and they used to fill in the grave while you'd stand there—then to the pub for drink. They used to *all* pull up there at that pub called the Punch Bowl in Merrion there. The women'd all get *drunk* and they wouldn't come home till eleven that night."

Tales of ghosts and the devil held a serious place in the folklore of the tenements. Ghost stories were told in dark hallways and sightings of deceased souls were often reported, especially if they had met with a tragic or untimely death.

Every tenement district had its haunted houses which could be the source of fun or genuine fear depending upon the historical circumstances. Dealings with the devil, however, were especially unsettling, particularly if there was evidence of supernatural possession. In the Liberties there were several houses reputed to have been possessed by the devil. Mickey Guy remembers well that in one such house the local priest had to perform an exorcism and allegedly paid with his life for the act:

"When I was a kid me mother and father and half of Carman's Hall would go down at twelve at night to Mark's Alley. There was a house there that gave trouble. You'd look up at the tenement house and (see) the windows opening and the people in the house would be going that way (swaying) and the dresser and delph falling. Seeing is believing and I *really seen* that in Mark's Alley. And they'd send for the priest to go and banish the devil. It's true. Prayers and blessings and so forth. We were always told that the priest doesn't like going to banish the devil cause he only lives six months. And the priest was Father Donoghue and that priest *died*—after banishing *that house*. That's perfectly true. It *did* happen in my time."

3

Oral Testimony: The Monto and Dockland

She was born and reared in the poorest tenements of Queen's Terrace where local men had to rob food and coal for their family's survival. When sent by her mother to the local pawnshop she was jeered by passing children from a posh school. But far more cruel were the abuses she had to suffer at home. Her father, a docker and local bully, would habitually drink, gamble away the family's few shillings, and brutally beat his wife and children. Though emotionally scarred from the suffering of youth, she is today a woman of healthy mind and admirable spirit.

"I was born in Queen's Terrace in 1913. Two-storey tenements all around. And the tenements were dangerous. See, they were over one hundred and fifty or one hundred and sixty years of age, could be two hundred. Up there on Fenian Street the tenement house fell—collapsed—and two pals was found dead. Children. They were locked in one another's arms when they were found, just after making their First Communion. I suppose they fell on one another. They were only seven. Ah, and there was a good few fires. Just around the corner the mother of two children just went out for bread and her two children were burned to death. But luck had it that she had two more and they were the *image* of them—two reincarnations.

"*All* tenements was poor. I think our street, Queen's Terrace, was the poorest cause there was so many families living in it. Eight families living in my tenement. I had four sisters and three brothers. Me mother's sister had twenty-one children! We grew up in one little small room and six of us slept in one bed. And we had no bedclothes, we mostly slept with me daddy's overcoats over you. Sure, the bed was loaded with bugs and hoppers and you'd be scratching yourself. One toilet in the rear yard for the eight of us families but during the night, naturally, in the winter you couldn't *dream* of going down. So you'd have to go and get the slop bucket. It was kept in the corner of the room and we put an old curtain around it. And in them times you used newspaper for toilet rolls. And when we were little we never had a bath. And we had scabies at that time.

But you know the barrels for the beer, well, they'd be cut down and we'd use half for bathing, like a tub. But we were only sponged.

"We had no handles on our cups, broken cups . . . broken everything. And I said the first thing I'd get if I was comfortable was a nice cup to drink out of. Now with me mother we had margarine, the *cheapest* of margarine. But sometimes she'd scrape up a bit of butter and when I went to Confession for me first time I said, 'Father, I robbed the sugar and butter on me Ma.' And I said (to myself) that the first thing when I got married 'I'll get a pound of butter and I'll dip it in the sugar.'

"My father was a docker and all me brothers was dockers. Me mother wouldn't let us play on the docks cause all the prostitutes was down there too. The boats would come in and they had their own men. And many of them (women) were even thrown into the river. Like if you and me (two prostitutes) was down there and I have me man and you took my man I'd kill you, and maybe you'd be thrown into the river. Oh, many a body I heard going in. But as children we'd go down to the docks and make slack balls. See, at the docks the men used to get shovels and fill up their coal tubs and naturally some would fall off and it'd be crushed completely, and the coal would go into slack. No one would be bothered with the slack, only us. We used to bring it home, mix the slack with water and we'd make slack balls. You'd light your fire and your slack balls would be beautiful.

"I remember the Black and Tans all standing around the corners with their guns. There was shooting and the bullets used to come in and me mother had a few miscarriages over the shooting. Sure, there was *holes* in our walls—you should have seen it! We all had to run and get under our beds cause there was shooting, I remember that. And in 1922 there was looting everywhere. During the war there was curfew and the butchers and all was closed. And me daddy and the others used to go and rob the meat across the way, break the door to get our meat, any shop that they could get their hands on. They used to go down and rob the coal at Ringsend Bridge because you could see it in big heaps. It had to be at night time. And the men'd rob stuff off the boats. A load of shoes come in and they got them off the ship. They'd put the new shoes on and put their old shoes into the ship (boxes)—and they could get a few more besides that. See, the stevedore might be gone for his break. And no one'd squeal cause they was all neighbours.

"The most hardship was that me mother wasn't getting the money in cause me father drank it and gambled it. There was no money. But *his* food *had* to be there—no matter where she got it. And years ago you got nothing from St Vincent de Paul and if you had a sideboard you'd have to sell it (before you would get assistance). Oh, yes. And me mother wouldn't take *nothing*—ever. She had that much pride. I started to work at fourteen right out of school. I went to domestic work. I was a nanny and I got half a crown. And I said, 'Oh, thank God, Mother, a half crown now, that's grand!' I never took it—it was for me mother.

"And she'd get loans off a money-lender. There was a woman down here and she had a stall with apples, oranges, and if you wanted a loan of money you *had* to take a dozen of the apples and they could be bursted apples, no good to you. Maybe get a loan of five pounds and if you paid your interest every week you'd still owe your five pounds. And one time there was a big row. I saw it at the corner. This woman (borrower) hadn't the money to pay her and this woman (money-lender) beat up the woman. And now there was a friend of mine and when she'd get a loan off a Jewman the Jewman would knock and she'd put black crepe on the door. See, years ago when you're dead they'd put a crepe on the door. So she'd get a crepe and put it on the door and she'd get a young fella to answer and say, 'Oh, she's dead.' So it happened one day she did this and she got under the bed—but he saw her *feet*!

"I went to school on Baggot Street, Our Lady of St Joseph's. The upstairs was for the well-off children, it was called 'Our Lady's', and the poor went downstairs and that was 'St Joseph's'—that was for the poor. The children upstairs weren't from around here, they were more posh, like from Rathgar. And the children wouldn't mix. They wouldn't play with us. We knew we were poor, of course, and we talked about the posh but they wouldn't come near you. And they used to have lovely jumpers with pom-poms, like round balls, over their little pinafores. And I'd none. I'd be wearing any old thing. Mother always got our clothes second-hand at the Daisy Market and the Iveagh. And one day I found two pom-poms, only two pom-poms, and I pinned them down there (on clothing) and I had an idea (how it felt). But I had no jumper. And they pulled the pom-poms off me! I felt sorry for them . . . cause they were so hurtful. And I was going to the pawn for me mother one morning and when you'd be going to the pawn and you'd meet someone you'd say, 'I'm going to me uncle's.' See, the pawn was always christened your 'uncle' by everybody. So when I was going to the pawn that day the children from Our Lady's was passing and when I got to school they wouldn't recognise me. They wouldn't even look at me. And my heart was broken! I'm still emotional.

"Up to the time Daddy died at seventy-odd he drank and gambled and me mother wasn't getting any money in. She'd have to pawn his suit and she didn't want him to know. She got a hanger and put a piece of paper *over* it in an old wardrobe so if he opened the wardrobe he'd *think* his suit was there. Yes. But he'd come in *locked drunk* and he'd be in bad form and if he discovered it she'd be beaten. *Brutally* beaten! All her life beaten. Me mother had black eyes. If she hadn't got a black eye every day he'd get a medal! He was a champion middle-weight boxer. He beat up everyone on the quays. They were all terrified of him . . . *we* were all terrified of him! Ah, we got a boot in the face when we were small. He lashed one of me brothers with a strap and he went away. And he had never missed a day in school, *ever*. I lost me mind when he went. We had a *terrible* life. My father'd fight just to have a row, at home as well. Me mother, she'd run out . . . she'd *run*. She'd *have* to run or she'd be dead! Her sister and her aunt had a shop and she'd run over and run under the counter and they'd save her. Her father wanted her to leave him, but she wouldn't. So we said, 'Wouldn't that be grand, Mother, if he died.' Because you *couldn't stand* (to see) the beatings. We were too young then (to help).

"Women was slaves to the men. But the *next generation* wouldn't stand for it! Cause my daddy, when we got older—*he* had it! He was like the little bird. And she never spoke to him. He tried to. And *we* never spoke to him, we *couldn't*. Never, ever, *ever*! So when my father died I kept me mother, God love her. Me mother died at ninety-one, from heart-break. She always wore a shawl, always dressed in black. The neighbours always used to call her 'nice little Missus' . . . she was so gentle. Everybody adored her. No one in this *world* had the life she had. Many a time I cry over her. The hard life she had and she never lost her temper in her life. Never! And my mother couldn't cry. *Ever*! She never cried in her life . . . she was so good. And if I was ever on television and was asked 'how did she live till ninety-one?' I'd say, 'from *beatings* . . . beatings and cruelty'. And never cried. Oh, God, the sadness in her face."

TIMMY "DUCKEGG" KIRWAN—AGE 72

For thirty years he laboured as a docker and was known to all as "Duckegg". In his time, nicknames stuck for life and that's the way he wants it on his tombstone. Reared in a tenement on Corporation Street, he didn't wear shoes until the age of fourteen. Back then a lad had to be 'handy' with his fists and he became a junior member of the local animal gang. As a schoolboy he would walk past the kip houses where prostitutes would lower money from their windows in a tin can on a string to induce the lads to fetch them cigarettes and stout— and keep the change.

"I'm Timmy but they call me the 'Duckegg' for short. They called me the 'duck' cause I was never out of the River (Liffey) over here, I'd swim across it. Then another fella put in the 'egg'. From two years old they called me that. I worked as a docker down there for thirty years and everybody had a nickname who worked on the docks. You'd only know him by his nickname. Oh, that ('Duckegg') will be in the paper when I die. If you put 'Tim' down in the paper nobody'd know who I was!

"I was *born and reared* in a tenement on Corporation Street. All tenements at that time. Eight or nine families in a tenement and maybe ten or twelve children. There was ten of us sleeping in the one tenement room not three-quarters the size of this. You slept on mattresses made of straw. Get ticks with straw and change the straw every week. But sometimes you wouldn't have the money and you'd have to shake out the straw in the yard to air it out cause the houses was walking with vermin, and then put it back in again. The place was walking with vermin, bugs, and rats. One toilet in the yard and you'd be coming down there at night-time in the lashing rain on a cold winter's night and no shoes or nothing on you and the rats running up the stairs under your legs. And when you were young you'd see shadows and things and you'd be afraid. And I heard the banshee, a wailing sound, and there was a death that night. I swore to God that was the banshee—I *know* it was. Now she wouldn't do you any harm but the little grey-haired woman she'd sit on that window sill with a comb and she'd moan all night. And you could hear that moaning no matter how far away you were.

"I often slept out in the lobby because me father wouldn't let me in when he'd be drunk. Slept on the landing with an old coat over you. Ah, the wind going through the tenements was terrible at night. And there used to be policemen that'd go down at night time looking for anyone lying on the stairs . . . the poor old souls. See, the people in the tenements used to put paper in the hall for them, to cover up with at night time. And they'd (the dossers) tidy up the paper before they'd go out and leave it in the same place and nobody'd touch that because they'd know who owned that. And people in tenements used to give them a cup of tea and bread in the morning. People were great. But this policeman—he was called '9C', that was his number—he had a black tar stick and he used to go around looking for poor souls laying in the tenement houses all night. A big Mayo man. He'd go around at twelve at night and he knew every lobby where the poor devils would be asleep and he'd have his flash lamp and he'd hit them across the back with that, the poor old souls.

"We were very poor. You could go selling papers and you might bring home three shillings and that was the dinner for the house. You'd get a pig's cheek for a shilling and a good few potatoes. And we'd go over to the stew house on Buckingham Street and you got a mug of stew over there. And as a young kid I'd *rob* the bread cause me mother had no money! We had nothing. Then on Monday morning the landlord would be coming around looking for his three and six and he'd have a rent book and knock at the door. And people'd be watching him through the window and *hiding* on him cause they hadn't *got* it. Oh, he'd come back about five or six times to you knocking on the door. So maybe you'd just have to go to the pawn office with a pair of shoes or something to get the rent. The pawns were great. I seen a man pawning his wooden leg to get a drink. He'd take off his wooden leg and get his two crutches and carry the wooden leg under his arm to the pawn office. He'd go in there and get twelve shillings and go into the pub and get a few drinks. And he'd sit down, he wouldn't stand up, cause he'd fall when he got drunk. Then he'd get his wooden leg out when he got his army pension.

"I didn't wear a pair of shoes till I was fourteen years of age. We *hadn't got them*. Oh, out in bare feet in the depths of winter in freezing cold weather. If you stumbled to hit (kick) the ball playing football on the setts and hit the sett the whole top of your toes would come off. And you got terrible stone bruises from playing on the setts. We had stone bruises day and night. Oh, terrible pain. A boil on your foot you got and your daddy had to let it go (drain it) at night time with needles and, My God Almighty, *terrible* pain. Lance it with a needle to let it go. Then you had hot breading poultice. Mash the bread up in hot water and a bit of sugar and make the poultice and the next morning it was *gone*.

"I worked as a docker for thirty years and dockers were the best pint drinkers in the world. They'd drink at seven in the morning and half twelve at night without a bother. They'd drink about five pints before they'd go to work and come out and down to the pub again at beero hour, that's ten in the morning. Two or three more pints and back off to work again. Then at dinner hour some of them wouldn't go home—straight into the pub again! This was their life. The crack was great. Most labourers drank together, people who worked hard. But the tradesmen would drink together. Never drank with us. See, the tradesmen, they were the 'gentlemen' of the trades . . . they never classed us. Snobbery.

"Now the children around there, their fathers used to send them down for the jug of beer. A child could bring down a begging can or a jug and he'd (the publican) know who you were and he'd say, 'do you want two pints of stout in that?' Plain porter. And you had to put it under your coat because if the policeman seen you coming he'd be charged for serving you under age. And before children'd come back to their father with the beer they half drank it and some of them'd put water in it. And they used to give babies a sup of stout to kill the maggots inside of them, to kill the worms inside of them. That's what they used to say. Yes, it was a cure. Now most publicans was very good, I'll say. If a person died and you had no money you'd get a sugar bag and go into the pubs and make a collection and the publican would help you. And if a person was being put out over rent—an eviction—they'd do the same, make a collection as well for them. They often did that at that time.

"Oh, there used to be some great sing-songs and hooleys and wakes in the old tenements. Saturday night used to be the great night when they'd all come out of the pubs. Singing outside the pubs first and then go up to their hall doors of the tenements, all singing and harmonising. A man would have an accordion and another man with a banjo and one with a fiddle and, well, them three got together with the fellas singing and they'd all be dancing. And then play cards there *all night*, sitting down, until bright daylight. And in my time wakes was better than weddings—to pass the time. At a wake you got plenty of drink and you'd play games and go knock on people's doors. And if there was a policeman at the corner you had to go down and call him a name and run back into the wake. But a man had to go with you to *see you do it*. Now this one fella was four days dead and no one came to claim him and the body and the smell was getting terrible bad. And these two lads—they were terrible—they took him out of the bed and put a hat on him and a pipe in his mouth and put him sitting by the fire, and a coat on him. And they didn't say anything to the young ones coming up. And this fella got into the bed in yer' man's place. And the young ones thought that was Bollard (deceased man) in the bed and they all come around beside him and *up he comes*! Oh! They were more happier times . . . better than all the flats today.

"There used to be fights with different neighbourhoods—animal gangs. This one man, they beat him and killed him and so they were called 'animals'. Got a bad name. The police put that name on them, the 'animal gang', that was in the paper. Most of the animal gang sold papers around age nineteen and twenty. Different gangs used to meet in dance halls at night time after selling their papers and a row would start and it'd end up in the street here. Then they'd go off and fight other crowds, gangs from different neighbourhoods. You had Gardiner Street, Corporation Street, Townsend Street, and Sheriff Street. And the Liberties now, they had their own gang, they were the racing crowd. Now the animal gang around here, about twenty in the gang, they had their own dance hall called the Ardee in Talbot Street. They owned that. They'd run it as a dance hall in the night time and then they used to play House—you know, Bingo—in the daytime. But the police took it off 'em because there was too many troubles there.

"Now years ago when there was a row and two men were fighting there was no wooden bars or chains. And all the fellas was *very handy*, they could use their hands! *No need* to use weapons. They were great, all in boxing clubs. There was a lot of boxers. They were called the 'bread and tea' boxers because they had no food. They used to leave school and be selling papers in their bare feet and they'd go home and get their bread and tea and go down to the boxing club room. With two men it was hand-to-hand and they'd shake hands when they'd be finished. Oh, but *gang* warfare was a different thing. Oh, yes. Ten or twelve fighting. And *then* they'd use weapons. *Murder*! I seen that all the time. Now the police were afraid of them. Now and again they'd go against the animal gang, but they always lost. Sometimes they wouldn't walk down their street. Oh no, they'd leave them alone. And when there was gang warfare they wouldn't interfere. The gang (members), they'd get maybe twenty stitches in the head, maybe more. See, they'd go to the hospital for to get the stitches put in but they wouldn't go back because the police would be looking for them. They'd take the stitches out themselves after five days. Sit down in their house with a needle and take them out.

"The animal gang, they were *Robin Hoods* in the neighbourhood! They used to take up for the people in their own neighbourhood. Cause they'd get a bit of stuff and give it to the people. One time we were on strike on the docks and we'd no food or nothing. So they went in and robbed a butcher's shop and took two cows off him, off the hook, and cut the cows up in pieces and delivered it to all the people at night time. Another fella broke into a bakery down the street and took bread and brought it to the people. We used to call them 'Robin Hoods'.

"And there was evictions at that time. I seen it hundreds of times. They couldn't pay the rent and they were taking the gas money out of the metre to buy food. Things was that bad. Anything to *live*, you know? Well, the sheriff'd come along and throw you out into the street in the snow and everything. That was the way it was and the Corporation didn't *care*! There was loads of people put out. Throw bed clothes and all out into the street. Ice and snow coming down and them poor people sitting out in the street in the chairs. And maybe they'd lived there for twenty years before that and reared a family there—and someone else'd take over *your* room. But then all of the sudden people got together. And when the sheriff used to come then the animal gang used to come in then—now you had it! They battered the sheriff. And he had the police with him. And the funny thing, the sheriff, he was always a red-neck, a *culchie*. Ah, they hated the sheriff, didn't like them people. So you had hand-to-hand fighting up and down the streets and people'd stand beside the animal gang and throw water and all (down from windows). And them sheriffs wouldn't go back to that area for a while! And that gave them time to collect money for that woman or family, you see?

"We used to see them, the animal gang, and they were all great singers. I lived facing them . . . great harmonisers. You'd hear them at about half twelve at night when they'd come out of the dance halls and all. They'd all get together and sing, like 'We were strolling along . . .' and they played the spoons and all. They were great. People'd be looking out their windows all night looking at them and listening to them. You'd hear one voice maybe and they'd say, 'What a singer!' Most of the animal gang when they got older they all went to London, this was in the thirties. They *had* to get out. And they worked over in London together and were together in the same pub, the Green Man pub, over in the east end of London.

"Now we were younger members of the gang coming (up) along. See, living in the neighbourhood we'd be all kids looking at them and you couldn't help following them on. We used to wear caps and knew all the action. And they used to tell us when we were only kids, 'Never get out in the middle of the road to fight a man or fight two men. Always put your back agin the wall so nobody comes behind you.' That was a rule. And '*Never take off your coat* when you're fighting' because if there was a knife getting used or a weapon the clothing protects you. I was often in fights meself, especially fighting the police. I was never afraid. In the neighbourhood you're never afraid, you know? We were great. And the next day the policeman might pass you and you might say 'Hello'. Now (Guard) number '123', that was Byrne, he was strict on us. Wouldn't let the men play football or cards or nothing. I'll tell you what he'd do. At night time he carried a gun on his hip and a baton—he had a gun! And he'd take out his gun and hit 'em across the lip with it. He hit one fella across the lip with his gun and he got thirty-six stitches. And he got into a few rows himself. Oh, policemen would get in rows.

"Now there was a man named Johnny and they were playing cards out there and this policeman comes down and took out his baton and hit this chap. But this fella took the Guard's baton and kept twisting it cause, see, he had the string in his hand. And the lad had the baton and he kept *twisting* it and the string went around his (the Guard's) hand and stopped the circulation of blood going through him and he was on the ground. And yer' man *murdered* him on the ground, gave him an awful beating. See, he knew what to do to a policeman coming in with a baton to hit him. Just took the baton and kept twisting it. But then he had to clear away to the States. See, that's the way it was around here.

"In them days the whole area was called the 'Monto'. It was a red-light district. See, it was Montgomery Street when the English was here and that's how it was called 'Monto' for short. It got a bad name. These places were called kip houses, the red-light houses. The kip houses were for prostitution and drink. And then you had the shebeens and the speak-easies, they were just for drink. Then you had hundreds of porter sellers, people selling porter after hours. See, there was no all-night drink at that time so what they done, they left the pubs and went into these places. After hours, after you were put out of the pubs, you'd go to these places if you had money and you'd ask for a drink. Now in shebeens there were girls working there as well, collecting glasses and things, and a lady looking after the girls, and the bouncer was there. And at speak-easies you wouldn't open your mouth cause the pub would be open after hours and it'd be 'shhhh!' Now the shebeens and the porter sellers, see, they used to hide the drink in the manholes, in the sewers. Hide the drink in the manholes . . . of Pudding Street, Railway Street, lanes. And they'd go and lift up the manhole and take out the whiskey or whatever was there and bring it in for whatever was ordered. There was a woman who sent all her sons off to the States and Canada to be educated out of the money she made off of drink after hours.

"Now at the kip houses the madams, they kept the girls there. I knew all the madams in the Monto . . . knew them well because I lived among them. Now where they came from I don't know but they used to speak with a Dublin accent. The kip houses, you had Becky Cooper's, Polly Butler's—she lived beside me—and May Oblong. The best kip house you had was Becky Cooper's. Becky Cooper was a lovely woman, she was six foot three. She was eighty-three when she died. Local people didn't mind the madams. And they were the best in the world for helping the poor. Oh, yes, if you wanted money for food or anything. Now May Oblong, she'd see you down-and-out and she'd help you. She had a big heart. Ah, she was over six foot two and she used to wear rings on every finger. If you hadn't any food she'd give it to you on the slate but she wouldn't charge you a lot of money for it, instead of going to these money-lenders. And the madams had the old people in the neighbourhood working for them, cleaning the delph and collecting the glasses and all . . . giving them a few bob. The poor people worked for them, they *had* to do it. My mother worked for them, cleaning up and scrubbing and washing the house for to make a few bob for the family. The tenement house we lived in was owned by a man who owned kips. He was a landlord. He made his money out of that and his family was sent to Scotland for a college education. Oh, they were able to do that for their families.

"Madams had seven or eight girls. And they were lovely girls, mostly country girls. Some were beautiful. They were about twenty or twenty-four, around that age. And they dressed very well. See, the madams dressed them and looked after them, made sure they were washed and clean and all. They were called 'unfortunates' . . . 'unfortunate girls'. The girls were very decent, very good natured. They were *kind* people. They'd take children in their bare feet and buy them shoes and boots. That's *right*. And you'd be going by with your baby in your arms and they'd take the baby out of your arms and take them around to Talbot Street to the clothes shop and *dress* the child for you. Yes, they *did* that. Now the madams would lock them up in these houses and we'd be going to school in the morning and we used to see them roaring out of the windows. This was all around Montgomery Street and Railway Street. And they'd let down a can with a string on it and money'd be in the can to get them cigarettes and matches. And then coming back after school you'd go down the same way again and they'd let down the can again with a string on it to go off and get them a gargle at the pub, to get the stout, and hand the can up agin. And they'd tell you to keep the change for the pictures.

"All the ships would come in here to the quay on the northside of the river and the sailors would come in and it was, 'let's go over to the Monto!' China-men, Norwegians, the Frenchmen, Americans now and again, coming out of these ships and they'd go into these places during the night. It was about a sovereign (the prostitutes charged). Oh, there was sailors and gentlemen went into these houses. Oh, yes, some of them 'big-shots' . . . gentlemen and Lords and everything else and they'd come in on a hackney cab, a horse and cab. And they'd hide inside the covered-in cabs cause you could pull the curtain over them and they'd say (to the driver), 'Go to number twelve.' It was night time and nobody'd see them and they'd open the door and go into the house and the cabbie'd wait up the road a bit till two or three in the morning. Now the sailors, bouncers could throw them out. Ah, they were *fighting* men. Big fine lads who could use themselves. And then you had fellas lying on the ground after being rolled during the night and their pockets inside out.

"You had policemen in these places drinking all night as well! They were from Store Street. I knew most of them. All Mayo men, all big men. And they were "on the take"—or them places wouldn't have been *open at all*! They *should* have been closed up. But they closed their eyes and they got that (money) every night. See, they'd come on duty and they'd slip into one of these places and they'd be drinking there all night and they'd get their back-hand then the next morning before they'd go out. They were able to sit in them places all night. And there was fights outside the houses at nine in the morning when they'd all be coming out stupid drunk. Ah, the police drunk as well! Never sober. You had the police and other people coming out and they'd have an argument and they'd strip off and have a go . . . the men and the police. No weapons, it was hand-to-hand. It'd be a fair fight. We'd be going to school in the morning and we'd see all this. Some-times they'd just go out in the lane and it'd be 'bang, bang' and it'd be all over in a minute. Knock him out and then the women'd wash them up. And we'd be all standing there going to school."

ALICE CAULFIELD—AGE 66

She lost both parents at age twelve but kindly neighbours looked after the orphaned children and they remained together—but it was a struggle. When food was short she used to rob bananas from the boats or snatch a few potatoes from a shop stall to be cooked on an open fire in a tin can along the street. She also delighted in sneaking into the picture house for a Tom Mix matinee. These were the small joys of tenement life that she fondly remembers. But telling of her four sisters lost to tuberculosis is emotionally wrenching.

"I'm from Newfoundland Street, that's down by the docks. All tenement houses and I had one brother and four sisters and we only had one small room. We were *very close* now on that street. My mother used to take epileptic fits and another lady in the house used to look after us. When we'd come home from school and our mother wasn't there the people next door would give you a cup of tea and a bit of bread. They'd take you in if your mother was sick and look after you. Me mother and father died when I was twelve. He died when he was forty-five and my mother died when she was forty-four. The people who used to mind us looked after us. We had our own room, our own place, underneath them. One of them would give us our breakfast and one would give us our tea and the other would give us our dinner. I was the youngest. Some orphans would be put into a home so we were lucky that we had friends to look after us.

"We hadn't enough space, only a small room. Five of us used to sleep in the one bed, feather mattress. In bed there was three at the top and two at the bottom. It was like a spring bed and that'd break and you had to tie it up with twine and rope and stockings, *anything* you could tie it up with. You couldn't afford to buy a new one. God, I think we only had a bed and a chest of drawers and a little box for coal. And my father used to have a wooden butter box and maybe we'd sit on that. We used to have an oil cloth on the table and on the mantle-piece. Holy pictures and statues of the Sacred Heart and Our Lady and a little red lamp lighting them all the time. Hang clothes on the back of the door. And to dry some of the clothes you had a bit of twine along the fire under the mantle board and you'd hang the clothes on that to dry.

"There was a lot of hardship. Like food, we didn't get enough food. A man used to come around with the milk with the horse and cart and churns. People went out to him with a jug and he'd take up his scoop and give you a pint and then he'd say, 'There's a drop for the cat,' that bit extra. A 'drop for the cat' he'd call it. And one woman had a shop with a half-door and she'd sit inside looking over and she'd sell crab apples. They were bitter but we used to eat them. They'd be hard, sour. We managed them. She'd give you about twenty of them for a penny. My mother'd make apple dumplings out of 'em. Sometimes we'd go mitching down to where the banana boats would come in and take a few bananas. Bring them home and shove them under the mattress to ripen. Take about two days. Now when rations come out we used to get two ounces of tea a week and two ounces of butter for each person in the house. But a man'd come around and sell the black market tea. One time we went down to this man to get the tea and when we brought it back up there was only about that much (thin layer) tea—the rest was horse manure. He put the tea on the top of the horse manure on the bottom of the bag. Just put a bit of tea on the top to fool people. And then he was gone!

"Now we also used to go to a shop and I'd take a potato and someone else would take a carrot, someone else would take a leaf of cabbage. We took it off the stall outside the shop. Never got caught. We were about seven or eight. And we'd put that in a big tin and we'd light a fire up on a hill called Condry's Hill. And we'd throw it all in together—wouldn't wash it. Put everything in it, cabbage, potato, maybe an onion and even an apple we'd throw in . . . without peeling it. We used to stir our dinner with a bit of stick in just a plain tin can. And when it was done about four or five of us would eat the lot. Get a bit of glass to cut it and a bit of cardboard off the ground and put it on the cardboard and eat it. I remember one time we lit a fire and we seen a policeman and we hid and after a while he called us out and he said, 'You shouldn't run away because you're burning your dinner.' And he was stirring our dinner with a bit of stick.

"Oh, we played in the streets. There was lamplighters and you'd get up and swing around the pole and if the rope was slipping down he'd tie it up for you and put it around the two hoops. And I remember we'd go to the watchman's hut. You know, if the road was getting dug up he'd have a hut and he'd have a fire and we'd be sitting around the fire telling all haunted stories, ghost stories. At night time cause the man'd be in the hut all night. We'd sit outside the hut and he'd come out and start talking to us. He told us one time about the banshee. Told us that she'd sit on a window or a wall and comb her hair and if you stayed too long she'd throw her comb at you. So he said, 'I'll bring you down one night and I'll *show* you.' And we thought it *was* a banshee. But it was an old lady that used to come out and comb her hair.

"And we used to play shop. We'd have a bit of cardboard on the kerb with a stone under it and that'd be the weighing scale. And there was an old lady and she'd take a drink and she'd open her window and call down and tell you to go down to the pub and get her a pint of porter in the jug and take it up to her and she'd give you a farthing maybe. And there was this other woman and she'd come out and say, 'I have a load of sovereigns for you.' That'd be a plate with a gold rim around it (to be broken into pieces) and those would be sovereigns. And she used to say, 'Now play there at my door and don't go away. And if a man is looking for me just say 'that woman is gone out'.' That would be a man that she'd be getting money off of and she wouldn't have the money to pay him back. A Jewman. She'd give us the plate to actually break it ourselves just so we'd be there to tell him she'd gone out. 'Now tell him I'm not in,' she'd always say to us.

"Then we'd go to the picture house. Oh, we'd get excited. I liked Roy Rogers and Gene Autry and Tom Mix. We used to go to the Elec, that's under the arch there on Amiens Street. Sometimes we'd go to the Rotunda picture house and the Mayro up on Wolfe Tone Street. At the Elec this woman would be selling apples outside and we'd try and get up near her and push her and say 'hurry up' and we'd take an apple off her. Then we'd go to the Rotunda and you got tins, like a washer with a hole in it, to show you paid. Maybe four of us would go in together and we'd only give (the usher) two, and we'd hide the other two in our hand going in. And the rest of our gang would be outside and they'd go around the back and we'd open the toilet window and hand them the two other tins and they'd get in. And maybe you'd be enjoying the picture and it'd break down, go off. And we'd all tramp our feet and say, 'Show the picture or give us our money back.' And sometimes in the pictures there'd be hoppers on you (from seat cushions) and you'd be *scratching* all night. We used to say 'If you went in a cripple you'll come out walking' . . . with scratching all night. Those days were poorer but we were happier.

"My father used to be on the coal boats, he was a docker. And me mother'd put his tea in a billy can and put his dinner in a bowl and put a cloth around it, a red handkerchief, and she'd give us a penny to go across (the Liffey) on this ferry to bring it to him. It'd be maybe a coddle. But we wouldn't go cross on the ferry, we'd *keep* the penny and walk all up along by the Custom House and across the Butt Bridge. And we'd get a penny savings stamp at the Post Office or we also used to put a penny into the shop for toys, kind of a (savings) club. And when the bomb fell on the North Strand we were crying because the Post Office and the shop was bombed and we couldn't get our money. We didn't realise that we'd still get it. And if we were saving up for such a thing we'd take the top off the brass bed and put the money down the leg of the bed, to *hide* the money. You know, maybe one penny, farthings, ha'pence . . . put that down the leg of the bed. But then when we'd want it we'd have to get me father to lift up the bed and take the wheel off to get it out again. Oh, God, if you had one of those brass beds now!

"I was in school till I was twelve. Some of us couldn't read or write very well. And I had diphtheria and I was in Cork Street Hospital. Oh, Janey Mack, it was for a good while. Then I was (back) in school but I used to go down to Clontarf and work for one of the teacher's sisters, do the housework for her. I used to get ten shillings a week off her. And I had to bring in a form then every three months to the school and get it signed to say that I was in school at the time—but I *wasn't* in school.

"I remember when I met me husband first—I was nineteen—and I went up to his mother's house for dinner and they were better off than we were. And I remember I got roast beef. And I went home and says to me sister, 'I don't know what's wrong with them, I think the meat was bad.' And she said 'Why?' and I said 'Well, it was very brown looking, not like the meat we get.' Cause we always got corned beef and pig's feet. And then I said that we got little cabbage heads—and that was sprouts! See, we never got that. And then I got jelly and ice cream! And I thought that was *great*. A big treat. I said, 'Oh, they must have *loads* of money . . . jelly and ice cream we had.'

"My four sisters died of TB. Two of them was twenty-two when they died. And you were sent to the Pigeon House in Ringsend, that was a hospital. I remember going to see them. Some people was afraid to go and they didn't bother. But I used to go and see them. And I remember one of them and I went up and just as I was going in the nun says, 'You can't go in yet, we have to get her ready.' So I said, 'All right, will you be long?' 'Ah', said she, 'I won't be long.' So she comes out again and says, 'you can go in now.' So I went in and when I went in she was laid out in a habit—she was after dying. And, see, it was really only meself and her left. Oh, God, I nearly went mad . . . cause it was just the two of us left."

CHRISSIE HAWKINS—AGE 83

She grew up in a Railway Street tenement, slept on the floor, and lived on soup, stew, and shell cocoa. Her neighbourhood was teeming with children—one woman had an even two dozen! At age fourteen she left school and became a housemaid for a woman who tried to entrap her into prostitution. A caring policeman set her on the straight course just in the nick of time. After she was married and began having children only the local pawnshop kept her out of destitution. Losing her baby daughter and seeing the men carry the tiny coffin away down the street still stirs great sadness—"she was only that size . . . so small."

"Railway Street was all tenements. Only one room people had. Six children me mother had. Some had twenty children. One woman had twenty-four! Me mother and father slept in a bed and my brothers slept in a little bed under the window but me and me sister used to sleep on the floor. My brothers was in bare feet up to ten or eleven and we used to go to the St Vincents to get clothing. Cause people had no money to buy them. We had a big fire with coal and you could use turf too on it and me mother'd always make stew and soup and then she'd have a kettle of shell cocoa. We were *poor* . . . poor but honest. Happy and innocent.

"The landlords, they needed our rent. They wouldn't take half, they'd have to get the whole. There were people put out years ago, for rent. Neighbours would help if they could but not in regards the money for the rent. They couldn't. But they'd bring them in and give them something to eat. They were very good that way. Well, I'll tell you about this old lady. She was a country woman and never mixed with anybody. And to look at her you'd think she was going to grab you, you'd be afraid of her. She was a very strong person. She was married to some big-shot off the railway but he died and she must have went (mentally) when he died. Her whole mind. And the Corporation come to put her out because she wouldn't pay a penny rent. So they put her out. So she comes out of the house with a big, big bag of money. It was that size (pillow cover). A big, black bag *full of money*. Every kind of money. And nobody *knew* she had money, they thought she was poor when she was getting put out. So she left the house and went all around Foley Street and somebody gave away on her and said it was money she had in the bag. And one man got a knife and slit down the bag. Didn't hurt her but just ripped it down and all the money fell out and everyone grabbed it! And took it. She *could have* paid her rent.

"Now I was never out of pawn offices, always in them. Monday was the big day cause we used to have to pay our debts. And back on a Saturday to release things out of it. And the pawn was always *packed*. There was a pawn office down here in Corporation Street years ago and Mr O'Shea, he knew me and you'd put any old things in. Years ago you'd pawn anything, like shades with Our Blessed Lady and the Sacred Heart. I remember fastening up Sacred Heart books and I'd say, 'That's the book for me mother's pension' and he'd say, 'Now, Chrissie, you needn't open it.' He gave me six shillings on it. He trusted me. Now isn't that awful. And I'll tell you one thing I used to take to the pawn for me poor mother—me father's photograph! It was a big one. That's true. Oh, in a lovely frame, a big frame. I just carried it through the streets, I didn't care if anybody knew it was me father. I got a half a crown on it and she'd release it on a Saturday. And then I'd pawn it back again. And I pawned me wedding ring the day after being married! I did. And I got a half crown and that went for me breakfast. I didn't care as long as I got something to eat. I released it and then I pawned it back. And then I *never* got it out.

"I went to Rutland Street school. They were very strict, really very, very strict. We were afraid of the teachers. If you done anything you'd be put outside the door and left standing there all day. That was the way they learned you manners. But they weren't cruel unless you did something very bad. I never got many slaps off them cause I was afraid of them. Afraid for me life to look crooked! I come out at fourteen and went to work for a woman on Talbot Place doing housework. I always done housework. I took to it. Housework always kept me going. A lot of them fancied the factory work but I fancied housework. So I was cleaning the house and cooking a bit of food for her but she kept me too late at night. I'd have to go in there at eight in the morning and I was there till twelve in the night-time and it was pitch dark and I was nervous. And I heard the banshee one night. Ah, I heard a *terrible* cry from her. That's what made me turn around, the crying. I didn't see a thing cause she was up on the top of the building where the smoke comes out of the chimney pot. I didn't see her, thank God, but I run and I never stopped till I got home.

"So I done all the housework for this woman and she worked in Mountjoy Prison where the women was taken for robbing. But she fell down the stairs and broke her leg and it never could get mended. Then she wanted me to stand outside the door and see was there anybody (men) wanted a room upstairs—and for me to go up with them. Wanted me to go up there with a man. I didn't *understand*. I was innocent. It seems that she done it with two or three other girls and they didn't realise until it was too late. So this policeman from Store Street says to me, 'where do you live? Have you got a mother and father? You look like a nice little girl, will you tell your mother and father when you go home not to let you come in here anymore?' So I didn't go in anymore.

"You see, there were unfortunate girls around here years ago in the Monto. Mostly country girls, lovely girls. Some of them very young girls. Stayed in all the big houses along Railway Street. There was an awful lot of them, indeed there was, God love them. Oh, ships coming in from all parts of the world and gentlemen would come over here to Railway Street. I'll tell you, the unfortunate girls, if you were short of anything they'd give money to you. Oh, they were very good. They were all very good and kind to the poor people. If anyone died and they had no money, no insurance, they'd go around and collect money to bury their husbands or their wives. Very kind. Some married . . . and more didn't.

"Back then children was born at home. Mrs Dunleavy, she was the midwife, I'd send for her. She brought home *thousands* of children. Oh, she brought home my children. Now I buried a lovely little girl only a year and seven months old. Rather suddenly . . . she had trouble. I think she was born with a bad heart. I brought her to Cork Street Hospital and she died from pneumonia. This was on an August Friday, I'll never forget it. I went to the doctor and says, 'I want to take her home.' And he says, 'I'll let you take her out on permission that she's getting buried in the morning.' 'Yes, doctor,' says I. But I didn't bury her till August Tuesday. Oh, she was dead when I brought her home. All me friends and neighbours went up and collected her. She was only that size in the coffin. The men carried her. She was four days in the room. Just got one candle for a little child. All the neighbours would stay up all night. Then the men carried her and buried her . . . carried the little one to Glasnevin. She was only that size . . . so small.

"At the wake the room was packed with all neighbours. They were really great neighbours. And one old lady, a lovely old woman she was, came and had a little sup of poitín. See, she was an old lady at the wake and some of the men had brought the poitín and gave it to her. And it was *strong* at that time. See, she very seldom drank—but when she *did* she *liked* it. But she wasn't really used to drinking and she didn't know what it was. So he just gave her a little small glass. So she fell asleep. And then for a *month* after every time she was drinking water she was getting drunk after that stuff. When she'd take water she'd be getting drunk again. Oh, she was drunk for a *month*! She was very old. And she'd say, 'Oh, I'll *never* go into your place anymore.'"

JOHNNY CAMPBELL—AGE 68

Today he sits peaceably before the television in Our Lady of Lourdes Old Folks Centre intently watching the World Cup soccer match. But in his youth he was a real hellion on the mean streets of the Monto where he grew up. At age seventeen he was sent to Mountjoy Prison for three years for breaking into a public house. It was a harsh sentence, he feels, noting that the legal system today lets young juvenile offenders "get away with murder".

"I'm from Corporation Street, a tenement, and when I was seventeen I went to prison, went to Mountjoy. I broke into a public house and got three years. At that time, see, the sentences was tough, strict. If you were drunk, aggressive like, you got a month. Oh, God, a young lad next door to me robbed a jar of sweets off a counter and he got five years! Yeah, for robbing them and running. Justice now . . . you'll see young lads robbing a poor woman's handbag and they get three months, or probation. In my time if you done robbing you got five years, nothing else. Now they let them get away with murder.

"The police was tougher then, they had their batons. Oh, they used them in a melee. All the toughest Guards was at Store Street, all fighting men and boxers. In those days they'd no walkie-talkie, only a whistle. Oh, they got a man down and hands behind him and they could drag him along so he couldn't kick. Sometimes they'd drag him by his feet. And if you were aggressive they'd beat you. Ah, they *would*. Oh, I got beatings myself, I got a hiding. Next morning I had black eyes in the court and they'd say, 'That's the way he was when we arrested him.' Now once I knew *well* (upon being arrested) that I was going to get a hiding at Store Street—and what did I do? I took sick on the street. Now I wasn't sick at all but I was brought in to the hospital. So I took off me clothes and says to the doctor, 'Are there any marks on me?' And he says, 'No.' Says I, 'This is a policeman and I'm going to the station and I'll probably get a beating-up, so will you be in court in the morning in case I'm scarred?' Says he, 'I will.' The doctor said that. Wasn't that clever?

"But Guard '123', Christy Byrne, he was a great man. He'd fight you before he'd arrest you. Ah, he *would*. And he'd say, 'If you beat me you can go and if I beat you I'll bring you in to the court and I'll get you a fine of a pound.' That was the way he did it . . . but you *never* beat him. He'd call 'em down from the buildings (Corporation flats). They'd be throwing dust bins and all down on him. And he'd say, 'Come down' and he done it all himself. I seen him fighting *two men together*. He was tall but very thin. There was stronger policemen than he was but the others *wouldn't go* in there! He'd give you a fair go. Oh, '123' was well liked.

"Back then you went outside a pub to fight, didn't start fighting *in* the pub. And it was a fair fight. You'd strip to the waist and take off your shoes and just fight in your stocking feet. Ah, no kicking. And when you were finished you went back in that pub and the man (barman or publican) would give you a towel to wipe your face and he'd put up two pints. Then they'd shake hands. Now a fella named Whelan and a fella named O'Shea, they were two *tough* men around there, two of the toughest. And every Saturday night you'd always see a continuation of the first battle they ever had. *Same* two men, *every* Saturday night. It was up there at the Honey Palace. They'd be there and one man'd say to the other fella, 'right, let's go!' Take their coats off, hang them on the railing and they'd *battle* with their hands. Men'd gather around and the police wouldn't interfere. No, because they'd be afraid. See, the men'd stop fighting themselves and start fighting the police—and they'd *win*. But the police would be across the road. I remember once just standing beside these two policemen and one fella says to the other, 'Go over and stop this.' And the other says, 'Jesus, *you* go!'

"Now there was also mobs fighting against one another, animal gangs. There were four gangs that would go against one another—Stafford Street, Ash Street, Sheriff Street and here, the Monto. Most of the animal gang was dockers, nearly all of them. The dockers were the toughest men in Dublin. Ah, they *were* because they were going through the mill themselves with the big tubs of coal and everything. And, oh, my God, they could put away maybe twenty pints . . . the coal dust and all. Now there could be a big melee on a Saturday night near Paddy Clare's or Jack Maher's (pubs). There could be twenty men fighting. They'd have razor blades and iron bars and knuckle-dusters and flick knives and hooks off the bales, for the dock work. And you might see a fella taking off his belt and start swinging it. Like McCauley, he was a ringleader in the Monto and he got his eyes taken out by a fella named Browne who hit him with a belt, took his eyes out. Browne got nine months.

"Some women you'd see in the public house. Snugs was for the women. But older women, they'd send a young lad down to the pub for a gill of porter. That was three pence. They'd bring it home for the old woman and she'd give him a ha'penny and he was happy—he was a *millionaire*. And she'd get the poker red (in the fire) and put it into the porter and that put a good head on it and she'd drink it. And it was a vitamin in itself, putting iron in it. And sometimes women would have rows. Maybe they'd have an argument over the little kids doing something (wrong) and one woman'd hit another's child and one mammy'd come out and be fighting the other woman. Pulling hair and all. But no weapons. They wore shawls back then and big boots with buttons on them and they'd try to hit one another with the shawls, try to blind them. Swing it. A shawl will blind you. Sure, then you'd see them in the public house that night and you wouldn't think anything had happened.

"Now in the tenement houses there was red lights (brothels). People that run them, the likes of Becky Cooper, she had whiskey and all for the sailors. And in the street people'd *know* they were prostitutes but they'd talk to them, so's not to make enemies with them. All fine looking women. Oh, *immaculate*, kept themselves clean. And they were kind to news-vendors and all. If they got a paper off you and the paper was only a penny they'd give you a half crown. Now in them times they'd take a woman in for prostitution and it was six months. And you had to go to hotels (with men) cause boarding houses wouldn't take them. They'd catch a fella when he was drunk or bring him into the pub and let him buy the drink and they'd put more lemonade than whiskey in it (their own) and they'd let on to be drunk with him. Then just went off to the small hotels like Moran's down there on Gardiner Street. The porter, he'd let them in for a couple of hours and then you had to get out. See, he'd be on night work and had a room of his own and a bed and couples would come in the room and *he* got the money. See, you hadn't got to sign the book and when his boss would come on the next morning the book would be just the same. *He* got the money, that was put in his pocket. And there was a lot of wallet robberies at that time. Maybe during the night she'd slip out on you if you were drunk and maybe go with your wallet and all. That's the way it went."

MARY WALDRON—AGE 80

There were eleven families in her tenement house on Gloucester Street and when she lost both of her parents before the age of eleven neighbours helped to keep the orphaned children of the family together. Back then, she recalls, you had to be resourceful to survive. People made sheets out of flour bags, ate rabbits and eels, and relied on home cures when sickness struck.

"I was born on Gloucester Street in 1913, the year of the big strike on the quays. Terrible strike. My father worked in the Custom House docks. He was a Ringsend man, they were very clanny. My father died when I was only nine and then my mother died about two years later—she fretted after him. I had four sisters and three brothers and when she was dying she sent for her sons and she told them what she wanted them to do, that we weren't to be put into a school or a home. We were to be *kept together* until we were able to do for ourselves. So it was the *neighbours* that looked after us.

"Gloucester Street was great. All tenements. There was eleven families in our house. Oh, *packed*. And the Black and Tans used to be flying up and down Gloucester Street in cars. During the Rising they barricaded the streets and we would be hopping in and out. We thought it was great, you know. We could have been blew up! But we hadn't got the sense to be frightened, we hadn't a clue. Once me mother was carrying me up the stairs and 'bang, bang'. It was really dangerous. People were in the shops looting stuff like tea and sugar and all that and bringing it home. I looked out through the window and seen one woman dragging a sack of sugar and another one dragging tea to their homes. It was all food mostly. Oh, everyone was looting at that time . . . because they were *poor* and never had anything. I'd a brother and he was knocking off whiskey and another brother who was knocking off chocolate. Oh, we et it! We enjoyed it.

"The women were great years ago, absolutely great. The mothers, they always done *everything*. Up at half six in the morning. Cleaning and washing, always ironing. When they'd do their washing a woman would have enamel vats and washing boards. Bring up the water from the yard and do it in the house. Have the hot water there and then they'd make up a bucket of blue and starch—a blue square and it'd make the water blue and bring the clothes out bright. Shake them out and hang them up. We used to have a line pole on the window. Monday and Thursday was the two big wash days. And marvellous hands years ago the women had at doing things. All able to sew in them days and great knitters. Me mother was great at sewing and knitting and used to make all our clothes by hand. And she'd make sheets. She'd buy flour bags and open all the bags and steep them in cold water to get all the stuff out of them. Then wash them and boil them and put a handful of washing soda into the water to get the colouring out. And she'd dry them and she'd sit sewing them with her hands and make sheets out of them for the beds. Four big flour bags would make one big sheet.

"When I was young the butcher's shops had big tables with sheep's heads and cow's heads and lumps of beef. And you had flies and blue-bottles all around. You'd get a sheep's head for four pence. Get it cracked and bring it home and wash it and make *gorgeous* soup. And you'd get a rabbit for eight pence. And the market dealers from Parnell Street used to sell fish, and all the women wore shawls and different colour aprons. The women'd be out at four in the morning to go to Howth. They'd *walk* out with their cars (barrows). And there used to be eels at that time and eels was very nourishing. Parnell Street was a great market then and they had big stalls and sold vegetables and apples, oranges, bananas, melons. Used to cut the melons and sell them a penny a slice.

"The women were very fond of the pictures years ago. Here in the Lec (cinema) on Talbot Street on a Sunday night a couple of women would go in together, three of them maybe, and bring in one or two bottles of stout between them and *hot* pig's feet. Oh, yeah, bring it in under their shawls. And they'd be looking at the picture and eating them and drinking the bottles of stout. Now when the pictures went dear there was black market tickets. They'd buy the tickets on a Friday or Saturday and sell them to you for so much on a Sunday because the pictures used to be *packed* in them times. And they'd charge you ever so much for them. The police was always up and down but they'd always disappear if they saw a copper. They were never caught.

"At that time they used to do the tenement houses down, distemper them, twice a year. The toilet was in the yard but at night time you'd use the slop buckets and empty them down in the morning. And the houses was very, very bad with bugs. Because when them walls was made there was all cow hair through them and that's how they were *warm*, the cow hair used to keep the heat in them. And sometimes the wood got buggy and they'd come through the wall, little brown bugs. So halls was painted a brick colour, it was a pink distemper, some kind of powder they'd mix in water. There was a great smell off it.

"Oh, and *plenty* of rats. Absolutely. And then we'd plenty of cats around. People kept them mostly for catching mice and rats. And some of the rats was very big now, *very* big rats. We had rats in the room we were living in. They'd chew the wood. And you might walk on one of them on the stairs going down. And in the yard the rats used to play in and out and up and down and we'd be standing in the hall door looking at them playing. Me mother always used to say that a rat would never hurt you unless you hurt it. Oh, but people'd say that a rat went for a body's throat. See, if you were coming down the stairs you'd block its view and the rat would be trying to jump over the shadow . . . see, it was blocking their light and they'd go to jump. And people'd say they were trying to grab their throat.

"And years ago people had different cures for themselves. Great cures. If they got a headache they used to get a sheet of brown paper and soak it with vinegar and wrap it around their heads and put a scarf around it to keep it on. And if their children was a bit knocker-kneed they'd get the backs of a ray fish and boil them down and wash their children's legs in the water. It was supposed to be good for the bones. Now if you had a goose, the grease off the goose, they used to keep that in a jar and if you had rheumatism now or any such pain you'd rub it well into you for the pain. And get tallow if a child had a complaint on his chest, like a cold. They'd get a big sheet of brown paper and make a kind of vest and stick pin holes in it and rub the tallow all on the chest and put the paper over it and put him into bed. And if their noses were stuffed they'd rub the tallow on the bridge of their nose. And I remember me sister putting mustard behind the ear for a toothache. Great cures years ago.

"And people in tenements was very particular about their windows. Oh, very. They used to clean their windows ever so often with soap and water. Some used to clean them and polish them off with newspaper but mostly they used the soft paper that'd be on apples. They used to collect them out of the vegetable and fruit shops and clean their windows with that. They *always* believed in their windows. And they had flowers on their window sills. *Beautiful* flowers, different kinds and colours, like pansies and buttercups. And if there was railings on the window they used to have creepers growing up around it. My mother used to call it the 'rambling sailor', that was the name of a creeper. And very particular about their curtains and laces. At that time there was lovely lace curtains, all scalloped at the sides. And bird cages outside the window. Open the window and put the cage on it and the bird would be chirping. And people used to talk to their birds. Oh, yes. Now a man on Marlborough Street had a lot of birds. He had a blackbird and it used to whistle after the girls. And you'd think it was a *fella* whistling! It was *very* good. Girls going to work, they'd be looking around . . . didn't realise it was a bird.

"People used to save up money. There was a penny bank up on Gardiner Street near Mountjoy Square and me father used to give us a penny on a Friday and we'd go up and put the penny into that. We'd get a little card and they'd print your penny into that. And then when you'd be drawing it out you'd go up and get whatever you had in it, maybe three or four shillings. That'd be as much as you'd have from a penny every week. Women would put in, say, a shilling a week. Oh, crowds. And some people had little tin boxes with a lock at home and they'd save up in that. But some people used to open the side of the mattress and shove their money in and save it, say a pound note or a ten shilling note. Stitch it back up and no one would know it was there. I remember this woman once getting a new mattress in for the bed and she sold the old mattress for a *shilling*. And when her husband come in she said to him, 'I'm after getting a new mattress.' And he said to her, 'What did you do with the old one?' Says she, 'I sold it.' 'What?', says he. 'I sold it.' 'There was a *hundred* pounds in that mattress!' And he nearly went crazy. Never got it back, not at all.

"We played *all* on the roads. It was horses and cars, very few motor cars then. They were great days. On Gloucester Street we'd make chalk beds on the middle of the road and we used to put a rope on the lamp-posts and swing. We used to get a big straw rope for a penny. You'd be swinging around the lamp-post and sometimes the rope, it'd break and you might be flying out in the middle of the road. That's why the policemen if they caught you swinging on a lamp-post they'd cut your rope and you'd have to run. Then we'd go to Sandymount and pick cockles. You'd have to wait for the tide to go back and then you'd get two little pin-holes with a blue mark around the sand. Well, you'd root that up and take up your cockle. We'd all go along and we'd pick up a good few, a big bag full, and then we'd wash them in the water and then going home we'd be screwing them open and eating them. You'd get your knuckles in the shell and twist them and open them and suck out. And we'd often get home and we wouldn't have none left, they'd all be gone.

"At night-time we used to play games on the stairs. Light the candle and stick the candle on the wall and we'd play like concerts, singing and dancing. We were supposed to be all musicians sitting on the stairs. One was supposed to be playing the fiddle and one playing the tin whistle and one girl would sing. And we used to be all sitting telling yarns. There were stories around, like about some woman and she died and it seems that she saw where she was going—she saw *hell*—and when she died she *screamed* and tore the hair out of her head. Everyone was talking about it . . . 'Imagine, that woman saw the devil!' Now whether she saw the devil or not and saw hell . . . but they *say* she did. But, oh, I heard the banshee. I *heard* her . . . oh, God. Now I always heard cats crying and dogs howling and this was different. It was *unmerciful*. They say she was a little woman with long hair, used to sit down on the walls and keep combing her hair and crying. But, my God, when I heard it it was *really* shocking. It went through you, it really did . . . and you got cold.

"Now there was a woman from Kevin Street moved into our house and she was telling us about the fellas going around late at night playing the mouth organs. They used to do that years ago. It seems that the fellas was joking going along and they saw the banshee sitting on the wall over on Kevin Street and one of the fellas dared the other fellas to take the comb out of her hand. So, one went over and took the comb out of her hands and the next morning he couldn't get out of bed. And they got the doctor for him. But the doctor could find nothing the matter with him. So then they got the priest and the priest blessed him and all. So one of the fellas told the priest what happened the night before and the priest went to him and said, 'You'll have to get out of that bed and go back and give her that comb.' So, anyway, they helped him up and he went at the *very* hour that he took the comb off her and put the comb back in her hand and came back home. But died. Now I think that really happened.

"Long ago couples would go behind the hall door. And years ago when you were getting married you used to have to go to the priest to get the 'letter of freedom'. He'd ask you personal questions like, 'Did anything happen before you got married? How long were you going with him? Does your mother approve of it?' Girls got married and never knew a thing about married life, not a thing. Oh, I never knew a thing about married life. But I never had any trouble, thank God and the Blessed Mother, and I had twelve. Women . . . oh, some of them had twenty-two children. Years ago they just got married and had their family and that was it. Women daren't say 'no' to their husbands. He was your husband and when you married him you had to do what he *told you*! Like it or lump it! Or you'd get a few punches. That's the way it was years ago. I seen them getting kicked now by their husbands, falling on the ground and getting kicked along. Oh, nobody'd interfere. Oh, the men used to give *shocking* treatment in an argument to the women . . . *banging* them. Police might be called but they were never charged or anything. And they couldn't run home to their mothers. That was always battered into you from your own parents when you were getting married—'don't forget, you *made your bed*, you *lie in it*!' Even though there was murder and one black eye. And then they'd be happy as Larry next day . . . like nothing happened."

BILLY DUNLEAVY—AGE 86

He grew up on Foley Street and later Gloucester Place where he had many an unfriendly encounter with the dreaded Black and Tans whom he openly hated. He contends that in a fair fight many of the local men could have whipped the Tans but dared not do so because "they'd shoot you". He was a great supporter of the "real Sinn Féin" who were active in his Monto district at that time and Mayor Alfie Byrne was a great hero to the poor.

"The old days, they were poverty-stricken. *All* tenement houses here and *packed* with people! Oh, it was a great thing in Ireland years ago, big families. There was eight of us but some families had twenty. My mother was a midwife and she looked after all the poor people when they had babies. My father used to cut cow horns in a factory to make rosary beads and combs—that died out.

"*Everyone* was living in poverty. On a Monday morning there'd be queues going up to the pawn. It was mostly bedclothes and a suit. And the poor people that was really hard up, they used to give a bundle in and it'd be nothing but maybe an old brick. They'd get their two bob. And we'd no gas, no light. The first man that got us electric light was Alfie Byrne, the old Lord Mayor of Dublin ten times. A *great* man. All the poor he looked after. If there was anyone down here in trouble he'd be down *that* night, in the 1930s and all. He was the best politician we ever had! Oh, for the Lord's sake, when an election would come along he was *always* put in. Everyone in poverty and the rent might be only a shilling a week but they couldn't pay it—no money to pay the rent. The Corporation'd get the police down for not paying your rent, put you out on the street! And you had no one to come to your assistance at that time. Well, the neighbours would take them in. See, then we had the Sinn Féin, but it's not the same Sinn Féin that's going now. They were the *real* Sinn Féin and looked after the social part of the country. *They* used to stop them (evictors). Oh, they got *fed up* with it. Oh, they wouldn't let them in.

"Kids would be knocking about the streets. We used to play handball against a big wall. If you got caught you'd be fined two and sixpence. For devilment I done scutting on the cabs and all the trams. And if you mitched from school you'd get a hiding. Oh, the (Christian) Brothers were rough, tough . . . used straps on you. Horrible men they were . . . very ill. Oh, that's the truth. And if you mitched five or six times you'd be sent away to Artane for three or four years. But everyone come out of Artane had a trade. And they had a place out there in the mountains, Glencree, and that's where you were sent for robbery. If you went to Glencree you wouldn't go back the second time! Oh, it was hard. You got up at six in the morning and out in the fields digging for turf and all like that, in the winter. I had a cousin was sent out there for robbing a bit of lead and he got five years. And do you know what happened to him? He was (working) on a machine and his arm got caught and he lost his arm. And he only got £300 for it.

"We were only kids then but the Black and Tans I remember them. People *hated* them. The British soldiers were different altogether, they'd go out there and be maybe talking with people. But the Black and Tans was all a gang of criminals, all gangsters out of the prisons. All riff-raff out of prisons. Always ten and twelve of them together in armoured cars. You couldn't get out in the night (curfew) cause they'd come along and give you a hiding. They were tough with the gun but if you met in a fair fight they wouldn't be tough. Not at all! They used to run through the place in the night-time and break people's windows and all. That's what they called fun, do it for fun. What could we do? If you went out they'd shoot you! Do what they liked! They'd steal anything, do anything. Go out on drunken orgies. They'd go in kip houses and *rob them* if they got the chance at any money. Oh, yes, they were all a gang of bastards. Horrible things they used to do. There was a picture house around there called the 'Lec' and on a Friday evening these two chaps—they were just seventeen or eighteen years of age—was coming out of it and the Black and Tans come up alongside them and took them away in an armoured car. The next morning they were found in Drumcondra with a bucket over their head and about fifty bullets in them. The Black and Tans killed them, *riddled* them with bullets. For doing *nothing*! He just had a Kevin Barry song in his pocket! They were a gang of murderers the Black and Tans.

"I remember the Rising well. I was over in St Stephen's Green that morning and these men come along and says, 'Go on home now, there's going to be a bit of trouble.' So naturally enough we went home. We didn't think it was going to be a *Rebellion*. People couldn't come out, there was a curfew on. Oh, I seen everything. In 1916 there was looting and everything going on on O'Connell Street where all the good shops were. Men and women and all, they had no grub or nothing and all hemmed in for over a fortnight. They *had* to go out and get it. Anything they could get their hands on, carrying different things. And the IRA chaps, they all run down this way and some of them wounded. There was a chap with a horse and car and he took four of them up to the Mater Hospital that was wounded.

"The IRA was the best men we ever had at that time. The Tans used to go around in the tenders with a wire over the top and if it was going by up there in

Talbot Street they'd (IRA) say, 'Get out of the way, *quick!*' and they'd throw a hand grenade into the car. Now Phil Shanahan, he owned a pub there on the corner, he was a great man and he used to hide them after they'd been out on a job. He had cellars and all the IRA men used to go in there and hide their stuff and all. But nobody *knew* who an IRA man was. Oh, no, you wouldn't know who an IRA man was around here at that time at all. They were all very secret. They *had* to be that way. Your neighbour could be an IRA man. On a Saturday morning this big fella, he used to give information—he was an *informer* against the IRA—and two men come around that morning and riddled him in the public house, riddled him with bullets. The IRA killed him. But they were good men and they wouldn't kill any innocent people.

"This place was all the Monto. Oh, there was about seven or eight kip houses, we lived next door to them. And a good few girls in them. Oh, they were grand looking girls, seventeen, eighteen, maybe twenty. The kip houses were just ordinary houses but you seen the men going in and out, in and out. Oh, men'd come in with big cars and all. Big-shots . . . businessmen, British soldiers, officers in the army, British *generals*. Big-shots! It was safe enough. Men wouldn't stay all night. But some of the girls would *rob* them. Got 'em drunk. Take his trousers away from him and take his money. And the kip houses had bouncers—whore's bullies we called them—and if a man didn't give up the money he'd get a hiding. The Guards knew what was going on but they couldn't do anything. But if the kip houses were selling bottles of stout the Guards could get the bottles and break them up. See, there were manholes out there, you know, where the water goes down. And they'd (kip owners) put the bottles of stout down the manholes when the police'd be coming. Now your bottle of stout at that time was only about eight pence but if the men brought a girl to Becky Cooper's kip they'd be charged about a *pound* for that bottle. The police knew where the porter'd be hid and they'd raid and take them and break them.

"Now the madams, they were Dublin people. And the madams all stuck together. You had Becky Cooper up there, she was a kip keeper, and May Oblong . . . indeed, I remember May Oblong. She was a madam and she had a shop up there. A big stout woman who used to sit out there with a big white apron. She owned a car and she had a man for driving her around in the car. Oh, May Oblong had a temper if you done anything on her. And she used to lend money too. And you had to pay nearly *double* what you got off her. If you got a pound you had to pay two back. Her husband was working at Guinness's at the time and he had all them Guinness men hooked, getting the lend of money off her. And if they didn't pay the money back to her she went up to their jobs and got them sacked! Oh, some horrible things used to go on years ago.

"It was a hard life for them girls. They were really all country girls that got into trouble and that's where they finished up. A girl (unwed) with a baby, she was in trouble . . . from farmer's sons. There was a convent around there and they was put in there for twelve months with the nuns. They had a hard time. Scrubbing floors and everything else and the nuns standing over them. Oh, the country girls got a hell of a time of it, that's why all the girls was 'on the town'! That's where they finished up. Now the madams had them dressed in good new clothes, that was the attraction. But when they got the money off the men and didn't give it up to the madams they took the clothes off them—stripped! They'd *strip* them, take all their clothes off them and put them up in the rooms in the houses.

"They had a bad *occupation* but they was very decent, very, very kind the girls. You wouldn't hear them cursing and they might give the kids a penny or tuppence to buy sweets. Respectable girls. The wives around here would even say 'hello' to them and be friendly enough. But we had a hospital here then called the Locke, over here on Townsend Street, and you know what they used to do with the girls (with sexual diseases)? Smother them. When they had syphilis and all . . . *incurable*! They used to be smothered. See, there was no such thing as pills at that time. They couldn't cure them. Smother them to take them out of their pain, or give them some kind of a needle. They were that far gone and at that time there was no cure. The hospital was built for that purpose. That's right. They wouldn't do (smother) them all, just an odd one. They'd be nearly gone dead before they'd do it."

NELLIE CASSIDY—AGE 78

She grew up on City Quay where her father was a docker digging coal boats and her mother worked like a "slave" in a stifling sack factory. It was then a dangerous area where the Black and Tans raided her home tearing everything asunder. They once arrested her father in a case of mistaken identity and threatened to shoot him. Nonetheless, it was an exciting place to grow up as she saw ships and sailors from every part of the world. New Year's Eve was always exciting with all the ships blowing their horns and sailors and tenement folk singing and dancing and clasping hands in friendship.

"We lived in *happy* times and *poor* times. My daddy worked on the docks. He was a coal digger, a very hard life. My mother worked in a sack factory. There was fourteen of us born in a tenement house in City Quay on the dockside. We had one room, that's all. And we had beds *everywhere*. We used to put out four pull-out beds at night-time for the fourteen of us. Oh, we saw some hard times. I witnessed hunger in my younger days when we were very poor because there was no work on the quays and the men didn't get the Labour Exchange at that time. We had to *try* and survive. We all got some food if we had it but we often *hadn't* it, I'm not ashamed to say. And me mother got our clothes second-hand at Cole's Lane market. Now St Vincent de Paul never gave us a *thing*! We put in for it once and we were three weeks waiting on it. And the day they came my father was after getting a boat (to work) and he wouldn't take anything off 'em. That's *true*. It was the way we were being *treated* . . . *three weeks* left waiting. It was like we were begging. Oh, the old people had *pride*.

"I used to go over to the docks carrying me father's dinner. It might be meat and potatoes and onions and it'd be wrapped in a cloth and knotted so that you could hold it like a handle. And you had a can full of tea in the other hand. Me father'd sit out and eat that on the docks and I'd sit beside him and share it with him. I remember one day I was five minutes late and he sent me home. He wouldn't take the dinner off me because I was late. That's true. And me daddy used to be *black* when he'd come home. He'd take off all his clothes and he'd wash his own hands and face but you'd have to wash his back and make sure he was clean.

"We'd go over to the river and ships coming in from every part of the world. Cattle was being loaded onto the ships and they'd run into our hall and drovers'd get them out with a stick. Then the trawlers used to come up and we'd ask them for the fish and they might throw you two or three. They used to give it to us. And they'd let some coal spill over on the ground when they'd be loading it on the lorries. Anything that was loose on the ground we'd all go out with ordinary coal man's sacks and be robbing it—it was just outside the hall door there! Sweep up what was left on the docks, bring it up in a bucket upstairs and you had your coal. And I'll tell you what used to be on the docks—big, big trees (timber poles). And we used to go over in the evening and cut the bark off the trees for firewood. Put that into a bag and it done for the fire.

"It was a *lovely* place to live and we had all the beautiful ships coming up the river. You *name* them, *every* nationality. And I seen every colour of men, from every part of the world. And we used to go out dancing and used to have to be in by twelve and the watchmen on the ships knew us and they'd be watching over us. And if you were passing the boat you might get a whistle from the sailors and the watchmen would tell them to stop. On New Year's Eve the church bells would be ringing and the boats would be blowing. Oh, the foreign sailors would bring over plum pudding—they'd make it on the ship, the cook. And they'd divide it among us all sitting down and we'd have a sing-song till two in the morning. Oh, it was a great area.

"But during the war it was *dangerous* cause the bullets was flying everywhere. And you'd never know when the Black and Tans would arrive. I was only seven at the time but I remember it. They used to frighten the people terrible. They came into *everybody's* house and there was shutters on your window and they'd tear the shutters asunder to see if there was documents or anything behind them and frighten the life out of us. And children'd be playing in the street and someone'd shout 'here's the Black and Tans' and we'd all be brought in. Sure, me daddy was taken down by the Black and Tans, him and another man. See, there was two chaps belonged to the IRA that lived in the tenement house with us and it was them that they must have been searching for. They took me daddy and this other man down in their bare feet and just their trousers and put them up against the wall. And they said they were going to shoot them. And it was Christmas time and I remember there was a pudding on the table. Now I was young but I can remember we were sitting up in the bed this night and one of the Black and Tans saying to us, 'Could you give me a piece of your pudding?' And I said, 'If you give me back me daddy'. So they had them down for a long time and, of course, we were *praying* and *praying* and *praying* that we'd see me daddy come back. So after a while the two boys was caught and they let me daddy and the other man free.

"Now me mother had two children and she was told she had only one lung and was told to have no more children—and she'd *twelve* after that! And women were *slaves* . . . slaving. My mother used to work in Mooney's sack factory for to get a few bob for us, along with whatever me daddy'd earn on the docks. She used to hand sew the sacks with a thick twine for a half a crown a week. It was sacks for fertiliser to grow vegetables. And a lot of men lost their teeth and their hair shovelling that fertiliser. That's quite true, from the dust on the phosphorite boats. She used to go down at six in the morning and she'd have a young baby and she'd have to come home at eight and breast feed that baby and go back down and sew sacks again. Oh, we saw some hard times. And you could pawn anything, your clothes or a picture off the wall, your iron. Me mother had to sell her home four times cause there was no work on the docks. You'd sell your home . . . your *furniture*. She *had* to sell them for to get the money for food. Sold four homes! Sell it to Jewmen going around that'd buy them. Sold the chest of drawers, the sofa, the sideboard. Until we were able to get something else again. It might be two or three years. And we had only four beds and a table to eat off of and a few chairs to sit on. *Four times* she had to do it.

"Very few of the men had a trade, it was all dockers on the quays. All dockers and seamen. My father worked on the docks and I had three brothers worked on the docks and our next door neighbours worked on the docks. *All* the men in the neighbourhood had to be down there at eight every morning when the stevedore'd pick the men for the boats. Men used to stand in a group on the quay wall and the stevedore would stand on a chair and he'd pick your name and your name to work. There might be fifty or sixty men standing in a group for a read, out in the rain, for a day's work and he might call twenty— and the others was left standing there. Very heart-breaking. Because the men were *hungry*. There was no constant work. Dock life . . . ups and downs. You were lucky if you got a boat. And they were *tough*, the men, they *accepted* everything. They were used to hardship. And *hard* work. I used to *see* them. They used to work pitch (boats) and it burned out their eyes. They worked very hard and *earned* every penny they got.

"One of our next door neighbours worked on the docks and he went down (during 1920s strike) and took me father's job—he *scabbed* it! It was one thing for a stranger . . . but for your *own* to do it. And me father was a great union man. Oh, the union men used to throw them into the river and everything. Decent people stuck together and they'd know if you were a scab, that you were no good. And the women, once you took any husband's job they wouldn't look at you. No, cause they were taking the food off your table. And me mammy sent me down to me daddy—he used to drink at that time—to tell him not to go into any of the pubs along the quay cause all the scabs was in them, cause she knew he was hot-tempered.

"See, the scabs were your *own neighbours*. And here just as me father got to his own door didn't this man just after taking his job come out and say 'hello'. And now my father was a very quiet man in his own way but he had his shovel on his shoulder and he gave him a bang with his number seven shovel on the head and he cut his head. And, of course, the police was sent for. And when they came down they knew me daddy and they said, 'God, it's *not you!*—cause you went to the Christian Brothers school and all.' So he was arrested and mammy was expecting a baby. He got three weeks in gaol. And he told me mammy that when he'd come out either he'd *kill* Mr Hogan or he'd take the pledge. And he took the pledge for life and he died without ever touching a drink after that. That's the truth.

"Me father got hardening of the arteries and he couldn't walk and he didn't live too long. I was glad he died quick because he couldn't get out and he didn't drink nor smoke and he'd *go mad*. And that's the way he died after digging coal boats for them years. They (friends) carried him to the church and the neighbours made a collection to buy a wreath and have a Mass said. Funerals was horse-drawn cabs and the hearse would stop outside your door and then come up to the side of the ship and the men'd always knock off from work till they'd pass by, out of respect. See, the way it was, if *one* was in sorrow, we were *all* in sorrow. *Everybody* knew everybody else. It was a *community*. They used to be buried at one o'clock in the day. It was Dean's Grange out beyond Blackrock. Everyone stood around and they used to fill in the grave while you'd stand there. You had to stand till it was all filled in. Maybe throw a piece of gravel in, or a flower. Then to the pub for a drink. They'd go into a place called the 'Punch Bowl' in Merrion there. Cabs used to bring the people. Buried at one and go off and the women'd all get *drunk*. If they had the money they would. And wouldn't come home till eleven that night. Oh, the women'd be looking forward to it!"

Elizabeth "Bluebell" Murphy—Age 75

Hers was a brutally hard life. Her family was evicted from their tenement room on Corporation Street by a greedy landlord who put them out on the cold street. When she was a young girl her parents died within one week of one another and she lost two sisters to tuberculosis. She grew up having to sleep on straw, empty filthy slop buckets, cope with bugs and rats, and cook with soggy turf. Nonetheless, with absolute conviction she asserts, "if I had a tenement house now I'd go back and live in it."

"Oh, my name is Elizabeth but years ago we used to walk in a procession down at the church and me mother always bought me bluebells, flowers with little blue bells on them. And the woman next door christened me 'Bluebell'. And I never lost it, even when I worked at the sack factory on the quay. The boss even called me Bluebell.

"I was born and reared in a three-storey tenement on Corporation Street. We had only one room and I had five brothers and sisters. We had only one double bed and we had to lie on the floor on straw. One toilet in the back yard for everybody and a little chamber pot that'd be taken down and cleaned in the morning. Saturday night you'd have a kettle and filled it with water and bathe the kids one by one in front of the fire. We only had a dresser and a table and a little chair and we used to bring them downstairs in the yard and scrub, scrub. Plenty of soap and hot water and a scrub brush. And we had to get down on our knees and scrub the wood floors and scrub down the stairs twice a week. Kept spotlessly clean. But we were put out. The landlord evicted us because he wanted that room to open a shop. He *did* that, put us out on the street. And put our things out on the street—until we got another little room.

"Me mother'd do the cooking. Just an ordinary fire, no grate. During the war we had turf but it was wet. Try and light a fire on that! It was pitiful to see it getting done but they done it. Then we had gas in the house but during the war the gas would go off but it left a little glimmer. Now you weren't supposed to use that—but they *knew* it was getting used. There was a glimmer man and he'd come around and check on you. He'd walk around and you'd know him. Oh, you'd have to watch for him, keep your eyes on him, cause if he caught you using the glimmer you'd get the gas taken away *altogether*. Mostly the dinner would be a coddle or a stew. And we had chickens and hens and there was a goose named 'Fanny'. And me mother used to boil rabbits and there'd be a rabbit stew. Now I suppose you'll laugh if I told you . . . but my mother and father used to eat off the one plate. They were that close together like, you know. They were very happy together. Me mother died on Christmas week and me father died at the end of Christmas week. Five days between them, they were that close.

"The men was always on the docks, had to work hard for the few shillings they made and women used to go out to the fields years ago and pick potatoes and vegetables. That was very hard. But no matter how poor they'd be on a Saturday night they'd be sitting outside. People'd all come around and sit on the steps and they'd get pig's legs or a pig's cheek or ribs and they shared it. Shared everything with one another. Same with births, deaths, and marriage, they all came. Everybody helped. Children would be out playing and the parents would be together. And we used to have a lot of street singers. There was a woman used to play the banjo and she'd come along and sing and there was a girl that'd play the violin and she was great . . . just to sit and listen to her. And we'd have sing-songs. And Paddy Clare's pub was on the corner and I used to go for me father with a jug, a big jug, to get a pint after his dinner. This was called his 'pint in a jug'. The kids often sipped off that going home.

"We all worked in this sack factory over on the quays. *All* women, maybe a hundred. It was Keogh's on George's Quay. It was more than a sack factory, it was a second home for us all. You started at fourteen for ten shillings a week. Give it all to me mother and she'd maybe give us a shilling back for the pictures. We used to wear smocks and worked from nine to six. We were doing both the making and the repairing. We made jute and cotton bags and we used to make the big tarpaulin covers for covering railway wagons and all. And old second hand sacks we took them in and had to examine them and take out all the dirt and grain out of them. Turned them inside out and clean them and darned them on sewing machines. We even had to get the bags from Guinness's to mend them. And we'd have a sing-song when the machines would be all going and we'd be all singing. Just to pass the time. And if we were in a hurry we used to sing that song, 'I love to go a wandering across the mountain track' and we'd go on quicker to that tune.

"Oh, it was great to get into Keogh's. But I don't know how I'm alive with all the dirt and dust. Definitely. Had to scrape everything off the bags to be darned and the husks of the grain would get all over you and we'd be *sweating* doing the darning. And we went to Tara Street baths (once a week). Oh, that felt *great* after a week in the factory. It cost about sixpence but it was *worth* it at the time. *Beautiful* big, big baths and plenty of water, as much as you'd want. And we were able to go dancing that night! There was a dance hall up on Parnell Square. We'd all go together and meet the fellas at the corner. Fellas was more shy then. But every one of the girls around was great dancers. I worked there at the factory from the time I was fourteen to when it closed down in 1970. Mr Keogh, he was marvellous, *outstanding*, you couldn't ask for anybody better. But he walked out one day, one Monday morning, and he never came back! Never heard tell of him from that day to this. He was never found. Never seen him since. Nowhere!

"It was hard on women back then. Oh, large families they were. Twelve, thirteen, fourteen children. *Every year* some of them'd have children. When children would be out playing parents would be together (intimately). You couldn't say 'no'! You were *obligated* to have a lot. But you never complained. At that time it was the natural childbirth and they just had to put up with it (pain). And I think it was the natural childbirth that was the cause of the mother and child being so close. The bond between them was so tight. I think that the pain of having the child was the cause of the closeness. Mrs Dunleavy, she was a midwife, and she brought home half the neighbourhood. She was great. The midwife would do everything. But you had to have the water boiled and bedclothes and sheets ready and *plenty* of newspapers for the bed. Then the mother'd be churched. See, churching . . . years ago the old people said that you were likened to the beast in the field after having the baby and then by churching you were brought *back* to the Church—purified! That's what we were told. Oh, the woman wouldn't be allowed to do anything in the house till she was churched, especially take up a knife and cut bread or anything like that. She wouldn't be *let*. Cause it was *wrong* till she got churched.

"There was an awful lot of TB around, that was the killer. An elder sister went on an excursion and it was lashing rain and instead of coming to change her clothes she kept the wet clothes on her and that turned to TB. Another sister, she went to work when she was only thirteen and she got TB. So the two of them died from TB. A lot of young girls died. And very sad when a child was laid out. They'd have a little table and another little table on top of it like a canopy and they'd have it all done in white and then all around they'd have blue paper all done in bows and crosses, all in blue. It'd be lovely. And a little white pillow and the baby lying on it. It used to be gorgeous. Now at that time it was an awful thing for a woman to die at birth. And there was one woman died on the birth of her babies and it was twins. The three of them died. Oh, I'll never forget that. And she was laid out with the two babies in her arms, one on each side. They were there lying in the coffin and everyone crying. One baby on each arm she had. Oh, terrible sad . . . that was awful.

"Now in the tenements at Christmas there was really no one down-and-out—no matter how poor you were. Everybody helped everybody. The poor people, there was always something made out for them. If they didn't have it someone else would give it. You got your Christmas candle, *always* red, for nothing where you bought your groceries. And the man at the dairy across the road where we used to get our milk and butter, well, he always gave us a goose for Christmas. And everybody made Christmas pudding. Each week you'd spend a few bob and put it by until you got all the ingredients. You'd start collecting raisins and currants and the cinnamon and the nutmeg and spice. Then you'd get a big calico cloth and you'd grease it first with butter—or margarine—and then put it all in and tie it and boil that for about six or seven hours. Then leave it hanging for a few days and it would be so *beautiful*. And on Christmas we'd put up all paper chains and silver bells and coloured balls. Windows would be all done up, all painted, and paint the hallway door. The doorways was nearly always painted green. And in tenement windows they'd put holly and ivy and your white lace curtains.

"The shops used to be beautiful all lit up at night and the windows lit up with everything Christmas. And you could go window shipping at *any* hour . . . three and four in the morning. Oh, we'd be out all the night. We always went up to Clery's to look in all the windows. And there was a shop there on Talbot Street, Guiney's. Well, the man that owned that he'd tell you to go over late at night on Christmas Eve and he'd give toys that was left. He was a lovely man. And he'd give the mothers little toys that'd be left there for to be divided among them. Oh, yes, he gave them to us for free. On Christmas Eve just before they closed. Oh, sure, and then we'd always have a party and always a sing-song. Maybe an accordion would be brought in and we might go out on the street and sing. Oh, everybody'd be dancing in the street on Christmas.

"It was a hard life . . . but I wish I was back in it again, in the tenement again. When they started tearing the old tenements down it was like tearing *us* apart. It tore *me* apart. It broke me heart. We were all one family, all close. We all helped one another. If I had a tenement house now I'd go back and live in it . . . yes, I would."

4

Oral Testimony: The Liberties

NANCY CULLEN—AGE 71

She grew up in a tenement house on Cook Street beside coffin makers and clay pipe makers. Bare-footed children danced with delight around the street balladeers and organ grinders. When children were injured they were lifted into a big old pram and wheeled furiously off to the local hospital. As a girl she played in the ancient dark, dusty vaults of the Viking site discovering archaeological relics which today would be promptly placed in a museum.

"On Cook Street there was a row of tenements and three shops. My mother had a small little green grocer's shop and we lived in a tenement room in back of the shop. Me father worked in Guinness's brewery in the vat house. There was a *terrible lot* of poverty then in the thirties and I had five brothers and two sisters and we'd only one toilet out in the back yard and slop buckets . . . *horrible*. But you could go into everyone's house and no one was ashamed, even though they were poor. And you wouldn't see anything dirty in their house. People had just bare boards on the floor, no lino, but, honest to God, they'd be like milk, scrubbed *white*. And keep the tables clean by putting newspapers on them. Oh, and the women were very proud of their washing and it was always lovely and clean. Most people went up to the Iveagh wash house to do their washing. Big iron sinks for boiling their clothes. Ah, it was *very* hot and steamy. And the women would be chatting with one another and shouting and some would be singing and some would be giving out! Then they'd have a line stick, a pole, shoved out through their window to hang their washing on. And very critical of one another in them years. If they put out anything that wasn't washed well they'd say, 'Ooooh, look at her wash!'

"In me mother's shop on Cook Street she used to sell cabbage, onions, potatoes and cigarettes and coal and turf and sticks for the fire. And she sold a lot of paraffin oil cause most people only had oil lamps. Me mother'd give food on credit. She might get it back, or get half of it back. And in me mother's time there was an awful lot of coffin makers in the street and clay pipe makers. Lots of people used to smoke clay pipes. They were white clay and they made them in the fire and they'd polish and clean them. I think they used to cost a penny. And there was Kelliher's coffin makers on the street, an open-front kind of shop, and you could see the coffins and some would be up against the wall. We used to often run in and jump into them when we were kids and Mr Kelliher'd chase us and we'd *run out* again.

"Oh, and there used to be a lot of people used to go around the street singing. A man used to come around dressed like Charlie Chaplin—Gannon was his name. Dressed in swallow-tail coat and a little moustache and he used to have a melodion. He'd put all the kids sitting along the path and he'd be out in the road and do Charlie Chaplin and dance and sing and play the melodion. Then he'd go around with his hat and all the people at the windows that'd be looking out, if they had a penny of ha'penny they'd throw it out to him. And he'd be going around picking up all the pennies and ha'pennies. He wouldn't get a lot but he might get a couple of coppers. And there used to be a barrel-organ-grinder man and another man with an ice cream cart and you could buy a cone. He had a cart with two shafts on it and two legs and then he stopped and he'd have a bugle and he'd blow his bugle. And, of course, naturally, when the bugle went *all the kids* went out.

"Children used to go around running in their bare feet, no shoes, and most of them would have stone bruises. And I remember if a kid fell and hurt himself and it was badly cut they'd shove him into a pram—no matter *how big* he was—and push him to the hospital. They were the old-fashioned prams. Even with a big kid that'd break his leg or cut himself, he'd be picked up and just put in the pram. There was one lady, a youngish woman, named Kitty Gorman on the street and when a child was hurt she was the one that'd run with them most of the time. Just *throw* him into the pram and *run* to the Adelaide Hospital in Bishop Street.

"There was very little for children then. But you could go around and pick up bricks and build a house up to maybe here (three feet high) and get four or five bricks and build it up and make a table or chair and put paper on it. And maybe you'd have a brick for a doll. You know, make a doll out of a brick, get a bit of coloured paper and put it around it for a bonnet. Another thing we used to do as kids was bring down potatoes and a stick and maybe a bit of coal and we'd light a fire in an old house and we'd make a stew. Maybe in a tin can we'd find. Used to peel it and put it in the water and boil it. And half raw it used to be eaten! It was all only innocent and we thought that was *great* . . . you know, making a house and having a bit of stew.

"We went to High Street School, a National School and Catholic. Very small school, two rooms. It was by the Vikings. Our school was on one side and across was a vault, a big, long, dark place with only just a kind of opening in the wall, where they have (now) the Viking Centre. Well, we used to call that 'the vault'. And we weren't supposed to go into it when we were kids but we thought it was grand. But it was thick with dust and if you went into it you'd come out *black*. So we used to run over in the vaults and go in the slits. I suppose we hadn't any sense. But we used to go up in there and we found an old sword and we chased one another around. I suppose if it was found now it'd be an antique. And another thing we found was a skeleton's head. And we were kicking it around playing football, actually *in* the vault. Now our teachers didn't know this.

"Then there was the 'trigging hall' in a tenement house. We used to call it a 'trigging' hall but it must have meant 'tricking', cause you could run through it. See, there'd be hall doors on one street and when you'd come in through that you'd go through a yard and come out through another street. So for devilment we used to run through it and out the other side. And if we were playing relieve-io we could go in one door and run through the yard and out into the next street. Now there was a house next to ours and it always had the name of being a *haunted* house . . . *always*. And we used to go up there on a winter's evening and we'd bring a candle and sit on the stairs and tell haunted stories. We'd be about nine or ten. And we'd be sitting there telling haunted stories for ages and everyone afraid to move. And then everybody'd *scramble down the stairs*! Everyone'd run together. And then the kids had to go upstairs to their own house and the hallways were very dark, no light whatsoever on the stairs. Pitch dark and you had to feel your way. And we'd stand at the door and say, 'watch for the banshee'—*frightening* them. But that was the fun of it.

"There was people and they'd say, 'Oh, I heard the banshee last night, there's going to be a death.' And *surely* there would be! Or somebody'd say, 'I heard three knocks.' See, three knocks, that was a sign of death. Those were superstitions. Or a black dog symbolised the devil. We always used to be afraid of a black dog. And I was afraid of me life of cats. Now there was this one cat, it was a wild cat, half Persian. The cat didn't belong to our street but it always came into our yard through a hole. And one day my mother was afraid to go out and she just threw a scrubbing brush, not *at* the cat, just for to get him out of the yard. And that night he *attacked* her! It was *wild*. And it attacked another woman beside her. I remember this actually happening.

"To me, all the women back then looked the same. They were dressed the same as an old person . . . shapeless. Wore long, heavy shapeless skirts down to their ankles and underneath the skirts a petticoat. And shawls. And you'd never see a woman going around with her bare arms, unless they pulled up their sleeves to wash. There'd be women with their heads out the window talking to one another and then on a summer's evening they'd all come down and sit at their doors and be talking in a group. Bring out chairs or boxes and they'd all sit talking. And if a woman smoked in them times—and a few of them did—they'd only smoke Woodbines cause they were the cheapest. You could buy a Woodbine at that time for a ha'penny, or five for tuppence. Buy two for a penny and you'd get a match with it. But they never smoked out for the people to see them. They always *hid* it. They hid it and smoked under the shawl. And even then it'd only be a puff and that cigarette might have to last them for the day. They couldn't afford to buy any more. When I think of it now I think that was the only recreation they ever had.

"Now I remember me granny and she was blind and very old at the time. She lived up on Bridge Street on her own, wouldn't live with anybody even though she was old and blind. But she had good neighbours and they'd come in and clean up and do messages. And when she'd get her pension on a Friday we'd go up to her and she had a begging can with a lid on it and she'd say, 'Go down to Mr Quinn and tell him to give you a nice creamy gill of plain—and tell him to give me good value.' He was a publican. We'd run in and give him the can and have to wait outside the door cause you weren't allowed in a pub at that time. And he'd bring it out and Mr Quinn would walk you up the hill. He wouldn't let you carry it. He'd walk with you a certain amount and then tell you, 'Go on, *run*,' cause he'd be in trouble if he gave porter to a child. So me granny'd get that and then she'd send us for her snuff. She used to snuff when she'd take her gill. She'd have a little box, like an old-fashioned mustard box, an oblong shape, and she'd send you over for an ounce of snuff. I think it was three ha'pennies and that'd probably do her for a week.

"At that time when we were kids there was an awful lot of poverty on the street. I didn't think much of it *then* but it was only since I got older that I realised that it was terrible poverty. I remember that there'd be men sitting playing cards and they'd be playing for buttons. And they might have one or two cigarettes and one'd be handing it to the other to take a smoke out of it. You'd see a man puffing at a cigarette and he'd put the cigarette behind his ear and then puff on it again. Take a puff, put it out, and then put it behind his ear. And light it again then in an hour or two. And I remember one day saying to me mother, '*Why* are the men sitting there and my dad has to go to work?' I thought it was terrible that he had to go to work. And she was explaining to me that there was just no work for them. They'd be paying cards there for *ages*, only just for buttons. And then they might get up to play a game of football and the football would be a roll of paper maybe put in an old sock. In them times many of the men was idle but very seldom you seen a man with a dirty shirt or a dirty collar on his shirt. They were always very clean.

"Now for the Eucharistic Congress of 1932 five or six men were idle on our street and they built an altar. *Every* street and every house decorated and you had altars outside. And holy pictures and pictures of the Pope. And you wouldn't find a piece of paper on the street where we lived. These men decided to build an altar with steps going up, from pieces of wood from these old broken houses, and it was a *beautiful* altar. We collected (money) from all the shops around and we were able to buy all the stuff for the front of it. And Mr Quinn, the publican, he had electric and he let them put the light bulbs on his wire and it lit up the whole altar. And the church gave them a red carpet and we had an old-fashioned gramophone and some of the kids we'd be all singing and we were winding up the gramophone all day and that went on for a week. It was absolutely great. And do you know that them five men after that *got jobs*! And me mother said it was good luck.

"There was a lot of illness then . . . girls of my age. But when we were kids we didn't realise what they had. They got sick and some of them were no time sick and they'd just die. There was a couple of girls died around our age. When we were about fourteen. One particular girl died of TB and we used to go and see her in Rialto Hospital. We'd go up and sit with her. But she died after. We didn't even realise what she had! And they didn't call it TB then, they called it consumption. But I'll tell you, years ago if there was anyone had TB there was an awful stigma attached to it. And if a girl would be getting married then if someone belonging to the boy (family) had TB, *oh,* the family wouldn't like them to marry. Cause there was really no cure for it at that time. A stigma . . . people'd be afraid.

"I only barely remember me own sister dying. I must have been very young. I know that the child died suddenly. She must have been sick because she was always crying . . . always crying. And I remember me mother walking the floor with her all night. She'd be in her arms and she'd be walking all up and down. One morning we just woke up and the child was dead. That was all. She was only a *year.* I suppose I was about six. I remember her being (waked) in the corner and white bows. There wouldn't be a funeral for a baby, like now. A child would be brought out at seven in the morning and just buried. Carry the coffin out. Only the father. I don't think the mother used to go. And sadness.

"If a big person died they'd wake them at home. There'd be a white sheet up around the wall and black bows. It's awful morbid when you think of it now. There'd always be snuff and holy water and a feather and people used to stay up all night at a wake. And as a child we'd be going and robbing the snuff! Now on Cook Street when we were little kids all the men would carry the coffin on their shoulders to the church. If a funeral was coming we'd run in and say to me mother, 'Here's the funeral' and she'd run and close the door of the shop. Oh, everybody'd close the doors till the funeral passed by. And there was a man and he used to have a short leg and we used to call him 'Hoppy' Gaynor and he was *always* in the front of the funeral. Always. If it was anyone lived around Cook Street or Bridge Street he was in the front of the funeral and he kind of made the pace so that no one'd go too quick. They couldn't walk too fast because he was always put in the front. And we'd be watching for the funeral to come along and someone'd run along and say, 'Here's the funeral, here's "Hoppy" Gaynor.' We always knew that it was the funeral coming down the street when we'd see Hoppy. But we didn't know . . . we were too young to understand it. Being a child we didn't realise. We used to say, 'They're gone to Heaven.' There used to be a girl near us and she had a little brother named Christy and Christy died. And when we'd be sitting out in the night-time and she'd look up at a star she used to say, 'That's our Christy up there.' Kind of innocent, you know? And we used to *believe* her."

PADDY MOONEY—AGE 72

He was born on Whitefriar Street in the midst of red light lodging houses, mean money-lenders, and shell-shocked war veterans who would rave and bellow about the streets. Paddy was a typical tenement lad—resourceful and scrappy. He always had some scheme for making a few bob, be it singing in the streets or scrounging around for cigarette butts for men's pipes. Back in the hungry Depression days people tried to make money in any way they could. He remembers that you could actually "hire a child" from a neighbour family to go out begging. As a youth, he lost many close friends to tuberculosis only to discover as an adult during a medical examination that he, too, once had the dreaded "consumption" but somehow survived it. He is today a man of wry wit, gentle character, and much dignity.

"On Whitefriar Street we lived in the back parlour but then we 'elevated ourself' to the drawing room, that was the front room. The houses were brick with plaster walls with horsehair to bind it together and there were bugs *everywhere*, on the walls, in the beds. They were a brownish colour and a terrible smell off them. And rats were a problem. Some people, if they could afford it, used poison for to get rid of the rats and then you could *smell* the rats that'd die. I remember one time my father was shaving and there was a scratching on the floorboard. A knot was gone from one of the boards and it was a *rat* going for a piece of bread that was near the hole. And I remember me father took the boiling kettle off the hob and just poured it and that rat squealed and then died.

"There was a place across the road on Whitefriar Street, a lodging house, and I always looked through the gate and I would wonder what goes on there, seeing all these girls (prostitutes) going in. Used to go out *every* night of the week with fur coats and all that, extremely well dressed. See, in the common lodging houses nobody asked any questions. If you just wanted the bed for the night you didn't even have to give a name. And some people wouldn't be married and they'd just team up together. Oh, it was *common* practice. Like there was this fella and girl and they were living with each other and they were both reared up in orphanages. Now they decided that they would get married and they done a bit of research and, be Jesus, they found out that they were brother and sister! And there was this priest after them saying that they'd have to get away from each other. So they left the house because the clergy was after them and I don't know what happened to them after that.

"Years ago it was mostly bread and tea we lived on and there was beef parings you could get maybe for four pence and have a good stew. And there was penny dinners—always stew—on Meath Street run by the Quakers. People'd come along with their jug or bowl and some women used to hide it under their shawls to bring it home. People were ashamed to get the free food. Most of the poor people wouldn't buy a Sunday dinner until very late on Saturday night because the meat was auctioned off then. See, they (butchers) hadn't got the refrigeration and they didn't want this lying over the weekend. My mother used to go down about half past nine on Saturday night and the meat would be auctioned off for four pence or five pence. And she used to go up to the bakery and buy yesterday's stale bread and split loaves that'd be broken apart. I remember as a kid they were on strike and I'd have to go up there and pass the pickets and they'd read, 'This bread is baked on blood and sweat!' on the boards they used to carry around. But I'd pass the picket and go in for me bread.

"The Iveagh baths were there for whoever could *afford* it, and then there was the penny baths in Tara Street. Now the Tara Street baths were near the docks and all the fellas digging the coal boats they used to be *black* from head to foot from the coal dust. Well, they'd get in there and *you'd* get in there and when you got out you'd be as black as they were going in! See, they were swimming baths and you didn't have showers before you went in. But we used the canals. And I had this friend, Freddy, and he was a Protestant and when he became fourteen he got a job in Christ Church Cathedral. So Freddy says to me, 'There's an awful lot of olive oil there in the church, I'll get a bottle.' He *stole* the oil. And we'd go to the canal and smear ourselves all over with olive oil and dive into the canal and get out and we didn't have to dry ourselves, didn't have to have a towel, cause we were oily all over.

"And scutting was the way you went everywhere. Now if I was going into the centre of town I'd just jump on the back of a lorry passing by. It was common practice . . . and many a young fella lost his life over it. Now for devilment fellas took potatoes from Lalor's shop at the corner of Whitefriar Street. So these fellas (friends) took about a quarter of a stone and got an old pot that was in this derelict building and made a fire and boiled the potatoes. Now Mrs Lalor *knew* who took them and they were brought up and charged in court and they got five years in Glencree. Five years! And there was a priest up in Inchicore and a young fella stole an apple out of his orchard and *he* got five years.

"Now when I was a kid I was always earning money, *always*. I was even out singing in the streets. And there was this man in our house on Whitefriar Street and he had a wooden leg and he had a war pension and he used to smoke a pipe. And he'd say to me, 'Get that jam jar and fill that up with butts.' So I'd fill the jam jar with butts I'd find in the street, take the paper off them and put the tobacco in his pipe and earn a ha'penny or a penny. Now he used to put on this artificial leg in the morning-time when he'd get out of bed. And he had two different legs, you see. He had a Sunday leg and a weekday leg and he used to keep the legs under the bed. And I'd get under the bed for to get this leg for him and he'd say, 'That's the f—— *Sunday* one, get the other one!'

"At that time if a man had two pounds a week (wages) that was considered very good. But if you had a job and you were sacked there was no pensions from the State and you had to resort to the relieving officer. At that time I don't think they were trained in *any* way. So you went and begged to get maybe a few shillings from him to tide you over—but it wouldn't tide you over for a day! And you could be turned away. When me father died we went on relief and me mother had a half a crown for each child. But I can remember when I was two and a half years of age and me father was working at this time—see, there was a lot of time he didn't work—and he bought a box of balloons and we had so many balloons that we could afford to blow them up until they burst. It was so different from the other times when you'd buy a balloon and you'd be very careful about it so that it wouldn't burst. So we burst them all over the place!

"People had very, very little money then and some had tenement rooms for as little as three shillings a week. And you could be evicted for not paying. People'd go to Jewish money-lenders but their *own* people were also money-lenders and they were worse than any Jews. See, you could come to an agreement with a Jew. Oh, yes, our *own* money-lenders were worse than the Jews in regards to exploiting the people. Then there was the penny bank, that was the poor man's bank. There was a penny bank at the corner of Francis Street. And you could get a savings box, they were metal boxes, very heavy. Oh, they'd hold quite a number of pennies and you could put shillings into it if you had them. You'd put your pennies in at home and then take it into the bank and they'd open it. See, you didn't open it yourself. But my wife's mother *did* one time. Oh, she got a *hatchet* and she made *sure* she opened it!

"When the Depression set in in the late twenties and early thirties people had to try and live as best they could. At Molloy's lodging house across from us, a family in there had fifteen barrel organs that they used to hire out at a half crown a day. You could also get a child for to go begging—*hire a child*! Yeah, it'd be one of their own, maybe around two years of age and they wouldn't be much of a nuisance. Take them out for a half crown a day, carry the child around in a shawl at that time and you went around begging. Then there was this man in our house and he never worked in his life with the exception that he used to make bird cages in the bed. He'd be lying in the bed making bird cages because there was a bird market not far from there. He wouldn't get *out* of bed, never worked any place else. And the people in the back parlour, she was French and he was English, used to sell hair restorer. You used to see them going around and she'd always stand on a box. Now she had her hair all tied up in a big bun but when she dropped her hair it went right down to the two cheeks of her arse. So he was selling it and she was showing what this *could do*, what it done for *her*.

"And then there was a lot of cripples around and men that came back from the war shell-shocked. They used to go around in maybe threes and fours playing music, playing instruments, through the streets and people would throw them a penny or a ha'penny. There was one man used to go around with a stick and he'd roar 'Eeeeow'. And, of course, his nickname was 'Eow'. There was another man—and, Christ Almighty, it was terrible looking at him—sometimes he'd go mad and start bashing the metal rails along Whitefriar Street School with his fist and you'd want to see the *blood* gushing out of him! That's the way he was affected with the war.

"Back then every second street had a boxing club and fights were very fair. All the fellas would stand around and nobody'd interrupt them. And if a fella fell on the ground he'd be let get up before you'd hit him again. I remember a most unusual fight with the Murphys, a father and son, along Pimlico. Well, this father and son, they came out of a public house and I don't know what sort of an argument they had but they fought—and they fought for a long time. And the father was a hard man, he was. Anyhow, the son eventually beat the father. Well, the father was going around *boasting* for months, bragging and boasting, 'Only me *own son* could beat me! There isn't a *man* around here could beat me, only my son.'

"Then there were the animal gangs that went around. And if they didn't like you you were beaten up. They never went around on their own, they were always in groups of maybe six to twelve and they'd all stand at corners all together. You knew it was an animal gang and you'd keep your distance from them—and a very *respectable* distance. There'd be dozens and dozens of them round about twenty to thirty years of age. Unemployed men. Anyway, there was this fella I knew and they caught hold of him and beat him into bits. And it led to a battle that lasted day after day, for weeks. There was *hundreds* of fellas fighting all around Pimlico, Marrowbone Lane, all around the area. They always had something in their hands, knives, bicycle chains, forks of bicycles. And people who had little huxter shops that would sell sweets, potatoes, paraffin oil and everything, they had to put up their shutters over their windows.

"But Lugs Brannigan, he was *unafraid*. If there was a *hundred* of them there he wouldn't be a bit impressed by them. See, Brannigan, he was a boxer but he used to wear black gloves and he always had knuckledusters (under the gloves). I actually witnessed this now at this pub. I saw Brannigan going over and there was six of them (animal gang) outside this pub and he put his hand out and says, 'nobody run.' He was *unafraid*, I'll say that much for him. He did beat a lot of them and he was responsible for bringing a lot of them to court. Many would be brought up to court but few would actually go to prison.

"Years ago in the tenements it was as many as would fit into the beds and the rest would be on the floor and a lot of children died of croup. And we went through a very bad period of scabies, it lasted for a couple of years. Oh, it was terrible. If you were diagnosed as having scabies the house you were living in had to be fumigated. And *everybody* had to go for a sulphur bath, down to the Iveagh baths. Oh, when I got it I was in a terrible state. You'd tear yourself and bleed, every part of your body and in your hair. But *one bath* and you got rid of them. Just once in there and it killed them. And people had coughs, colds, warts, corns and the Mushatt brothers, chemists, they were Jewish and they made up all their own stuff and it didn't matter what you had, they'd get rid of it. They came from *all over* the place to the Mushatts. People *really believed* in them. They wanted *his* stuff, what he'd make himself, always in the back. No matter *what* was wrong, they'd go to Mushatt. People *swore* by the Mushatts.

"Oh, and TB took an awful lot of life. But it was a sort of *accepted* thing. You know, you'd say, 'That family has TB' and you didn't throw up your hands in holy terror. But what struck me was the way some families were wiped out. I remember Brigid. Ah, she was a lovely looking girl she was, about fifteen or sixteen years of age when she died. Then her brother, he was coughing up blood and he says to me, 'I don't have TB, not at all.' But he *did* have it and, of course, he died of it. And then the father died and the mother died and Maureen (daughter) died of it. Families just *wiped* out. It was the conditions under which we lived at the time. I remember one fella and he had TB and he used to get his (relief) money on Wednesday and it was only a few shillings.

And I said to him, 'Would you not try to spread it over a few days?' And he says, 'Jesus, I'd only persecute meself. If I go in and drink it—just get drunk—at least I've forgotten one day of the week.' And he died of TB. I remember when I was being examined (as an adult) and the doctor says to me, 'When did you have TB?' And I said, 'I never had TB.' And he says, 'By God, you did, your lungs are all scarred.' So a lot of people got it and didn't know they had it and lived through it . . . in whatever way they fought against it.

"There used to be burial societies and they'd come around and collect each week and you'd be insured. Now there was these two people, 'The Scald' and 'The Mooch'. The Mooch, she was married and her husband died and she'd no husband. Now The Scald was an ex-British soldier and he had some sort of pension. Anyhow, he got married to The Mooch. Now he was an awful man for the drink, do anything for the drink he would. So he went down and knocked up Mr McInerney (burial society agent) and says, 'Mr Mack, The Mooch is dead. Would you be able to send up the drink? There'll be a few people coming in for the wake.' So he got the drink—big bottles of stout and small barrels of stout and he got ale and a couple of bottles of whiskey brought down. But McInerney, well, he went down and knocked on the door and who opens the door, only The Mooch! McInerney nearly dropped dead to see the corpse opening the door. And there was The Scald and all his mates all drinking away! Well, McInerney charged him and got him to pay for all the drink he got.

"I remember when me own father died. I was ten years of age. He had been ill for a good period of time. He had dropsy and something went wrong with his kidneys and his heart and a whole conglomeration of diseases. And I remember his legs going very bad and they used to be tied up, elevated, at the end of the bed. Just tied up with rags because we weren't in a position to get treatment for him. Now there was this idea years ago, no matter how poor the people were, always this idea that, 'We don't want a pauper's funeral if we can possibly avoid it . . . we'll do without food just to pay (the burial society).' And I'll never forget this as long as I live . . . when my father died we didn't have the money for the coffin. Now I'll tell you this because it's nothing to be ashamed of because I wasn't responsible for it. But he had a son that I never met from his first wife and he bought the coffin. And then there was no money for the hearse. So me father went in the 'black hearse', that was the pauper's hearse, and was buried in the pauper's grave in Glasnevin. Because we weren't in the position to get money and nobody *gave* us any money. The hearse came from the South Dublin Union, a workhouse. One horse and a great big black box of a hearse. No windows on it, just a big black box. And *one* horse. That was a very glaring exhibition of poverty."

HARRY MUSHATT—AGE 83

"I was known as the fellow with all the cures," he proudly proclaims. Actually, it is a modest boast because to the tenement poor around the Liberties he was truly the saviour of the sick. His matchbox-size chemist's shop at number 3 Francis Street became an institution and people from all over Dublin swarmed to his door. As Pete St John affirmed in his book Jaysus Wept!, *the Mushatt brothers "had the greatest collection of cures and herbs in Dublin". Harry and his brother treated everything from common colds, skin rashes, chilblains, toothaches and baldness to headaches and hangovers. Intones Harry, "there was tremendous faith in us."*

"Between about 1834 and 1880 Eastern Jews from Russia and Poland started coming to Ireland and they lived around Clanbrassil Street and there was a synagogue in St Kevin's Parade. My father was a credit draper and came over here in 1886 from a small town in Lithuania. He married my mother and we were a family of seven. My eldest brother became apprenticed to a chemist and got a position as an assistant in Mistear's Medical Hall, a pharmacy. Mistear made a lot of his own preparations and my brother was putting medicines together all day long, what we call compounding. My brother qualified when he was twenty-two and a few months after that my father found a shop for him in Francis Street that was idle. The landlord went and asked the (local) chemist, Mr Farrington, that was around the corner, 'There's a Jewish fellow wants to take that shop around the corner, have you any objection to me renting it to him?' 'Ah', says he, 'let him fire away—he won't last three months.' He wasn't worried a bit. But after twelve months he was bloody well worried!

"We established our shop in 1922 and we retired in 1967. I was there as a young boy of fourteen and used to go down and help my brother after school. Then I went into the shop when I was fifteen and served my four-year apprenticeship under my brother. If I asked him for more money he'd turn around and say, 'Sure, I served my apprenticeship for *nothing*, you're lucky that you're getting three shillings a week.' I washed the floor, I washed the bottles, I cleaned the window. Whatever donkey work was to be done, I did it. And he did his share, no doubt about it. We pulled along together. I left the house in the morning at a quarter to nine and didn't come home until ten or eleven at night. The 1920s and 1930s weren't easy years to knock out a living.

"Now I'll give you an image of the shop. It was in a tenement house. The shop was about twelve feet long by six feet wide with shelves on the back and the mahogany counter in the middle that took up, say, three feet. We'd no fancy bottles, we'd no *room* for fancy bottles! In the back room we had the dispensing counter and all our chemicals. We had a window and we'd put out Mushatt's Skin Soap and a big painted foot on a card for Mushatt's Foot Paste, showing the sole of a foot. Out little shop was number 3 Francis Street and then there was a hardware shop and a pub named Dowling's— 'Don't be always growling, go into Mr Dowling.' In those days the publican was *everything*. He had to have stamps and a telephone for the people. We didn't have a phone when we started and we went over to the public house to use the phone and paid him the penny or tuppence. Now down the street there was a bootmaker, Paddy, and he was a great tenor. He used to sing opera. And many a night going home he'd still be hammering nails into the footwear and we'd go in to say 'hello, Paddy' and he'd give us a bar of a song. Oh, there was great talent around there.

"A good lot of our customers were tenement people. All around Francis Street and Engine Alley they were all tenement houses. They were great people. But tenement people came from *all over* Dublin. They came to us because they really couldn't afford a doctor. 'Go to Mushatt's,' they'd say. The shop was never empty. We worked like *slaves*. Oh, there was a bond of trust. I suppose if we served one customer we served three hundred on a Saturday. *Packed out*. It was mostly women . . . women took care of everything. And still wearing shawls. Some of them in those days were very poor and hadn't even got a blouse to put under it when the shawl was wrapped around them.

"They were poor days and they all lived in one room and the average was between seven and ten children. And in tenement houses sanitation was a bad thing, and dampness. Ah, it wasn't healthy. There was lice and bugs and vermin. And during the war years the scabies was quite prevalent, you know, with the soldiers coming back after living in the shelters and all. And you got men coming back after the First World War with malaria and shell-shock and many of them got very fond of the drink. And they'd do anything for drink. They even used to put on a show on the street, two or three of them, and sing and dance and go around with a hat and get a few bob—and *into* the pub for a drink. There was a fella, Cal was his name, and he was a character. He was in the army and shell-shocked and he'd go around mumbling and shouting and sometimes he would go off the deep end and come in with a cut across his forehead and 'Mr Mushatt, put some plaster on that for me.' Or even if he *hadn't* got a cut he'd say, 'Put some plaster on that.'

"I was known as the fellow with all the cures. We made our own medicines. My brother and I made up forty-four different preparations in our shop. Oh, we had a book that all the formulas were written in. So they'd come to us because they really couldn't afford a doctor. We sold all these preparations over the counter and they'd come in for a penny's worth. Oh, they'd bring their *own* bottles. Come in with a baby Power's bottle and they'd want tuppence worth of camphorated oil for their child that was coughing, tincture of iodine if they had a cut. The *big* part of the business was people coming in complaining they had stomach trouble or a skin rash or a toothache or scabies. So we made up different preparations from skin ointments, psoriasis ointments, to foot pastes for removing corns and calluses and warts, to stomach bottles, tablets for kidneys and headaches . . . *all* different things. What we did well with was our stomach bottle, Mushatt's Creme of Emulsion, and we had a stomach bottle for flatulence, acidity. And we had an iron blood mixture, for anybody that was kind of bloodless, let's put it that way. And there was Hippo Wine and Squills for a cough and we made our own teething powders and worm powders for children. And there was a lot of chilblains then from the cold and frost. People hadn't got gloves in those days or proper heating. Your fingers would swell or your feet would swell and get kind of red, like frostbite. So we'd make up a rub from sweet oil and ammonia, make it thick, and put a little wintergreen oil into it to give it a bit of heat and they'd come in for that. And if somebody came in with a cut finger or a bit of dirt in their eye or met with an accident we'd dress the cut or burn. Oh, yes, we were that way.

"Now for a hangover we'd give them Black Draft, as it was commonly known, a mixture of senna pods and Epsom salts. It was a liquid, sixpence a draft. Give 'em two ounces of that. This man came in one day and I measured out two ounces, handed it to him and he drank it down. And he says, 'If it works I'll come back and pay you,' and he walks straight out. What can you do? Then we had our hair tonic that was a stimulant for to make your hair grow and be free of dandruff. Oh, yes, the tonic was to grow hair. Oh, we had *some* success with it. There was a man used to come in, a bricklayer, and one night he came in and takes off his cap and says, 'I want something to make hair grow.' So my brother takes down the hair tonic—now my brother was bald!— and after a few moments he says, 'I'll tell you, Mr Mushatt, *you* use it on your scalp this week and I'll come in Saturday night and if it does you any good I'll buy it.' Another night a girl came in for a tuppenny box of face powder. And a half an hour later a little kid was back with the face powder and she says, 'Me sister sent me back with the box of face powder, she wants the tuppence back.' So I says, 'Why? Does she not want the powder, is she not going to the dance?' 'She's going to the dance but the white wash off the wall will do . . . the *gas* has gone out.' See, she wanted the tuppence for the metre on the gas.

"When we retired in 1967 we were sad. Oh, we missed the old faces. We had a bond. But after forty-five years we were *tired*. After being behind the one counter you're *worn out*. Because they came from *all over* Dublin and we worked like slaves. There was tremendous *faith* in us. We had parents, children, grandchildren. Oh, they were loyal. I go to various places now and the minute I mention the name 'Mushatt' they know it. It brings tears to my eyes. As one representative (pharmaceutical supplies) said to me one day, 'Mr Mushatt, you have an *institution* around yourselves.' And that's what it *was*. Nobody else had got the name. 'Go to Mushatt' . . . that was the *name*. I'll tell you, I feel very proud that we had such a good name cause my father, God rest him, was anything but a rich man but he said, 'There's *one* thing I'll leave you and that is a good name. Guard your name, your name is worth more than money will ever bring you."

MARGARET BYRNE—AGE 72

She remembers both hardship and hunger as a child. Some days she and her brothers and sisters had only a single boiled egg for their daily meal. Other days, "we didn't really have a meal." One Christmas Eve her father was dying in his bed but her mother was so desperately in need of money that she had to go to the house of a woman dying of TB to do her washing for her to earn a few shillings, risking her own health. In those days, says Margaret, you did whatever was necessary for basic survival.

"I was born in St Augustine Street, off Thomas Street, in a tenement house at the very top. We just had one room. There was four of us children—there were more but they died. We had iron beds with straw mattresses. And these red bugs, they'd make a home there in the bed, kind of nesting. Oh, they were terrible things. And my mother always had a cat cause there was rats in the house. We had a lovely cat but I *hate* cats now, I'm terrified of them to the present day. The reason is cause we had a coal box, it was a tea chest, and the cat had kittens one time in the coal box. Now the coal was down low at the end of the week and I was just a child and I leaned over this thing and *fell in* on top of the cat and the kittens and the cat tore the life out of me.

"We had a coal fire and two hobs on the side and we were able to have two big pots simmering on the one fireplace grate. You had an iron kettle and a marble in the kettle to keep the rust out. Sunday was our big meal. We'd have corned beef, cabbage, and potatoes. Or we might have a stew or coddle. On a bad day she'd have to go down to the shop and get a half dozen of eggs and that'd have to do for the father, mother, and four children. And we had that for a meal then, a boiled egg. Some days we didn't really have a meal, maybe just bread and butter.

"My mother always done her washing on a Monday morning. And you hated Monday because everything was getting done in the one room. She stood over a big vat of washing and there was a washing board and she was washing and scrubbing. Then she'd put the clothes into this big pot on the fireplace, bring them to a boil and she had a stick and she'd beat the clothes down as the water was boiling up, making sure they were *snow white*. And a good rinsing in cold water. Oh, she was very particular about her whites. Now we had lines (cord) from this end of the room down to the other end—where we were eating and sleeping—and the clothes was all put there. And then she'd iron them. She had two irons, they were very heavy, and you'd put them into the fire. One you'd be ironing with and the other one'd be on the fire. And the sweat would be *pouring* off her it was so hot. On Monday she'd be in terrible bad form . . . she was *so tired* and so weary.

"I remember on a Christmas-time my father was dying and this nun used to come to my father and give him morphine injections to ease the pain. And this nun, to help my mother out, asked her if she'd do a bit of work. She was a little bit proud but she had a dying husband and four children so me mother said 'Yes'. So this nun gave her a job to go to another house where there was a young mother dying from TB. Oh, there was an awful lot of TB. You were supposed not to, but people *did* go into those rooms. Go in to help the person even though they knew they were risking their own lives. So my mother had to do a load of washing for her on Christmas Eve. Had to stand over all that washing on a Christmas Eve and she got a half a crown. And the poor woman died two days after that. And my mother, it was an *awful risk* she took. But God was with her and nothing happened.

"Orphans were taken care of by neighbours . . . this is going back to TB again. I remember one family and the mother and father died from TB and there was eight or nine children. The eldest girl, she was twelve or thirteen years of age and the baby was about twelve months. And that elder girl of twelve or thirteen, well, she was called a 'mother' because she was looking after all her little brothers and sisters. Now the neighbours in that tenement house on St Augustine Street looked after that family and helped that girl to rear that family. People'd come in and help her and they used to bring in meals and things. And those children *never* had to be sent away from home.

"My mother was left a widow when I was twelve years of age and there was no widow's pension. Me mother was getting a thing called 'relief'. She had a very hard time. She often took the quilt off the bed for the pawn shop. Washed it and bring it down to the pawn shop and would get a shilling on it and that was a meal for us. Anything you could get a shilling on went to the pawn. Now St Vincent de Paul was good to some people but St Vincent de Paul *was not* good to my mother, even though she was a widow with a young family. They visited us and said we didn't need any help—but we *really and truly* did need the help! If you had furniture in the place they'd say you didn't need help. You had to have *nothing* in your room before you'd get help from them. So I went to work in a sweet factory when I was fourteen and me brothers didn't do school even to fourteen. They got messenger boys jobs for five shillings a week.

"Now when you came to fourteen years of age and during your period your mother told you that it was a blessing from the Blessed Virgin and that you were going into womanhood. But you were *very* ignorant. Now courting, you'd be in the halls and you'd have to go with a fella for a long time before you'd kiss him. But you didn't know *anything*. I remember one time a fella come down on me chest (with his hand) and I *beat* the hand off him! I thought I was supposed to have a baby. I was in an awful state. Even when I got married now and was pregnant, I didn't know where the baby was going to come from. I thought they were just going to cut you here (stomach) and lift the baby out. Until you had your baby you didn't *know*. I only had two children. I didn't see the face of the first child. He was dead. And the second child only lived for three weeks. The child was laid out on the bed and then early next morning that child would be put in a coffin and the father and a couple of men would carry that coffin from the house up to be buried. Oh, there was an awful lot of deaths at that time.

"I remember in our house this girl had a baby out of wedlock. Her mother remarried and she had a stepfather. So she becomes pregnant and that girl was out in the street! Completely put out of the home. Out of shame and embarrassment. So she went to live with an aunt who kept her. Then she had the baby, a lovely little baby. But that aunt died and she came back home with that baby to live. And that stepfather put that girl out *four* times. She used to sleep on the landing with that baby in her arms. And you were afraid then to interfere, to take her in, because her mother and stepfather was living next door to you, do you know what I mean? But you'd take her a cup of tea out on the landing, and took her porridge. But my mother used to take the little girl in. Oh, she *did*. My mother'd sneak her and the baby in at night-time and sneak her back out in the morning. And her mother didn't know that she was after being in our house. There could have been *terrible* trouble. That child died at a very young age but that girl got pregnant again and eventually she got married at night-time and she wore a loose jacket to cover herself. The stepfather had TB and had left the house at this time. He was in this sanitorium and the mother was there in the house with her four children. So she got married and she bought a few penny cakes and a few bottles of milk and we all had a wedding in the house. So what they done that night they like barricaded in her mother's room, put sheets across, and her mother was in the one side of the room and the girl and her husband slept on the other side . . . separated by sheets. That was their wedding night."

JOHN-JOE KENNEDY—AGE 75

He was born in Engine Alley and earned his place in the folk history of the Liberties as one of the original animal gang members of the rough 1930s. He was arrested for his part in the melee at Baldoyle and sentenced to three years in prison. Back then it was nothing to be ashamed of because "you had to be tough to survive." Today he lives off Ash Street and is such a gentle, grandfatherly sort that it is hard to imagine him in bloody street combat fifty years ago.

"Oh, Engine Alley was all tenements and lodging houses and a hell of a lot of TB in the tenements back then. It was the dampness, the walls was *reeking* in dampness. A tenement room back then was half a crown a week. And some terrible fires around. Cause it was all open fires and you might put on a lump of coal and there'd be a 'bang' and you wouldn't know where the sparks had gone. Ah, there was people burned to death in the tenement houses.

"There *really* was poverty in them times. Very little work at that time and kids walking around the street in bare feet and the arse out of his trousers. I was the same. Oh, *common*. I remember they used to give out free boots in the schools—the *Herald* Boot Fund—and we used to scrub our feet nearly bleeding and put them out in front of the teacher like that to get a pair of boots. And then there was the police clothes, like a jersey and corduroy trousers. Used to call them the 'police clothes', get them down on Pearse Street. Oh, you were a tough guy you when you had them on you! Ah, it wasn't good then. But money went further in the old days. Cause I remember when I was only a kid and me mother'd give me a shilling and I'd go over to 'Cocky' Roche's across the road there and I got a pig's cheek out of the barrel and a thing of cabbage and potatoes. For a shilling.

"Engine Alley was *walking alive* with rats. Cause there was three slaughter houses around here and people had pigs in the yards and that drew the rats in. Oh, they were *huge*. Me mother-in-law had hens and we used to sit looking at the rats robbing the hen eggs. Did you ever see a rat robbing an egg? One fella goes out and gets the egg and he turns over on his back and the other fella pulls him into the hole by the tail with the egg on his stomach. We used to see them. Oh, I was always afraid of rats. Now there was one woman, Biddy was her name, and she woke up one morning and she was only after having a baby and the next thing the rat was *feeding off her*! The rat was at her nipple. And she rubbed the rat, she thought it was the child's head. See, they always followed the mother when the mother'd be after giving birth. Sure, me wife was giving birth to the second baby and I felt this (movement) across me feet (in bed). So I took up the child out of the cot and the minute I put on the light the two of them hopped out of the bed. Two rats. In our bed. And we had two dogs, only two old mongrels, but the two dogs banged them. But the child died about three or four months later. The rats must have been putting their tails into her mouth.

"Oh, Engine Alley was a great street at that time, always full of children. We'd play football up and down the street and bet ha'pennies on cards, just to pass the time. And the organ-grinders played tunes and a lot of them used the monkey for picking out fortunes. Cost a penny. And we used to have a great sing-song at one or two in the morning up Engine Alley. We'd all just stand around at the corner and there was a girl there, Lizzy, and she used to have an old melodion and there'd be a sing-song and dance till maybe three in the morning. Nearly everyone up around Engine Alley would be there from the tenement houses. Women all in their shawls and you'd see them smoking, it'd be underneath their shawl. A small little clay pipe, a 'scutch' they used to call it. It was cut down like to a small little thing that they could hold in their hand. And people looking out the windows and listening. We'd be out there singing like a nightingale. Them nights that we used to have, they were terrific.

"For courting you'd maybe go up Mulligan's Lane. But the priests around here were very tough on drinking and sexual and all this game. Like 'Court a girl openly and don't go into dark places.' Oh, terrific sermons reprimanding you. Especially the Passionate Fathers and the Jesuits, oh, terrific sermons. I used to go to them. They'd frighten the life out of you, they would. But there was a man here and he had a girl that was crackers about him. And they used to roll around in the streets, the pair of them hugging and kissing and rolling around on the ground . . . do it for devilment to torment the old people. To *torment* the old people! And you'd hear the old people . . . 'them *dirty* pair of sods . . . ought to be *ashamed* of yourself.'

"There used to be lodging houses and the country girls—unfortunate girls— they'd leave home and come up here looking for work and some of them used to go wrong, go 'out on the town'. Men would take them out. They'd stay out all night. Some lovely looking. There was girls then, honest to God, I'm not codding you, film stars had nothing on them. Oh, they were lovely. A *shilling* (they charged)! One we used to call Veronica Lake, long blond hair. There was one girl with a man and she had to go in first and have a bath and the next thing was the gentleman come out and he'd two bunches of scallions and she had to *beat him* around the table with the scallions. And she was nude. All she had to do was beat him in the nude around the table with the scallions and she got *twenty pounds* for that. Now another woman (a madam) says she was passing the chapel on Francis Street there one time and she got 'pushed' moreless into the chapel. That's what she *said* happened to her. Now what happened nobody knows. But she went in and got her Confession heard and she went religious after that. Oh, very religious.

"Years ago there was poverty but people were very close. They shared. But there was some *bad* people too, people depriving you of a bit of grub. Like this woman, she went by the name of 'The Grey Mare'. She was a very vicious woman. Ah, very envious she was. At the time there was a relieving officer and you got relief, maybe five bob. Well, before the relieving officer'd go to the people he used to go into the shop she had and she'd say, '*They* don't want it.' And he'd go by *her*! So you wouldn't get your five bob relief that week. And at times there was people left *starving*! Due to her! That's the truth, I'm telling you the truth. Oh, she was bad . . . we called her 'bad'. She even got her own husband put away umpteen times. For *nothing*. He'd be in the pub at the counter and the door would fly open and she'd start off (screaming at him). And he'd run out after her—now he had a wooden leg! And he'd run after her with a razor but he'd never get *near* her. And there was air raid shelters around here years ago and she used to go into the air raid shelters and hit her head off the wall and come out split and go down to the police station and say her husband was after doing it. An out-and-out liar. That woman, the Grey Mare, was a *demon*, that's what we used to call her.

"We used to have to go over to the northside for the Labour Exchange, the dole. I was eighteen. But we used to have to go over in mobs, in gangs, cause a couple of us did go over on our own one time and we got a hiding. Every time we went over there there was a row . . . battles. So there'd be about ten of us that'd go over. There was so much trouble that eventually they built a Labour Exchange here in Werburgh Street for us on the south-side. They were the animal gangs, all that mob, a crowd of northsiders from Waterford Street, Gardiner Street, Corporation Street, Foley Street. They were all in their twenties and thirty mark. They used to call them 'animal gangs' because they used to carry blades in their caps, in the beak of the cap. Blades sewn into the beak of the cap and they used to take it off and give you a crack across the face with it. It was like a knife across there. Oh, very dangerous. And they wore these black shirts with white ivory buttons. Oh, you could spot them a mile away.

"One time we went to the Mansion House to a dance and there was a couple of northsiders there and a crowd of us and there was a row there. One fella got throwed off the balcony! And another night a crowd of us were at the Tivoli (picture house) and a whole crowd from Stafford Street come over and we sneaked out the back of the picture house and met them and there was murder on Francis Street! Fighting with fists, boots, knuckledusters, anything you had to defend yourself. Oh, you had to be tough to survive . . . *had* to be. Then the coppers used to come flying on us. And Brannigan, he was the top-notch, a hard man. He was rough and feared *nothing*. If there was a mob there he'd go right in, digging in, digging out anyone that'd be there. He was about six foot four and real boney, skinny. He went in for boxing as a young bloke but he wasn't a great boxer, he was a *punchbag*. 'Canvas' Brannigan we used to call him when he'd be boxing. But he could *take it*, he could take the punishment.

"He got his reputation from fighting, going in and out of the likes of the tinkers, the itinerants. There used to be a couple of old yards and there was about ten caravans there. If there was a row with them he'd go in and he'd fight the best of them. And they were hard men, them fellas. They could fight. And it was all bare knuckle. The minute a row started Brannigan would be up there. Like a shot! He'd come up by *himself*. Most of them were chimney sweeps, like the Wards, and we used to love to see them (fight). And the women were better that the men! Ah, the women used to spar off just the same as the men. And the men'd make a ring for the women to box. And one man (husband) would be roaring, 'If you don't beat her I'll do this and that to you.' Might just be a family feud, an argument between them. No hair pulling, actually boxing! Oh, they were *better* than the men. Sure, they used to fight the men themselves, the women. Oh, yes. And some-times two families. But it would be all fair fighting. You'd just watch it, you wouldn't interfere. But Brannigan would give them two warnings, 'Stop and go home!' Then he'd walk in between them and they'd stop. Oh, they had the respect for him.

"There was five of us one time went down to Shelbourne Park and the whole of the northside was there. Spike McCormack and all. They hated the southside, *hated* us. And there was only five of us against about two hundred. Oh, the crowd stopped it. So we said, 'we'll finish this in Baldoyle!' So we all got here (in the Liberties) in a public house around the corner and the Hannigans was throwing beer into us. There was four of them (families), all bookmakers, and they had a couple of shops there in Meath Street. The next thing we were all three-quartered (drunk) and the taxis was called. So we went down to Baldoyle and finished the row. And there was killing. There was only twenty of us—against the whole of the northside. We were drunk . . . didn't know any better. They *weren't*, but we were. We had the false spirit in us. I was twenty. Oh, we all had weapons, the northside and the southside. Oh, everything was involved. We had walking sticks and bits of lead pipe and knuckledusters and there was knives. And there was a French bayonet. You know, a bamboo cane and a snake's head on the top and when you pressed the snake's head a blade shot out. The row started at the last race and people all started to run. People running everywhere! There was two people stabbed. One stabbed and lucky he didn't die and the other fella stabbed in the leg. Funny thing, eight of us was arrested and only *one* of the northside gang. And we all done imprisonment. I got five years. We appealed and got two years off our sentence. It was reckoned that it was the harshest sentence ever for a gang war."

FRANK LAWLOR—AGE 66

He was one of the dedicated young men who joined the St Vincent de Paul Society to assist the poor during the war years. He and another Society member went around in pairs on their bicycles to visit the needy in their ramshackle rooms. Their job went far beyond merely handing out vouchers for much-needed food, clothing, and fuel. It also involved sitting awhile to listen, learn, sympathise and counsel. Most important, he feels, was to instil in the people a sense of dignity. Over time he became good friends with many of his families and at Christmas time got loads of lovely pudding on his rounds.

"I'm from Arbour Hill originally and I started working for a coal merchants in Pearse Street when I was about nineteen. The accountant there asked would I like to join the Vincent de Paul Society and that's how I joined. The area I was attached to was Moira House on Francis Street. Wonderful people in the Liberties and very clannish. Conditions then in the forties were very, very poor. Most of the houses were very ramshackle . . . but still standing. Rooms let for two and sixpence and a toilet in the back yard. Very unhygienic. By today's standards it wouldn't be tolerated. And ten and twelve children, three or four in one bed. The food was bread and butter and jam, maybe a bit of bacon and cabbage on the weekends. The money-lender and the pawn office was a way of life. It was hard times.

"The poor themselves applied for aid. They'd drop a note in a box in the parish church or to the priest's house saying, 'Could someone call on me? I'm in a bad way, my husband is out of work.' And as quickly as possible we'd call. We always went in pairs, that was the rule, to avoid any embarrassing situation that could arise. We'd go around on our bikes. Areas that had bad names, policemen would only go down there in twos, but the Vincent de Paul men went down there and they were welcome. They would know you in the district as the 'gentlemen' or the 'Vincent men'. You'd spend some time with them. It wasn't just a case of 'There's your voucher, see you next week.' You'd spend about twenty minutes with them. And there wasn't always a chair to sit down on. They felt that somebody out there had heard their cry for help . . . you were a *friend.*

"You'd ascertain how difficult things were for the woman and how many family they had and what was the major needs. And it wasn't recommended that you visit regularly at the same time every week because it meant that they would be ready and maybe hide anything away. Like they could rent a radio then for about one and sixpence a week and I heard that these Vincent de Paul men came and poked under the bed looking for this radio and said, 'Wait now, you've enough money to spend on this radio.' Now that was a terrible thing that there were some members like that. We didn't go around looking under beds. We'd *see* a need and try to meet it. And it was vouchers then, not cash. A voucher for maybe three and six or five shillings. For food and clothing. And it wasn't supposed to be for any cigarettes. You wrote on it, 'For provision for Mrs so-and-so' and addressed to a specific grocer. And for clothes we'd write a voucher for the value of a dress, frocks, shoes. Sometimes vouchers were issued to coal merchants and vouchers for furniture. I did know occasionally of the vouchers going into the public house. It was a three and six voucher and it was sold for two shillings. There's no doubt they did that alright.

"What you really aimed for in the Society was to give the poor *dignity*. That was *much* more important. There wasn't a set thing you had to do. Like if you could give the man a job or a horse. We bought a horse for a man because he had a cart and had the opportunity to carry bundles of sticks or something else. So we gave him the horse on practical grounds as well as giving him *dignity*. We hoped our members would have this sensitivity. But there was a poor lady living in a tenement in Marlborough Street and her husband died and somebody said that she was badly off and perhaps the Society would call. And some members did call and she had the place beautifully set out and they said, 'Oh, I don't think there's anything you need here.' She was *insulted* and humiliated. And *she vowed* to them that however long she lived she would *never* allow a member of the St Vincent de Paul Society inside her door. Now there's a case in point of the pride of the poor, after being so badly hurt by a person that was so indiscreet to treat her like that. But that was the exception. You don't have an organisation with 10,000 members that you don't get a few bad ones.

"It was always the woman's job to meet with us. The men got out of the way, wouldn't be hanging around. If it wasn't for the women there wouldn't have been a family! That was my experience. Sure, they never got out, *never* got out. And very raggedy dress. You'd very rarely see them with a change of clothing. Women were worn out from work and worn out from having children. Sometimes we would give them the money to go to the pictures—get a break, get out! Wonderful people and they worried about one another. A wonderful community spirit. Oh, fantastic! I remember one lady now in Francis Street and she won the top prize in the lottery, which was ten pounds. And she said to me, 'I don't need any money this week cause I won £10.' So I said, 'Oh, I'm delighted. Go and have the night out, go to the pictures.' 'Oh', she said, 'it came in very handy because Mrs so-and-so downstairs, her daughter is making her First Communion so I sent her down £2 to get shoes for her. Now she would do it *for me*.' And then she gave some to a person who was worse off than her so she wouldn't have to go to the money-lender that week. And then it was *gone*.

"At Christmas-time we'd give a double or treble ticket and a food parcel with tea, sugar, cake and maybe bring them in a roast chicken. You'd bring that to them on your bicycle. And inevitably when you called the week after Christmas there was your Christmas pudding handed to you. Oh, a lovely pudding. But your conference said, 'You don't accept anything from the poor. They owe you nothing. It's a privilege for you to be their friend.' But you *had* to take it, cause you wouldn't insult them by saying you couldn't touch it. Oh, yes, that was a tradition and you'd get tea. That was great. So that was house number one . . . and then there was house number two and . . . So then you'd say, 'Would you mind very much if we took the pudding from you and wrapped it up?'"

MARY O'NEILL—AGE 84

When she grew up along Chamber Street early in the century it was all red brick tenement houses, weaving factories, and a few huckster shops and pubs. Her mother died when she was sixteen and it was her inherited duty to look after her twelve brothers. This meant rising every morning at four and spending the entire day preparing meals, washing clothes, ironing, and scrubbing floors. Although deprived of most normal childhood pleasures, Mary bears no resentment explaining that it was simply her expected role in those times when the mother had died. After rearing her siblings she married and had eight children of her own.

"My father worked in O'Keefe's the knackers where they used to slaughter the cattle and any sort of animal, boil down the bones and make glue and different things. The heads of fish and all. I had twelve brothers and there was three sets of twins. I was the only girl. Me mother died when I was sixteen and I had to look after me brothers. I used to get up at four in the morning. Ah, cook the meals and wash and scrub . . . everything, from morning till night. All washing on the washing board. I have me washing board yet.

"In 1910 Chamber Street was red brick tenement houses and four shops between them and a public house. And there was a lot of silk weaving factories around us. You had to do your stairs every week, scrub them down with black soap and a scrub brush. Down on your hands and knees, put your apron around you, maybe a piece of cloth under your knees and a bucket of hot water and you scrubbed down them stairs. Every week. People had great pride. Big halls in the tenements and women would sit in the hall doors with their shawls around them and be chatting. And they'd be sitting at their windows looking out and be chatting with the woman at the next house (window) and they'd have a chat with people walking around (below). And we had a great landlord, Mr O'Leary was his name. Every New Year's day we'd (children) all stand outside the doors waiting for our pennies (from O'Leary) and we'd get *brand new* pennies, every one of us, all the kids in the street.

"We had a big old heavy hall door in the tenement and the Black and Tans kept hammering it down. Oh, I remember the Black and Tans. There was curfew and we had to put up a black sack or wrap at the window for to blacken it out. And they'd raid homes. I remember them coming into our house and me father had been in the Leinster Regiment and had a (British

23 Men could earn a marginal livelihood from selling papers.

24 Street in the notorious Monto prostitution district. (Chandler Collection)

25 Charwomen of the tenements.

26 Typical provisions store in Dublin and Belfast during the tenement period.

27 Shawled women seemingly waiting for pawnshop to open.

28 Yard in Morgan's Cottages where the sanitary facilities were minimal—documented by Sir Charles Cameron.

29 Swift's Alley in the Liberties.

30 Marrowbone Lane where local residents battled with the animal gang in the 1930s.

31 Children of the slums. Such photographs were used by humanitarian groups to show the appalling living conditions of the tenement dwellers.

32 Wares displayed for sale at Mason's Market on Horseman's Row. (RSAI)

33 Wares set out for sale at Anglesea Market. (RSAI)

34 Cole's Lane looking towards Henry Street. (RSAI)

35 Stirling Street in the Liberties.

36 Patrick Street women traders, circa 1906.

37 Children gathered at Blackpitts.

38 Cobblestoned Ash Street in the Liberties.

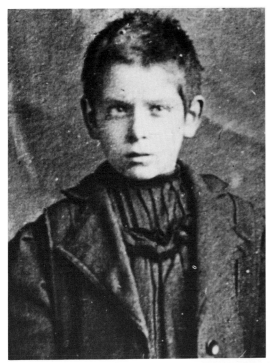

39 & **40** Ill-clad children of the tenement slums.

41 Circle of men participating in a "toss school" on the docks.

42 Tenement room on Newmarket. (RSAI)

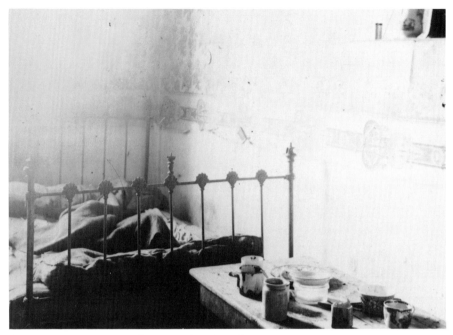

43 Tenement room in the Coombe. (RSAI)

44 "Furnishings" in tenement room in the Coombe. (RSAI)

army) picture over the mantelpiece and the fella says, 'I see, I see . . . it's all right.' And he went away. I was only a little girl and I was *terrified*. I saw them going up and down in tenders and seen them taking a man out of a pub up beside us and he was supposed to belong to the IRA and they put him into the armoured car and took him away. And they *murdered* him.

"I used to get up at four in the morning. Had to get up early to get one brother out to the ice stores and then get me daddy out and then have to get another chap up and then another fella up and then one for school. A big plate of porridge and plenty of milk on it for them. And tea and toast and maybe an egg—if you could afford an egg. One brother, he was a grocer's assistant and I had to have a shirt for him every day and dipped the collar into the starch and you'd iron it with a handkerchief over it and it'd be glossy. Then I used to have to bring one brother to school and maybe he'd get halfway there and he'd say, 'I'm alright, Mary,' and he'd go off *mitching*. Go down to the quays to carry bags for the men, or playing football or scutting cars. Then in the summer they used to go up to the canal and then 'box the fox', rob the apples from the orchard. Climb over the wall and get up in the trees and get the apples, maybe pears, stuff them in your pocket.

"When I used to get the meals for the boys we always had stew. You'd go up and get a couple of pounds of leg beef and sheep's head and an ox tail and you had a big three-legged pot that size and you'd fill it up with dumplings you'd make out of the flour, round little balls, and put them in the stew. You had a big open fire and iron pots and an iron kettle and two marbles in the kettle to keep it from rusting. And years ago now with the big open fires when you'd peel the potatoes you'd leave the potato skins at the back of the fire and throw the cabbage leaves the same. That was to keep away sickness. We used coal but sometimes the roadways were made with tar blocks, the wooden setts, and when they'd lift them up the Corporation would give them to you for the fire and they'd blaze up in the chimney. And we used to get butter boxes from the shops and they were put around the fire and you'd sit on them when you'd be cold and damp.

"Now when I got married in 1934 I moved up to another tenement house and had to pay three and six rent. My husband worked in an iron foundry and it was a dirty job. He'd come home black and I had to have a big kettle of boiling water for him to clean himself and a lump of soap. I had eight children and I had a handywoman called Ma Lakey. Everyone knew Ma Lakey. She'd do everything for you. You'd have the newspapers for the bed and she'd get the hot water and everything. You just had to bring the child into the world yourself, no pain killers. She'd just stand beside you and hold you down and the baby'd be born. Then the mother'd get a bowl of gruel. She'd look after your baby and do your washing and come in the next morning, for the whole nine days. A half a crown (payment). And dare you get out of bed—she would *not* let you! The baby'd be put in a little cot or a drawer with a little blanket or a pillow. Kept it warm. And the baby was christened in a little gown and little bonnet and the Godmother'd take the baby around to the neighbours and they might give threepenny bits or sixpenny bits and maybe you wouldn't see the baby till night-time.

"Now I remember in 1943—and I was four months pregnant and expecting a baby meself—and the woman over my head was expecting at that time and it was two in the morning and she *hammered* down on the ceiling and I run up and she says, 'Oh, my God, Mary, will you run for the doctor?' So I *flew* around the back of Guinness's—four months pregnant meself—and when I got down to the Coombe (hospital) I said, 'I want a doctor immediately.' And he said, 'Would you be able to sit on the cross-bar of me bike?' And I said, 'Yes, doctor.' Now we couldn't get a midwife and it was his first baby and that doctor was in *pieces*. Now he *was*! The poor man. I sat on the cross-bar and we rode the bicycle up. So I was with him till that baby was born and he gave me the baby—and I'll never forget it—he said, 'Give it a few clappers on the bottom.' So I helped bring that baby into the world.

"I knew one poor (unmarried) girl now who had a baby and her mother and father gave her a hard life . . . a *hard life*. She was put into the convent on the Navan Road and she had to work. Her hair was cut tight and she wore a big heavy convent skirt and big old boots. I went there to see her. She was made to work like a slave, the water dripping out of her. Her mother wouldn't take her, nor her father. And the baby was given out for adoption. Her mother wouldn't have anything to do with her but her granny took her and reared her. And that poor girl was going around the street, her poor mind gone. And she was a lovely girl. And do you know what? She used to put an old cat in a little pram and drive it around, God love her. Her mind went! If it weren't for her granny she'd have been dead years ago. And when the granny died, then she went."

JOHN O'DWYER—AGE 70

He was born in the Liberties, began his apprenticeship in his father's pub at age fourteen, and went on to own his own public house. During his early years he served behind the bar in two "real rough and tumble" tenement districts—York Street and the North Quay. Dockers and drovers could be a rowdy bunch but once you got to know their nature they could be handled with a bit of diplomacy. In those days of great poverty and meagre meals, John explains, "drink was their main diet . . . it was food".

"I was born in the Coombe, the heart of the Liberties. Then my father had a pub in South Earl Street, just a corner pub, and the whole family was living over the shop. I started working for my father when I was about ten. Oh, I used to go in and pull pints in short pants. I left school at thirteen and did my apprenticeship for five years. My father gave me a half a crown a week. My first job in the morning was cleaning the spittoons. It was a *horrible* job, especially during the TB epidemic here. Then in the early forties I served at Kennedy and Lalor's (pub) in York Street. York Street was all tenement houses, a real rough and tumble area. I remember going into a house in York Street and there was twenty-four families in it and only *one* toilet for the families down in the yard. Very little they had, didn't own a thing. I don't know how some existed at all. Oh, but great pride.

"Now the people on York Street, they had *nothing*. They were all fighting for the one piece of cake and it was very small. At the time I worked there *all* the money came from England because the people had gone across to earn money in the factories and munitions factories. And there was all sorts of things going on, like women going off with other fellas and their fellas coming home and finding them in their rooms and so forth . . . there was always a row. They were rough, tough people on York Street. Oh, *really* tough. We called the pub the 'Glass-go Inn'—the 'glass went in' every night! In my early days on Saturday night the pubs shut at half nine, so for rows *Friday* was the bad night. But it was very difficult to bar people in that particular area because if you barred one fella you were barring the whole family, a family of maybe ten or twelve and their cousins as well and then they'd *all* leave. Cause they were all so closely together and related.

"At that time all life was related to going to Mass, going to the pub, going to work—in that order. The centre of life was all in the pub at that time. Men had full control of the wages and they always had enough to drink . . . always. When they finished work they never went home until the pub closed. The women were *slaves*. Oh, sure, they were slaves, had to be home *all* the time. They never got to go any place. They dressed very poorly and never had money for any incidentals. Women worked very hard and I don't know how they stood by the men. It was part of the *culture* at that particular time. And whatever happened in a tenement house would always drift back down into the pub. It was like a confession box. Like a woman with a black eye wasn't allowed outside the house but we'd *know* about it, we'd know what was going on because conversations always come back into the pub. Oh, the neighbours would tell you, alright, you'd know all about their families and everything.

"Where I was there were women dealers and they used to sell oranges and fish and so forth and a second business for them was lending money, always done outside the pub. There was one particular woman I knew in York Street, Rosie was her name, and she was well-known and they used to come from everywhere for to get money off her. Oh, dealers always had plenty of money and they'd come in and have their drinks. And old women with their shawls on, they'd come into the snug where they wouldn't be seen and get their pint put into the jug and the publican always had to put a 'tilly' in, a drop extra. That was the way it was done. Now on Sundays, for Sunday dinner, the locals *queued up* with their jugs. Oh, yes, there was a special jug kept in every house, a delph jug, and always *beautifully* coloured, that'd hold a pint. And some of them had their initials on it, they'd get it done. They were all women in shawls and wouldn't go near the bar at all. Sometimes little children'd come with the jug and we weren't supposed to serve children with the jug but no one noticed, it was overlooked.

"Kennedy and Lalor's had another pub on the north quays and I used to work in that pub as well. A complete docker area. And drovers used to come in and they'd put a glass of whiskey into a pint of porter. Desperate people they were. Always had a big ash stick with a big knob at the bottom of it. You'd be afraid of them. They got out of control, you know. Always have this ash plant with them that was part of their trade, you see, and you couldn't take that off them. Oh, the police used to be afraid of them. Now the dockers, they had *nothing*. They *lived for pints*. Drink was their main diet, it was *food*. They used to call the pint 'the liquid food'. That's what they called it. They were living from day to day really, they'd nothing, no possessions. All they had was what they walked around in. And dockers were all paid in the *pubs*! That's the way it was in those days. Oh, I saw it meself many times. See, cause they (stevedores or foremen) had to have a centre point to pay their men, so they thought the easiest way to do it was to get them all into a place that was out of the rain. The pub was out of the rain and that's where they paid them.

"Oh, it was a terrible system. Sure, those dockers, half of them, never brought any of it home. Oh, their wives and children were starving. I'm not saying *all* of them now because there were some very good people but there was a percentage of them that wouldn't even *dream* of handing over the wages. I remember going to a docker's funeral and he had nine children and no one went to the funeral. No, nobody went at all. His children hated him because he never brought home a penny. There was no feelings for him at all. I remember going to that funeral and the priest was there and a couple of grave diggers and maybe two customers—and that was it. Nine children in that family and not one of them went to the funeral. Very sad . . . shocking.

"The local people, back then it was the publican who *married* them, *buried* them, and *christened* them. When people were getting married the booze was given to them for a party and then repaid later on a weekly or a monthly basis. No extra charge, it was just a way of life. Same thing if somebody died and had no money to bury them. My father'd take over the burial and organise the burial and when it'd be all over the family would come along and pay him so much until the debt was cleared, normally about three years. With christenings the same thing applied, to get a party. *All* these things were celebrated . . . death, christenings, marriage, and the local publican, he was the *man*. And if you didn't attend a local funeral they'd go to the pub next door and you lost their trade. You had to be there. You *always* went. One year, I done 240 funerals meself.

"And if a fella was going for a job and he wanted a character reference my father would take on the job of writing out and saying his name is so-and-so and he is a worthy type of character. And he used to sign for people to buy furniture and stuff on the payment system. Oh, I did that myself many times. See, they had nothing in the tenement houses, they owned nothing, really. So they had to get a guarantor. Oh, they had great respect for the publican. They could even confide in him. A publican was a man who, if there were difficulties in a family, maybe the people might call him outside and tell him that they were having terrible trouble at home and ask him (for advice) and he'd listen and give them guidance. Ah, he was next to the parish priest."

TOMMY MAHER—AGE 81

His father was a carter with horse and dray and his mother was a street dealer hawking fish in her wicker basket car, so Tommy had to be left in the Poor Crèche on Meath Street each day when he was an infant. At age ten he left school to help his mother sell on the streets. He spent his life working the streets of the Liberties and claims that the best free "shows" were the wild brawls between women dealers who would nearly "pull the scalp off" one another in their fury.

"I was born in 1912, when the Titanic went down. Born in Garden Lane just off Francis Street. Heart of the Liberties. It was all tenements . . . *rough*. I had two brothers and four sisters and my cousins. Their mother and father died and my mother took them over and there was four of them. All my aunts and all lived near one another in this lane and it was like a little country place. The women, in the evenings they'd bring out a stool and sit there talking with the shawls around them. A good shawl, a big brown shawl was called a 'teddy bear'. My mother had one of them.

"Where we were in Garden Lane, the Keogh's bacon people owned it. They were the landlords and they were very good. It was two and six a week. They'd have to keep the yard clean and the toilet but the tenants done the stairs. Sometimes landlords would get the chimneys done but then sometimes we'd have to pay for it ourselves. It was a couple of shillings. People had fear of fire. Sweeps would come around with a bicycle. Jemmy West was our sweep. Put a big sack around the mouth of the fire and there'd be holes in the sack for the rods to go through and the brush. Many a fire was started over candles burning. Very bad fires. People'd get out the best way they can. I took a woman and child out of a house that was burning. I got over the wall, in the back door, and up to the back room and I took this woman and this boy out into the yard. And there was a cousin of mine and we were all playing in the room and she wore these calico bibs and the parents were away and her bib caught fire. Poor girl, she was very, very disfigured. A lovely looking girl and she was disfigured, all her face and all. Never got better.

"Me father was a carter with a pony and cart, carrying stuff for people and selling some oranges and apples and bananas. We had a yard there on Carman's Hall and kept the horse there. My mother used to go out on the road with a bit of fish in a basket car, like what Molly Malone'd be doing, sell around house to house as far as Clondalkin. My grandmother and all them people was traders. Traders on Patrick Street, they'd be fighting over one thing or another, like over my stall or your stall or whatever position it'd be in. Oh, they could *curse* all right. And throw off the shawl and they had petticoats and skirts. Mostly hair pulling, catching 'em and pulling by the hair. I seen women in Francis Street nearly pulling the scalp off their heads. I *did*. I seen where the scalp was coming up on a woman's head.

"Now I was in the Poor Crèche. The crèche was in Meath Street. If your parents were going out to work they'd put the children in. For a penny. A penny or whatever you could give. Women'd take care of you, only about three or four of them. Then I went to this school here in John's Lane. To be straight with you I didn't go much to school. Came out when I was about nine or ten, helping my family selling and all. They'd (the authorities) leave me alone cause I was a good worker and I was more important to the family than I was for education. I had to look after the horses for me father and when I got a bit older I used to bring me mother out in the pony and cart selling oranges and apples. Oh, I could handle the horses, God yes.

"I played in the Iveagh Market as a boy. I'd romp around there and used to jeer poor old 'Daddy' Aiken, a poor little man with a Corporation cap on him, an attendant. You'd jeer him and he'd chase you. You could play football in the streets but if you were caught you were summonsed. The Guards would be on a bike. Oh, yes. You'd run and they'd chase you on the bike and maybe give you a smack. Could take you to the Children's Court and you might be fined a half a crown. Or you might be left off with a caution. But they *knew* you had to play in the street cause we'd *nowhere else* to play! So we'd play soccer and there was some 'tomboys' we called them knocking around. Oh, they'd play soccer just as good as the boys could do, curse every bit as good and play cards and all. And I went to the canals but I didn't like swimming— too dirty. People'd throw a dead dog in or an old mattress. I'd get pinkeens in a net, a penny for a net, with a long cane and put them in a jar just for fun. And I'd play around the locks but it was dangerous if you slipped in. I remember a fella drowning up there, he was drunk and dived in for a swim.

"In Francis Street there was two barber shops, Mr Fox and Mr McDonald. Just an old shop. They'd cut your hair for sixpence. Your mother'd say, 'Take the lot off, just leave a fringe.' The (front) fringe, if you saw a priest you'd go (lift it) and say, 'Hello, Father.' Some men had their shaving mugs with their names on them and open razors—'cut throats' we called them. And barbers had singing birds. Some of them had birds that'd *fly around* in the shop. A lot of birds in the tenements, it was a bit of colour and life. Hang it (the cage) out the window and he'd be singing all the time. Now we lived beside Deegan's pub over on Francis Street and there was a window in the toilet of the pub and you could hand the drink out of there into our yard. See, we could get the gargle out through that window on a Sunday. We had steps up to it and you could go up and put your hand in. The publican lived in the pub and he'd be there on the Sunday morning, hand it out. Cause, see, the pubs didn't open till two. So my father and some other men'd be there on the Sunday morning getting the drink out of it. No one would catch that.

"Some of the men around the Liberties they'd get a few extra drinks and they were very bad. Plenty of family rows. Drinking . . . it was the *whole cause* of the trouble. And living in tenement rooms, it created an awful lot of stress. And husbands would *beat* them (wives). Yes, they would, they'd ill-treat them. But you wouldn't want to interfere. Family or relations could interfere. And there was rows in Francis Street *every* Saturday night. Ah, we'd go down every Saturday night to have a look. In the street . . . husbands and wives and maybe sons and daughters and uncles. *Every* Saturday night there was a show. Cause they'd get a few extra drinks. Oh, there was always something on, never a dull moment. And, oh, you'd get a father and son at it alright. The family might separate them. Drinking was the whole cause. Because they wouldn't fight unless they had the false courage from the drink. Then the priest'd stand up on the pulpit and (give) sermons on drink. Oh, God, the missions, they were very rough. Stand up on the pulpit and, 'We'll run Red Biddy out of this country!' Red Biddy was a cheap wine. Then he says, '*Everyone* in this parish is going to die!' And this one fella was laughing. 'What are you laughing about?' 'I don't belong to this parish.'"

LILY FOY—AGE 60

Lily was born and reared in the Liberties but now lives happily in Stoneybatter with her husband Leslie, one of Dublin's premier handcraft signwriters. But her roots across the Liffey run deep and she never tires of telling tales about her legendary granny who lived to be nearly a hundred years old. Around the Liberties she was saintly. She brought babies into the world, cared for the sick, and waked the dead. And, as Lily puts it, "she feared no one." Indeed, she would not hesitate to burst into a tenement room when a drunken husband was beating his wife, scream at him to halt, and even strike him a terrific blow if necessary. Everyone loved and respected her and she was idolised by Lily who likens her to Mother Teresa.

"I grew up off Pimlico in the Liberties. Top of the Coombe. My mother was a coat-maker and my two aunts were weavers but my grandmother was the boss. She was the head of the whole family. My grandfather died young of kidney problems—a lot of men died young at that time—and she was widowed at thirty-two years of age, left with three girls and a boy. And my grandmother had no pension, she got nothing. If you were that badly off you got two loaves a day in the poor house, as they called, in James's Street. You got nothing else. You were supposed to exist on bread. So she got a few pigs cause she knew how to rear them and had them in the back yard and she reared her family on them.

"It was all tenements around, big houses full of people. And I remember granny had a big bath out in the yard and a big wooden wringer. Oh, she was a great washer. Big white linen sheets. But that vat of water was never thrown out. That water would be taken by a neighbour next door that was very poor and they knew that our clothes were very clean and they'd wash their clothes in it. And then they'd take *that* water and start at the top of the tenement house and scrub down the stairs. One woman would do her flight and another hers. And the floors would be like milk. You could eat your dinner off the stairs in the tenements. They were poor but they were very clean.

"My mother had nine of us. But I don't remember her ever going to doctors. Just didn't bother. Pregnancy was nothing to a lot of women. The older women, the grannies, helped. Me mother would be scrubbing and cleaning up the room and getting all ready and we'd know there was another baby coming. Then me granny would be running in big pots of hot water. There was no anaesthetics or anything. Just tell them what to do when they'd get a pain, to hold on and push down. They used to tie a sheet on the end of the bed for the women and let them pull on it. They'd know that it had to get worse before it got better. Me mother was two days in labour with me and I was her first. Now there was girls around there that had babies before they were married. My granny went in and helped them. We never knew until later on, years after, when I was a married woman, that children I was reared up with, that their mother was (in reality) the eldest daughter. We always thought they were brothers and sisters. And they wouldn't tell one another. They even got them christened as brothers and sisters.

"My grandmother, she always went to people who were having babies. And she reckoned that some of the mothers around there didn't get enough to eat. They'd give it (food) to their husbands and the kids. And we used to have hens and if anyone had a new baby we wouldn't get an egg for our breakfast. Those fresh eggs were kept for the woman because granny used to make egg flips for the woman. It was an egg, milk, sugar, a little bit of butter and you'd heat the milk and break the egg and flip it. And if you were very comfortable you could put a sip of sherry or brandy in it. It was a tonic, supposed to be very good for your blood. So Granny used to give them egg flips for the so many days they'd be in bed. Because mothers didn't get enough food. And if they were breast feeding their baby Granny would make them drink a glass of stout. Go for the stout in a jug. Plain porter. It was cheap at that time. Drink that . . . that's how a lot of them nursed their babies.

"It was hard times on women. Men were the *big noise*. They were the boss. They got the meat. The man never done anything. Couldn't do anything. Never minded the kids or anything. Fathers would be out drinking and the mothers reared the kids. Men would give money to their wives but maybe have more money in their pocket for drink. Give the wife £1 and have £2 for himself. Myself, I reckon women kept homes together. Mothers kept the peace in families. Everything goes back to the mother. It still does. And I remember that the men over there at that time were very hard on their wives. He'd be killing her if he knew she was going to the pawn or if she got into a money-lender who used to go around. They'd drink a lot and come home and beat some of them (wives), beat them up. They were the boss. But my granny, they weren't *her* boss. My granny used to always tell us, 'Even if you're only that height and a fella is the size of Nelson's Pillar, *never* let him hit you. If he hits you wait until he's in bed and kill him!' And I saw men not only hitting but kicking their wives. If they were hitting their wives my granny, she'd go in—no bother to her—and say, 'This'll *stop*! You're not going to kick your wife and children while I'm alive.' I often seen her running in and daring fellas, big fellas, men six foot, to hit her. They wouldn't! Wouldn't raise his hand to her cause he *respected* her. I remember running down to me granny and telling her that there was a certain man up there hitting his wife. And my granny—and she was only a smallish little woman like myself, but blocky—running up to him and I saw her giving him a punch as good as any man gave a punch. She feared no one.

"They'd always run for my granny if there was trouble. Or if children were sick or for people that were dead. I remember when there'd be anyone dead my granny always kept white sheets and pillow covers and she had a big apron and she'd tie the sheets and stuff underneath that so nobody would know that she was loaning to the people. And she'd sit up all night with the sick. When there was smallpox in Dublin she'd go into people's houses and people would say to her, 'Oh, you shouldn't go in there.' And my granny just said, 'If you get it, you get it, but you have to help people.' And my granny and her children never got it but that person that said it to her got it herself. And her whole face was marked forever. And my granny used to say that's what you got for not helping.

"Me granny lived to be ninety-six. My idea of God and goodness is Mother Teresa. My granny was like that. Like sharing an egg. Charitable. I reckon Mother Teresa is like her."

SENAN FINUCANE—AGE 73

He came from a farming family in Clare in the late 1930s to join the police force in Dublin. He was soon walking the beat in the Liberties with his mate the legendary Lugs Brannigan whom Senan calls a "God among the Liberties people". Together they disbanded toss schools, cracked the secret door-knock code of public houses serving patrons after hours, and battled the animal gangs with batons flying. When the German bomb fell on the northside in 1941 he was immediately dispatched to the scene where he witnessed in horror body parts being retrieved from the wreckage. He loved his life in the Liberties where he became a much liked and respected "copper on the beat".

"I'm from Clare, I came from a farming family. There was ten in the family and I left in 1939 and came to Dublin by bus from Limerick. I was never in the city before. Arrived here, waked up the next morning and we got measured to see that you were the right height, and a stiff medical test. Then we went into training right away for six weeks. Oh, it was like the army. We lived in barracks, about fifty of us, in Kevin Street. Up at seven for drill, a long walk, in for breakfast, boots and brass buttons to shine, and a haircut every week or so . . . oh, *tight*. There was never a dull moment.

"My first impression of the Liberties was, of course, the tenements. Down on Francis Street and Bride Street and the Coombe, they were the *worst* tenements in Dublin. And in back of Kevin Street there was an old tenement house that collapsed and there was two killed. Oh, and big families in the tenements, ten or twelve children in a room just the size of this. I saw a girl of eight and she was minding two younger children while her mother was a dealer in Camden Street. She was *rearing* those children, at eight. They had a lot of hardship and only the bare necessities to cook. One outdoor toilet and slop buckets and you'd often see the toilet overflowed and people there getting all kinds of diseases and fevers. I was assigned to the worst, most *horrible* places there and you'd get a feeling that you were going to get disease out of it. But I never got nothing! We had O'Keefe's the knackers who'd buy animals that would be dead and make bonemeal and crush it for manure. They'd skin the animals first and maybe twenty or thirty cattle in a big container boiling and you'd get a smell off that. And you'd see a fella sitting skinning an animal and he'd be taking a mug of tea and a cut of bread while he was actually doing the job. But the people around there maintained that the smell kept down disease.

"A lot of hardship. Traders going around selling fruit and fish and the men then would go out to the dump and collect jam jars and bottles, bits of coal and timber and everything else and fill it into a bag and take it home on a pram or bicycle. And clothing was scarce during the war. Women'd go out tugging with their prams knocking at doors asking if they had any old clothes. Come back with a bundle of old clothes and wash them and re-sell those again. And a lot of discarded military clothing, trousers, tunics, during the war. No coal came in for a few years and so you just kept turf for the cold weather in winter—and only *very cold* weather. Lots of people went out to the bogs, up in the Wicklow mountains, fifteen and twenty miles away, to cut turf and there were hawkers with turf for sale during the war. And some fellas would cycle out maybe ten miles to snare rabbits and bring them back for food and sell them. Rabbits are very nice if they're properly done. Oh, I ate rabbit myself.

"Children all in the streets playing football and handball. They *shouldn't* have been but they'd just give a signal that the police are coming and they'd run. And children swinging on the lamp-posts, that was dangerous with the lorries coming along. And scutting was highly dangerous. We always tried to prevent that. See, they went from one traffic stop to another but sometimes they couldn't take a chance of jumping down off the lorry, couldn't get *off* cause it was going too fast, and sometimes they'd be taken away down into the country ten or twelve miles!

"Men'd sit down in the street there and play cards and pass the time. That was harmless, only small stakes. But we'd get lots of complaints about the toss schools around Cork Street, Kevin Street, different places around the Liberties where people would lose all their wages. Wives would complain that they were losing all their money. See, on the penny there was a head on one side and a harp on the other and they'd be tossing that. It was 'heads you win, harps you lose.' Now at a big toss school there might be sixty or eighty people and the place would be full of silver, half crowns. Often there'd be a hundred pounds or maybe two hundred pounds on the ground, a *lot of money*. So emotions were high. And a row was often started at a toss school because they'd have pennies with *two heads*—where you can't lose. So we'd have to raid that and you'd want to go pretty fast with a force of maybe ten or twelve Guards and get that place cleared. They might have a lookout and then we could go to plain clothes pretty fast. Oh, I often seen *buckets* of money.

"And we'd check for publicans doing after-hour trade, keeping them (customers) inside doing the drinking. Because other publicans would complain. Or their wives might complain too. Certain places didn't see that the Holy Hour was observed. Even on Christmas day and Good Friday we'd have to be out and try and prevent it. But people could be *sneaky* in keeping out of sight and there could be thirty or forty people inside the public house during the Holy Hour. It's *amazing* (how quiet they could be). We got seventeen in the public house one day and we couldn't hear a *thing* outside until we knocked on the door. And, see, they had code knocks and they'd change the code. It might be two knocks, a single one, and two more. Or it could be three and two or one. The publican always had code knocks so they could get in. But we used to break the code. Oh, yes. One time we knocked with the right code and went in—and to their *great surprise!* We could hear *nothing* outside but when we went in they were all *jumping* all over the place, out the back door and over the wall.

"The poorer classes would drink the cheap wine, only a few shillings per bottle. There was what was known as 'Red Biddy', a cheap wine. *Cheap* wine. And you'd get *so drunk* on it that they could be operated on without an anaesthetic! Cause those drunks in the street, they wouldn't feel the pain. They'd just go unconscious with the drink after a pint of cheap wine. Oh, they'd be sleeping in the lobby of tenements and you might go into a hallway at the night-time and walk over a fella in the dark. I saw a fella sleeping down there at Christ Church for two or three years. And do you know what his pillow was? A cocoa tin and a piece of rag about the size of your fist. He'd be lying down on the concrete and *that* was his pillow. A bit of rag just like a pin cushion and he'd rest his head on that. He'd a red face and never bothered anybody.

"In those days if there was a row they'd say, 'We'll go down the lane here and fix it' and it'd be a fair fight. Then shake hands and maybe have a drink together. And we had Jim Brannigan here. Oh, I was stationed with him for twenty years. He was like a God among the Liberties. He *was*! They all knew him and he knew *everybody*. Jim knew them *all*—by name. Maybe a fella throwing a bottle and hitting a fella's head and Jim'd say, 'Don't run away, I *know you*, come back!' Now in family rows we wouldn't interfere in nine cases out of ten. The husband might come in drunk and give the wife a kick. And the woman would be shouting and everything and the next thing was, 'I'll get *Brannigan for you*! I'll get Brannigan and he'll *chastise* you!' He'd enter rows and make them shake hands at the finish, you know, between husband and wife . . . make peace. And, of course, Jim was available night and day. He really loved the people and they *liked* him.

"The animal gangs were very strong then. They'd only fight among themselves, like rival gangs. You had a southside gang and a northside gang and they'd travel two or three miles over to the other side of the city and a row would start. Sometimes they'd get transport there, maybe taxis or (horse) cabs and go to the other side *just to have a row*. Could be twenty to forty to fifty in a gang. All ages, twenty to fifty, would fight. Most of them unemployed. There was knives and bottles and chains and their fists.

"And there'd be those supporting the gang—they had their supporters. Like even the *fathers* and *mothers*, go out and help their sons. Oh, yes, in a big row you'd often see maybe *two hundred* people in the streets, running in all directions. Any maybe one, chasing two or three that had no weapons. Some people, like the mothers and fathers and friends, would egg those lads on. Shout out, 'Good lads . . . good Joe . . . good Tom . . . *give it to them!*' Oh, yes, I saw women throwing stuff *out the window*. Oh, it was a good battle and people'd be hanging out their windows—it was a good show. Our orders, of course, were to deal with them as best we can. And to get *help* as quick as possible. You couldn't get into twenty fellas fighting each other there, you had to go and get help. And we carried only a baton. Oh, I often had to use that if there was a baton charge to disperse an unruly crowd. But we would only draw the baton as a last resort, against an animal gang or other types of fighting.

"Now when the war was on we had blackouts. They had to have a curtain there and if there was light inside, even if it was an inch out, there'd be a man (Guard) coming inside to fix your blinds. And gas lighting was only on certain times of the night. Back then the police did the rationing books, till the Civil Service took it over. Rations for an ounce or two of tea per week and sugar and all those items that were a scarce commodity. And, of course, petrol was rationed and paraffin oil for a lamp. No oranges or bananas or grapes because of the war, all those luxuries disappeared. But you could get things off the black market, smuggle it in some way. You were lucky if you got a few candles or tyres for bikes from the black market. We wouldn't do very much about it because people were in dire straits trying to get some little bit extra.

"Air raid shelters came along in 1940 but they weren't too great a protection in case of shrapnel or glass flying because they were all above the ground. See, if there was bombing they were to go to these shelters because the tenements were old and they'd fall to bits. A bomb *fell* just up the road here one time by the canal. We lost a couple of houses but no one was killed. We heard it that night, heard a 'whizz' and next thing the bomb exploded. You heard the whizz of the bomb falling, coming down from the sky. There was an awful explosion and we weren't used to that. But there was *terrible* excitement over on the northside when the bomb fell on the North Strand and killed thirty-six. We were all called in and it was one o'clock in the morning. '*Everybody out, get to the scene of the bomb!*' We had to walk over to the North Strand because there was no buses at that time of night. Everybody headed to that scene walking and it was just the same on O'Connell Street as during the day on Saturday. The whole of Dublin went over to see what was wrong and see if they could help. A lot of curiosity. The scene . . . oh, there was a crater in the road that you could throw nine or ten motor cars into it. A terrible lot of agony and crying and weeping cause no one knew who was missing. We had to direct the traffic so they could take away the bodies. There was houses demolished around there with glass everywhere and I saw some people working there with their bare hands taking out the bodies and all bloody. We saw pieces of bodies being taken away . . . legs, hair of the head maybe, and hands and everything else. It was a *terrible* sight.

"But I always liked police work, always liked to meet the people, talk to the people, mix with the people. They were *born* with very little and the luxury was not there, from the start. They *hadn't much* but they were quite happy with their lot. Oh, great pride and great respect for religion and very good-natured. Like if somebody was sick or an accident they'd go around and collect for them. If somebody had an accident out there on the road you'd have somebody come out with a chair and a blanket and maybe a drop of whiskey to revive them. And if anybody was drowning in the Liffey you'd have two or three diving in. And they kept their *tradition*. I saw a football match one morning in Lower Kevin Street, at three in the morning, and I was wondering where the crowd came from. Fellas just put down their hats and coats and went into the street to chip the ball around . . . at three in the morning! I asked what they were doing. And, of all things, they had come over from a *wake*. They were great years. I would do the *same* again if I was starting life over . . . even walking the beat."

CHRISTY MURRAY—AGE 86

Christy was one of the fabled barefoot street urchins of the 1920s selling newspapers out in the cold and snow along Westmoreland Street. Selling papers was one way a poor tenement lad could earn a few bob. The few shillings he earned were always given to his mother so that the family could "have a feed" of potatoes and bread. In those days he had to cope with trams, horse vehicles, and rowdy Black and Tans. But he remembers well the kindness of people back then who would give him a bit of food and tea when he was looking hungry.

"I was born in 1908. We lived in Werburgh Street, that's off Christchurch Place. That's history there with Strongbow and all those big shots. My father worked on the docks. It was a poor life. You had to struggle to exist. At eight I was selling papers outside of Bewley's in Westmoreland Street. My brothers, Dinny and Jack, used to do the papers. They were older than me and brought me onto the papers. I was selling the *Mail* and the *Telegraph* and the *Herald*. They cost eight pence a dozen and I'd sell them for a penny apiece and you'd earn four pence. It was all according to the weather. When weather's bad papers get bad and people don't bother. You'd often have to go without anything and you might get washed off the street. On a good day you'd earn a couple of bob. I had three sisters and three brothers and I'd give the money to me mother. Now a couple of bob would get a dinner for the lot in them times. We used to get potatoes and bread and we'd all have a feed. But I made me Holy Communion in the police clothes that you got free cause we were so poor.

"Westmoreland Street was a place where there was an awful lot of news-boys stood there. There was about ten newsboys. Oh, I sold in the snow and walked in the snow in me bare feet when I was small. Sure, I don't think I wore boots till I was fourteen. And your fingers would be freezing—freezing. I was often very, very cold. Oh, and you had competition all right. And you had to have a license. You'd get your license at the police station. It was like a piece of tin and a strap and it had a number and you had to wear it on your wrist. Once you had that badge you'd make a pitch of it and no one else could stand there. If someone tried he'd be in trouble he would. He'd get murdered. Oh, there was often boxing matches over fellas claiming pitches, a row over it. Now I done four days in the 'Joy' (Mountjoy) over the license—I wouldn't pay the five shillings for the license. I was only about sixteen years of age. I wouldn't pay, I said 'No' and I done the four days. I went back on the papers again but I had to get the license. Or they might give me maybe a month then and I didn't want that.

"On Westmoreland Street I used to jump up onto the trams to sell papers. Just hop on. Used to go up to Nelson's Pillar. I'd jump on and dash upstairs to see who wanted a paper and then hop off and then onto another tram. I was young like a hare and I'd dodge the horses and traffic. The conductor might say 'No' and put you off. But if he was alright he'd let you jump on and sell the papers. And, ah, I'll tell you, Bewley's Oriental Cafe was a grand place. They'd give you a cup of coffee or tea on the 'QT', you know, and you'd drink it and out you'd go. They were very nice to me. And at that time there was a gentleman there, a fella named McKenzie, and he was a broker. He took an awful liking to me at that age and he used to always give me two shillings for the paper, every day. He used to go into Bewley's for his coffee.

"People in them days were great. They had more feelings, more nature. My brother Dinny, he got a sovereign of a gentleman on the tram one day and he said, 'Go and buy boots for yourself.' *That* was a gentleman. Gave him a sovereign to buy boots . . . I'll always remember that. And sometimes I'd get fed when I'd go around with the papers. See, I used to serve the shops with the papers. I'd get me dinner up on Earl Street from a woman, Mrs O'Reilly, and they had a shop. When I'd serve her with the papers she'd say, 'Sit down, Christy' and she'd give me a bit of ribs and cabbage and potatoes. It was her nature. The *nature* was there. Oh, the shops, they'd look after you. Loaves and cakes and everything you'd get. I was well known. And the pubs would give you pints. Oh, you'd be like a fella drunk out of his mind going home.

"I joined the army in the war years and after the war I left Westmoreland and went on Thomas Street. Thomas Street and Meath Street, ah, great streets, the Liberties. I've only been off the street now for eight years. I got crippled in the legs with arthritis in both knees. The bad weather will cripple you. But people in them days were great . . . people had more nature. The old times were glorious. The *old times are gone!*"

BRIDIE CHAMBERS—AGE 66

Around her Meath Street neighbourhood everyone in the tenements relied upon home cures to treat ailments. When she was sixteen her arm became seriously infected and doctors at the local hospital could find no remedy. After weeks of severe pain, her mother turned to a local woman healer for help. The woman concocted a curious looking thick black paste and applied it to her arm—at exactly three o'clock—and three days later she was cured. But the woman refused to divulge her healing power and secret potion to inquisitive doctors.

"I knew the hard times. We were reared in the tenements on Meath Street. All very, very poor. Some had beds to sleep on and some hadn't. There was no work really. Men might get labouring work, digging the roads and that. Women used to tug with an old basket car. Oh, *miles* they'd go for old clothes. Oh, and the women'd bring the younger baby with them. Have the baby sitting in the car. They'd wear shawls. But shawls started going out in the forties. When the war came they all got glamorous!

"They were very poor days around here at that time and the wife always in their home. Never went out anywhere. Had your washing and ironing and cleaning and get your messages and cook the meal. Oh, and on a Monday they'd be queued up from six in the morning for the pawn. He used to open about half eight. We had a pawn around the corner on Ardee Street and one beside the old Coombe hospital. People used to pawn everything at that time, old hand irons, hobnail boots, pots. And they'd be telling one another their troubles! Everyone seemed to be *happy*.

"We enjoyed ourselves skipping rope, marbles, swinging on the lamp-posts out there, that was our enjoyment. My mammy'd sit on the path and swing the rope for me. And Lugs Brannigan was the head man around here. He was very good, very kind. I always found him nice and he used to talk to us. A fine big man. Very strict. He saved a lot of children. He didn't take the boys in, he used to slap them and he'd say, 'The next time you do that I'll put you away for a few years, if you miss school another morning I'll put you in Artane.' And they were afraid of their life from then to do anything wrong. Oh, everybody had respect for him. A big strong man and he'd have a go with anybody. He'd *box* them. And if he caught a man ill-treating his wife, hitting his wife, he didn't let them get away with it. I often seen him taking a man in for rowdying and carrying on and lock them up for the night.

"People courted in the tenement hallways, for privacy. And courting we'd go for walks, go to the Phoenix Park, maybe go to the pictures. And if you'd no money for the pictures you'd go and buy some chips and go for a walk eating them. You'd link arms, not hold hands. All innocent like. Curl your hair with curling tongs you had to heat. And when my mammy was courting they used to have paper on the walls and there was red roses on it and my mammy used to wet it and she'd rub it on her face and that was her make-up for the night. You'd go for walks and there were organ-grinders around the streets with the little monkeys and the monkeys nearly talking to you! Oh, the monkey'd have his little hat and all and he'd be jumping all around us and all the children would be dancing. And here in the tenements when the public houses would close on a Sunday Billy would get out and he'd do his dancing and then Biddy Kavanagh would start and then the accordions would start and the banjo. And they'd all be sitting out still drinking their bottles and eating cabbage and pig's cheeks and the accordions and all—playing . . . that was the street.

"Now there was a red lamp lodging house over there, Lynch's, and they were all unfortunate girls. Mostly girls from the country who were after being in (domestic) service and went wrong . . . and then they had to do what they had to do. They'd go out on Grafton Street and around the Green (St Stephen's Green) and go off with an old gentleman for the night. Big old gents and businessmen. And some men used to murder them. Oh, yes, before they'd pay them they used to murder them. Some girls used to come in dirty and with black eyes. And they were all nice girls, very decent. They never hurt nobody and were very kind to children. If you went for a message for them they'd leave you the change and if they had a good night they'd maybe buy you a frock the next day. Lovely girls they were and they used to be lovely dressed. And *spotless*. Oh, and the girls used to go to Mass on Sundays. You never heard anything against them . . . they never done nothing on us.

"People in the tenement houses, they always had their own cures. I remember when I got the mumps my granny had an iron pan and she poured salts into the pan and burned it and let it cool and put it into a silk stocking and tied it around my neck. And one time now I had a *very bad* arm and it was hanging down here like a lump of tripe under me arm and I was about four or five weeks going back and forward to the hospital. I was about sixteen. Oh, God, I was very sick and couldn't eat. Now Mrs Hendron, a healer, lived on Newmarket Street, a big tall woman. She was just an ordinary woman that used to sell coal and potatoes in her shop. But she was very handy if anyone was sick. Up where she lived it was all tenements and she was very kind to everybody up there, very good. She wouldn't refuse them. And she says to me mammy, 'She doesn't look too well. Come up to me today at three and I'll dress it for you.' And me mammy says to me, 'Oh, she's *very* good.' And she wouldn't start till three. So I went up to her and it was like a black thing she made up, a paste. She didn't let me see her making it. And she put it on the paper they used to wrap butter in. She put that all on top of it and that was left on for two days. Then on the third day I went back to her—at three—and she cured it. But you'd want to see what she got *out* of it! An abscess, it was *that* (eight inches) length. I'll always remember when I went back to the hospital I had it covered with a bit of bandage and this big stout nurse when she took it off she kept looking at it. And she went for the doctor. And the doctor came down and looked at it. 'What did you put on that!' Says I, 'The woman down where I live, she put her stuff on it, she made it and put it on.' Says he, 'Ask her what it is.' So I said that to Mrs Hendron . . . 'Oh, I *couldn't* give that to anybody. I have that all me life. That was me mother's, I couldn't give it.' Her mother handed it down to her and she said 'No'. But she cured it. And the doctor would have *loved* to get hold of it!"

JOHN GALLAGHER—AGE 60

Everyone around the Liberties knows John and his limitless energy and dedication to helping others. He is the most active community worker in the neighbourhood, helping every social group from young children to the elderly. He was born on the Coombe and even as a young lad recognised the appalling system of segregation in the local school system between the poor tenement children and those from better-off families. He regards it as a terrible tragedy that tenement children were made to feel inferior. As an adult he helped to break down these discriminatory barriers by working with the nuns and educators. Today he is one of the most respected men in the old Liberties.

"I was born on the Coombe in a house beside the Weaver's Hall. At one time to mention that you lived in the Liberties around the Coombe, that was the *lowest* place to live. *Now* the Liberties is very famous. But back then all the way down the Coombe you had tenements, terrible poverty. People were paid very little, a few shillings a week, and in some of the bigger Georgian houses they might have ten families. The biggest number of people ever in a tenement house in the Liberties was in Braithwaite Street and there were a hundred and something living in the one house. But you had great community in the tenements.

"In most of the houses there was only one toilet in the yard and no running water, just a tap, and the yards were in a very bad state. But some tenements would have been better than others. There might be a good tenement house where the hall door would be closed at night. See, the lowest place to live was where there was no lock on the door—they were at the bottom of the ladder and had down-and-outs sleeping in the halls during the night. That was the worst form of tenement. So there were distinctions between tenements . . . and between *residents* in tenements. There would be the level of the men who *did* have jobs, and they'd always be that little bit better off and their children would be better dressed and *looked* better and others would be envious of them. And like if a woman dressed nicely some other woman would say, 'Who does she think *she is*? She only lives in a tenement!' So the idea was that if you lived in a tenement you were really of the lower order. And some of the children if they lived in a tenement and they were sent to learn music they'd be *jeered* going through the streets—trying to be *above* your class.

"If the conditions were bad you'd try not to stay in the tenement that much. The children would be out playing. The streets, they were the playground. And you hadn't got the *scourge* of the twentieth century—the motor car— which destroyed cities. Back then you had horse traffic so you could play in the streets. The other thing was that Dublin was *small*. Like if you went beyond Dolphin's Barn you were nearly in the *country*. People would walk. It would take you twenty minutes to get from the Coombe up to Dolphin's Barn and you had little rivers and things. So you were living in a *slum* which was dirty but twenty minutes walking would take you out to the country. That was a *great* thing. And a lot of children, you'd have them robbing the orchards and that'd be their meal for the day, that's how they'd keep going . . . and a great sense of adventure for them.

"They started off here with the National School run by the British but then the nuns came here and built beside it a private school. And you had the extraordinary situation of this terrible class distinction. You had the children from the tenements walking up to the yard to the *back* that was the National School, and at the *front* the children of tradesmen or shopkeepers or people who worked in Guinness's or Jacob's and they would consider themselves better than anyone else and they'd go to the private school. But the tenement children would go to the poor school . . . a bad thing, this class distinction . . . a terrible tragedy. Children who went to the poor school wore old clothes and many of them would have been barefooted. And the other children wore a uniform. If you went to the National School you weren't as well dressed and weren't as well fed and you looked inferior . . . you *felt* inferior. And the children, they weren't even supposed to *talk* to each other. Segregated!

"Sanitation was *appalling*, lots of bugs and vermin, and you had children coming to school with dirty heads. Now once a nun brought a child from this (private) school up to the National School and she was stripped off, with all the petticoats, to show *how clean* you should be. And the tenement children, their parents would have very few clothes for them and hard to keep the clothes clean. That was the thing, you were living in dirty *conditions*. So this nun took one child and showed the children at the National School how clean *they should be*. That actually happened. It was a dreadful thing. Now I'm not criticising the nuns—it was the *system*.

"Money was always very powerful to the poor. Their position was that if you got a factory job, like in Jacob's, it was *great*. But most got jobs maybe cleaning or in a terrible sewing factory, and for men it was mostly manual work, construction work, where you had to use the pick and shovel. Some men, even my father, they'd walk maybe from here to Rathfarnham to do their day's work and then walk back. It was really hard. And the husbands would drink more than they should and there was a lot of drunkenness. It was a form of escape because it was the problem of going back to the dirty tenement, the cold, nagging wife and a lot of children around crying. To *get out*, to get into a pub, it was a different world—*escapism*. Much better being in the pub. It was a man's world. And a lot of deals were done in public houses, a lot of jobs were got in public houses. You'd hear about jobs in the building trade. You'd go into a pub and somebody'd say, 'Look, we're starting work and we're looking for a few men' and you'd give him a drink for that bit of information. Then you'd be out there early the next day waiting for the start. So it was like a little *club*, used for escapism, and it was also used to get information for jobs and things.

"But women were great. Women really kept the families going. As well as working they'd take in washing and do some cleaning (for others). *Really* kept things going. They had a hard life, most of the women, and sometimes the wives would get beatings. It was a very bad thing. They were really second-class citizens. I can remember *vividly* in one of the houses where the father was a painter but he didn't work all the time. There were five children in the family and he'd come home in the evening when he was working and the children wouldn't have got any dinner during the day—they might have got tea and bread. He'd come in and there'd be just *one* dinner, one plate of food, and he'd sit down there and the children would sit around the table and if he felt like it he might give them a potato. The idea of the wife was that she had to keep him in good health, had to keep the bread-winner in good health. So he'd get the *good* meal and the children would be next and she'd be the last. She'd sacrifice and maybe get no dinner at all. That's how a lot of women would be in their thirties and having a lot of children and be really old-looking.

"You had this great community in the tenements and you had the three generations (together) and you might have an aunt or an uncle living in the next tenement. So if you had a row with your mother you could always go and stay overnight with someone else. That was a great thing. And you didn't have electric lights then and so you went to bed when it got dark and you'd be comfortable because you'd all be in the one room, you weren't isolated and you weren't *afraid* because there was somebody beside you. Everyone slept together, it was a great feeling of unity. I mean, the poor people were never alone in the bedroom cause they'd all have to be staying together.

"Sometimes when you have very little you have a great sense of well-being. If you don't know what it is to have a lot you can be happy. If you never got a salmon you're happy with a herring! So they were happy. And you always heard singing in the tenements. If you had a little money you had a gramophone and then they'd have this sing-song. And they all had their records of Caruso and McCormack. And they'd *sing* these songs. The *extraordinary* thing about the tenements was that you'd hear operatics coming out. And the great thing here on a Sunday morning was a woman who lived in number eight on the Coombe and on a Saturday night she might take a drop too many but on a Sunday morning, no matter *how late* she was up drinking the previous night, she'd start singing and she'd sing for maybe two hours. And *everyone* would listen to her. *Beautiful* voice.

"In the public houses around here now at the weekend you'll see people who were moved out of here who come in from Tallaght and Kimmage and all. They come in and they want to *talk* . . . roots in that one street. Like my mother. She'd go to church, she'd do her shopping, maybe go in and have a drink at one of the pubs, meet the people, and it was like a pilgrimage each day. But when she had to be (moved) up to the top of the street here it was the *end* for her. She never recovered from moving. It made *that much difference* to her . . . moving a quarter of a mile. It was terrible for her. Moving changed her routine. Now what difference did it make to people having to move six, seven, eight miles? The people who were moved out of here, they *left their heart here.*"

MICKEY GUY—AGE 72

He's a bona fide "Liberties lad" and proud of it. Most days he can be found in Swift's Pub on Francis Street sipping his pint and chatting away with a few old cronies. He likes to tell how, as an enterprising youth, he made a few bob catching huge rats for local men who used to turn them loose in back alleys and set their dogs on them for sport and betting. One of his most vivid memories is that of two local tenements reputedly possessed by the devil. People in the houses mysteriously swayed back and forth while furniture and delph flew about the rooms. "Seeing is believing," avows Mickey—and he saw it himself.

"I don't know how people managed in them times. Six and eight children reared in these tiny tenement rooms and very dark inside where the sun wouldn't be shining and seven and eight families using the one toilet in the rear yard. Oh, God, it used to be *fierce*. And the women done everything. They tugged and went up to the plots at Dolphin's Barn out in the country and they used to work for the farmers pulling cabbage for a half a crown and they'd get a few potatoes and a few heads of cabbage going home. People in the tenements, they were poor but they looked after one another. Everybody shared. If there was a death in the family people'd be going around from door to door with this black sugar bag—it was always a black sugar bag—collecting to make up the money for the burial. The *greatest* people.

"On a Saturday night Francis Street would be *packed*. The Iveagh market used to close at eight and the women dealers used to take their bundles of clothes out on the steps and there used to be rows like Moore Street. Women out with their big bundles of second-hand clothes to sell and people'd be coming and going and there was five pork shops that sold pig's feet and there was nine public houses on Francis Street. And the lamplighter'd be on his bike and he'd put his pole up to the lamp and the children'd see him coming and it was, 'Billy with the light, out all night, watching his sweetheart' . . . they had a song about that. And the lavender man, God bless him, he had round feet and no toes, like a horse, just a hoof. And he had lavender in a little bag tied to put in your clothes in the wardrobe and you'd *smell* him. And during the war years there was the glimmer man, the gas man. We were cut down to only certain hours to turn on the gas and we were using only the glimmer when the full power of the gas wouldn't be on. You weren't supposed to have the glimmer on, but people did it. It was dangerous. You were taking a chance cause there was danger cause air could get into the pipes and *blow* you.

"Then there was the coal blocks sold and the turf men come in from Co. Kildare, the bogs, with their clamps of turf and twigs for to keep the turf lit. Go around the streets and they'd say, 'Turf, turf!' and it was tuppence a dozen. Some would come over there in Smithfield and they used to lie (sleeping) under their carts and the horse just standing there. Or get his few shillings and on the way home along the Lucan Road he'd lie in the cart asleep and be drunk and the horse used to ramble all the way home. And, see, there was trams running out there at that time and, sure, there were some of them killed on the Lucan Road. That's how it came to be the 'Dead Man Murray's', the public house, outside Palmerstown, cause there was always accidents with the turf men.

"Me granny sold in the Iveagh market and she lived up there facing the market. Now it used to be an old brewery and it was knocked down (before the Iveagh Market was built). See, people sold out on the cobblestones at that time and Lord Iveagh built the market for them. Now me granny told me that when she'd be looking out of the window at twelve at night-time the rats would come in *droves—millions*—walking up Francis Street. And they used to go into the old brewery there for all the dampness of the porter draining underneath. *Millions* of rats. *All around* the Liberties there was rats. I wasn't afraid of them because you were brought up with rats in the locality. Sure, it was a regular thing with women having a baby, (breast) feeding a baby in the bed, and the rats smelling the person (milk) and many a person had the rat in their beds. I remember this mother when she was feeding the baby and the rat's in the bed on her *breast* and the father got a hold of it and the rat *clamped* him. A rat gets a hold of you with his teeth, he locks on you. The only way to get him off is to put him into water and he'll open. And he went off to the Richmond Hospital at three in the morning with the big rat hanging on him. So the doctor runs to get a basin of water and puts him into the water and he opened.

"Oh, men used to bet on rats. Used to keep rats alive and be betting on them. Here in Garden Lane two men, they'd have dogs and back a crown and let 'em out in the lane and the two dogs would run and get the rat and tear at it and *sling it up* and it'd come down and it died. One man had a great little dog and he always won his half crown. They kept rats in cages. It was a hobby for them. The rat would run from the dogs and five or six men would be watching. As a matter of fact, if I caught a rat I got sixpence off Mr Blake, a caretaker at the Iveagh Market. He used to buy them off you and he'd boxes of rats. He used to let the rats out and put the dogs on 'em. Now I had a brother, Paddy, that worked in Keogh's, the bacon yards, and his hobby was to go up to the slaughter house and there used to be big cobblestones with rat holes. And he'd find a nest of maybe fourteen or fifteen only small rats and the she-rat would be running away when she'd hear the noises and leave 'em. Well, then he'd pick up all them small rats and put them into a can, pour water on 'em and boil 'em and it'd be like a solution. Boil them into a solution just like a jelly. Well, the next day they'd (brother and friends) go up and roll up their sleeves and they'd put this solution on their arms and they'd put their hand *into* the hole and any rats there used to come to them . . . the scent. They'd catch them one at a time and they'd bang them. And they'd be killed and dumped. It was just a hobby they had.

"We all come out of school at fourteen years of age and we were brought up that we couldn't walk over the bridge to the northside. Cause the northside crowd, they were a rougher crowd than we were here. If we went to the Mary Street picture house, well, we'd get a hiding off them. But you never seen doctors, you could go to a chemist. Even if your throat was cut he'd give you a cure for it! He'd put a dressing on it. Daddy Nagle was in Meath Street and Mr Mushatt was in Francis Street. They were the *masterpieces*. Daddy Nagle, he was known as the 'Lucky Man' cause he had some kind of (healing) ointment. And Mushatt had the brown plaster for a bad back or bad chest and it *burned* the skin off you. But from north, south, east and west people'd come to them. And the only dentist in my time was a man named Mr Carey. It was a half a crown. When I went to get mine (tooth) out he'd say, 'Give me your money.' Oh, then he'd pull the head off you! He'd put his *knee* up on you. And he'd pull. Just ether and pliers. Now he'd no wife but a big family of boys, and a maid. And what he'd do in case you'd be crying—if your mother'd be outside— he had his sons playing music in the back, playing instruments and fiddles, so the mother wouldn't hear the roaring. That's what he used to do. And then— and this is *history*—he died and the *maid* took over pulling teeth. One man died of some infection and she was gaoled.

"In my days *everyone* had a loan off a Jewman . . . on the 'QT'. Because they weren't *supposed* to. But the money-lenders used to be the only people they *had*. The Jewmen money-lenders used to come around with their jarvey cars on a Monday or Tuesday to collect. And one woman who lived over there, well, she'd have other people's books, like *your* mother's book and *her* mother's book and you'd leave the money with her for the money-lender. See, she was a cover-up for them. She used to pay for them so that their husbands wouldn't know about it. Because the Jewman wouldn't be going to your house, he'd call to *her* house. Now there was another woman in the tenement houses named Kelly and she was a money-lender and she'd be sitting in the pub drinking from ten in the morning till ten at night and the poor people'd be looking for money. She'd be sitting there and she'd lend you so much money and you had to pay your interest. And back then people'd hide their money, in the chimney and under an oil cloth and timber on the floor. As a matter of fact, my mother done it. When she died they were looking for £25. She was saving it up for a sister of mine having a baby and she wanted to buy a pram for her. I was clearing out the place and she was dead and I was rooting and rooting and I found the £25—up the chimney breast!

"When I was growing up you were afraid of your life of the priest. Father Hayden had a blackthorn stick and if he caught you as a young fella taking a shortcut from the front of the chapel out to the back you were *dirtying* the churchyard. And you'd get the blackthorn on your legs. Oh, I got it meself off of him. Oh, he'd frighten the life out of you. And priests would get up on the pulpit about gambling and bookie shops and that. Now there'd be four or five of us tossing a ha'penny up nearest the wall and Father Pickett or Father Donoghue would be coming from the park (Phoenix) after riding horses and they'd have their whip and they'd jump off their bike and *lash the legs off you* with their whip. Cause you were gambling. Oh, you'd have to run when you'd see them coming. They were *worse* than the police. And they were the biggest gamblers when they'd go to the races . . . the biggest gamblers of the whole lot!

"We were always told that the priest doesn't like going to banish the devil cause he only lives six months. Now there was a house down there (Francis Street) and it was closed up for *years* when I was a child. It was called McAllister's house. They were pork people but it was closed up. And there was another house there in Mark's Alley the very same (as McAllister's) that gave trouble. And when I was a kid me mother and father and half of Carman's Hall would go down there a twelve at night-time to Mark's Alley. You'd look up at the tenement house and the windows'd be opening and the house going that way, back and forwards, and the people *in* the house would be going that way (swaying) and the dresser and the delph falling off. I *really seen* that in Mark's Alley. And they sent for the priest to go and banish the devil. It's true. And the priest was Father Donoghue. Prayers and blessings and so forth. And that priest, Father Donoghue, *died* . . . after banishing *that house*. That's perfectly true. Seeing is believing and I really seen it. It *did* happen in my time."

Margaret Coyne—Age 72

She was born along Protestant Row into a family of street dealers. While her mother was out each day selling she had to stay home from school and rear her younger brothers and sisters. She sacrificed much of her early life caring for her siblings. But she smiles when recalling how her mother, granny and aunts would head out in the morning with their basket cars of fresh fish to sell and often ending the day enjoying a few "small ones" in the local pub—then straggling home contentedly singing at the top of their lungs.

"On Protestant Row there definitely was some very bad poverty, and all large families. One mother had nineteen. The older one took charge. I reared all my sisters and brothers. I was never in school, I was always minding them cause me mother was out working, she was a dealer. I certainly didn't get a chance to go out and play. That was life!

"First thing in the morning you had to carry your slop bucket down to the toilet and empty it. Then go down to the yard with a white enamel bucket to bring up clean water to use. In the summer you could wash yourself under the tap if you closed the back door and had someone stand in it and not let anyone else in. You *had* to do it . . . privacy. Men could go to the Iveagh Baths but women used the tap. It was a way of life at that time and a woman had to be *quick*. You'd use Sunlight soap. Wash your hair and all. Women's hair, they never really wore it down, it was always in a bun. They had long hair and my mother used to wear her hair all back in two big buns in the back. Wrap it around her finger and then curl it in a bun. And women usually cut one another's hair.

"In the winter-time you had to bring the water up and heat it. Very cold in the morning in winter-time. Heaping coats on top of you in the bed and, oh, you were all on top of one another and you dressed yourself under the covers. And you'd use newspapers and coats at the door to keep out the draft and stuff papers around your windows. There was no waste. I'd use the newspaper on the floor to keep it clean and you'd cut up newspapers for the toilet. Cut them into squares cause there was no toilet rolls in them times. But it was very respectable. We all had open fires you cooked on and you grew up with that. And, oh, by God, we used turf from the bog and the water'd be running out of it. We were really bad in them times with that turf. People who lived on the Coombe, they used to go and collect the turf and sell it. They'd carry it in sacks. They'd bring it back and the water'd be *dripping* out of it, and they'd expect you to buy it. You *had* to take it, and we were glad of it at that time.

"On the (ground) floor of the tenements there were huckster shops. They sold everything, tea, sugar, bread, butter, paraffin oil, coal—everything from a needle to an anchor! And everything was sold loose then, tea, sugar, and the milk was in a jug, no bottled milk. Food wouldn't keep so you had to go to the shops every day. We'd no fridge. You used to put the milk in a bucket of water to keep it fresh and put the butter in the shade in some corner. And the place was full of mice so if you could get a biscuit tin you'd put the tea and sugar in the tin. And you had to be very careful of the bluebottles and you had to place a piece of gauze to cover all the food to keep the flies off in the summer. There was Lalor's Dairy and he had a big yard with the cows and we'd go for a pint of milk in a jug and it would be hot, only out of the cow. And, God forgive me, I often put the jug to me mouth and would drink it, it'd be that nice. Shopkeepers were very good and they gave credit but this one man had a sign up in his shop and it said: 'I had a friend, I thought I could trust him, I lost my friend and I lost his custom—credit is dead, bad debts killed him.'

"We went to St Brigid's School down on the Coombe. Believe me, discipline was tough. They had a leather strap and we'd get a slap from the nun. The leather strap would be hanging from her belt on her habit. Some of them had a bit of lead at the bottom of the strap and you were belted. And they'd have a pointer, a cane, too. Oh, your *poor hands* used to be in an awful state. Oh, they wouldn't use it for anything trivial now, but for talking in class or something that you didn't answer or if you were after being mitching. Oh, we mitched. But I was never in school, always minding my sisters and brothers. I think that mothers favoured the sons and the girls were there to work. Boys had more time to go out and play. They were spoiled, they *were*, really spoiled. You'd have to have dinner on the table for the sons and the husband when they'd come in and I don't think they were asked to do *anything*. I even had to clean my brothers shoes.

"In the tenement houses the mothers budgeted the money. First thing she'd put away would be her rent and food and then she'd see what she had for the week. And they used to put money every week in a didley club and you'd get that on a Christmas. Someone'd have a club up and you'd trust them. My aunt used to have one. And Mrs Hannigan, she used to have a *big* didley up years ago. You'd start giving her money in January, start with a penny and maybe it'd up to about five shillings. And she wouldn't give it to you before. Oh, no, a *good* didley club owner wouldn't give it to you. This would make *sure* you had something. But there was a lot of people done out of (their) money at Christmas. Some unscrupulous people, they'd go off with the money. This was done a couple of times. And if they came back some people would have a go at them.

"Mothers . . . they had to be saints in those days. At that time Crumlin was all fields and women used to work for the farmers with cabbage and potatoes for a half a crown a day. Walk out, God help them. They worked very hard. My mother, she was a dealer and she used to go out at six in the morning and go all around Stillorgan and Carrickmines wheeling a basket car selling fish. Hail, rain and snow she'd go out. I remember often seeing me mother in the snow up to that (ankles). Now me grandmother and me aunts sold fish too and they'd all go into O'Hare's pub over by the Daisy Market, in the snug, and they'd drink whiskey, a couple of small ones, if they had the money for it. It was cheap at that time. Now *we'd* think they'd be gone out to sell their fish but they'd get a few whiskeys and they'd be coming home off the booze and singing!"

PATRICK O'LEARY—AGE 70

In his old-fashioned chemist shop on Thomas Street he made most of his own medicines and tonics, serving four generations of Liberties folk. He treated everything from nappy rash to old-age pains. He had a special tonic for tenement mothers who suffered from malnutrition, weariness, and stress. And his hangover remedy worked miracles for those men who, as he puts it, were in an "advanced stage of decomposition". But he admits that the better part of his life behind the counter was spent just listening to them and dispensing advice about every imaginable problem in life. He felt great compassion for the poor and truly became their friend, confessor, and counsellor.

"I started at sixteen and did a four-year apprenticeship with a chemist called Browne's on Stephen's Green. Their pride was that they made up a lot of their tonics like cough mixtures, ointments, teething powders, pills. Actually making their own round pills by *hand*. Oh, I made them up till I was dizzy! I got very good training. I qualified at twenty-one and got a job at Toomey's of Denmark Street. Then I was coming to the time when I wanted to start on my own and I put an ad in the paper for a shop. And I got one reply, just one, and it was, 'I have a shop in Thomas Street that might be of interest to you.' I went to see the shop and it was slap in the middle of Thomas Street, on the left hand side. As they call it in Thomas Street, one side is called the 'sunny side' and the other side is the 'money side'—that's Liberties talk. And I remember thinking, 'By God, if *ever* there was a spot for a chemist shop it's here.' I looked at it and couldn't *believe* my luck. *Slap* in the middle of a very, very busy street. That place is absolutely *steeped* in history. You can't go back deeper into Dublin than you can in the Liberties.

"Around Thomas Street and Francis Street and Meath Street it was tenements, like in Sean O'Casey's plays and all. It was the original thing. Going up four storeys and being afraid of your life going through the stairs. And you wouldn't *dream* of leaning against the banister. Everybody had big families. One woman on Thomas Street had twenty-two children. And you'd get them living in the one room and in a lot of cases it would have been rat-infested. Oh, tremendous congestion. You went up in the winter into a *damp* room, a cold, damp room, and they had a turf fire, and drafty and maybe a roof leaking and the walls damp. A toilet down in the yard and the *smell* of the place was the smell of the unwashed, both the person and the building. They had *nothing*. They just hadn't the facilities. And they were death traps! If the place went on fire they didn't have a chance! That's gone now, thanks be to God.

"A lot of their illnesses were born of the fact that they weren't properly nourished. Their diet was bread, margarine and tea. It wasn't a sufficient diet. And to a great extent it would be hereditary because their father and mother had lived on tea and bread and margarine, so they start off on the wrong foot. They were much more liable to infection because they hadn't the *resistance*. They were wide open and caught any infection that was going around. You got an awful lot of chest complaints and coughs and colds. And they'd be pale and red eyes and a very pale complexion. They were generally run down. And skin complaints would spread like wildfire. Scabies, that was the big thing. Dirt caused scabies, these little itchy spots. It used to be unbearable, the itch. I sold a cream for scabies . . . you've *no idea* the amount of ointment I sold, and very effective. And head lice. We had a lotion and shampoo. The lotion killed the lice and you were left with the dead lice in your hair and then you shampooed it and fine-combed them out.

"Young married women . . . *always* under stress. And we sold head and nerve tablets for nervous strain. I think, first, economic stress and then a lot of them got married too young. The husband might be going from one job to the other and then being unemployed and starting to drink and she having one child after another and they were living in the one room. She never got a *rest* from it. Never got a rest from the stress and strain. They were *run down*! I gave them a straight-forward old-fashioned iron and vitamin tonic, the *old* formula. And some men were hard on the drink. One totally tragic case, a woman who came in and it was appalling and you felt you wanted to do something about it. She used to come in and she'd have black eyes and bruised face and she just didn't know who to turn to. And she'd come back the day after and she'd be worse. Very hard on the women. Religion was their total anchor. They had a faith that was beyond all reason . . . a rock. Nothing affected it. They would restore your faith in humanity. They're *literally* the salt of the earth.

"They came to me for my own stuff I'd make up. Make up my own ointments, tonics, corn cures. I'll put it to you this way, we were *nearer* to them than the dispensary doctors. If they had a headache or a cough they'd come in to me, didn't have to go to a doctor. My cough bottle would cure their cough. Or headache tablets. That's another thing, I always priced my tablets *each*, sell them, say, at tuppence each. And if they had only five 'P' they can end up with a few tablets. Just give her two for fourpence. I very often did. And I *liked* doing it . . . we're supposed to be a *servant*, not just a business man. That's the very *essence* to me . . . an old tradition in the old part of the city. And if somebody came into me and they were short of money I'd take care of them and say, 'Give it to me the next time.' And you were a friend for life! People weren't that well-off but very hard working, very honest and they'd appreciate *anything* you'd do for them more than you could imagine. You had complete *trust*.

"And if they got hurt they'd come in. *All* the time, an everyday thing. Cuts from people that fell on the street or butchers that missed and got his finger, girls in factories with machinery and children all the time falling with scrapes and scratches. Oh dear, *straight away* into the chemist. I never charged for that. There were two men used to come in, brothers in their seventies, to get their nails cut. We'd have to use scissors and when you'd cut you'd hear the nails landing, hitting the far wall. And oftentimes I'd have to stop women. They'd come in and say, 'Here, I have something wrong on my breast here, let me show you' and they'd start to take off everything. And I'd have to say, 'Hold on a second, just a minute now' and I'd give them an ointment for it. See, they could come to me *free*. Ah, sometimes you'd want to have a strong stomach. This woman came in and says, 'Oh, Mr O'Leary, you know that stuff you gave me for his nose, that was something great.' See, it was for her husband who had a catarrh. 'That was something great . . . after he took your bottle the snot came down his nose in ropes.' Talk about being graphic!

"For hangovers there'd nearly be a queue outside the door, all the fellas that had been out the night before and were in an advanced stage of decomposition. When I'd open the door they'd be after me like a flash. They'd want this bottle I had for settling the stomach and a couple of these tablets for the head. This bottle for the stomach had a big name and the stuff I put into it I *knew* it was going to be good. It *had* to be good. I won't tell you too much about it but a lot of it was based on alcohol! You know, there were a few strong tinctures in it which were good for settling the stomach but the tinctures were made of alcohol. So when they'd take a dose of this they'd go, 'Aaahh . . . that's grand . . . a couple of pints of that now and I'll be alright.'

"They'd come in sometimes not to buy a thing at all. I'd spend most of my time *talking* to them—or *listening* to them. By *far* the biggest part of my day! It's somebody just to listen. And family problems. I've been told everything, the *lot*. If *half* the husbands *knew* what I've been told . . . you have no idea. I can tell you some stories too. Like I bought a house for one person. She said, 'Mr O'Leary, I want to buy a house, how do I go about it? Do I give them the money?' Now another woman, a great-grandmother, she was a great character. She was a dealer out in the street and couldn't read or write but she made a lot of money. She had a daughter when she was sixteen and *her* daughter had a daughter when she was sixteen and *her* daughter had a daughter when she was sixteen. Anyway, we were great friends. She was a most gentle person, spotlessly clean, a lovely woman. Now she had no formal education but she was a money-lender—unofficially! This woman made an awful lot of money and she would come in and talk to me and she'd tell me that she was afraid to go out. And I said, 'Why are you afraid to go out?' 'Oh', she said, 'you know I have a few thousand pounds around the house and I worry and can't wait to get back in case they've broken into the place.' She had £8,000 *stuffed* in a statue of the Sacred Heart! '*He'll* look after it for me', she said. Eventually I said, 'Put that into a bank.'

"*All* my life I've been listening to the price of oranges and apples. From the dealers outside. The traders were out in all weather, they were as hardy as they had to be. Standing out there in the rain with piles of stuff they'd have to sell. But the dealers enjoyed life and would be shouting up to one another. Oh, and they'd be in great voice after half two when they were after being in the pubs. I remember one woman who was outside the shop and she was selling cabbages and there was another woman up the street who was selling the *same* lot of cabbages. But the woman near me started to undercut the one up the street. And they were using these knives to cut the ends of the stalks off the cabbage. The next thing, the one up the street discovered that the woman down here was undercutting her and she comes down, as they say, 'with her boots on'. She came down with her knife like this (raised) and she *gave out*! Oh, she went on for about five minutes telling her what she thought of her—and she didn't repeat herself once. I've never heard such a stream of language in my life . . . 'and if you ever do that again I'll break your f— neck' and all that kind of thing. Oh, the whole street was stopped. And they were at each other at a *foot's* distance, the two of them looking at one another. You could have heard them down on O'Connell Street, their shouting. But this woman was shouting at the other one telling her what she was going to do with her, break her bloody neck and carve her up and all, and the other one was silent, you see. And do you know what the logical answer from the other one was? 'And *who* are you living with now?' And she vanished.

"They had fantastic wit. And they absolutely *vandalised* the English language. Do you remember the Millennium? That was the 'aluminium year'. *Vandalise* the English language. Maybe that's just their way of getting back at the English! To make a shambles of their language. I *did* enjoy it. I'm terribly sorry that I didn't write down all the *things* I have heard in this shop . . . if I'd *only* written them down! And I've *absolutely no doubt* that Sean O'Casey didn't invent a single thing. All he did was keep his ears open. Because when I go to the Abbey or the Gaiety and I see an O'Casey play I hear all the Americans and the Irish bursting their sides laughing at the way they mangle the English language. Well, I was listening to it *every* day! It's *totally* authentic.

"Fantastic wit. Now I have to tell you about these two women that came in, two old women who had seen it all, and one of them had a great sense of humour. The two of them came in and I had an ointment that was famous all over the city for women with an itch, as they say, 'down below'. An ointment that people from all over the city with 'an itch down below' were coming in for. In any case, this woman came into me with this friend of hers and she says, 'Mr O'Leary, pardon your presence, but I have this itch down below'—and her friend now was just behind her—'and it isn't just me, *all* the women up on Watling Street have it . . . I don't know what it is.' And her friend says, 'Go off on that now, Mr O'Leary, *I'll* tell you what it is—it's the new temporary postman they have going around!'

"There's been four generations here. When I came there was a little kid of eleven standing outside the door selling. She was a typical kid—under-nourished, pale, frozen cold on a winter's day in December, standing beside her mother's stall—gaunt, cold but still selling. First of all, her mother was bringing her in to me for tonics and cough bottles and all the things that go wrong with somebody who's undernourished. Then about six years later she got married and next thing she's bringing her child in with nappy rash, then windy stomach, then teething—I know all the steps. And before I was finished *that* child was a mother and was bringing in *her* child. The fourth generation. Generation after generation. Oh, and then the grandmother takes over from the mother and she comes in with the grandchild. Oh, she completely takes over—'Give me that child' and she takes the child and bends the child up like a stick and says, 'Look at his little arse, Mr O'Leary, isn't that in a shocking state?' And the mother says, 'Oh, mammy, don't talk like that.' And she says, 'Sure, what are you talking about? Sure, I had *your* little arse up there!' It's life.

"I'll tell you about the Liberties people in two words—practical Christianity! Caring about one another. It was the most *natural* thing in the world the way they helped one another. I don't see it anywhere else. They're a breed unto themselves. Their *loyalty* to one another is absolutely tremendous, a very close community. And you know the thing about the family being the rock of society? Well, that is the way it is with them. Religion was their anchor. And their *pride* in being Liberties people and pride in their traditions. The *memories* that they have . . . hundreds of years passed by and it's only like yesterday.

They're a special people, a special breed. *Total* dignity. If I had to start again I'd go straight back there again. My life has been enriched *tremendously* by being privileged to be among them."

JIMMY OWENS—AGE 68

His mother was a fruit dealer on Thomas Street and at age eight he was out in the cold and snow of winter helping to hawk her wares. By thirteen he was out on his own selling women's hairnets for a penny each. Later he graduated to selling fruit to the crowd at Croke Park on match days. Being out on the street in the fresh air was more healthy than being confined to his unsanitary tenement room. He is proud to have come from the tenements of the Coombe and earned a living from street selling for more than sixty years.

"I was born and reared in a tenement house in number 16 Coombe Street. Me mother was a fruit dealer on Thomas street and I was on the street (selling) since I was eight years of age. I had six sisters and two brothers and a brother that died. Very hard times. It was all poverty then. The majority of people used to pawn in them times, pawn clothes and all. And up along Thomas Street there was a penny bank, a *penny* bank now. A penny bank for to save up a penny cause it was a poverty-stricken area.

"All around that locality there was no work and the men were all on the Labour Exchange. I'd say that 60 per cent would be getting that and only about 40 per cent working. But the trading woman always had *something*. She had to go out every day and bring in the money. Me mother sold flowers and fish and poultry and fruit, cabbage, potatoes, onions. She had her pitch and the permit cost a shilling a year in me mother's time, and we're there ever since. And nothing ever went to waste. Bananas and pears used to come in wooden boxes, and oranges, and you'd break up the wooden boxes for firewood. And there used to be a rope on the boxes and we used to cut the rope for to hank the onions. I learned an awful lot of experience from looking at what went on. All shawls they'd wear and the women would hold the baby in the shawl and then put the child in a basket or box. To breast feed it she'd have to go into a hall cause they were very modest in them days. They were all friendly and they'd go in and have a gargle at the heel of the evening and go and maybe buy a pig's cheek or a couple of pigs' feet to make a feed for the family.

"I didn't get much education and I was often half hungry going to school. Hundreds of children went to school in their bare feet walking on nails and lumps of glass cutting their feet. Their mothers hadn't got it (money for shoes)! And school was very bitter, a hard, hard, school—if you were a minute late, he'd say, 'Go in there' to this room and you'd get a hiding. The minute that bell would strike. A load of us used to be lined up on a cold morning to get a few leathers. I had to come out of school when I was thirteen cause me father died and me and me brother had to provide for them. I sold women's hairnets on the street for a penny each. Then I sold cabbage and potatoes and fruit. I was only a little boy at the time. I sold in the snow, out in the snow and the *freezing* cold in January and February. If you earned ten shillings for a week it was a lot of money in the 1930s. Some days you'd go out and hardly earn. Very hard times . . . but we always fed ourselves. I'll tell you, it was *hard earned* money.

"Then I'd go to a football match on a Sunday at Croke Park. I was about fourteen then. Used to push me two-wheel handcart. I used to hire it for a shilling from Granby Place and you'd bring it back in the evening. At Croke Park there'd be loads of people. Now they didn't let you into Croke Park, the police'd stop you. But you'd still get in over the stiles (sneaking). Then throw the basket over the wall. One fella'd throw it over the wall to the other and we'd catch it and then you'd go around and sell. Put the basket around our neck and go around hawking to all the crowd. It was hard going but there was salesmanship and all. Everyone got a few bob and you'd get a living out of it. And I handed the money to me Ma . . . I was *delighted* to give it to her to buy the food."

Elizabeth "Lil" Collins—Age 91

She was born at the turn of the century in Marrowbone Lane and at age sixteen went to work for Harry Sive, the legendary scrap-collecting Jewman in the Liberties. For the next half century she spent her life sorting out mountains of second-hand clothes, bottles, jam jars and God knows what else, brought in daily by a small army of women tuggers. She attests to Harry's kindness to poor tenement folk, but her fondest memory is that of the rousing Christmas parties he held for his workers where there was great Irish dancing and everyone would end up "mad drunk".

"I was born and reared on Marrowbone Lane, all old tenement houses. I have four brothers and five sisters. Life was terrible hard. I can remember Jim Larkin's strike. Me father was working in the malt stores on Ardee Street. They were on strike and they'd go down to the North Wall and they'd give them food and me father used to bring home a little bag of food. Me mother had a little shop. She used to sell cabbage and potatoes and pigs' cheeks. But she gave that much credit pitying the people that she got broke. She used to give the credit to anyone that had children, if they had children she never refused them. She *gave* it to them. They never paid her back and she got broke.

"I remember the Black and Tans. We had to put out all the lights, a curfew. Me father was sick, he took a stroke, and he used to sit outside the hall door. It was nearly all half doors in the tenements. And we used to have to *whip him* from the door cause they came with their rifles up the street. I was only a young one I was, and afraid of the Black and Tans. And terrible excitement when Independence came. They'd have big gramophones out through the windows and banjos and all and they'd be all singing and dancing and waltzing around the street. The accordions would be playing and the gramophones roaring and blaring and the men playing the mandolins and banjos. And a big bonfire and things of beer and all the doors wide open.

"I lost me father and had to work for fifty-five years. The Jewmen around here they were never without a day's work for you. I was sixteen when I started working for Harry Sive. He had a shop there (Meath Street). He came from Russia and got this little business and when he started he used to sleep on a wood table, he'd make that his bed. Now Harry was only sixteen the day he opened those doors and I was only sixteen. First he asked me sister to go to work for him and then he took me in. I was fifty-five years with him. It was a rag store but he'd take everything in. You name it and Harry bought it. Bales of clothes and cloth, whiskey bottles, stout bottles, jam jars, brass and copper, kettles, aluminium pots. It was very hard work. Women done the work on the clothes. Cleaning out the clothes, tearing out linings and the pockets with knives. Huge, heavy bales of clothes to sort out and put the clothes in and boil them. He had two big boilers of hot and cold water and girls or men scraping the labels off the bottles and jars and washing them. And taking in copper and brass and cleaning it and hammering it. Always something for you to do. I was an all-round worker, did *everything*. I often worked till two and three in the morning for him if he was terribly busy. And all day Saturday. You worked very hard but you were never without a day's work.

"He had (eventually) twenty-eight women working for him and nine men. And paid good wages. I got a half a crown a week when I started. We all wore smocks for working, he got them for us. They were blue and pink. And he'd buy dungareens for the men. But the floor was hard, cold stones and in the winter you'd be freezing. And before we'd go into work in the morning he'd be on his knees lighting the fire for us. And when you'd go in there they'd be all working and the fellas would be singing and running up and down and putting their arms around the women and kissing them, and always singing. You could hear them out in the street singing, doing their work. Every song you could think of . . . 'Take Me Back to Dear Old Brighton', 'It's a Long Way to Tipperary', 'Danny Boy', all the old songs.

"Oh, he had about thirty or forty tuggers bringing him stuff, women and men tuggers. They used to call the people that went around with the basket cars to doors 'tuggers'. He used to have forty-six of the basket cars lined up by the store. Had a big wheel at the front and two side wheels. He didn't charge them for the push cars. Tuggers used to come up in the mornings and get their basket cars and they'd be out all day. Oh, God, they'd go *miles*. As far as Newbridge and off to Bray . . . walking. To all the big houses. They'd be out all the day, come in and have their stuff weighed up and sold and then next morning they'd be out again. They'd give people delph. And if a tugger went into Harry on a Monday morning and had no money to buy the delph or little ornaments—they used to call it their 'stock'—Harry would give them the money for to start out the week. He never turned anybody away. Very, very charitable and very kind to children.

Some wouldn't even have left school and they'd have to go out with their mothers. Some would be from nine years old, go around knocking at the doors. Their children were reared up to tugging . . . generations of tuggers all the way up. Oh, some of them would be fifty, sixty . . . oh, some of them died at tugging. And tuggers might go for a drink and pawn his basket cars. He used to have the 'Waste Salvage' on his cars and an 'S' for Sive. But he never got mad at them. 'Go over and get it back!' Oh, he was very kind.

"When tuggers used to bring the rags and bones in they'd mix the bones in the rags. We'd be going through the stuff picking out the bones and put them in a big basket. Bones from the meat. He used to sell the bones to Keefe's the knackers and Keefe's used to grind them up and make them into manure for flower beds. Harry'd collect bones and the rats were in from every direction. Oh, there used to be rats in the store. I once run out into the street and he got the whole place fumigated and got rid of them. But some of the clothes from the big houses was nearly new and he'd give it to you. When new clothes would come in everybody'd be grabbing for them. Oh, there was always excitement when you'd find anything. We'd go through the pockets. Oh, you used to find money or a bit of jewellery when you'd search it. Now once I took this big top coat up and very, very dirty, like coal. Filthy and dirty and full of coal. And I said to meself, 'I'm not going to put me hands into that with all the dirt on it, God knows who's after being wearing it.' So I throwed the coat away and I felt it very heavy. And I ran over and I took up the coat again and searched it and there was a wallet in it. And then I put me hand into another part of it and I found a lot of silver. And it was *filthy dirty* because coal men used to go around with the loose coal selling it and they'd have their old coat on them and the money they'd get they'd stuff it in their pocket. And there was £19-odd in it! And, says I, 'God, what'll I do? Well that man might come back for his topcoat, I'll keep it and give it back to him.' So I kept it for nearly three weeks and nobody never came near it. So I said to meself, 'I'll keep it.' So I kept it.

"Oh, we got plenty of handbags and all. There was a girl working beside me one time and we was sitting down on the ground, about six or seven of us, and there was this handbag and for weeks it was going around and we were playing with it, throwing it from one to the other. Says she, 'I'm tired of looking at this, I think I'll open it and see what's in it.' And when she opened this handbag she was picking out ten shilling notes, half crowns, shillings, two shillings, pound notes . . . filled with money. And we were just passing it around playing with it. I'd say there was about £20 in it. Oh, God, she got to keep it. Oh, we were all mad that *we* didn't open it. But she shared it with us, five or six shillings she gave us.

"There were other Jewmen—Mr Wolfson over to Bride Street, Mr Taylor of Fumbally Lane, Mr Tolkin of Mount Pleasant Place and then Benny Coleman in Tailors Lane. Great competition between them, especially for good workers. But tuggers were always very loyal to Harry because he always gave them a good price. Now some of the other Jewmen, they were very mean. Oh, he'd *fight like the devil* with Harry Lipman (leading northside Jewman). Always fighting over stuff. Oh, there'd be murder between them, maybe over customers. Oh, and sometimes he'd get mad at you. He was fighting with my sister one time and she got a basket car and pushed it after him. She was his foreman and they were always fighting. Me sister Kitty was honest and straight and he liked that. Always fighting. She'd say, 'You crucified Our Lord but you're not going to crucify me!' And he'd say, 'I didn't do it, me forefathers done it.' He liked her.

"I'd say Harry was a millionaire. Ah, yes. But very charitable. Oh, very kind to the poor he was. There was destitutes that died over in the lodging house there and there'd be a collection for to bury him and Harry would always be the first to give his donation. And if any of the fellas around the street or any of their sons got into a bit of trouble and went to court Harry'd always give his name to bail them out or give them a bit of work and put them on the straight road. Now that big bell on Catherine's Church on Meath Street wasn't ringing for years and the church couldn't afford the money to have it restored. And Harry used to give donations for the bell. Every Monday morning he had an envelope ready in his pocket and he'd say, 'Bring that up to the Father.'

"Oh, he loved the Catholic religion and the nuns. And whenever a priest or nuns would come into the store and you know the way people'd be cursing—even the best of us—he'd say, 'I'm warning you'se all now, your priest is coming in and your nuns and I want to hear no bad expressions in the store.' Oh, he used to give them a good donation, bring them into the store, entertain them, spend hours with them and then walk them out to the gate there. But I'm ashamed to say now but when the Rabbi would come he used to *hide* and say, 'Tell him I'm not here.' Oh, but he loved the Catholic religion and used to love the rasher and sausage and all fried, and black and white pudding. *They* don't use that kind of stuff but he *loved* it. And his wife, she never knew he used to be eating all that.

"And, oh, he loved his bottle! His wife was always fighting with him for taking the drink. Oh, he'd go and slip off for a couple of days or maybe a week. Sometimes he'd go out for a message and maybe would be gone for maybe three or four weeks. Oh, on the drink. And his wife would be looking for him. Harry's wife was always trying to keep him down and he'd never let her inside the (shop) door. Go off and have a few drinks and so we'd run the business. And when he was out on the beer he used to bring the workers out and get them drunk with him. One time he went to the Royal (Theatre) with a few of the workers and Gracie Fields was on. And she was a Jewess. So Gracie was singing some song and he didn't like the song she was singing and he took off his shoe and threw his shoe at her! And they put him out. And he was missing for a fortnight and they were looking everywhere for him. And we were working and who walks up the lane but Movita and Jack Doyle! See, Harry brought them out drinking and having a good time for about a fortnight, drinking all the time and running up bills in Harry's name. And Jack Doyle saluted him and says, 'I'll see you again sometime.'

"At Christmas-time he'd give us a party in the store. We used to get a Christmas box off him. For Christmas he'd give us a box of chocolates, a bottle of port, and an envelope with a few bob in it. And the men, he'd give them big boxes of cigarettes. And drink for all the men and all the women and big cakes and get fish and chips brought in and he'd pay for it. And all the night we'd enjoy ourselves. *He'd* get drunk and the *workers* would get drunk and they'd *all* get drunk! And there'd be Irish dancing. But he'd get them all *mad drunk*. Then when everybody'd be gone home then he'd have to face his wife.

I worked with him up to the last day he shut up the store. Started with him and ended up with him. We were a *family*. He died among us. He was part of the community. He was over seventy-odd. Oh, he was very kind. I often say that he was the best Jewman that I ever knew, the best Jewman in all the city. Harry . . . he was one of our own."

Stephen Mooney—Age 65

As a young lad growing up along Pimlico he and his pals would pass the time tossing ha'pennies against the wall, playing cards on the corner, and keeping a vigilant watch for the "coppers". To flee the scene they would dash madly through the maze of tenement "tricking halls" and vaporise from sight. One of his favourite haunts was the city dump site where hordes of children would competitively scavenge about in search of prized jam jars for their entry fee to the picture house matinee. In his refined, gentlemanly manner he still likes sharing memories of youthful devilment, local characters, and the escapades of local "vicious" animal gangs.

"We lived on Pimlico and as kids we'd be pulled around in an old boxcar. It was made out of a butter box, about twelve inches high and two foot long, and wheels of an old pram. And for devilment there was scutting on the backs of cars. There was a fella used to drive a dray and he used to take sixteen-stone bags of wheat and he'd sit on the cart and control the horse and he had a whip. This fella was quite good with his whip and the handle was about four or five feet long. And he'd wait for the kids with this big steel-lined whip—he used to really *encourage* the kids to get on the back of the cart—and he'd *lash* the *hands* off you, the *back* off you, the *face* off you. Oh, he was a vicious bastard he was. Also for devilment there was knocking on tenement doors to torment the cranks. Cranks was people that responded to you, challenging you, coming down after you with a big stick and chasing you all over the place. And, see, we used to use the 'tricking halls' for to get away. And we always picked old people, I don't know why. It's the demon in kids. But if they caught you you could get a licking!

"Now the Jews at that time were all money-makers and they'd take bottles and jam jars and rags and metals off you, for selling. Harry Sive was in the rag business in the Liberties so if we wanted to go to the pictures we had to go out and collect jam jars for him. Now we had a tiphead—a dump—in Crumlin where we used to go as kids. You'd get a bit of bar or something to dig with. Ah, it was hard work. Now you must remember that there were *ninety million* kids making for the dump. And you needed the where-with-all to forge out your own area for digging. Oh, there'd be 200 or more kids, all digging for things, and there'd be blood flying left, right and centre! See, big fellas would come along and they used to rob us. And *men* and *women* there. Adults would mark out a terrain and if you ambled into it you'd get a hiding. Anything was brought back in a sack. The only treasures I found were jam jars. A large one, that was a guarantee to the pictures. And at the early stages of the war we used to collect cinders, the coal bits, in the dump and fill a bag of them. Then knock on somebody's door and sell them for two bob.

"Then you started gambling at about six, pitching up to the wall with your ha'pennies and pennies. Then you graduated to different kinds of card games, the likes of Don and poker, which involved you in more money. Quite a bit of money and it led to stealing in the homes, stealing money off the mantelpiece where your mother'd leave money. You'd steal it to get back the money you lost. Oh, it passed the time. We'd play in the night-time in the tenement halls with candle light but mostly we played on the street corners under the gas-lamps where you could watch for the police. We knew them by name and their nature as well, so you could nearly forecast the times they'd be arriving. Now if the police were chasing you this is where the tricking halls in the tenements come into being. It might be six houses of halls all with rear yards back-to-back and you'd run in through number 1, we'll say, and you'd bee-line it all the way to number 6 and hop up onto the toilet roof and scamper over the wall and you lost them . . . *tricking* halls.

"And there was a good few characters around our area that was shell-shocked and would chase us. There was one fella that'd come down Marrow-bone Lane and we'd call him names and he used to run after us and froth at the mouth. He'd chase us and actually beat you up if he got hold of you. Then there was Jembo-no-toes. Jembo was shell-shocked but a very fine cut of a man. He lost some of his toes (in World War I) and his balance wasn't perfect. He was inclined to waddle along. But he used to periodically go off the handle, roaring and shouting. Now one time this fella Osso Dougherty, a (local) comedian, stole the latch key off Bang-Bang and told him that he'd only give the key back to him if he *stuck up* Jembo-no-toes. And he *done that*. He come around behind Jembo coming up the street and sticks the key into Jembo and he let out an unmerciful roar at Bang-Bang. It was like dropping a bomb beside Jembo and he went stark-raving mad and chased him in and out of this concrete air raid shelter. In the shelter Jembo found the end of a brass bed with all the bars in it and picked up the thing and belted Bang-Bang. Now Bang-Bang was very fleety on the feet but Bang-Bang thought he was *playing* with him. He could have got *killed!*

"Now for entertainment there was films and telling stories. Now 'Slim' was great at telling stories about films. He was a slight bit older than us. If you hadn't got the money to go to the film and he *did*, well, Slim would describe the film from the beginning to the end. *Named* everyone, *provided the music, told the story.* Oh, kept you totally involved and would break in periodically with the music. And there was *venues* for all this—the school steps, the steps at the fountain, the wall where you'd sit with your backs up against the wall listening to him. And he'd *command* your attention. It was semi-dusk and dark and you were huddled together and there was no distraction. Oh, he was known as a great story-teller. And once you knew the likes of the characters he was talking about, like Errol Flynn and Randolph Scott, well, you were sitting there in the saddle with him. We were in the film *with him*! And he'd spend *hours* on it. And he'd say, 'They snuck in around where all the dynamite was'—and you'd hear the music going—'and John puts his hand down inside the box and pulls out a stick of dynamite and says, "this'll do the job!."' Oh, he was *great* at it. And he'd do the explosion and all the sound effects and everything. He was a *master* at that. His pleasure was in telling it and it was our pleasure listening. Ah, the *big* fellas liked him and the *small* fellas liked him and he was never in trouble with anybody.

"There were dozens of huckster shops at the bottom of the tenement houses and had wide windows. That enabled you to look in and see the wares that'd be put on a couple of bread boards, a bit of a display, like sweets and cigarettes. *All* kinds of sweets and the queerest names like 'honey-bees' or 'bulls-eyes' and all. They had a system worked out where it was six for a penny or six for a ha'penny. And cigarettes. There was a certain cigarette called 'Tento'. Now I don't know if you've ever tasted Nosegay in England, that's the nearest thing to burning leather and stockings at the one time. Well, these Tento cigarettes were a hundred times worse. Strong! Why did we buy them? Cause you got *two*. Used to sell them two for a ha'penny, and a match. Now Nanny Roche and Mary, two elderly sisters, had sold paraffin oil, coal, sticks, sweets, cigarettes. Now for two old ones they were witty. But they were very miserly with one another and now Nanny and Mary they'd only one set of clothes, that's all. We knew about the one set of clothes from me granny. See, they wore the same clothes. So you'd never see the two of them at the same time! So if Nanny had gone out somewhere and you came in the shop she'd (Mary) shout at you from the back of the shop, 'Come back, I'm busy.'

"People went into the tenements on the stairs, the halls, for intimacy. It was great for courting. It was so *pitch* dark. And no shadows. You could actually be in a hall and people could go up and down and pass you by and they wouldn't even see you! Great for courting . . . and there was a hell of a lot of women made pregnant. And now a man could be married and not get along with his wife and then date another woman and he'd be described as having a 'fancy woman'. Or vice versa! There *were* women who had fancy men. There were a hell of a lot of men who were meeting other women slobbering over her and kissing her and all, but if a man would bring another woman into his tenement house the whole lot of the house would take *umbrage*—even if they were all blackguards *themselves*. It was very common, having a fancy man or a fancy woman.

"Now there was once a row on our corner with two women, over a man. On the cobblestones. Around their thirties. One woman challenged her, like a man, out on the road, on the cobblestones. And it came down to a fight like a man. I never seen anything like it, the way they tore one another to bits. And the fellas were kept away from the fight. The women formed sort of a circle and they'd say to the men, 'Keep away, keep away.' Oh, hair pulling, biting, kicking and you name it. I never seen anything like it. Now this other woman, Nan, had *several* fancy men. Now her husband, a fine cut of a fella, it was commonly known to the menfolk around there that he was a 'rig', a man with one ball . . . *unserviceable*. And when Nan found out, that was it! When he was out, other fellas would be *in*. *Everybody* knew. She was a lovely looking woman and she stayed with him and I think he was happy enough that way.

"There were all different gangs and cliques of kids and you'd see a group hovering around and you didn't go down to them because they were the *tough guys*. They were very rough down on Ash Street and down at the end of the Coombe. If they seen me with money, going for messages, they'd stop me and take the money off me. Your parents would be docile and say, 'Oh, forget about it!' cause they didn't want to become involved. Now there was this Charlie fella, a head like a bucket and good with his fists. Well, Charlie went across to the Mayro Cinema (Mary Street) and the Mayro was a borderline cinema for two gangs. And Charlie went there and they were lining up on the queue and the northside gang seen Charlie in the front and there was a battle royal took place. Oh, they nearly killed him. Well, then Charlie—fair play to him—he went over again himself with a *chain* and he waited till it was their turn to be lining up and he just *lashed* into them. And they thought it was *great*! The northside thought it was great—cause he was unafraid! Charlie was the *hero*. Charlie was like a mediator then between the gangs when there was rows.

"Now the animal gangs, that was a different thing from kids playing on the street. They went up to their forties. See, at that time unemployment was rife, in the thirties and forties, and men was hanging around the corners. And then they'd get bored and no money for this, that and the other. So animal gangs used to go out of the neighbourhood and terrorise—involved in racketeering. They threatened to burn shops and stop people from going into them if there wasn't a sum of (protection) money paid. Ah, sure, they were all gangsters, all liked to be tough guys. And you must appreciate at that time the films that was coming out of America, the prohibition films kind of thing and they'd think, 'Oh, that's something we could operate *here*.'

"Now there was a money-lender who used to live in Meath Street, Ma Flanagan (pseudonym), and she was responsible for the formation of an animal gang. She was lending out money and it didn't seem to be coming back. So what she done then, she sought out in the vicinity of Engine Alley and Vicar Street, down to Carman's Hall, the *tough* guys who were unemployed, who would do anything for to get money. And she put it to them that if she could shake a few heads the rest would pay up. And then she had seven sons and those married in and they were all connected and she controlled the whole family and they were vicious bastards, now that's the best I can say. *Vicious animals!* Physically animals, they were. So she'd get the heavies and they'd beat up the husband, beat up the wife, and they'd *wreck* the house. Now it was only one room but they'd wreck the room. And anyone else that owed them money would say, 'Jesus, I don't want that to happen to *me.*' So they'd go off to the Jewman and borrow money to pay her off and then they were struggling on. She was tough, like that Ma Barker (in films) in the States. She wielded the power and helped to formulate the animal gang. They realised their own power when they were amassed together and they ventured into the protection racket then on their own. Now people reported them to the police but there was no way the police could do anything about it because it was all done under the *threat.*

"The animal gangs, they terrorised the district all right. But then the Marrowbone Lane gang—just ordinary folks who just banded themselves together (vigilantes)—says, 'We're not going to have this anymore!' And they went to war with the animal gang. About thirty-odd men from Marrowbone Lane and there was a lot of mature men . . . *and women* from Marrowbone Lane against the animal gang. And they came out on top! Oh, I *seen* it, they used our street as the venue for fighting. And this particular woman that led the animal gang up Pimlico she was what we called a 'mot', a girlfriend, you know, of one of the animal gang fellas. She wanted to show off to the other girls in her neighbourhood that she was as tough as them men. So she led them up the street with a big chain in her hand. She was about twenty-four. And the two gangs *battered* one another, with chains, razors, bars, knives. Oh, yeah, they had *bayonets* and everything. Tommo Finn, he led them (Marrowbone Lane gang) and he was about six foot four. And a mate of mine found a sword and it was rotten with rust and they cleaned it up with sandpaper. And at the time the fighting took place somebody mentioned it and says, 'Give me the sword'—like one of King Arthur's swords! It weighed a couple of stone. Now there was no edging on it, with the rust, but, by God, I'll tell you, he split many a skull with it!

"Anyway, the protection rackets was running and it (rivalry) was coming to a head and two animal gangs met up in Tolka Park and there was a battle royal there. One man was killed. And this one fella from the southside was responsible for cutting a 'V' in a fella's skull and nearly killed him. The court said, 'I want these fellas brought in and *that's it*, we'll deal with them in the courts.' Now Lugs Brannigan, he was instructed to go out and bring them in. Lugs was known for his fearlessness, that he would go *among* them. In his early days he was a boxer and he was battered from one end of the ring to the other—but he was *game* for a fight. So Lugs went out with eight or ten policemen, which was quite a lot at that time, and they'd wade in. And at that time they didn't waltz you down to the station. A fella would be batoned to the ground and I mean with a *big* baton. Oh, break his skull with them they would. And when they'd put you down they'd pull your trousers and your long-johns *down* and twist it to drag you. You were *dragged* in. And they bashed you on the ground as you were getting pulled. I can guarantee you that this is the gospel truth. They *bashed* you all the way down . . . and your head hitting kerbs and anything. You were 'resisting arrest'! Whether you were unconscious or not! This is the way they done it. They went to court and there was savage sentences handed out and they ultimately nailed the animal gangs. And that's the way they done it."

5

Oral Testimony: The Northside

PADDY CASEY—AGE 65

As a raw police recruit aged eighteen coming from the fresh country air, he confesses that the northside tenement slums were a shock. He walked the beat along some of Dublin's toughest streets—Queen's Street, Parnell Street, Dominick Street—where he witnessed "savage hardship" but met the greatest people. What he remembers best about the northsiders was their community spirit, deep religious faith and marvellous wit. When the Corporation uprooted them and moved them out to the sterile suburban estates he believes that it "changed the heart of Dublin" forever.

"When I came to Dublin it was a *shock* to me. I went into training when I was eighteen years old in Phoenix Park and went to the Bridewell (station) and spent thirteen years there. It was an extraordinary experience for me, coming from the country with green grass and country air. We thought we were quite poor in the country but when I compared it with Dublin we were very well off. Like food. We'd plenty of food, a lot of it home-grown. And we'd plenty of space and plenty of bed-clothing and you had plenty of heat, you were warm. But Dublin . . . it was a *shock*. Like the O'Casey plays *The Plough and the Stars* and *Juno and the Paycock*—that was *exactly* as it was when I came to Dublin. Old Georgian tenements and a mother and father and maybe ten children sleeping in one room. Sheets or blanket put across on a string to divide off the male and female. Ordinary old spring mattresses, if they were lucky. A lot of potatoes and vegetables, that was their staple diet. People were terribly poor. I saw some *savage* hardship.

"I was around Capel Street, Queen Street, the quays, up to Heuston (then called Kingsbridge) Station. And I had Dominick Street, the markets area and North King Street. A poor area . . . a rough area. Oh, I've been in those tenements. It was *terrible* at times. Sanitation, just one toilet down in the rear yard which could serve forty people. There was a mixture of smells . . . stale urine, both human and cat, the smell of damp on the wall, the smell of paraffin oil, stale cigarette smoke, the smell of B.O. as well, every sort of smell. Another smell that was *awful* was the Jeyes Fluid, a disinfectant used for the hallways and stairways, an abominable smell. And fleas, you always learned not to sit down on a couch or anything which might have fleas. But it was amazing, you know, that you could go into even the worst tenements and you'd find beautifully kept rooms. And the front steps washed down. They were quite clean in their own way. Everyone had their own little ornaments on the mantel-piece over the fireplace and always religious pictures on the walls. And a lot of them had the window box with the flowers in them and the windows always had to be *clean* . . . it's amazing.

"The people had terribly rough times. Poverty was not having anything to eat, rationing yourself to so many slices of bread a day, putting water into the same tea leaves for the tea, children going to school with no shoes on their feet. *That's* poverty. The problem in the poor tenement was a lot of unemployment. People *lived* out of the markets buying second-hand clothing and shoes and pawnshops were doing a *booming* trade. It was a way of life. On Friday and Saturday you'd see them queued up at the pawnshop to get a few shillings for the weekend. And a problem then was people breaking into their gas metres inside the houses cause they were short of money. The total might be about thirty-five pence but in those days it would have bought food for a week for those people.

"And turf was a staple fuel back then when coal was non-existent. To have a fire for the winter some men cycled up to the Dublin mountains, maybe fifteen miles, and they'd spend the day cutting turf. Some poor people wouldn't even have the bicycle to do that. People from the poorer areas, they'd survive by getting old boxes out of the markets for a fire. And I remember that there were wood setts on the streets to dull the noise of the iron-clad wheels which were used in those earlier days and those setts went down about four inches and were coated in pitch for long wear. And I was here in 1947 which was a terrible, terrible difficult winter with long bouts of snow and the poor people would come out with picks and *hack up* the street and take up the wood setts in sacks for fire. An awful lot of poverty.

"But the inner-city was *great*. You just went along—one man walking the beat then—and at that time people *spoke* to you. And there were street traders and paper sellers and buskers on the street playing banjos and singing songs and selling knick-knacks. And we had balladeers, fellas writing ballads and getting them printed in a sort of cheap printing house and selling them for a penny or two pence each, songs and his own sort of unbelievable dribble. But *still*, he made a shilling or two out of it. And there were characters. Oh, I knew Bang-Bang well, running all over the place with his key and shooting everybody. Children had so much fun with him. Then there was 'Johnny Forty Coats'. And he *had* forty coats on him! And on warm days. He had so many coats on him that it was just unbelievable. And there was 'Cyclone' Warren, he was a black boxer. I think he might have been American. But he had very bad feet I remember. He used to always wear boots that were split open. He must have had corns or something on his feet. He was always around and he was terribly quiet. They were respected, funny enough, those people.

"And three-card trick merchants. Did you ever see those fellas? It was *illegal*, of course. You have the three cards and it was sleight of hand. They'd have this little collapsible table out on the street so they could fold it up and put it under their coat. They'd go along and get a group of people if there was no police around and open out this table and take out those three cards. There were two ordinary cards and a queen. The idea was to find the 'Lady'. They'd catch the three cards, one in one hand and two in the other, and they'd mix them around. You'd watch the queen and they'd flick them around and say, 'Which is it?' And they'd probably have some friend there and the friend would point and always pick the right one and he'd be paying him—but it'd be a *pal* of his. And, of course, all the people would say, 'Oh, this is simple.' Gullible people. And then you'd pick and *invariably* you were wrong, of course. You were *never* right! It was illegal but that and gambling and penny tossing in the street were means of making money.

"It was a hard home environment and family rows were a problem. In those days the wife had the babies and it was up to her then to look after them and the Irish men were quite prone to drinking a lot. The men were inclined to go to the pub and then they'd come home drunk and the wife would start giving out and it would involve a fight then. And you'd be dragged into it a number of times. Now sometimes if the granny or sisters were called in the man came out *worse*. But you went up there and had to assess the situation and you'd try to stop it at the source. I think a policeman's life is one of psychology all the time, assessing a person and 'how's he going to react?' When you treated people fairly they treated you fairly. You made respect for yourself. The best thing was to go and say, 'Listen here, forget about it now because the two of you are fighting now but in the morning it'll be all together again.' And *invariably* they came around to thinking that way. Even if it might be a serious case of assault by a husband on a wife, if you'd bring him in and arrest him and charge him and bring him before the court the next morning the wife would come down and say, 'He was drunk last night, Your Honour, he's OK today. He's the best in the world until he gets a few drinks.'

"There's more civilised drinking now. But in those days I always regarded a public house as a cow or horse stables, you know, where men went in and they'd have *stalls*. Like when you bring the cattle or horses into a pen or big barn, strangely enough, every one of them has their *own* place and they'll never go any place else. Well, it's similar with men when they'd go in drinking. They went into their own little place and if you were an outsider and went in and would take up one of those spaces you weren't very welcome. That was *their* territory. And the publican was the lord and master and what he said was *law*. They weren't supposed to give credit but invariably he'd put it on the slate. He couldn't do business without it. And it's amazing now but at that time public houses had to close a full day on St Patrick's Day, on Christmas, and Good Friday. They were the three black days of the publican's year. But *invariably* we were going to catch somebody in a pub on St Patrick's Day and Good Friday. The pub was always shut, the doors closed, but there'd be people inside that he'd let in. Always a few people inside having a drink. And that drink, I think, was better than any drink they had that year!

"Now you (Guard) could go into a pub to eject a man if you were called in by the publican. It would only be if he wasn't able to eject him. There was particular pubs where that sort of problem arose. Generally, publicans were reasonably strict about people getting drunk on the premises and they'd say, 'Out, you've had enough!' And they'd throw him out. For some reason public houses were sacred ground and they just didn't fight in the pub. The fighting took place on the street outside the pub. There would have been some argument that took place within the pub but they'd come out and it was a *civilised* fight. Just punching and the best man wins and shake hands and go home! Nowadays there's a knife or a bottle or something else. Oh, I've seen fellas with their shirts off and all banging away at each other. Generally, in those days when a uniformed presence of a Guard came they sort of growled at each other and stopped, put on their shirts.

"And there was prostitution then. Prostitution was a problem going on. I remember Dolly Fawcett's well. It was next to where the Bolton Street Technical School is. Dolly's was regarded by some as a brothel, which it wasn't. It was a shebeen. What happened there was a fella'd go there for a drink and meet a girl there and take her out. They'd go to a lodging house that were brothels at the time. They were a mixture of country girls and Dublin girls, generally uneducated girls, who might have been exploited by her employer. Then they'd 'go on the game' and they had an awful, sad existence. Oh, it was very sad.

"Although the people were terribly poor and had terribly rough times they were lovely people. They had great community spirit. And extremely religious people, it gave stability to their life. Even men that'd be fond of the jar—and tough men—when the priest came along and spoke to them they could be meek as lambs. Lovely people . . . and they were *extraordinarily happy* for people who were so savagely poor. In those days you had a phrase—and I don't know whether it was a good idea or a bad idea—that 'The poor knew their place.' But it was a *fact*—they knew their place. They knew that their place was on the bottom of the ladder and they were happy to be there and they wanted to stay that way. They didn't seem to have any great ambitions to go up to the middle class. Quite happy to stay. That was the extraordinary thing, they were fulfilled. They loved this thing, particularly the women, of sitting on the steps of the tenement there on a summer's day chatting and the children running around. And the men'd have their jars and sing at the drop of a hat. They *liked* that. And unbelievable hooleys at weddings and Christmas and the wakes. You can imagine in the tenement, probably six or eight of those rooms, and *everyone* in the house joined in. The houses next door even joined in and they'd sing songs. The parties were *unbelievable*.

"I had a wonderful time with the people. Most of those areas, like Henrietta Street and Dominick Street, are all gone now. And along Parnell Street it's gone. Completely gone now. They were all moved out to places like Bally-fermot and Finglas . . . and it changed the heart of Dublin. And *none* of them wanted to go. I suppose anyone who has been torn up from their roots it's a very sad experience. And it was funny, you could move a man ten miles out and on a Saturday night he'd come back into the old pub for his drink."

CHRISSIE O'HARE—AGE 76

Her parents sold newspapers on O'Connell Street and after her father died her stepfather ill-treated her. To escape his wrath she married another newspaper vendor who eventually abandoned her. She was left penniless with three young children, one of whom died shortly thereafter from meningitis. Today she lives in a flat along Summerhill afraid to venture outside for fear of the menacing youth gangs who prey on the elderly. She feels imprisoned and lonely, confessing that there is little joy left in her life.

"My father was a news-vendor. So was me mother. They were at the corner of O'Connell and Earl Street. Me mother wore a shawl and never went to a doctor. *Never.* A doctor never knew her. There was thirteen of me mother's children that died at home before they were born . . . they were coming into the world too fast. Died at birth. There was just a boy and a girl (survived). But me mother was eighty-nine when she died and had all her teeth. Not a bad tooth in her head!

"I grew up in a tenement house on Lower Gardiner Street. My father only paid two and eight pence for our room a week. Water leaking in the winter was always a problem. In the winter-time there was slits in the windows and the doors and you'd roll up papers and put them in the slits cause the draft would be blowing in. Some people wouldn't have blankets and they'd sleep in just their clothes. Everyone put coats on the beds and some of them just lying on the floor. Then in the summer-time rooms were very warm and everybody had their windows open. Sometimes you couldn't sleep and you'd be sitting out on the steps till all hours of the morning. In the tenement it was hot and we never had fridges and you couldn't keep anything. So you'd have to go out every day and buy your food. Even your milk, it'd get sour. You got milk in a jug and people used to put it in basins of cold water to try and keep it fresh. And people'd go into a pub and ask for ice to keep the butter and cheeses cool. He'd have just a few blocks for his drink and maybe he'd give you a glass full. And we used to suck that ourself.

"Me mother had the morning paper and the evening paper and me father only sold the evening papers. Me mother had to get up at half five. Her papers was dropped over at the corner there. It was a hard life . . . in the winter it was. But she *liked* it. We had enough money to have our dinner every day. When me mother'd be out in the mornings a friend kind of reared us. We called her 'granny' and she looked after us. We had chickens and we used to get fresh eggs and I had me own chicken. And I come home from school one day and I'm looking for me chicken everywhere and I couldn't find it. And I says, 'Granny, I can't find me chicken.' My father was *roasting* it! To me it was a pet. But he didn't understand and he cooked it. I couldn't eat it . . . and never since either. Cause I still see the chicken.

"I went to Rutland Street school. I have a good few memories of my teachers. Mrs King, I was with her for first, second, and third class and I'll tell you this much, she never left the cane out of her hand in her life. *Never*. Oh, she was a devil. She got me and another girl talking and gave us each thirty slaps with the cane, fifteen on each hand. Just for talking, chatting. Oh, I'll never forget that. I didn't get much schooling because I had sore eyes as a child. Something happened when me mother brought me to the seaside. She used her big apron, big stiff apron with starch, to get the sand out of me eye and the starch cut me eyes. Then I used to rub it and it got infected. And it spread to the other eye. I come out of school at thirteen. It was no use to keep going.

"At the 1932 (Eucharistic) Congress *all* the houses and streets were done up in buntings and all. And all the windows done up. All colours of paper and cloth, and on the railings. And the doors were all done out with holy sashes and holy pictures and statues in the windows. Now Mr O'Toole (tenant) decorated our house on Gardiner Street. Fairy lights wasn't out much at that time because we never had electric light but he got a battery and put all electric lights around our place and all down our front window because we had a creeper. We all had boxes made for flowers and we had the lights all around them. It was beautiful. And we'd stools for all the people that'd come to sit down and look. Even a lot of Americans here looking around. People all walked up and down dressed up and said the rosary. Oh, it was very hot and the Scouts, the boys, would help anyone passing by if they were tired and sitting down, help them and give them water or get the ambulance and get them taken away, because of the heat. The Mass was held in Phoenix Park and everyone sat on the steps and listened to it because it was broadcast with John McCormack and all. On all the lamp-posts you had these things like loud speakers. The Government done that, the broadcast, with the Mass and the singing and John McCormack and all. There was more of them loud speakers in O'Connell street which was all decorated. It was beautiful. You *never forgot* it.

"Me father died when I was eighteen and me brother and me lived with me mother and me stepfather on Corporation Street. Oh, from the time me father died me life was hard. I had to lie on the floor cause I had no bed. And me mother had to pawn me own clothes. When me father died the corner was mine and I took over the papers but I just couldn't do it, just wasn't able. Oh, I sold them for about two years and then gave them up. I *hated* it. Me mother used to say, 'Ah, you'll never make a news-vendor.' I wasn't there long with me mother cause her and her husband had arguments and he put me out. I was the one put out. Then I picked up with this chap and got married and got a room on Corporation Street. Me husband was a news-vendor and he made colours (rosettes) too for the matches. And made hats too. Oh, we made everything and I liked selling the colours and the hats. Cut the cardboard with scissors and get this coloured paper and make loads of hats. You'd get up real early to Croke Park along the queues going in and I just put the box around me with a rope and I used to carry about eight or nine dozen hats. At that time they were only a shilling. I'd stand there and it was very exciting.

"The next thing, me husband goes from selling the colours to minding the bikes. 'Go sell the colours yourself,' he says to me. See, the men that parked the bikes, that started up around Croke Park. My husband started that nearly. We was up in Croke Park one day selling and there was a fella going in with a bike—and this was after a bike was being robbed the last week—and me husband says to him, 'Now leave it there with mine.' And then he started getting the bikes in, got a pitch. He could mind maybe sixty bikes. He used to give them a little ticket and it was about sixpence a bike at that time. And if someone didn't come back for the bike he'd have to carry it over to Store Street (police station). Then he started minding cars *and* bikes in the night-time in Abbey Street.

"I had three children but me and me husband started to argue and he ran out. Went away to England. Stopped sending us any money. And the relieving officer wouldn't give me any. St Vincent de Paul, they often give me a three and sixpenny order to get milk and eggs and bread. And then I lost a girl at eight months, of meningitis. I don't know. They said I left it too late, but I was after going to all the hospitals and they said there was nothing wrong with her, said they could find nothing wrong with the child, that I had imaginations. But I knew something was wrong because she was just lying and not taking the bottle. I brought her to this doctor and she was very sick and he says, 'You're after killing your own child. This child has meningitis.' I took her to Cork Street Hospital on Tuesday and she died on Saturday. Buried her from the hospital. I got a coffin at Farrell's (undertakers) and they brought it to the hospital. They carried the coffin from Cork Street to Glasnevin, the men. I wasn't let go to the funeral. I was at me mother's with me stepsister. Oh, I was in an awful state. I *wanted* to be there, but they wouldn't let me. They said the mother shouldn't be with the child. She was buried in a (poor) children's plot and me mother didn't want me to know where she was buried. They wouldn't let me go and they wouldn't tell me where it is. Oh, I went out there (later) . . . but I never seen it."

John V. Morgan—Age 70

From his little butcher's shop on North King Street he looked directly across to a dense tapestry of tenement houses. On a Saturday as many as five hundred women in shawls would come in and carry away their meat parings wrapped in newspapers. He remembers the tenement folk as the "grandest neighbours in the world".

"This shop was started by my father more than eighty years ago. I was born here in 1923 and did an apprenticeship around fourteen. We had our own slaughterhouse here at the back and I learned how to handle knives, how to kill. We were doing about seven cattle a week then and around twenty sheep in the back. We actually walked the animals down from nine miles out in the country. You had a pole-axe and you'd have to hit them between the eyes and they went down. In a poorer area like this what they had was mostly stew. There was a great go on leg beef and stewing beef, beef heads, sheep's heads, kidneys and things like that. Sheep's heads, take the hair off and the head would be split in two and make stew, very nice. Newspapers to wrap it up and put it under their shawls and carry it home. And they'd go to the market and buy cod's heads, fish heads, and boil them and shake them and all the meat would come off. It's amazing the amount of meat in cod's heads. And they'd have a *good* dinner for a shilling.

"Now over there (North King Street) in those tenements there were 700 people! All big families and the space they'd have in those rooms wouldn't be any bigger than this (10 by 12 feet). You couldn't sit down to read a paper or anything in it because the kids would be on top of you. There was a widow in one house and a widower in the other and they got married and had twenty-six kids between the two of them. They were a glutton for punishment! Can you imagine the daddy staying in that house and trying to do anything? So what the men did, they adjourned to stand outside or sit outside and they were called 'corner boys'. Oh, God, big men, *adults*. And over at that corner they'd be singing away. And the women'd be there too and they might sell fruit or periwinkles and they'd have a chat. But the poorer people around here, they had literally *nothing*. At the pawn offices sometimes they wouldn't have the suits to put in and they'd wrap up newspapers or something else. Could be *anything* in it. In fact, there was one woman and she put a dead cat in it. Wrapped it up. That's the only thing she could roll up and put in. But she got the money.

"Saturday was our busiest day. We could have 400 or 500 customers. Mostly women. No such thing as fridges or freezers and people would have to use their meat the same day. Ah, sure, most of them cooked on an open grate. And there was no trimming the fat. None *whatsoever*. They wouldn't *take* lean meat in those days. They'd think it was poor and it wasn't healthy . . . wouldn't touch it. See, my theory about fat in the olden days was that we were all nabbies. A nabby is a working man, a man that works on shovels or hard work, and the women had to wash and scrub and kids had to walk to school in the wet and cold and miserable. Now with all that it meant that people used up a terrible lot more energy. And there was no way of heating yourself. The only heating you had was fire. So, *fat*, basically speaking, is heat-giving. That's why people ate fat I reckon.

"Tenement people, they were the *grandest* neighbours in the world. Very decent, very hard-working and very charitable. And some of those tenement houses were called the 'coffin boxes'—it was *reeking* with TB. The *finest* of young lads and girls and in about twelve months they were gone! It was terrible. Big families they had and if, say, the father died or the mother died the first thing that would happen after the funeral, they'd adjourn to the local pub. And the women would get together and they'd say, 'Now, Maggie, what are we going to do? Poor Lizzy has gone.' And one woman would say, 'Well, look, an extra mouth in my house never did any harm, I'll take one (child).' And they would *distribute* them children around the locals. To keep them together. That's right. Rear them up until such time that they were old enough to go back to the father to take over. The people were lovely.

"Now my father was down on O'Connell Street on his bicycle during the troubled times and one of the dangers in years gone by would be if you were stuck in the tram tracks. When the wheel of the bicycle went in it was the same as putting on the brake and *straight over* the handlebars! Anyway, daddy came along and went over and was knocked unconscious in the road. Now one of the oldest neighbours around here, he was coming along with a horse and cart with a load of pigs, young ones. And when he saw daddy on the road he let the pigs out on O'Connell Street and lifted daddy up and put him into the thing and brought him up to the hospital. Put the pigs out and put daddy in! That's the kind of neighbours we had here."

PEGGY PIGOTT—AGE 65

She devoted her life to teaching poor children in the red brick Victorian Rutland Street School. Every morning her children would straggle in from the surrounding tenements, their "tummies empty and all raggedy". She understood that their home environment, poor diet, and illnesses made schoolwork difficult. And she came to realise that most had no hope of ever getting out of the tenement slums. Her duties went far beyond just teaching—she was a surrogate parent, counsellor, confessor and friend. Many other teachers departed in frustration but she stayed the course. In retrospect, it was a richly rewarding life.

"I started in Rutland Street School in 1947 out of Trinity College—and stayed for forty years. It was a National School built in 1912. A very tall red brick building with big rooms and wood panelled stairs. I wasn't familiar with that part of Dublin at all, really. Oh, it was all considered slum tenement area—Summerhill, Gardiner Street, Sean McDermott Street, Gloucester Diamond. But I think I had some sort of *feeling* for those people there . . . it developed afterwards that I had a great feeling for them,. They *depended* on teachers so much and looked on you as a surrogate parent really. I taught children from about eight to fourteen and a lot of them would come without anything in their tummies in the morning because they were so poor, and all raggedy. I taught sixty children and I was *unleashed* into this. And I was only nineteen. And, you know, teachers to them were *older* people. They hadn't had a new teacher for years and they queued up to look at me. One child said, 'Ah, you could be our *sister!*'

"You had to think what conditions they had. Twelve, thirteen, fourteen children in families all sleeping together in a bed, if they *had* a bed. The diet and nutrition, it was hopeless. Tea and bread and maybe porridge. Some would come to school without a breakfast. They had open fires and they lived on coddle or cheap cuts of meat that they would stew. They'd look pale and small and they'd be delicate. They got a lot of illnesses—flues, colds, sore throats. And consumption at that time was rampant in certain places. And they were all raggedy. They were *all* needy. In the old days Cumberland Street market was a *Godsend* for the people because it was all tuggers and clothing piled up and you could get something for very little. And they'd jeer each other, the children . . . 'You got that from the tuggers.' Then there was a thing called 'police clothes' and they'd be jeered, '*You* got the police clothes.' Oh, yes. And raggedy shoes. When the shoes would be very bad, the soles, they cut a Player's cigarette box and put that on the soles. I remember a past pupil coming back and telling me that, 'Oh, we were very poor and my father used to put this cigarette box in the soles of my shoes' and she said that she was *ashamed of her life* going up to Holy Communion because she'd kneel down and they'd see this.

"Tenements were let out in rooms and the toilet was downstairs and outside and they had to go down to the yard for water. They had no hot water. They were always very smelly . . . very smelly. It wasn't that they were unhygienic but they were the 'great unwashed'. That's a hard thing to complain about. It was very hard to wash yourself in those conditions and you had to tread very carefully because they were very *proud* people. If their hands were dirty you could get them to go to the washroom to wash them. You could do *that*. But dirty heads was another thing. Their heads were terrible. Hair very dirty, nits and all. You'd send for the parents and they'd bring them to the chemist to get something put on their hair that would kill the nits. Then a kid would shake her head and they'd all fall down on the desk behind her and the desk would be *white*. And the Corporation doctor used to examine the children in the school and there were various injections they'd get. And on the day of the injections it was *murder*! First of all, there was a card that the parents had to sign, a consent card, and some of them would just put an 'X', they couldn't write. But we'd *never* tell the children when the day of the injections was happening because they'd all be mitching. And there'd be lines of kids all *roaring*.

"Their homes were noisy and there were no books at home. And the parents probably weren't able to read very well. Education was something they had to get, it was compulsory. Very many of them—*most* of them—came to school just because they had to. And their attention span was very short . . . their diet, you see. And behavioural problems were there all the time. I used to give what I called 'home treatment', what you'd get at home if you were bold, like a clap on the hands. In those early days they didn't appreciate or value education. It didn't *matter*. You know, to be able to read and write in those days never got them a job! Girls got sewing jobs and there was nothing open for boys beyond being messenger boys. Some sold papers. They had nothing to come to school for really. See, they were in the tenements and there was *no hope* of getting out of the tenements. They had *no* ambition beyond getting a little job and then getting married. They accepted their lot. They were all in the same boat. They didn't look to tomorrow or to next week, just this day. They stayed in school until age fourteen but if they could get away with it they'd leave at ten, leave for one reason or another.

"The family was very powerful, you know, very comforting. And the extended family with the grannies. The granny was the matriarch. She minded the children and told everybody what to do. She was very powerful and *much loved*. The fathers never worked. Never worked. Whatever income was coming in was gained by the mothers. Mothers did factory work and did sewing and making rosary beads down at Mitchell's rosary bead factory in Marlborough Street. Many women would be charwomen and maids, daily help. See, the older sisters were always minding the babies and couldn't come to school. *Always* minding babies. The eldest, they had a great sense of responsibility because the mothers were out working. It wasn't really mitching because they *had* to stay home and mind children. You'd see them out and they'd have three or four babies wheeling them and minding them. But their fathers were *never* there. And sometimes they'd come in drunk and beating up everybody and all that. But the women were *super* women, the way they'd protect their children. They were like mother hens the way they'd protect their chicks. And the mothers with drunken husbands going off and leaving them and that sort of thing. They did come to confide in us. They'd come and tell their stories. And we were there, I think for that purpose, to *listen* to them . . . because they hadn't many people to listen to them. And I'd lend them about four pence for the pictures.

"When they'd reach sixth class we used to give them some sort of, you know, sex education. Well, not 'sex education' but we'd tell them where babies came from. But that was as far as it would go. Oh, they had *no* knowledge at all. Now with unwed mothers, that's where the grannies came in. See, a girl had a baby and her mother minded the baby. So that you wouldn't know *whose child* the baby was. And there was never any discrimination between children that were born out of wedlock. Now a little black child appeared in the school, she was coloured. A woman came in and she had this little black child, her grandchild, and she explained the black child to me by saying, 'T'was a little mistake of me daughter's.' Oh, she was lovely. Black, black hair and she was a lovely child. And now this will tell you how naïve I was when I went there first because I *couldn't* get over hearing the Dublin accent coming out of this child. And I remember when she was making her First Communion and they *queued* up to see her because they knew she'd be beautiful in white . . . that she'd be different. Oh, no discrimination, they loved her.

"The teacher, *always* throughout my career there, was a very important person in their lives. They looked on you as a surrogate parent, a confessor you 'gave out' to them, you corrected them, you did an awful lot for them. Teaching was the *last* thing you did there. I remember they said to me, 'You live in a gorgeous, respectable house with a closed front door!' They presumed (that) because, see, teachers were middle-class. No resentment, just putting two and two together. They probably *pitied* me that my front door was closed because there was a great camaraderie there and they were great for helping each other. They *knew* that they were disadvantaged, that they were underprivileged, because they were *told* that by the social workers or maybe the press. I suppose they felt a certain stigma, alright, coming from the tenements—if they came into contact with middle-class people. But they were very self-contained. They *didn't know* Dublin beyond their own environment. And they were all married around, like somebody in Foley Street was married and had a flat in Sean McDermott Street. See, they were all *interwoven*. So there was a lot of community . . . company. They had *great* community, great fun, great humour. They had a *dignity* and a pride.

"It was hard . . . very, very hard, really. Some teachers didn't like it, didn't last there. But others, like me, couldn't *leave* it. I *understood* them. Oh, many times I'd get discouraged but I had the facility to forget about it when I'd go home and start each day new. They *depended* on you so much, they really did. You were *everything* to them, you sorted out *all* sorts of problems. A motto in our staff room sums up: 'We, the unwilling, led by the unknowing, are doing the impossible for so long and with so little we are now qualified to do anything with nothing.' But it was rewarding there and I had a great feeling for them. When I was retiring there was a Mass and presentations and all and I was replying and I said that one day I was going down Rutland Street and I saw a dog in front of me and I said to myself, 'That's Toby Daly—I know every dog and "divil" in this community after my forty years.' I did!"

MARY CHANEY—AGE 84

"God be with the tenement houses", Mary likes to say. Her family was expelled from their room during the Rebellion when violent blasts from the big guns shook the brittle, decrepit tenements and threatened to bring them tumbling down. At age fourteen she went into a shirt factory for five shillings a week. On weekends she and her pals would walk Grafton Street to watch the "style and grandeur" of the posh set parading up and down. But there was no resentment as she accepted her social position without question. Despite the early hardships, Mary feels that she had a rich childhood, far more memorable than the spoiled children of the present day.

"You'll often hear people say now, 'God be with the tenement houses.' Everybody was generous to one another. Doors was always open, no locks nor keys nor bolts. No robberies or nothing in the tenements. And you'd know every foot that went up the tenement stairs. Everybody was generous to one another. Knockabouts would come into the halls and sleep on the stairs and all the tenants would bring them out a cup of tea in the morning.

"But it was a hard life, alright. We lived from day to day. All only tenements around us on Hammond Lane and all my family worked in the Corporation market, *every one* of them. See, the three markets is together, the Corporation, the Daisy, and the fish market. My father was only a labourer carrying sacks of potatoes in and out. My mother had ten of us and we slept on straw, not springs. Running around in our bare feet and go to the pipe in the yard to wash our feet. Every Saturday night we had to bring the water up from the yard and we had a big galvanised sink and we'd be each washed in turn. We were kept very clean and tidy. We used to have pots of stews and soups and on a Sunday when you'd come back from going to Communion me father'd have a whole lot of cups around the table with senna (purgative) medicine and the *minute* you'd come in you'd have to take that. It was a laxative, made like tea. We used to *dread* that. Once a week, on Sunday. Then we'd get tea and bread and butter. Then you'd be on an excursion for the day and our outing was to the *toilet* all day. Toilet parade!

"Our mothers, they had *no* social life at all. They never went to the pictures, never went to *any* place. Mothers could sit and chat, that's all they had. And they used to go to the rosary *every* night and when they'd come out they might stand at the corner and have a chat before they'd go in. A hard life. Never a holiday, had to be there with their families all the time. Me mother'd be up about seven, get us all ready for school. She used to get police clothes for us and they'd be stamped so the pawns wouldn't take them. But the pawns were the best neighbours going. She'd make up a bundle and go down and get a shilling. This woman, Big Maggie, her husband was a tough fella and she used to pawn his shoes every Monday morning and release them for Saturday because he used to be all done up on a Sunday. But he found out that she was pawning them. So she used to put a *brick* in the box and he'd (the pawnbroker) just say, 'A pound for Maggie.' Now there was another woman around our way—and this is as sure as God I'm talking—and she used to do a desperate thing. Well, you know when a woman or a man died they'd put pennies on their eyes for to keep them shut? Well, she used to go up to St Kevin's Hospital and she'd go and knock off all the pennies off all the corpses' eyes—to *go to the pictures*! The pennies off their eyes cause they'd die with their eyes open. They were dead now . . . when she'd take the pennies. They were the good old days.

"Oh, but the Black and Tans were *buggers*. They were young men with tam o'shanters on and their rifles on their shoulders. There was a blackout and you used to have to put a big black shawl over your windows, lights out, and if you were caught putting your head outside they'd be on you. And they used to do *desperate* things . . . oh, for *God's sake*. They shot a lovely big dog because he was barking. Now when the Rebellion was on and they were fighting at the Four Courts they had an eighteen-pounder (gun) that shook all the houses. Shook the foundations. We lost everything. We'd *nothing*. All our cups and plates blown to *bits*. See, the concussions of the guns and all. It was all gone. *Nothing*! We had one chair, a broken chair. And we couldn't go back to them houses because they weren't fit for habitation. So the British soldiers came in and told us that we *had* to get out, that we were in danger that the houses might collapse. Well, we couldn't come out of the front of the tenements because we'd be in the direct firing line. So the men dug a hole through the wall in the rear yard and we had to get out through that into the next yard. *Hours* we were waiting for the men to dig the holes through the big brick walls to get us out, away from the firing. And we were only young and our mothers holding on to us. All had to get out, one after another, and we got into Mary's Lane and then scattered. Oh, we were frightened, of course we were. We lost our sister for a week. All up Beresford Street there was men lying on the road for a whole week when the Rebellion was on. There was a woman shot in Greek Street. She was shot coming out of her tenement house to get water and they couldn't drag her in for a couple of days. Oh, we were *nearly dead* . . . the shooting and all. I don't know how we're alive *at all*.

"We went into a factory at fourteen making shirts. We had to serve four years (apprenticeship) for our trade. We were at sewing all our life. Started at five shillings a week. We used to give that to our mother and maybe get sixpence back. But you could go into the pictures for a penny then. Very little made us happy. And you'd walk all about, all around the town. Grafton Street was real posh. We used to go up and look at all the styles of the nobs, people that was in the money, cause it was a famous street. We'd wear just ordinary clothes. We never used to mind them . . . but you'd feel that you were shabby with all the style and grandeur coming down and they used to be in carriages then. And for the 1932 (Eucharistic) Congress every street in the city of Dublin was done up. That was the *loveliest* summer we ever had. We were in Beresford Street then and we were sewing for weeks and weeks to make buntings, all different colours, for on the tenement buildings all around. Everywhere was done up. Hall doors done up in frills and draped with paper, paint the railings and steps, put up window curtains and holy pictures. Men and women and kids and all done that, anyone that could hold the brush. Not the landlords, not at all!

"Then during the war years you had the ration cards. Got only a half ounce of tea per person and an ounce of butter per week and you'd have to get that marked on your ration card. Got it done in Talbot Street. So people'd get ordinary carrots and boil them and make tea. It was *awful*. And we used to have shell cocoa then. We burned turf during the war years and many a times it was wet turf. We used to have to go for the turf ourselves to the depots, bring it back in hand carts or prams. Big, high prams that you could fit three or four children into, two at the top and two at the bottom. Anything heavy you'd bring the pram with you to bring it back. There was a hundred and one things you could do with a pram. So we'd bring the turf back and leave it out to dry in the open air. And during the war we got the gas masks. We never had to wear them, thank God. It was for emergency, if there was an air raid or anything. We got them after the bomb dropping on the North Strand. It was like a big snout thing. We used to laugh at them. You couldn't pawn them—Government property!

"It was a hard life, alright, but we were happy just the same. Very little made us happy. Any old person you talk to will tell you the same. We'd nothing, but we'd a good childhood. My grandson now, he's twenty-five, and he comes in and says he needs so much for the disco tonight and £5 for the pictures and I say, 'What? We used to go for a penny or fourpence.' Says I, 'When you come to my age *what* have you to talk about? You've no childhood!' We had a *lovely* childhood. Very, very little . . . *nothing* . . . but a *lovely* childhood. The children today, they've *no* childhood. We can go back, but what can they go back to, they've nothing. We hadn't much but we had peace . . . we were happy."

FATHER MICHAEL REIDY—AGE 76

He joined the St Vincent de Paul Society nearly sixty years ago and has spent his life caring for the poor. In the 1930s he found raw poverty, serious malnutrition and TB in the tenement houses he visited. He could only help the poor to "survive". The mothers and grannies, he remembers, were heroines for their caring and sacrifices. He presently resides at Belvedere College.

"I've been a member of the Vincent de Paul Society from 1933. I was a boy of fifteen in the Junior Conference of the Society. The inner-city was unknown to me until I joined. Most of the work was visitation of the poor around Foley Street, Gloucester Diamond, the Liberties, Wolfe Tone Street, where most of the poverty would be at that time. The Monto and prostitution was ending and employment prospects were very few. See, the thirties was a time of depression in Dublin and men used to get casual employment on the docks and as carters with a horse and cart. They hadn't much education and they just took whatever came their way. Women worked in sewing factories and did cleaning and that. You'd see tremendous poverty.

"My first exposure . . . I remember going into those houses and a baby had just been born. There was the mother with her baby in her bed in the one room . . . it just struck me. It was dreadfully depressing conditions to live in. Oh, sanitation was very poor because there was only one toilet and a bath was unheard of. And large families. I saw eighteen or nineteen children in a family and some people lived in the basements of a slum area and they were really bad conditions. They were damp, they were dank and you had a light on for most of the day. Bread and tea would be the basic diet and problems with ill health, and TB was rampant at that time . . . really depressing.

"Families contacted us. Letters would come from the father and mother saying they wanted a visit. Sometimes you would hear of cases of people who were in really bad need, then you would visit them. We went on a Tuesday and a Friday to visit homes. We walked right into it, walk in and sit down, chat. You'd see tremendous poverty but some of them had beautiful little homes, even if they were only one room. Always a statue of the Sacred Heart, of

Our Lady, and an altar in the room and the Sacred Heart lamp. Everyone had that. At first when you'd visit them they were quiet. We'd ask how they were getting by, what their health was like. Food and clothing were the needs—to help them to *survive*. We used to give out vouchers, a little card, for food and clothes. And a lot of people with funeral expenses, they were helped by the Society. And there were penny dinners at the parish on Gardiner Street. And the penny, it was just to keep up their independence, the fact that they weren't getting it *free*. They'd get stews and soups and a mug of tea and bread. I remember one case where a couple were suffering from malnutrition but they were too *proud* and would say, 'I don't like taking charity.' But afterwards it was accepted. We got a wonderful camaraderie with these people. Without a shadow of a doubt, many of these families would have gone under without the help of the Society.

"People living in the slums, they were great neighbours. These people, they *helped* each other. The saying was, 'You can live without your relations but you can't live without your neighbours.' The poor woman next door, they sent her in her dinner. And women were heroines, they struggled on day after day in conditions of just living in one room and washing, cleaning, cooking. The grannies were tremendous because of the maturity and wisdom which was beyond what the others had and they had a very steadying influence on the family. But the women hadn't got much relaxation, just a bit of chat. Cause there was no Bingo in those days. They sat outside the tenements to have a chat. And they never got a holiday—their holiday was to go out to Sandymount or Dollymount and they'd walk out and get the bus back then. And then there was a lot of problem with alcoholism (husbands) and it was the mother that would keep the family together. They had resilience and spirit . . . such a marvellous spirit. The mothers, they were heroines."

ELLEN PRESTON—AGE 65

She is the stereotypical Dublin street dealer hawking her goods "through streets broad and narrow". Born in Gardiner's Lane into a family of street traders going back more than a century, she began selling fruit on Parnell Street as a child. At age nineteen she married, began having children, and decided to set off on her own with a rickety pram to sell on Henry Street. After forty-five years she takes pride in having raised her twelve children from the street, out in rain and snow and always returning to her pitch only days after giving birth. As she simply puts it, "You had to do it".

"The street is what we were all reared out of. Street trading goes well back in my family, over a hundred years. My mother had fourteen of us and times were hard then . . . very, very poor. There was no work for the men and the women traders they held the families together. They were the whole upkeep because they *had* to go out. Me mother and grandmother sold on

Parnell Street, sold vegetables and fruit and fish. Oh, there was loads of street traders. They wore shawls then and with children in their arms. And had large families. There was Mrs Boyle, she had seventeen. In them times you had *nothing* at all. It was the women who really made it. I used to be out selling fruit and potatoes and flowers on Parnell Street when I was about twelve years of age, one had to get out and try to help.

"I got married when I was nineteen and then the children started coming along—I've twelve children. Children started coming along and things was very hard. Parnell Street was starting to die out and there was nothing down there any more. So after two or three kids I said to meself, 'I'll just go off by meself and sell off me pram.' On a Monday I just went and got me pram and set out on my own and went to Henry Street and I've been there ever since. Selling fruit and flowers. Every day I pushed me pram, *every day*. Just push your pram on the road in the traffic, and there was horses and cars. Just keep walking. People knows us and where we're going with our prams. And we used to have to push the prams over the cobblestones and it was really very hard it was. But it was a living and we reared our families. See, if you got five shillings from the pram in them days that'd get you loads of bread and butter and milk. But you were just making ends meet.

"Anybody out on Moore Street or Henry Street, they all work very hard. All out in hail, rain, frost and snow. They earn money and look after their families, help their children. When it'd be cold I'd have a coat and a scarf and you'd just be doing this (rubbing) all the time with your hands for to keep the heat in them. And buy a cup of tea and hold your hands over the cup to keep the heat in your hands. Some days was miserable. I often came home with the rain beating off me. You'd come home and you'd be drowned. But you *had* to do it. Five shillings, that was a *great* day for me, a few bob in your pocket to feed your family. God was good to me and I was never sick. We got through. Only when I was in the hospital having my babies, that's all. One day I went out to sell and it was snowing and I remember the snow getting into me shoes and I was expecting one of the babies at the time and I brought me little parcel with me and I went straight to the hospital and had me baby. And I was out on the street again then in a week.

"I used to go out on the street, leave the street about five, come home and do all the evening meals for the whole lot of them. I didn't get away from the cooking till nine at night. Then I'd clean up and do the washing and do all me housework and fall into the bed. And I'd be up for seven o'clock Mass next morning. It was very rough. You just got used to it. I always made sure they had a good meal and got dressed and had a clean bed. I remember once, when I was about thirty-six, and I was brought into court for trading (without a licence). There was this judge and I went up in front of him and he said to me, 'How many children have you got?' And I had nine at the time. So he said, 'I'll only fine you half a crown. Just go home and make sure you keep them in school.' I never did let them run the street. See, I tried to keep them in school as long as I could, that's why I really went out selling."

Thomas Lyng—Age 70

In the vernacular of the tenement days the pawnshop was the "people's bank" and he was the "uncle". He began his apprenticeship behind the counter at age fourteen. In those days there were still nearly fifty pawnshops in Dublin. The local pawn literally saved the poor from hunger and eviction. Though pawn days were absolute chaos, they were also a great social occasion for the local womenfolk. Proud that he always treated customers with dignity, he believes that the pawnshop was an indispensable institution in the city's history. Today he is the manager of Carthy's pawnshop on Marlborough Street.

"In 1938 when I came into the business there were around fifty pawnshops in the city. There were two on this street. Most of the people were living in tenement houses in Dublin and things were at a very low level with regard to living conditions. They were hardship cases at that time. For a lot of them it was mishandling of the little that they had, because the husbands used to drink a lot and the women had to stay home and fend for the family. It meant that the women had to do all the running to the pawn office and accumulating any few bob they could get.

"A pawnbroker would take in almost anything then. It was always called the 'people's bank' here in Dublin because the ordinary person could come in and get a few shillings just like that, just by taking off their coat or anything. There was a tremendous competitiveness between certain pawnbrokers in Dublin for business. They'd all have their own customers and if one of the customers brought in a ticket from another office (by mistake) they'd really give him a great telling-off for going to another office. And a funny thing, nearly all the pawnbrokers were Catholics. There were no Jews in it at all hardly. And nearly all pawn offices were handed down to these people from their fathers. Very rarely did you see a pawnbroking establishment up for sale, very rarely.

"In the old days it was really a weekly business—in on Monday and out on Saturday. On a Monday morning they opened at eight and worked all day until six. Absolutely loaded with customers. Now when I went into it in the thirties I was just fourteen and in short pants. The place was like going into hell, really . . . packed from morning to night with women. All women wearing their shawls and their petticoats. Very rare to see a man in the place. When the men would come in they'd be shy of coming in among the women and so we had a sign for 'men only' and they could go off on their own and pawn whatever they had. Women were coming in with bundles of clothes and shoes and old suits and wearing apparel and pawning all kinds of sheets and bed clothing. There was nothing new and all that was taken in was old and *smelled* and the sheets and clothes would have fleas and everything in them. They just threw their clothes on the counter and the pawnbroker would just have to try and sort it out and take in whatever he could. And everything would be in *chaos*. It would be pretty rough, you know, but you wouldn't mind at the time because you were young and glad to be working.

"Every pawnbroker was filled to the very top of the house, every room packed with clothing of all descriptions. Even open razors, they used to pawn those for sixpence. See, most people were looking for the last penny. And the pawnbroker was dependent on the interest more that anything else. There were articles being pawned that weren't worth a quarter of what they were being pawned for . . . old shoes, suits full of holes and threadbare. But they'd still get the money on them every week because they knew the customer and they knew that it would have to be taken out at the end of the week. Sometimes they would try and cut the price down a little bit and there would generally be a bit of a squabble over that. I remember taking in shoes and they would be so worn that the best part of them would be the laces. People didn't have the money to buy new shoes then. I remember a man pawning his shoes and walking out into the street in his bare feet!

"We had queues going out into the street. And they'd be laughing and joking and that kind of thing. Women were very light-hearted about the whole proceedings in a pawn office. There'd be a great feeling of solidarity among them because they'd be all in the one boat. And there looking for money, you see. Nearly all the people went to one particular pawn office that was near them and you'd know them all by their names. They were used to being with the man behind the counter and most of the managers of pawn offices were all very easy-going, had a jolly kind of air so that they would be able to have a great rapport with the customer. Always a great sense of fun in the whole proceedings. A pawn office was never as strict as you'd get in other businesses. The man behind the counter who would be taking the property from the customer would always be having a great chat with them and a great sense of humour and this constant joking. That's what made it, I suppose, so easy to work in. I think pawnbrokers should be remembered as playing a very important role in the social life of the city, very active in promoting good relationships with people in need . . . with dignity."

Una Shaw—Age 61

She grew up on Rutland Street in the midst of the tenement world. Her school pals were tenement children and she developed a keen insight to the social and economic problems of poor families. She is especially sensitive to the plight of tenement women, their self-sacrificing nature, abuse by hard husbands, and the saving role of religion in their daily lives. All the long-suffering women she knew were "saints".

"There was terrible poverty, *dreadful* poverty. Oh, I saw it myself because my classmates lived in tenement houses in Lower Gardiner Street and when I'd go up to play with them that's what I'd see. Now we weren't an awful lot better because for many years my father didn't work and then he got a job as a porter in the bank. But they had terrible poverty. Very large families, anything from ten to twelve in one room. Little or no furniture and mattresses on the floor. Always the smell of cooking food permeated all through the tenement house and they used to lash Jeyes Fluid around the place. Terrible.

"They were very old houses and falling apart at the seams and landlords just did the *minimum* of what they had to do. Most landlords kept their houses just one jump ahead of the law. They didn't bother to fix them, didn't even keep them in reasonable order. Like the landlord was a law unto himself. He owned the house and the Corporation would go down (to inspect) but that's as far as they'd go. They never would actually take any action against him and say, 'We're giving you so many days and if you don't do that now you're going to court.' They used to get away with absolute murder. People didn't complain because they couldn't afford to pay any more. And once you'd see the furniture out in front of the house you'd know then there was an eviction. That happened. You'd see them outside. Usually it was because they'd be married to a man who drank everything and left them short. They didn't have the money. The only thing the neighbours could do was take the children in and feed them, look after them. But they couldn't help them with money.

"Money was *perpetually* tight here. There wasn't an awful lot of work for women in those days. A few dressmakers and they did that by hand, couldn't afford a machine. So women here did a lot of cleaning at the big houses like Merrion Square, Fitzwilliam Square, Blackrock. And those poor women they'd have to leave early in the morning and pay their own fare out and some would only be able to pay half their way and walk the rest. And it wouldn't be just to clean the house, they'd be expected to do the washing, ironing, the polishing—everything. Exploited . . . *absolutely*. Those poor women. And they *had* to do it. With such a big family you had to have the money. And the men in those days they'd collect the 'assistance' as it was called and they drank more than they do today and they might pop off over to the pub and come back with half of it gone. And he wasn't unduly worried about that either. So she'd have to make up the balance. And they weren't complaining, they kind of accepted it all as 'What can I do about it?' There's women in this parish and I'm quite sure they're saints in Heaven for the life they had.

"And in those days if the mother was getting a rough time of it (abuse from husband) you usually didn't interfere. People, they'd have sympathy but they didn't go and butt in—because you might end up with a fat lip too! Now there was two pubs on the corner of the street up there and every Saturday night there was a row. Too much drink taken. If they had a few jars there'd be insults traded and they'd circle and circle and never land a blow. Never actually hit one another. I don't think some were even able to see their opponent! And sometimes the wives would be sent for . . . 'Your husband's in a row.' And sometimes then the women'd start trading insults and it got to hair pulling. But the insults, they were fierce. Like they'd say, 'She has a mouth like a Malahide cod!' Or, 'She has a face like a vaccinated pig's cheek!' They were insults that were made up. And in those days dental hygiene wasn't very good and, of course, the teeth began to be discoloured and they'd say, 'Oh, look at her, if she had a white tooth she'd have a billiard set,' because they'd be green, brown. Things like that would come out.

"Very large families and some women they'd have one year in and year out. You'd often see pregnant women and they'd have to carry a baby in one arm and go all the way down to the yard to get the water. And if they lived upstairs they'd have to pull prams the *whole way* up. The pregnant mother would be doing it. And she'd have a baby and then she was pregnant again! I don't know how they put up with it. As a child I'd hear somebody say, 'How many children do you have?' 'Oh, I have three or four.' 'Oh, you don't love your husband.' *That's* what they'd come out with. It was considered that if you had ten or twelve children that you loved your husband. They just took it as the natural order of things. It wasn't a case of worrying, you know, how you were going to *manage*—you were pregnant and that was it! 'Ah, sure, God will provide.' They'd have ten children and maybe not able to cope with what's going on and she'd say (in Confession), 'Father, look, I don't want any more children, I really don't, but what am I going to do?' And the priest would say, 'Man is weak, man is very weak, so you have to do your duty.' *Always* the same thing they were told—'Do your duty!' The man dominated, *always*. Even though she'd be running the whole home. His word was *absolute* law.

"The children were very undernourished and very thin, *so undersized*. Their little legs were like matchsticks. You'd see boys out there playing football and the boots would be huge in comparison to their little legs, out of proportion. And a lot of children in those days suffered rickets and were bow-legged. We thought they were born that way but they weren't, it was malnutrition. They hadn't got the vitamins. But they were a *very hardy* little bunch. Usually the staple diet was potatoes and dry bread and margarine and dripping. If they had the money they'd go over to the butcher's shop and get the fatty pieces with little or no meat on it for stews. And there were food kitchens run by the Sisters of Charity and you'd see people going along with their little tins with maybe a bit of stew or rice. A *lot* of them in this area lived on that.

"An awful lot of infant mortality in those days. It was the diet and then the mothers themselves were often weak and tired and worn out in childbearing and sometimes the child just didn't survive. And no matter what was wrong with the children they seemed to have a better insight to them than doctors. I seen children and the doctor'd say, 'She's very ill, she won't live another week, we can't do anything,' and the mother would say, 'I'll look after her.' The mother would *never give up* . . . she'd *never* give up on a child. She'd work on that child and that child would grow up to be a healthy child. They relied on home cures. I often wondered was it just their *faith* in it? I mean, they'd *really believe* that it *was* doing them some good and they'd start to pull around and start to fight what was bothering them and they'd get better. But sometimes the child just didn't survive. But they accepted it all . . . 'Oh, it's

God's will.' It *wasn't* God's will, but that's the way they'd say it. See, religion was their mainstay. If everything else was gone, if you'd nothing else, that was the only thing they had when they were down and out. Just even to sit in a quiet church can take an awful lot off your mind.

"Women were the providers, it was *always* the women. The fathers were there but they seemed *invisible*. The women were the mainstay, they were everything. They were mother, father, counsellor, doctor . . . everything. An awful lot of saints. And once the mother was gone the home was never the same again. *Never* the same. That place was never filled. And if it was a young woman—and some of them would die in childbirth—there might be five or six or seven children left behind them and it would fall onto the eldest girl. She would never go to work and maybe never get married. She took the mother's place, that was the accepted thing to do. Because before the mother died she was the mother's helper. Mothers and (eldest) daughters were very, very close. They were more like sisters than mother and daughter. So she took the mother's place and she'd stay with them up until the time they grew up, maybe sacrifice her life to look after them. And then, you know, the father *leaned* on that daughter. And carried on his merry way."

CON FOLEY—AGE 75

His father opened the chemist shop on Parnell Street in 1909 and at age sixteen Con began his apprenticeship under his tutelage. The surrounding tenements were ravaged by sickness and disease and the local chemist was regarded as the man who could treat almost any human ailment. As he puts it, "survival of the fittest" was the rule in the tenements—and too many did not survive. After sixty years of treating the poor he still spends a few hours each week behind the old counter peering out his front window at the few remaining women dealers on Parnell Street.

"My father opened the shop on Parnell Street after he qualified in pharmacy in 1909. There were ten in the family and we all lived above the shop. Now across from us was the Blue Lion pub where O'Casey wrote *The Plough and the Stars*, and he was looking over at our place when he was writing it. I started my apprenticeship at sixteen under my father. There were 40,000 in the parish then, in that area. Oh, a *huge* number of people in tenements on Cumberland Street and Gloucester Street and Parnell Street. You could have sixty or seventy in a house. And incomes were so small that they couldn't afford to go to a doctor and hence the concept that the local chemist was naturally able to help people. The local chemist was the jack of all trades in medicine.

"Sanitation was very bad in tenements. With sixty or seventy in a house all using one toilet in the yard, toilets would get choked and a lot of sickness would have developed from that. The absentee landlords had a physically big man who collected (rent), like an ex-policeman, and he just ignored anything they said so long as he collected a half a crown a week. There was no law to make landlords do anything and the places were appalling. Rat-infested and a *huge* amount of flies around at that time and they were potent germ carriers—we should have been wiped out long ago! A lot of vermin around and it was a problem keeping the children's heads clean. Kids were generally sent down and got one of these real scalped haircuts. Sores on the face and rashes were much commoner because hygiene wasn't a big thing. We used to make up our own ointments for people with rashes and things. People'd come in with a baby Power's bottle and we'd make up medicine for two pence, that was standard.

"Now we had an epidemic of scabies years back. It's an old verminous thing that gets into the skin and is *frightfully* irritating and itchy. And fellas were coming in telling me that they used *paraffin oil* on it. That's what they did years ago. It was like, 'It'll burn the skin off me but it'll get rid of this thing as well!' And TB was a very big thing in the city at that time, consumption. Because of all the bad housing and poor food, and possibly there was an hereditary trait for generations. Even the hospitals we had for tuberculosis at that time, there wasn't much treatment. And then they had a *ridiculous* idea about tuberculosis that it was a sort of *personal slur* on the family, that maybe you had incest or something in the family. See, when you got tuberculosis they got *terrible* looking, lost weight and they were put into a back room and they were in decline. And people knew that it was contagious. Oh, a social stigma.

"When I was starting out it struck me about the malnutrition, just very poor feeding. I'd observe young children coming in, *tiny* things, that were sent over for messages. And you'd see stone bruises because they'd run through the streets and they'd no boots on them at all. And at that time there was all horse traffic and the droppings were all over the roads and they'd get gangrene if they had a cut on the foot because the horse's droppings is full of gangrene. Some of them lost limbs like that. Another noticeable thing you'd see was rheuma-toid arthritis. Working was almost all manual and the hands were *terribly* deformed, terribly gnarled . . . stiff nearly. It was nearly hereditary in some areas. And teeth were very bad. People used salt and soot for their teeth. They'd use their fingers or maybe use a cloth. Oh, indeed it worked very well. Dentists were virtually non-existent. If a person had a reasonably easy tooth he'd maybe nick it out. And some of the men (chemists) in my father's time would have just pulled them out. See, chemists were just sort of *expected* to be pretty competent.

"Saturday was the busiest day. In my father's time we were open till half eleven. See, the worker wasn't paid until it literally got dark on Saturday and by the time he got home and gave his wife a few shillings and she could come out to get what she wanted, well, you *had* to be there. All the shops in that area were open till that time. Now the street traders would all breast feed the babies in the street years ago and on Parnell Street there were about twelve or four-teen public houses and on a Saturday night there were some awful sights.

Unfortunately they might be fond of the drink and you'd often get the children standing in the doors of the tenements or the doors of the public houses and it'd be raining and the parents might be inside drinking. And women would often come in and you'd see them with black eyes and obviously they'd been beaten. You know, he'd been drinking. I think that because they had so little food that a few drinks could upset them very easily. And there was a great expression then, a threat to the fellow, 'Hit me now with the child in me arms!' That was highly melodramatic.

"When you were older you realised that a lot of the women going into the public houses were prostitutes. One of the features of the police at the time— the DMP, Dublin Metropolitan Police—was that there would be a bunch of recruits that could come in there. Well, they would be *marched* down to a hospital known as the Locke Hospital. It was for syphilis and gonorrhoea. Well, these young recruits were marched down there with some senior inspectors and *shown* these cases. Because, you see, these young men at night would be out on the beat. Oh, that was the best example you were going to get."

MARGARET BYRNE—AGE 81

Today the area around Sarsfield Quay is dilapidated and disreputable. But three-quarters of a century ago it was a lovely neighbourhood in which to grow up. Country farmers, their carts laden with heaps of fresh vegetables, streamed by to Smithfield and Haymarket. But living next to the Royal Barracks also meant that she was in daily contact with British soldiers, many of whom were "buggers altogether". After Independence, the new Irish Army band would parade past her home every Sunday morning on their way to Mass in full colour with bagpipes blaring. It was a grand spectacle to behold. Later in the afternoon everyone would perch at their tenement windows to watch the crowds flowing past toward Phoenix Park in all their finery. Today Margaret and her husband live in a small house on Benburb Street but the regal bands and elegant crowds are long gone.

"I was born and reared on Sarsfield Quay in a typical tenement. Old houses and one toilet in the rear yard—people survived. There was eight of us and the eldest died and the youngest died, so there was six of us reared. My father was a butcher but he had to give that up when he had an operation. We hadn't much wages in those years and you just barely got through. No one had anything. Oh, but people had *pride*.

"Mr Judge, he was a hide and skin merchant, he owned the house, he was the landlord. He was nice. He had a beard. He'd shout up, 'The rent!' And I often heard me mother say, 'Oh, come up old buggy beard yourself, for God's sake, you're able to come up quicker than I can go down.' It was only four or five bob at that time. Oh, he was a good person, a good landlord.

"But then eventually another fella took over and the personal touch was gone. Oh, yes. They wanted to get more rent. And they raised the rent and

45 Engine Alley off Meath Street.

46 A group of tenement children in Blackpitts.

47 Children playing in yard of Morgan's Cottages. Note chickens in background. (RSAI)

48 Children playing in McGuinness's Court off Townsend Street. (RSAI)

49 Barefooted children playing games in Stirling Street in the Liberties.

50 Tenement children suffered high rates of disease and mortality.

51 Sisters of Charity breadline—note the barefooted boys.

52 Shawled woman fruit dealer doing a flourishing trade with the "Tommies".

53 Sisters of Charity breadline—note the separate lines for men and women.

54 A bread counter in Gardiner Street near Summerhill during the War of Independence.

55 A sick woman being helped along by a relative and St John Ambulance man who is carrying her child in his arms.

56 Procession of the Papal League during the Eucharistic Congress of 1932. This was a major event in the lives of tenement dwellers.

57 School Street school class of 1938. (Mairin Johnston)

58 Mary Casey, one of the last of the old Iveagh Market dealers.

59 Cumberland Street open market, or "The Hill", is a surviving relic of the hard tenement days.

60 One of the last "tuggers" in the Liberties.

61 Eighty-four year old Nanny Farrell, doyenne of the Daisy Market dealers.

62 Daisy Market dealer Kathleen Maguire beside her heaps of clothing.

63 Derelict and abandoned Winetavern Street, once one of the liveliest streets in Dublin.

64 Some of the last occupied tenements in Dublin along lower North Great George's Street, 1981.

65 Tattered tenement houses along North Great George's Street falling into ruin and eventual demolition, 1981.

66 Georgian buildings along North Great George's Street which had become wretched tenement houses but have now been beautifully restored and preserved.

took me mother to court for arrears. Now there was a law for the rich and a law for the poor. It *seemed* that way at that time. If you were poor then and brought to court *they* had a solicitor but you'd no solicitor. So you couldn't argue. Ah, money talks. And, see, there were evictions. Me mother always used to say, 'Pay your *rent*, you can *eat* on the street but you can't sleep on the street. You must have your roof.' Me father come out of the court and he couldn't talk he was that disgusted . . . a law for the rich and a law for the poor.

"But this neighbourhood was lovely, *really* it was. I'm telling you no lies now. And Benburb Street was a very lively street. It was a complete market street and the country people'd come in with their horse and cart and go into Smithfield or Haymarket for the sales. They all came up with their produce and kids looked forward to getting up on the hay and all. And we'd be playing ball in the streets and hopscotch and swinging around lamp-posts. And we went up to the Phoenix Park where the chestnuts would be growing on the tree and the boys would be throwing sticks and knocking them down. Boys would have a chestnut with a hole in the middle of it and put a string through it and you'd hold it up and someone'd hit it three times and if you broke his chestnut you won. It was called conkers. Oh, there was all kinds of ways of making conkers hard, to see which one would break last. Some of them used to steep them in something and dry them with the heat of the fire and that would harden them. It was a great sport and it cost *nothing*.

"And up in the park there was a ha'penny toss school and everyone was betting on heads and tails. About twenty men, maybe more. There'd be a ring and there'd be a little flat thing, like a ruler, and all the fellas would have their own special ones and the ha'pennies were shined up real bright. Shined up with ashes and real bright and they'd throw them up and there'd be maybe ten or twelve shillings put down and everyone'd be covering it. Throw them up till he got two heads or two tails. Ah, there'd be even pound notes and all down there. And there was always a lookout. See, they played in an open space where they could see them (police) coming. Cause they'd break it up.

"The Royal Barracks was there then and the 'Windy Wilts' as they called them—the Wiltshire Regiment—was there. They were buggers altogether. They were British soldiers but they were a regiment that had a bad name. I mean, they thought *nothing* of us Irish. One time a friend had left some guns with my mother to mind for them and she had them hid in the coal house under the stairs. And my father didn't know about it. And they knocked one night, the soldiers, and it was very, very cold and they were looking for a man and she knew the man very well but she wasn't going to say that. And she had her back against that door under the stairs and so she pretended to get very annoyed . . . '*Listen*, I can't stand here all night, what the hell do you'se want?' Oh, she thought she'd never get them out. If they had got those guns under the stairs my father would have been brought out and shot.

"Now there was one shop, Flynn's, that had teas and fancy goods in it and soldiers'd go in there and have tea and *everyone'd* be *all over them*. You know, people'd be making a fuss over them and playing up to them—bar my mother.

She stood out on her own. *She* wouldn't, she stood on her own! Oh, definitely. Now I'll tell you, when those Wilts were leaving the barracks up there, all going back over to England, they came *up* to her and they said, 'You were the *only bloody woman* on this quay (that wasn't patronising).' That was their expression, 'the *only bloody woman*' on the quay. And before they departed they come up that night to say goodbye to her and her family, the Wilts did. Come up to bid her goodbye. And it ended up with a hooley. And I always remember what a lovely hooley it was. Dancing and a piano going . . . *terrific*! I remember them marching down there out of the barracks down to the quays. And for years after that they sent her postcards, believe it or not.

"Then afterwards the Irish crowd took over. *Our* army. They used to march every Sunday morning for ten o'clock Mass, down the quays, up Blackhall Place into Arbour Hill, into the garrison church. A company of soldiers and all in uniforms and the band would play. Oh, there'd be a couple of hundred and the army band would play and march and there'd be pipers. A *lovely* parade it was. *Every* Sunday morning. That was a tradition and that went on for years. And on a Sunday morning my mother, when she come back from Mass, she'd say, 'I want to hurry, I want to see the fashion parade.' There'd be *thousands* of people going up to the park in their finest, their Sunday best. And you weren't dressed in those days if you didn't have a hat and gloves and a bag, for a woman. And a lovely lot of people then going up to the flower gardens after dinner on a Sunday evening, that was a *regular* route. And she'd have the window open and be leaning out, looking out, talking to neighbours maybe passing by, or two windows beside one another and talking. You'd just put a pillow on the window and look out. It was a lovely sensation."

JIMMY McLOUGHLIN—AGE 50

His boyhood was so restricted to the Marlborough Place tenement community that he had "no visualisation about the outside world". Life revolved around street activities and he paid dearly for his pranks. He suffered a serious accident scutting the back of a horse cart and nearly lost one eye in an act of devilment. His mother, a small woman with a badly deformed back, worked her whole life as a charwoman and washerwoman to keep her family fed and clothed. When reflecting on his mother's hard life his eyes become teary and he pauses . . . "It hurts me to think what she went through." He still visits her grave weekly.

"Marlborough Place in those days was a very small little community sort of street where everybody knew each other. There were sixteen families in our one tenement house, a very old Georgian house. We never had a locked door, *every* front door on my street was left open. My father was a Howth man, a fisherman, and my mother, she was a charwoman and did the cleaning and scrubbing and she was a washerwoman and took in washing. We never called it poverty because we didn't *know* it was poverty. We just accepted our class.

We were all in the same condition. Actually, I think my house was the nearest tenement building to Nelson's Pillar, so we were near a better area. But we never played on O'Connell Street, it wasn't *our* world. And we never went to Stephen's Green. *Never* got to the zoo. I'd no visualisation about the outside world.

"We'd no playground in those days. We'd play ordinary street games. And I lived next door to a forge and great memories of that. The farrier, he was a *very* big man, very broad. Oh, work with their shirt off all the time and their bib. We'd stand there and smell the forge especially when he'd be burning the hoof. Lovely smells would come out of it. And on our corner the men might have a toss school. They'd come from all over the city for toss schools in those days. Toss the pennies and some people'd lose their wages. One man would keep nix on a corner of, say, Talbot Street and one man would keep nix on the corner of Marlborough Street—to see were the police coming. Oh, he'd give a whistle and they'd know. And the money would be taken up and they'd scatter. And then we'd all run around to see if any money was left. See, often they wouldn't get a chance and there'd be money left and you'd get a few coppers. And I remember then we used to go around looking for old jam jars or Guinness bottles. You used to get a penny for a jam jar and a ha'penny for an old Guinness bottle and we went to the Mayro Picture House—the 'flea pit'—cause it was the cheapest. The flea pit was down in the front. Oh, yeah, they were the hard seats. The rich ones went upstairs. They'd throw down sticks or they'd be spitting down on you even. I never went upstairs, always downstairs.

"One day I was scutting—we *always* done this when they'd (horse vehicles) come into the street, jump on it—and my leg went through the wheel, right through the spokes. Oh, I remember it. A *multiple* break. A man come around in a horse and car, a jarvey car, and they brought me to Jervis Street Hospital. Oh, I was awake but screaming . . . *screaming*! And my parents were angry with me for what I done. And for devilment—and this is how I got my bad eye, very gabby eye—there was this man, 'Hopalong' Cassidy, one of the local men and we used to jeer him. And we'd always say, 'Hey, Hoppy! Hey, Hoppy!' so we'd get a chase. He ran after us and we'd try and lose him. And he hit me with a belt, a buckle, and it knocked the pupil right across. I nearly lost the sight of my eye over a small prank like that. They sent me for glasses, just old wire glasses, that come free from the State. But I could never wear them cause people would *jeer* you, call you 'four eyes' and so forth. So I never wore those glasses and today I'm half blind.

"I was often close to barefoot. We used to put bits of newspaper or cardboard in the bottom of shoes. Even though the hole was big you wouldn't get them changed till the hole was bigger, till it nearly fell apart. And all our clothes came from Cumberland Street, that was 'the hill'. Local people'd sell the old clothes, they'd get them from the tuggers going around and knocking on doors. We only lived around the corner and I'd go with my mother and she'd just root out old trousers and stockings. Another thing I always remember was a bakery on North Earl Street and she'd give me a pillow cloth and a shilling and I'd go down and stand outside and ask for a shilling's worth of stale bread. And you were always told to try and get a currant cake if you can. And you'd go home eating it yourself and you got a clip across the ear for being so naughty. And I remember going to the stew house in Sean McDermott Street. You'd bring a galvanised pot with you and you'd have a shilling or sixpence and you'd ask them to fill the pot up. The sixpence actually covered your family. You'd bring it back in the pram. Oh, it'd be warm but then by the time you got it back in the pram you might have spilled *half* of it.

"My mother, she charred for the Italian community that was in Marlborough Street. The term 'charwoman' was still used in those days. She done the cleaning for them in their shops, that was her morning job. I often wonder how she done it, being out charring. Down on her hands and knees with a scrub brush and a big bar of soap. And in those days you *scrubbed*. And the frail lady she was. She was a very small person, only four foot ten and she had a very deformed back, big lump on her back. And my mother was also a washer-woman, she took in washing. Used to take the big pram and set off for Tara Street wash house. Big sheets and everything and she might have *five* or *ten* of those (loads) going over and she'd spend the whole day, from eight in the morning till seven at night. I remember her going in there and she'd take off her jumper and she'd be there *scrubbing* and washing all the day and I remember the *steam*. And for only a few shillings.

"On a Monday she'd give me the letter to get the St Vincent de Paul (men) down. I'd leave it at Marlborough Street Church and they'd normally come on a Tuesday. And they'd sit down and they'd say, 'Well, Mrs McLoughlin, what do you want?' And she'd say that she had no clothes or food. I remember my mother often crying when she'd be asking for stuff cause she was a decent woman and felt that it was a thing she didn't want to do. But she was actually *forced* to do it. They used to give us five shillings or a seven and six voucher to Home Colonial Stores. But they'd come in and sit down and ask, 'Why are you asking for help? Is your husband not earning enough money?' But *every-body* in my tenement got Vincent de Paul, everybody in the local *community* got it. I've always remembered those men, always very big men, and they always had this upper-class attitude . . . snobbish to a certain extent. They were always people that had *more* than we had. You called them 'gentry'. They wanted to look after the poor but they went into your home to examine your conditions before they'd give you anything. I often wondered how they got into this Vincent de Paul, why they were doing it. They *must* have had hearts . . . but I remember me mother crying when they'd come in and sit down.

"It's sad when I look back on that . . . it brings back sad memories. I never *realised* at the time what she *went through* to bring us up . . . it was only in later years when she died. We didn't *know* in them days. I only visualised it later in life when I seen her standing there and she was so boney. And my mother had nothing. *Never* socialised, never went anywhere. Oh, but you couldn't have got more love. And my mother kept her money in a little pouch in her bra. That was the safest place. It was always there and she divvied it up, and with my mother you always paid your (burial) insurance and your rent— first two things. My mother, she'd *never* miss (paying) those (burial) policies. And when my mother died and we went to bury her we went to get the insurance policy in a little shoe-box and we discovered she had nothing! Only six hundred quid—in *penny* policies—for all those years of paying, and her burial was £1,400. You wouldn't think it could happen. She thought that money would pay for her funeral. And now I think back what she went through in life . . . it hurts me to think what she went through. We *never done enough* for our mother. Nobody did! You took them for granted."

6

Four Tenement Tales

The four individuals featured in this section are well known throughout their parts of inner-Dublin as great reservoirs of oral history and gifted story-tellers. Their elaborate tenement tales illustrate the power of the urban oral tradition.

MARY DOOLAN—AGE 75

She is one of the last clay pipe makers in the old Liberties but she harbours no rosy illusions about the "good old days" in her Francis Street Tenement. One of thirteen children, including three sets of twins, her tenement was infested with rot, rats, and TB. "It was unhuman, brutal," she recalls. She and her siblings suffered the indignity of being called dirty "pigs" by an uppity neighbour a bit better off. But she relished the lively weddings and wakes around the Liberties. A woman of uncommonly strong will and spirit, she holds firm convictions about the downtrodden status of women in tenement society and the dominant role of men. Today she lives comfortably in a nice home on Ash Grove only a few paces down from her old tenement house. She is full of good humour and much wisdom.

"I was born and reared in an old tenement on Francis Street and my mother had thirteen children and she'd three sets of twins. And I'll tell you, they weren't the 'good old days'. *Not at all!* They were *brutal* days. Very poor days because the food wasn't there and people then lived in terrible places, horrible looking rooms. Anyone says they were good old days is a head case. It'd make you sick to think of them. Horrible . . . horrible. Oh, they weren't the good old days, Love, they were the very *bad* days.

"My father was a bottle washer in a factory on Bride Street. They made all chemicals and soaps and things. He used to bring us down to show us how hard his work was. All these bottles would be out in the back in sheds and in the winter-time he'd have to break the ice off them and they had an open fire going and they had to be put into warm water. He'd be freezing, his hands freezing. He had the worst job, a bottle washer. That was two pounds a week and he was the father of thirteen. My mother had a shop on Francis Street. She sold cabbage and potatoes and coal and sticks and paraffin oil. Very cheap old shop, you know. Now I'll tell you, the cattle always came up and down this street and the cows went into her shop. And she was very large, pregnant, ready to have her baby and this cow come in and breathed on her—didn't buck her or anything cause she was behind the counter—but the cow gave her a fright and she came into labour and the baby was born. It was the *fright* of the cow coming in. And do you know what me (baby) sister was put into? She was put into the scales that weighed the coal with a bit of newspaper under it and she was nearly twelve pounds!

"We lived in an old tenement, a kind of cottage at the back, and the rent was small, two shillings. It was a stone cottage, white-washed, and *soaking* wet. Rotten! The fungus would be up the wall, dampness all the way up. Oh, me sister and me brother got TB out of it. That's as true as I'm after walking from Holy Communion. Terrible places . . . *unhuman*, but you *had* to take them. When the cottage nearly fell down around us we were put up to another tenement, on the third flight. The flights of stairs were terrible, old wood and all woodwormed and shaky banisters and a few nails that a child could really go through. Old banisters thin and shaky and the men'd be drinking and going up and they'd fall. Very, very dangerous.

"Mice running all around and lice and bugs and flies. And hoppers, you'd be alive with them and your whole body would be covered with red marks and you had to use a powder. And *clocks* (cockroaches) running around. Did you ever see a clock? Big black, hard things and little legs. Me mother'd be killing them with *hammers*. True as God! And giving the rats the bang on the head with a hammer there was so many. It was alive with rats. Oh, you never seen the size of the rats in all your life. They'd come up the stairs like cats. True. I remember a man that was white-washing in the cellar with a bucket and a rat jumped up and caught him by the throat. He didn't die but even up to the day he was dead that mark was there that the rat did.

"We had three old iron beds. Horrible looking and springs on the beds and in bits and all. You had to get as many as you could in a bed. I was at the bottom and me sisters at the top. Oh, you could be more on the floor than in the bed. You could never have a night's sleep. We'd a paraffin oil lamp, put the wick in and clean the globe and that was our light. We'd no bath. You'd have to go down under the pipe and try and wash your face and your feet. But me poor mother'd wash our heads and all in a sink bath. She used Sunlight soap for the children and the carbolic soap, a red soap, done for him (father) and had a nice smell. It was only a basin filled with water and the kettle full of water over the fire. And there'd be two or three marbles put in the kettle to keep it from rusting. Now it wasn't glass marbles. No, these were like chalk, ten a penny. The marble would go in white and it would take on all the rust from the iron kettle and it'd be brown. And we (girls) was always robbing the marbles and she'd blame the fellas cause they were champion with the marble playing.

"Everyone used the toilet in the yard. Ah, it was *horrible*. The landlord, you gave him your rent and he done *nothing* (to clean). But me mother, she cleaned it and she'd have the toilet like milk. Oh, and you couldn't afford toilet paper. I never even remember seeing them rolls of toilet paper that there is now. We used to just cut up the *Herald* and the *Mail* in squares and leave it down in the toilet so anyone in the tenement could use it. And me father'd cut up another load of newspaper squares for smoking, cause he couldn't afford a match. He'd put the paper on a piece of twine on a nail at the side of the fireplace and he'd tear that to light his cigarette all the time. He used to smoke Woodbines. So you'd cut up the paper and have one set for the toilet and one set for smoking. And for the toilet it didn't matter if the print went on your behind or what!

"Having a big family you ate a lot. We got porridge every morning and me father and me brothers got the duck egg. Big duck eggs. Very big . . . green. Then at seven in the morning she'd say to me, 'Will you go down and get a bit of fancy?' You got a pillow case full of fancy bread at Kennedy's bakery down on Patrick Street for a shilling. It'd be broken bread and some would be stale. I was only a kid but I'd line up with the older people, delighted to get the fancy. And in the stew house on Francis Street we used to get a big mug of stew with lumps of fat in it cause there was no meat. Just fat. And you got bread and ham and a bit of rice. And you were glad of that. Everyone was the same in them days, you had *nothing*. Now we always had fish on a Wednesday and a Friday and did you ever hear of a garnet? It's a fish. Well, me mother had an old table in the back yard and she had all the fish on it and didn't this big white seagull come down and take the garnet up on the shed and was going to eat it. The blooming seagull got it! My mother was very poor and she *hadn't another penny* to get another garnet. And didn't she make me sister get up on the shed with a ladder. And my brother ate that garnet . . . he didn't know.

"All second-hand clothes we'd get at the Iveagh (market). And police clothing, I got them meself. You went to an old stable for them, where horses used to be. You should have seen the dirt, the filth, in the stable. You went to the stable and they'd hand it out to you. They'd look at them (children) and say, 'Here, that'll fit him.' A jumper and old shirt and trousers . . . dirty. *Horrible* dirt. You wouldn't want to put them on, but you *had* to. And there'd be a little stamp on the shirt and the number and all the kids would know that you got them off the police and they'd jeer them. And there was a woman, a hard ticket, a stuffy-nosed old thing—and we were such a poor gang—and she'd a young one going to a private school and her young one had a piano and all and she was looking down on us. She was hard on our family and she deliberately called us a 'load of pigs' one day. She was a snob. '*You're only pigs*,' she roared.

"Very poor days. And the children's teeth were rotten, from neglect of food. None of the vitamins like now. All black teeth. Like cinders. Rotten. I remember when I couldn't stick it (tooth pain) anymore and I went down to get it out. There was an abscess under it and my face was swollen. He put his *knee* on me and pulled that. A shilling for a tooth. They hadn't chairs or anything like today. Oh, the *way* he pulled it! They were like animals, the old fellas. And what were you handed to rinse your mouth out with? A bottle of *Jeyes Fluid*! That's the truth of God.

"And there was a lot of children with rickets and all, from food, you know. And they'd be knock-kneed and all. Very jaundiced and their little hands and their little legs . . . couldn't walk. Very delicate. And their heads big. And TB! Me brother had it. And me mother'd three sets of twins and two sets died. Now this one set, they were twelve months old when the other set was born. And this nun was praying over them in the cot and she looked at me mother giving birth to two more—and she already had a crowd of kids. Well, this nun was praying over them and within two or three days the two little children twelve months old was dead. So two was gone. Mother used to say that she (the nun) prayed to God to take them. She used to say that.

"My mother was a saint. I'm not telling a lie now—she was a *living saint*. My poor mother done her washing with her board and used to kneel down with a bucket and water and have things like *milk*. She never drank and she never smoked. And *never* had a holiday. But he'd (father) be out having the best of times. He *had* to have his drink. Men made sure they were kings. She never got a holiday but she used to go to the Moira Hall, the Mother's Club, and they got a cup of tea and a biscuit, and a rosary. And she lived for that every Tuesday. And they used to run an outing every year for a half a crown. Maybe to Skerries or Howth and a bit of dinner and they'd have a sing-song and have balloons and all and come back that night at eight. But live the *whole year* for that, getting ready with things like little bits of velvet on her hat and a little scarf . . . going for the day. And me mother had her hair down to there (knees) and, oh, she'd do it up with loads of hairpins in lumps. She used carbolic soap and she was spotless. But not a *trace* of make-up. Not even on her wedding day.

"My mother, she used to cry when she had no money. And Vincent de Paul, everyone got them but you could only get a bit of porridge and margarine in the shop with it. It was a little ticket for a half a crown. In my mother's day you couldn't have *nothing*. They'd say, 'When you get rid of that and that (any household items or furniture), you come to us then.' Oh, they were *demons* now. They were a dirty lot of demons . . . yes, I'd say it to their face! They didn't really do good, they really brought you *down*. They made sure that you were down. And in my day if you had a big bulb, a 100-watt up, they wouldn't give it (assistance) to you. You had to change it to a 25-watt. But they're not as bad today.

"We never had anything and me brother, the eldest, he used to look at her and say, 'Mother, if I ever win anything on the horses I'll bring you a gramophone.' Well, here one day me mother was up there and here she sees the door opening and a *big* horn, and him carrying the thing. He was after winning £3-

10-0! And bought the gramophone, His Master's Voice. Big, big green thing. Oh, we were *charmed*. And the first record that went on that was Jimmy O'Dea, sixpence ha'penny, and it was all about horses. Me mother, she had brown eyes and they nearly fell out of her head. And she kept kissing him. The whole £3-10-0! *On her*. That's all he wanted. He idolised her.

"Very poor we were . . . very, very poor when you think of it. See, you had nothing and there was no money for spending. So you had to go to the pawn. I used to go to the pawn for me mother, down on the Coombe. Oh, it was 'going to me uncle' and 'meet you at me uncle'. And there was *so much* of a queue. Oh, God, they'd be lining all over Cuffe Street, down the road and around. Women with prams and all the rest and kids *crying* and all . . . oh, Janey Mack. You're waiting on his suit and his overcoat and his shoes. He only seen them on a Sunday and they were back all the week in the pawn. And when the pawnbroker'd take in so much he'd stop and you'd have to wait until he paid all the rest out. And the pawnbroker'd be roaring out, 'I don't mind taking your pot in but would you wash the f—— cabbage out of it!' Oh, God. And you only got enough in the pawn to make a dinner.

"Back then everyone run the didley clubs for saving the money. Before credit unions. My mother was always in the didley. My aunt run one. A didley starts with a ha'penny a week and it went to a penny, from a penny to three, and, you know, up to about five shillings. Started in January and ended in the first or second week of December. My aunt would keep the money the whole year around. She'd have little bags of money and it'd keep going up. But you couldn't get it back in August or anything. She *wouldn't give* it to you early. You wouldn't get it till December for your Christmas. Then they'd all get their few pounds. And you might give her what you'd like.

"School . . . I *hated* it. Now I'm not very well educated. And we were idiots growing up. I say 'idiots' because the minute you heard your mother talking, you know, about sex, you got a box or a kick to get out. You knew *nothing*. Didn't know where the baby was coming from or how it got there. We'd say, 'Mother, the doctor's going up to Mrs Byrne and he's got the baby in his black bag.' We *thought* that. That's the kind of rearing we got. And, God Almighty, I remember this day in school and there was five girls and we were playing with this little doll and this one girl put the doll on the table and said, 'You're the doctor and you must bring me the baby' and all, you know? *Innocent* as can be. No dirt. And there was an old bitch, a (lay) teacher, and 'What are you doing?' And one girl says, 'We were having a baby.' Well, she took out her cane and kept walloping us all. She made an awful lot out of nothing, she was an old bitch. And we *did not know anything* about a baby or sex. *Innocent as can be*, I wouldn't tell a lie. Got her cane and gave us five (slaps) there (hand), five each. As hard as she could go with the cane. See there (fingers), she nearly paralysed it. Then she had the five of us sent over to Father Hayden to be forgiven and he was *worse*. And we still didn't know. As true as God, we knew *nothing*.

"Nowadays a girl's pregnant and she gets £60 or whatever. Good luck to them. But at that time you got sent away. Oh, you were *dirt* and *filth*. She'd be put away to a convent. I know five or six that happened to. I knew this girl, a lovely girl, and she was only about fifteen or sixteen and she kept getting bigger. She was innocent too. And she was three months pregnant and big. And her father hit her across the face with an apron, a smock, and he said to her, 'Here, *get that on you*, you shameless hussy, you *dirty, shameless* hussy! You'll not belong to me.' And she was screaming, 'Daddy, Daddy'. She was only a girl, lovely and fair-haired with big blue eyes. And she had to scrub (floor) boards, down scrubbing and she was near to her time. Now this girl *kept* the child. It was a *beauty*. And she married the father soon after. It was a happy ending.

"As kids we could stand on the wall and see all the weddings cause our tenement was next to the church. If you were in Francis Street you walked to the church and got married. The girl and the fella got married and come out of Francis Street chapel and you'd see them out skipping rope on the street. Married but skipping rope! They were innocent. The bride would play skipping and they'd all be running and jumping in and he'd jump in with her. This is the truth of God. And the groom would throw out a few coppers in a brown bag to the kids. Ha'pennies and pennies. Oh, Yeah, that was called the 'grushie'. Ah, they'd kill one another for it. And you came back and it was a bit of a house wedding with jelly and custard. The night before the bride's mother'd make a *big basin* full of jelly and a big basin full of custard. And a bit of a meal and a few drinks. Well, then they'd have a little room to go to that night cause there was no going off on a honeymoon. No one had any grandeur. They'd only a bed and table and chairs. And he went to work the next morning. Now some people was holier than others and they thought it was a sin for the bride to come out. They'd have to stay about a week in and the mother'd bring the few messages in.

"When I got married we'd only one little weenie room for two shillings a week. And in that room the dirt was *caked* into the floor. A blind woman lived in it and when she'd sweep she'd sweep into the one corner and it all mounded up. No matter what she'd have she'd throw it in the corner. She let the dirt pile up and it went into a hill. You had to get a shovel, it was like concrete. Dirt and mice running all around. Horrible looking room but you *had* to take them when you were getting married. And rats in the halls. Now I'm not ashamed to say that I got a bed, a spring bed, and that was the wedding present. My mother and father stood together on that and bought it for me. A spring bed and I had the lot of me children on that. I had four girls and three boys and I buried two. And we wouldn't have had the bed for six months when the spring gave away and I was pregnant with the first fella. My fella (husband) got a bit of wire, tied it up, put a washing board over the hole and then we had to put a good few old bits of blanket over that.

"You'd get your furniture on the 'weekly' from a money-lender and the Jewman. And you had to have an awful lot of security for to recommend you for a little bedroom suite. And you *had* to have a pram cause you lived in tenements and had flights up. And very hard to get a pram in 1944. My

Tony was born in the war and they—Jewmen—bought all the prams up and done them up and painted them in every colour and got *colossal* money for them. I'm after paying £12 for a pram for Tony forty-seven years ago that wasn't worth £1! He was a robber. He robbed *everyone*. He bought old dirt and got them done in gold and silver and every colour and you'd think you were getting a good pram and it fell asunder within four weeks . . . the wheels and all and it was rusty, in bits. Looked lovely but it wasn't nice. The minute it got the rain the hood and all broke. *Robbed* you with the prams.

"You got married and you knew *nothing*. You didn't know *how* a baby got there or *why* it got there . . . it 'come out of under a head of cabbage', that's the way you were brought up. Sure, this woman, she was me own age, and she was having her first in the old Coombe (hospital) and she thought the baby come out of the navel. She'd be sitting up and pulling up her old night dress and looking at her navel, waiting on the head of the child to come out of her navel, and she was cursing in labour, 'Oh, Jees, there's not a *sign* of it (baby).' And she was a married woman . . . young . . . she didn't know. We were innocent.

"And after marriage you *had* to have children. You *had to have children*. Oh, that's what you married a man for. You wouldn't have a word to say. They were the *men*, they wore the trousers. See, back then there was none of these TVs and videos, but beds—*that* was the entertainment. You know what I mean? That's how there was so many children! Now I know a woman, Mrs Hannigan, had twenty-one children and another woman up the road had *twenty-three*. Back then there was a lot of 'wet time' (for outdoor labourers). See, the builders, if it rained, that was 'wet time', they'd be sent home. Well, you could count nine months after that and there'd be a child there. Yeah, because it was *in* to bed. There was nothing else to do. That's the truth of God now.

"When you went to Confession long ago they were very strict and you were afraid for your living life. And the priests, oh, God. If you went into Confession and said that you wouldn't have sex with your husband—that's the best way to say it, but we didn't call it 'sex' in them days—he'd say, 'You're married and you have to suit your husband, that's it.' They'd tell you to 'Get out! I'm *not* giving you absolution.' You wouldn't get absolution . . . you *had* to have children. That was a load of crap now, wasn't it? And the man had *no* responsibility. He pulled up his trousers and put on his coat and off he went. And the men didn't bother with the births. Not till they'd hear it screaming. Like me father was playing cards on the stairs waiting for the pubs to open on a Sunday morning and me mother in bed and the baby nearly there. He was never with her for none of them births. *Had* to have his drink . . . but he was a good man. My poor mother, she had nothing, but he never struck her. But some men, they'd bang you with the leg of a chair. Seen all them things in me younger days. He'd be off at the pub and she'd be in watching the kids and she'd have two black eyes.

"Now on me first baby I was peeling potatoes and me aunt says to me mother, 'Did Mary get churched yet?' and me mother says, 'No, but she's getting it done on Friday.' See, the baby was christened but I wasn't churched. Now I didn't know what 'churching' *was*. And me aunt looked at me and says, 'Leave down them, you're *tainted*! You're tainted in the eyes of God.' She nearly killed me with fright. The way it was, you were like a *fallen woman*. Like a man and a woman (together) and I was a dirty woman cause I had the child . . . tainted. She more or less said that I was with the devil. That was the belief, it was a living *disgrace*. Truthfully. You were tainted unless you got this candle and (renounced) the devil and all his works. And it made you a Catholic again. See, you weren't a Catholic. *Stupid*! There's none of that now.

"Then there was the wakes. At wakes they'd all be coming and drinking stout, and sandwiches. That'd go on all night. And smoking pipes. At funerals clay pipes was given out for nothing. Oh, I was a clay pipe maker on Francis Street. They were made of soft clay and put in a kiln. And if they broke we sold them to the kids for a ha'penny for the bubbles. A clay pipe cost a penny. They could last . . . and then they called them 'seasoned'. And if a man let it fall it was clay and it'd break and he'd go *mad*. If too much didn't break away (from the stem) he'd try and smoke it with the little bit of it left, cause it was seasoned, burnt . . . *black*. And the new one he couldn't get used to. But the old ones (women), they all had their old shawls and they'd be smoking their clay pipes and drinking their stout at the funeral. And they'd smoke in their home with the clay pipe and outside on an old chair.

"They done terrible things in the tenements at funerals. This is the truth now. There was an old woman and she was called 'Julia the mangle woman'. A mangle was two big things that you rolled the clothes through and that pressed them and took the water out. You'd wash your clothes and take them to her and she'd do the mangle. People'd come to her from the wash houses. Two pence. Blankets and all would go through. Some women were tough, that's the way they made their living. Julia was a *big, big* woman. Anyhow, Julia died and that wake then would go on for a week. Now three or four people would lift the body out and they'd take everything off Julia and she'd be naked and washed and all. See, neighbours, strong people, would wash the body. And then she'd be settled back in the bed, a blue habit with 'I have suffered' on the front and tied in the back with strings and big black rosary beads in the hands. So one of them said, 'Go over and get Mammy Kelly.' Now we called her 'Mammy' Kelly, like she was every-one's mammy. But she was like a grand old poor one, you know, like a *skeleton*. So Mammy Kelly was put sitting on this seat and they were tearing off the sheets off poor Julia's bed and getting it ready and they told Mammy Kelly—and she was very nervous—'You're going to hold Julia.' And she *collapsed*. And they were only joking! About holding the body. See, Mammy Kelly was only about that (small) size and Julia was a *big* woman. Oh, she really fainted. But they brought her to and gave her some whiskey and all. But she flew home.

"Then there was a man up the street and his name was Jembo-no-toes. He played a melodion and his mother was *that size*. Ah, she'd be *easy* twenty stone. Had big old skirts and a big stick and she'd always look over her half door—couldn't move from where she was. Now they had pigs and big barrels and you'd throw slop in and she'd give you the tuppence for the pictures. We used to put bits of cabbage and potatoes in the bucket and put stones or bricks in the bottom for weight cause she was nearly blind and she only done it by the weight. God forgive us today. She'd say, 'Throw it in the barrel.' And the money'd be smelly, *stinking*. Anyhow, Jembo was always playing his melodion and poor Jembo died. And there was some hard tickets in the Liberties and they said, 'This one is nervous and that one is nervous, so we'll play a trick.' He was settled in the bed and the habit on him, so they took his hands out of the beads and it was an iron bed with bars and they put twine around like that on his fingers and put the melodion on his stomach. And a fella was *behind* the bed. So when these nervous fellas would come in he would pull it and 'Aaaaah!'—they'd *run*. Oh, some of them fell, and some fell on top of the other. This is the truth of God now. Put the melodion on him and you'd *swear* he was alive. And they said, 'f—— Jembo is not dead at all, he's *playing his melodion!*"

NOEL HUGHES—AGE 61

As he likes to tell it, "Now I drank a few times with Brendan Behan and he said to me one night, 'you are a living genius, there's more in you than in any writer, but it has to be brought out of you.'" He is indisputably a marvellous repository of local urban folklore on Dublin's northside. As a lad he had a reputation for devilment and as a young man was a rough-and-ready sort engaging in a good few pub brawls. He was also active in local affairs especially when it came to combating injustices toward the poor. He once took part in a violent street battle against what he calls "the posse" made up of the sheriff and his henchmen who were attempting to evict a helpless woman from her tiny tenement room. "We won the day," he proudly proclaims, by forcing the intruders out. He also knew well the notorious madam, Dolly Fawcett, and her disreputable dens known as the Cozy Kitchen and Cafe Continental. His roots along North King Street run deep and today he resides in adjacent Coleraine Street and he can recite the history of every street and building around him.

"In my district it was *complete* tenements, three stories high. There was a disaster where two tenement houses fell down in Church Street in 1913 and there was thirteen people killed in that, mostly children. My mother's aunt lost two of her children in that disaster. And the landlord who owned those two houses got out of the country to Australia. That gave an awful lot of people a fright in the tenements.

"Life was hard in the tenements. Hard on mothers rearing children because, see, so many lived in the one room. I can remember eighteen children and the father and mother and mostly what happened was they'd sleep on mattresses on the floor. You might get four children sleeping on the one mattress on the floor and the body heat, that was their means of heating. Mattresses would be shoved under the bed in the morning and pulled out in the night. Poor people used just the ordinary fire and they cooked on that and boiled the water on that. *Everything* was done on that fire grate. Wages was so small that to buy a bag of coal that was an awful lot of money, so you'd see them going out gathering sticks on old building sites, anywhere they could get them. Now showers and baths, an *unheard* of thing. People'd have a tin basin about three feet long and they'd boil water and put it in this vat and the children would be put in that and washed. I used to be put in those myself and washed. There was maybe four children washed in that water. And then the woman, she'd close the door and she'd have a wash herself in that. And her husband would go out for a walk and bring the children. Oh, God yes, they were very modest in those days.

"You seen mothers bringing down a bucket with slops—the children's urine and shit—and that would be emptied into the toilet. Because she couldn't take children down six flights of stairs to a toilet in the open yard when it was raining so severely or in frosty weather. The toilet had a door on it and wooden seating. You had your privacy and you had to knock on the door, 'Hurry up in there, hurry up out of there!' But sometimes dirty, filthy people would go in that didn't live in the tenement and use the toilet because they were all open hall doors. And they'd urinate on the floor and that was a disgusting thing to the people that lived there. The landlord used to pay a fella and he would go in and clean out these yards and get maybe a half a crown off the landlord. Now in our tenement there was a man—God, we didn't know his name—and we used to call him 'Five Minutes' because he used to be in such a hurry to do them tenement back yards.

"Some of the tenements were very, very clean but more of them you got a bit of a stink in. Some people had great *pride* in regards to scrubbing down their lobby and their stairs. We'll say two families lived on the one floor, well, one woman would take a turn scrubbing out the lobby and her stairs this week as far down as the next lobby and that would change over the following week. They used Dirt Shifter soap and the scrubbing brush. She'd be down on her knees and a little poem came out of the tenements here in Dublin and it goes, 'Ah, you see a woman on her bended knees, the more she bends them the more I sees!' So that house was kept lovely, scrubbed *spotlessly* clean from top to bottom. But then you had others and they didn't care about their tenement whatsoever, didn't care about keeping their lobbies and staircases clean. Now in North Anne Street, off King Street, you had that quite an awful lot, houses that wasn't kept as respectable.

"And they used to use a red raddle, a red paint, on the walls and landings of the tenement houses going up. Actually, it was only a powder, a white-wash dyed red, just very cheap stuff they had and a very brightish red. And when you'd hit against it if it didn't dry properly it would mark all your clothes. Come off on your clothes and you would identify anyone who was in the tenement that had been painted with this stuff. Oftentimes you'd see a girl that had been courting in one of the halls, with her back against the wall, and when she come out of it she would have the identified mark on her back—the 'mark of the tenement' on her back!

"A lot of vermin and an awful lot of fleas in the tenements. And these lice came out of the plastering on the wall. Because there was what they called 'hair lime' at the time, cow hair mixed with lime to make the plaster, and they got damp and the bugs came out of that. And when the wall dried the wood lice came out into the tenements and it was an awful problem for the people. Mothers couldn't do anything about it. And there was rats in the tenements on North King Street around the piggeries and slaughterhouses. That's where they used to come from. And I remember a drought coming—I was about fourteen years of age at the time—a heavy drought came into the city and the rats actually came up out of the sewers, because the sewers went dry. It was a *horrible* thing. They got this killer stuff and lifted the manholes and poured it down. And then they actually brought up water from the Liffey and poured it down these manholes and that made the rats follow the water away to where it would go out into the river.

"Hard on mothers rearing children in the tenements. With the husband maybe not working and life being so hard, so suppressed on them, that mothers, I often seen them in my memory worn and torn with trying to make ends meet at a young age. Young women, when they were only twenty-eight or thirty and wore a shawl around them, looked fifty years of age. There was an awful lot of women at that time lost their health. But mothers done the best they could for their children. And in them days the children had rickets, bandy legs, and what was known as 'khaki eyes', little yellow sores in the eyes. And the tenement was *rampant* with TB and it wasn't until Doctor Noel Browne set out his clinics and he was a great apostle to the Irish people. Noel Browne was a God, a *God* to the people of the tenements.

"The *main* thing with a mother in the tenements was that the children would have a good dinner. That's all she was interested in, the one good meal a day—for survival. There'd be a big loaf of bread cut up on the table with a bare scrape of butter on it and everyone was *so happy*. Or maybe a feed of bread and dripping. That'd be the juice off the meat let go hard and scraped onto the bread. I still use that because it's so delicious. And a woman, if she'd no corned beef herself, she would get the borrow of the corned beef water, what we used to call in Dublin the 'greasy water', to boil her cabbage. They'd get the loan of the greasy water and have a feed of cabbage and potatoes and no meat because they couldn't afford the meat. Or maybe they'd have a pig's cheek for two shillings or a good rabbit stew. We ate rabbits, your mother'd make a *hell of a good stew* out of that.

"Back then you got lazy buggers of men with their children half naked and hungry and they didn't care. These men used to stand at the corner instead of going out to look for a shilling, to earn a couple of bob. Then you got the other fellas with *pride* for *his children* and he'd be off and out searching. But mothers was mostly very decent and honest. And there was many a time the man would drink the money and come home and a row would start and he would *hit* the wife. There was an awful lot of hitting wives in them times. I seen many a woman in my time with black eyes. And what you *wouldn't* see, like she'd be sore around the ribs from a blackguard of a husband, a bowsy who would do such a thing. And he just didn't care. Women at the time, they put up with this persecution. Women of today would not tolerate such abuse, wife battering. The woman always got the worst of the wear and the poor children *screaming*. The children would be *screaming their heads off*, 'Mammy, Mammy, Mammy . . . Daddy don't, Daddy don't!' It was an awful disgraceful thing and I remember it very well as a child.

"Now an old man called Addie down on Little Mary Street, his wife was an awful nosey old one and he used to be always fighting with her. And she'd always be out the window looking out this way with the two hands out. And didn't old Addie give her a push! And she went out the window and down onto the ground. She wasn't dead but she was very badly injured. But what done away with him was another old one across on the other side from another tenement had *seen* him giving her the push. And two police-men come up and he was given three years for that, in the madhouse.

"Very hard on women in them days but you'd see a plant in some of the windows, what was called a garden box, that brightened things and gave their mind a little bit of peace. That was their little bit of garden to look after. A bit of wood nailed onto the outside of the window sill and they'd have the star of Bethlehem, a plant that grows into a nice flower, or the star of David. Or they'd have geraniums. But women, they never had any entertainment or break whatsoever. None. Oh, for a woman a wake or a wedding, that was a holiday on the Riviera! The weddings in the tenement houses, some went on for *three days*. There'd be a ham and pork and cabbage and potatoes and a sweet, like a big bowl of jelly, which was a luxury. And mostly porter. See, relatives and friends, they'd save up. Or maybe go to the Jewman or a money-lender. Well, they'd save up and maybe be on the drink for three or four days. And they'd all be singing!

"And Christmas in the tenements was a happy time . . . and a poor time. There was no turkey, there was no goose. There might be a chicken or a big lump of corned beef. Children might get a sixpenny stocking out of Wool-worth's. There'd be a couple of bits of cardboard stuff in it or maybe a small little car, cardboard games, some sweets. Many a child got nothing, only the love and care of the mother and father. But there'd be a Christmas candle and a Christmas cake and a pudding. Ah, a few drinks in the house and singing. On New Year's there was an old custom and people'd come over in the back yard of the tenements and they'd greet each other out there in the yard, shaking hands with each other, giving a hug to each other. Everyone would come down at midnight when the bells would be ringing because Dublin was a great place for the bells of Christ Church. Ah, they'd be singing and the ships would be down on the docks and you'd hear them blowing. And a lot of them would have a sup of drink in the yard, bring a bottle down in the yard to share. That's the way they'd celebrate and bring in the new year.

"Pawnshops was the biggest part of all life in the tenement. Oh, without the pawnshop you *couldn't survive*. There was the pawnshop in Capel Street there, Brereton's and you'd see the women bringing the clothes down to the pawn on the Monday morning. And when they'd come back from Mass on a Sunday the Ma would say, 'Take that (suit) off now or I'll be cut in the pawn in the morning.' That means, 'I'll get less money, keep it fresh.' I used to go into the pawn and get a bit of laugh listening to the women bargaining with him. And women'd be talking to theirselves and you'd think they'd be talking to someone else. Like, 'I'll get five shillings on that and I'll be able to pay so-and-so on that.' Talking *out loud* to theirselves. Me granny, she'd get a brick and wrap it up in brown paper and go in to the pawn and she'd say, 'Give me a half a crown on that, John.' Oh, he *knew*. But he knew my granny would come back because she was so trustworthy. So the system worked.

"And a funny thing now about the pawn, the women would rob their husband's clothes without the husbands knowing it. Now I remember Kitty Brogan and she robbed her husband's suit and pawned it. And home he came on a Wednesday night—I'll always remember that it was a Wednesday night—and home he came to put on what he called 'me old suit'. And he opened the wardrobe and there was no suit! And she makes the run over to me mother and says, 'Oh, Jesus, Kate, he'll f—— kill me! He'll *kill* me, Kate.' 'What's wrong with you, Kitty?' 'Jesus, I pawned his old suit and he's after coming in to put it on and he hasn't a bit of clothes.' I'll always remember that he came over to me father and says, 'By Jesus, I'll nail her . . . if I get hold of that old one I'll kill her . . . I'll *kill* her, I'll take her f—— life!' See, he needed it for to go to a meeting. And so he got the lend of a trousers and coat off me father and he had to double it from the top of the trousers where it goes around your belly.

"You could get a few quid off the Jewmen too. Some of the Jewmen, Harry Green and Mr Baker and Mr Spellman, they were money-lenders around here. But now they were done out of a lot of money too. Because someone would go and get a lend of a few quid and when the Jewman'd come (collecting) there'd be a 'make-up' husband—or maybe the husband was in on it. See, when he comes around they'd (women) get a man to stand in and he'd say (to her in front of Jewman), 'What are you borrowing money off Jews for?' And he'd give the wife a dig. And the Jewman would run out the door. And he wouldn't come back.

"Now me granny, she often got a lend of a few bob off the Jewman without my grandfather knowing about it. My grandfather was 'The Harrier' Hughes and 'Big Maggie', his wife, would get a loan of money off the Jewman but then she got 'Bill the Sailor' Connolly to turn around and act as her husband. And the Jewman came and knocked at the door and Bill had the towel around his neck and a razor in his hand and he's shaving and he says, '*What* money? What money are you talking about?' And the Jewman says, 'The money your wife borrowed off me.' 'You're *borrowing money* off them?' he says, and he gives a box to me granny. And he's *not* her husband at all, just a made-up husband. And he made a run for the Jewman and the Jewman runs down the street because Bill had an open razor in his hand. And he never come back anymore. That happened an awful lot.

"The women handled all the money. Women, oh, they always hated to see anyone coming if they owed him money. Now none of the landlords hardly lived in the area and they all had an agent they'd send around, an old fella, and collect the rent. Now the agents was nearly all old ex-policemen. He'd come around weekly, on a Saturday evening, and collect and get a half a crown or five shillings or whatever it was. Now if the woman didn't have it she'd say, 'I'll pay you on the double next week.' Now it might go that a person would let it run up and owe six weeks rent—and then she'd look for a room somewhere else! And they'd move overnight. And nobody'd say where you'd gone. They'd get the loan of a handcart from Granby Lane for a shilling and you'd see them *loading* all their stuff on the handcart and the father'd be in the front pulling and a couple of his children'd be shoving behind him. They'd put the dresser on first and then the bed on top of the dresser and something else on top of that. And the table would be turned on its back on top of the bed and then tie down the chairs and the whole lot down. He'd have it well tied down with a rope and well balanced. And then he might have to come back for another trip.

"Oh, I seen evictions. It's very hard if you get a family that lived in that house and all their children and their granny lived in that house and they were getting put out, and the other people in the tenements might be out crying. There was a woman going to be evicted out of a huge big tenement house and the woman was crying and she was a Church of Ireland lady, a Protestant. And she was told (by neighbours), 'You *remain* where you are.' See, in my district it was a ghetto of IRA and when the police came into the tenements there'd be banging of stuff (warnings). Now I remember the posse, the city sheriff. Now he didn't have horses or anything but they were called 'the posse', him and his men. So all the people gathered in the street and we went up on the roof and when the posse came galloping up he got a shower of bricks and the devil knows what flew down on them. And the people attacked them, *women* and all. Mostly women attacked them. Attacked these big old policemen. They run out of the street and they said, 'No way I'm going up there again.' We won the battle that day. I remember distinctly . . . because I'm one of them who split a policeman that day.

"And on a Saturday night you were always sure of a row in a pub, or outside of a pub. Two fellas would come out to fight. It'd be a fair fight and the next thing one fella might go in with his head, give the other fella a butt with his head. And then some fella'd walk over—you know, one of the real fighting men—and crucify him for using his head and say, 'You shouldn't have done that!' and give him a few clappers for doing that. But they were mostly fair fights. Some simple bloody thing would start it and maybe there'd be a digging match in the pub. But you'd go outside to finish it. They'd say, 'Alright now, *out!*' And they'd let them have a go at it. Then they'd shake hands and be the best of friends after that. Ah, I had a few of them myself. Oh, I did . . . quite a few fights. I seen meself with thirteen stitches in me, then shaking hands with the fella and going back in to have a pint with him. Then I had a row with another fella. He was 'Pig's Eye' O'Hara's son and his nickname was 'Turkey Hole' O'Hara—he was a moocher. And I had this row with him and he brought this stick to hit me and I took it off him and gave him a bang of this stick on the top of his head and cracked the stick. And gave him another few wallops along with it because he was a kind of a bowsy. But about a week after that I had a few bob and I came around and he was standing outside the pub and I says to him, 'Will you have a pint or will you have a fight?' 'Oh, I'll have the pint,' he says.

"Then there were prostitution dens, a few of them around Dublin. On the south side of Dublin there was a family called the Lynches and that was a prostitution den. But the Cozy Kitchen and the Cafe Continental had the two biggest names. The Cozy Kitchen was a place where you went in to either pick up a girl or have a drink. It was down in the basement of a tenement house in number 2 North King Street, into the forties and away up into about 1957. Now Dolly Fawcett, who I knew very well, and her sons had the Cozy Kitchen. Dolly, she was the madam of it. Dolly, when I knew her, was in her seventies. Oh, she was a fine looking woman, the appearance of a woman that was very good looking in her youth. She could be described as a 'madam' but she was a married woman and had two sons. Her son Stephen ran the Cozy Kitchen and the other son ran the Cafe Continental which was in Bolton Street. It was the same thing but it was more for prostitution in there than in the Cozy Kitchen. That was where an awful lot of people went into. Now the Cozy Kitchen was situated in such a way that there was hardly anything facing it and so you were sheltered there. But at the Cafe Continental it was more in the open and you *would* be seen. So to go in and see that you weren't seen you watched and had a look around and all of the sudden when the door was open you'd make a dash in.

"The girls would be around the place, at the counter, and a man would start chatting her up. They were mostly all country girls up from the country, from seventeen into their thirties. They weren't high-class prostitutes or anything like that, they were just ordinary commoners. I suppose they charged about two pounds. They'd bring the blokes off to a flat. Or take him around the laneway or around the back, somewhere like that. The whole neighbourhood knew of this—the whole of *Dublin* knew about it because the sailors off the ships used to go in there an awful lot. Men, they'd come from the docks and from all over. It was mostly all outsiders cause the men from the tenements didn't have money. And you had a priest called Father Crosbie and he used to go up the laneways with a stick and any couples he'd see he'd hit them with the stick. Oh, he was a terrible man altogether for frightening people.

"Now I was drinking one night in the Cafe Continental—they'd serve you whiskey in a cup—and I was only eighteen and I was drinking away and there was a knock on the door and who was it? My mother! She was looking for a taxi driver, the cabbie, to bring her daughter-in-law to the Rotunda

Hospital to have a baby. So Fawcett, the son, pushed me under the table. Oh, the hair stood up on me head and the sweat run out of me! Frightened the living daylights out of me. And the police raided it a couple of times but they got backhands. Oh, there was backhands going on at that time, paying policemen off. And there was a bit of an argument a couple of times (about closing it down) but nothing ever materialised of it. And then it just eventually closed up and the Fawcetts went off to England.

"Back then it was a cheeky woman who went into the pub amongst men, women did it in their homes. Now me granny would give me sixpence and a penny for myself to get her sixpence worth of gill in an enamel tin jug. And she'd say, 'Don't let the old fella see you'—that'd be me granddad. Oh, he'd give her a belt with the jug in a minute because he was a very vicious fighting man. But she'd do that behind his back. So Granny'd be preparing the cabbage for the Sunday dinner and she'd be watching the grandad and picking the old jug up (sipping).

"Now jarveys would keep their animals at the stables at the back of the tenements, in the lanes and mews. And there was a jarvey called 'Banker' from Church Street and his brother was called 'Red Pole', a jarvey as well. Now banker got his name cause he'd always say, 'Now I'll bank on that' and his brother got his name cause he used to park his cab and horse for hire outside of a barber shop and the red pole was sticking out, so that put the name 'Red Pole' on him. And there was another old jarvey named 'Lousy Cushion' cause someone got into his horse cab one day and he starts scratching and so he got the name 'Lousy Cushion' and that name stuck on him. Now my granny was twenty-eight stone and Mrs Tyrell, a good friend of me granny's was a good twenty stone and another woman called Meg Durham was around twenty stone. And the three of them got into Banker's horse cab and they're going along and Meg Durham says to me granny, 'Ah, look at that, Maggie,' and me big granny got up to look out the cab window and the wooden floor *went down*. and the pony was trotting and me granny's two legs was down on the ground trotting along with the pony and she shouting, 'Banker, *stop* . . . Banker, will you *stop*!. Feet went through down to the ground and she was something like six weeks in the hospital with her shins hitting against the axle. That is a truthful story, that happened.

"Another time I went with my two grannies and Mrs Tyrell and another woman to a funeral one day and I was only nine to ten years old. Oh, there was five of them anyway stuffed into one little horse cab and I was sitting up with Banker on the front, on the dickey. So we went to Glasnevin cemetery to the funeral and back we came and they said, 'Banker, pull in at Mike Bushe's,' that was the name of the pub. So Banker pulled in and they were drinking away. Then they decided to go out to a pub called Dolly Heffernan's. So they went out to it and they all *got drunk*. And Banker got drunk! And it was about five or six miles from the city. So they got them out of the pub and put them into the cab and put Banker in with them, with all the women. Now I was only a youngster but well used to horses all my life and so I was put up on the dickey and the reins was handed to me and 'Go on, drive home!' Now everyone was out looking to know where I was all day long. And I came home that night with five women and the jarvey sitting inside the cab—and I only nine year old and driving the horse all the way home—and I turned into the street where all the tenements was and me father looked at me . . . and *me mother* looked at me. And it was the *talk of the neighbourhood*, the laugh of the neighbourhood for a long, long time after that. It was a folklore of the neighbourhood after that.

"People at that time was very, very generous when anyone would die. Maybe there'd be no money and a collection would be made, what they called the 'sugar bag' collection. Oh, they'd go right around to the shops and houses in the tenements and they'd say, 'It's for so-and-so.' That's all you had to say. It was for the burial and the stout. They'd work out how much it'd be. The coffin maker lived across from me and where I lived they used to say, 'Ah, there's another one gone,' cause you'd hear a big saw starting up working on a coffin. And things were so hard and so poor in Dublin that there was poor people that was buried on the top of their friends in the grave. Because they didn't have the money to buy a new grave. Like they'd (friends) say, 'Put her down on top of me mother.' The hearse would come and pass by the person's house three times around—it was just a superstition—and then straight off to the cemetery with the horses.

"Oh, in my time as a youngster a wake would go on for three days. See, the person would be lying in the room for three days and three nights and there was no electric light in those tenement houses, it was an oil lamp with a big globe. And between the smell of the corpse and the smell of the paraffin oil you didn't know which was the worse of the two, a sickening smell all the time. A couple of women from the tenements would go in and wash down the corpse and the eyes would be closed and the mouth would be closed and they'd just be straightened out and hands joined with mostly rosary beads with the crucifix sticking up. And then the habit would be sent for and put on. There'd be a saucer of snuff and two candles lighted and maybe a saucer with holy water in it with a feather and you dipped the feather and sprinkled it over the dead. And when they took a pinch of snuff it was always on the left knuckle of the index finger. The thumb of the right hand and the index finger of the right hand would be used to pick up the pinch of snuff to put it onto the knuckle of the index finger of the left hand and they snuffed that. Then people'd kneel down and say a prayer and a real old friend would take the (corpse's) hands and say, 'The Lord have mercy on you, Johnny' or 'The Lord have mercy on you, Biddy.' Ah, there was heartbreaks . . . *heart-breaks.* See, cause they were old pals. Ah, and if the sup was there, the drink, they'd be up all night. Ah, they'd be sitting at the fire talking about things that happened a hundred years ago.

"And *everyone* would come. You got people who came that didn't *know them* (the deceased). If they heard there's a good drink they'd come and they'd have a drink. Didn't know them but they'd know they were going to get a couple of bottles of stout. See, there was an open door—you just walked in. It (news of death) seemed to go right around for a couple of miles. I know of a couple of occasions where a person came in and said, 'May the Lord have mercy on him, I knew him well'—and it was a *woman* that was dead! Oh, yeah, they were on the mooch, begging for a drink. Now we had a man in the neighbourhood, 'Pig's Eye' O'Hara—his name was Neddie but he had a turned eye—and he was an awful man for doing that. Another moocher too was Nicky Darcy and he was another bugger for doing it. And old 'Fish' O'Neill would do that . . . but Fish would give a couple of bob to the collection.

"Now I know of a thing that happened in my time. A man called McGuirk, he was a very crippled man, and he died bent up with the head forward like that. And they had to stretch him out and break his legs to put him down. And then he was tied down. And Jambie O'Neill came in—he was a three-card trick merchant—and everything was nice and quiet and calm and he says, 'The Lord be good to you.' And he had a razor blade in his hand and nobody could see the razor blade and he cut the cord to keep the keep the person tied down. He did it for a bit of *devilment*, for a bit of joking. And when he cut the cord didn't Mr McGuirk come up in the bed! And there was wind in his stomach and he come right up in the bed and 'buuurp!' And when McGuirk come up in the bed all of the sudden a woman fell against Lizzy Brophy and didn't Lizzy fall into the fire and burned all the side of her arm. And he got three months imprisonment for overdoing it.

"Now for devilment one time meself and me pal got two cats and tied their two tails together and hung them on the handle of a tenement door and knocked. And when the door opened didn't the two cats swing in on top of the old one! And when a woman's clothes would be out on the line and the big knickers would be out you'd fill them up with a bit of straw or hay and they'd be hanging on the line like that. Or you'd get a man's long drawers and filled it full of hay and got a carrot and stuck it out as his dickey. Just a bit of a joke. And you heard so much about the banshee and the devil that people'd be frightened in the halls of the tenements. Oh, people claimed to see the devil in the halls. I was nervous myself going into the dark tenement hallways. Now there was this one stuck-up girl and my pal and myself got an old dummy, the window dummies, and we got inside the tenement house and put the dummy standing against the wall and she come up the stairs and struck her match and the naked dummy was there and didn't it fall on the top of her. And her and the dummy fell down the stairs and she screaming for mercy. And the dummy was on *top* of her! And what they used to use at that time if they were going down to the toilet was a lump of paper folded up and they'd make a torch out of that. And didn't old Willie Taffe (girl's father) put that into the fire and lit it with his left hand and the poker in his right hand and he was down the stairs and *beating the shop dummy*! He thought it was a fella lying on top of his daughter raping her! And I was the instigator of that. I was about fourteen.

"Now another truthful story. A man had a mule and cart and 'Magso' Leonard was the name of the man. And Magso was an awful man for drinking. And what did he do, he went out and got stupid drunk and in he come to his room. So we took the wheels off his cart, carried the cart into the tenement to his room, brought in the wheels and put the wheels back on it, brought up the mule, yoked it up, put the harness on it and tied it to the bed. And Magso lying in the bed bloody drunk and never minded. And the next morning Magso woke up and he's wondering how he got the mule in . . . didn't know. For the rest of his life he wondered about that!"

MARY CORBALLY—AGE 72

"I don't feel any shame in coming from the Monto", she confides. From her tenement window on Corporation Street "we had a ringside seat" to view the raw Monto street activity below—prostitution, animal gang brawls, police brutality. She was the second eldest of fifteen children and went on to give birth to twenty-one of her own. Tenement life was harsh as she had to walk to school barefooted, survive on meagre meals, and empty horrid slop buckets. Yet, from her remarkable memory bank she delights in recounting details of Christmases past and the games and pranks played at wakes years ago. And she still holds to old customs and beliefs, describing vividly how she heard the warning wail of the banshee just before her husband died. Today she lives in Portland Place close to where she grew up and her home is a hive of children and grandchildren hovering around her. She is clearly a much loved matriarchal figure among both family and local community.

"Now I'm going to shock you when I tell you that we had fifteen children in the family and only one room in the tenement. We ate, drank and slept in the one room. There was two big beds and at night-time there was two mattresses pulled out, made of straw and covered with canvas. There was a fireplace with a 'Home Sweet Home' fender and a box with a bit of coal. The fire had to be put out at bedtime because if anything happened we'd be all burned to death because you'd be walking on one another trying to get out. So the coals would all be put out. And in the tenements there was a hall door and in most houses they were open and there was a nail on the floor or a brick or lump of rock at the door to keep it open if it was breezy at night so the door wouldn't be banging. Sure, we used to have fellas sleeping on the landing. They was neighbours. Like if there was a row and the son was thrown out.

"Oh, it was hard times. Me father was in the 1918 War with the Ulster Rifles. When he come home from the war he went to work as a baker in O'Rourke's Bakery but then work got slack and he was unemployed. Me poor mother died at forty-eight, always had her hair tied up in a bun and wore a black shawl up till she died. My visions of my mother . . . always cooking on the fire, a big open fire and a kettle on one side. It was mostly stew and coddles and people then didn't even use a knife and fork. There was nothing to use a knife and fork on! It had to be a spoon. And for brushing teeth we used soot and salt. For the water to wash yourself, that was brought up from the yard in a white enamel bucket to the kettle on the fire and on a Saturday night you had your bath. Had to make sure that all the kids was washed. The bigger ones done themselves and then the bigger ones helped the smaller ones. I was the second eldest. We all had to help. And we never had toilet soap, it was ordinary household scrubbing soap that we washed with. And then you used to have slop buckets on the landing, just a galvanised bucket. The bucket was just in the corner on the landing—no privacy. There was always a signal, like a cough or a sneeze or something, to let other people know that you were there. With small children you'd be afraid to let them go out in the lobby so they had buckets in the room for them. Slop buckets would be taken down first thing in the morning by the mothers.

"I often had to go to school barefooted. Ah, many kids was barefooted. But it was very few girls you'd ever see in their bare feet. Oh, yes, it was immodest. And newsboys that was barefooted, oh, God, they'd be only eight or nine years old. They'd come about fourteen and some of them hadn't got shoes. Some kids was out selling and their mothers didn't even know! Kids sold the papers just to get into the (Belvedere Newsboys) Club cause you used to get a mug of tea and a bun every night. In them years they called the paper a 'reader'. so you'd say you were going out to sell your readers. They were only a penny each at the time. Father Ryan, he was the priest in the Belvedere Newsboys Club and the boys loved him and *every* house in Corporation Street and Foley Street all had *somebody* that belonged to the Club. When Father Ryan was going away he left a little picture of himself with people and *everyone* got Father Ryan's picture. And the people then went and paid a shilling a week to have that done life-size. They call them now 'blown-up', it was 'life size' then. And Father Ryan was on the wall like the religious pictures.

"Stone bruises was on boys cause they was all in their bare feet. Me brothers all used to have them. They were a big white blister, hard and sore. They'd come from a prod, like if you walked on a piece of glass or stone or anything sharp that'll stick in you and this big white hard gathering would come. And there'd be a little black in the centre. Ah, you'd be in pain . . . terrible pain. But no one would bother because everyone had them. So they'd get this needle and they weren't sterilised or anything and they'd just stick it in it—they'd say it was 'letting it go'—and all this stuff would come out. Then they'd get the bread and hot water and squeeze the bread out onto a cloth and it'd be roasting—hot poultice they used to call it—and they'd put that on it and they'd scream. You didn't feel the needle going in and you felt relieved when this liquid would come out of it . . . until the hot thing would go on it. That was to sterilise it. But it'd cure it.

"They were all home cures then. Everyone had a cure cause there was very few doctors you ever went to. Like you used to get big lumps of black soap and you scraped the soap into a cloth and put sugar on it and that was good for boils. You could put that on stone bruises as well. And there was Maguire's Chemist in Talbot Street and Maguire's catered for all the poorest people and sold a penny and tuppence worth of everything. Like you could get tuppence worth of iodine for cuts or tuppence worth of Hippo Wine and Squills, that was for little babies with coughs. It was real sweet thick liquid, a light brown, and it'd loosen all the chests. And for babies with coughs or colds you could buy tuppence worth of tallow, a lump of dripping, and mothers'd get a brown paper bag, like a real hard brown bag that used to have sugar in them, and they'd cut the neck like in the shape of a little shirt, no sleeves, just to get over their heads, for on their front and back. And they'd cover that with the tallow and put their vest or whatever they wore over that. There was a cure in that. And TB, that was like cancer now. If someone had it they called it 'consumption' and you wouldn't use their cup after them. People didn't stay away from them but they just had their own cup and saucer and their own plate and spoon. You wouldn't wear their clothes. And their clothes would be burned when they died.

"There was no Bingo then for the women, they sat on the doorsteps, all sat out talking. And in pubs women was all in the snugs and they'd go in and get their gills. Now I often seen women in rows, could be in a pub, and there would be hair pulling and the shawls would be thrown off. Oh, yes, many a time. It could be over anything. There used to be a couple of women down on Corporation Street who were hard-goers and at that time their underwear was called 'shifts' and you'd see 'em fighting in their shift sleeves. Throw off the shawl and the cardigan and that'd be under it. Fighting in their shift sleeves the way men would fight in their shirt sleeves. And people might be separating them and then they'd be into it! They'd say, 'Ah, she got the worst of it and she was just separating them.'

"And there were fortune tellers around then. I'll tell you, everybody back then knew Gypsy Lee. She was in the caravan down on Foley Street and then she moved into Railway Street. She knew a lot. You could go to her if you were in a bit of trouble or difficulty. Oh, people took Mrs Lee seriously . . . all the time. Compared with anyone else her word was accepted as the right thing. She had the crystal ball, and she was a palm reader. Oh, people would come from *all over*. People used to queue up for her. She was highly respected, a *real lady*. You'd (as children) be playing a game and somebody'd come along and say, 'Do you know where the fortune teller is . . . Gypsy Lee?' And you'd go with them cause they'd give you a penny or maybe a ha'penny for leading them around to her. Oh, she used to have crowds waiting.

"Around Foley Street and Corporation Street all the fellas stood at Clare's (pub) and Brett's (shop) corner and stood at McCormick's corner. All corners. Just men, like me father. Not for anything bad. If it was fine weather and they were in getting a pint they'd come out and stand, but most of the men wouldn't have the price for a pint so they'd stand at the corners cause they'd no money to go in and drink—and there was no television. Just stand at the corner and be talking. You'd see them laughing and joking and trick-acting . . . cause they'd no money to go in and get a pint. The fellas that you see standing outside now in the summer, they're standing out for the air. But them poor men, in the winter and summer they stood there. Cause they didn't have any money. But they'd be with their friends. Or they'd go for a walk. My father used to walk *miles*, walk to Terenure and here and there. Maybe three or four men, never one on their own.

"Now the animal gangs, oh, they were a rough bunch. Everyone was kind of afraid of them. I'd say there was about thirty or forty of them, the *real* animal gang, around Foley Street and Corporation Street. And their opponents were from Wolfe Tone Street and King Street. I suppose 'animal' originated out of animals, the way they'd fight. The animal gangs fighting, it went on for ages and ages and there'd be sticks and stones and killing and everything. I'd say there'd be maybe ten or twelve on each side, and maybe more, killing one another. And then the police'd come and they'd be all scattered. See, we had a ringside seat cause our window—the only window we had—looked straight down onto Corporation Street. Now when the men would be fighting they'd be taken by the police and, well, you oughta seen *how* they'd be taken. The police would drag the men with their arms twisted and the men wouldn't walk for them and they'd drag them and their legs and their feet would be getting dragged along. And it'd frighten the living daylights out of you looking at them. Ah, they'd be stupefied drunk but they'd be pretty strong and they wouldn't walk for them . . . no, they wouldn't walk. I seen them giving them the batons and all. Oh, they'd be bloodied.

"The Jewmen, we couldn't do without them. Oh, my mother had a Jewman. I had one meself. In them days your first loan off a Jewman would be about two or three pounds and you paid five shillings to the pound. Oh, five shillings was a lot of money. The Jewman came to the door and he had a little card and he marked it. And you could hide on 'em, like 'Tell him I'm not here,' but that meant it took an extra week to pay your loan. Oh, they'd fleece you. But they were a necessity of life, you couldn't do without them. And Christmas was a time when everybody looked for money and you didn't care who lent it to you. Like the money-lenders, they were the *worst*—and they were your own neighbours! Some of them, if you didn't pay them you'd be met on the street and get a hammering off them, off who they'd have there.

"Christmas when I was young . . . ah, it was grand. We hadn't much but, oh, God, it was lovely. Christmas morning you were up at six and the beds all decorated. They used to have a white honeycomb quilt for each bed—but then they'd be taken off and pawned till the next holiday. And the pillow cases, you got them done in the laundry and the edges of the pillow cases were real stiff, like galvanised. And when you put them on they'd be so stiff they stood on their own. And the brass beds, they'd be shined up for Christmas. My father always shined our beds. Always washed the bed down first with paraffin oil and then he'd use the Brasso. Oh, it gleamed on Christmas. And we used to hang up the stockings on the bed rail and there'd be chains, not glittery ones like now, just paper chains and always a big red candle. Everyone'd go mad for a red candle. I still do myself. And me mother'd put a big red paper bell in the middle of the curtains. That was put in the window so that people passing by could see the bell. And at Christmas when we were waking up you'd be sitting up on the landing stairs with whatever toys you had, Woolworth's toys for maybe sixpence. Nearly always a doll for young ones and for boys motor cars. And a few sweets. And the little ones would all be out in Talbot Street singing Christmas carols. I can cry when I think of them years . . . happy years.

"All the courting was done on the stairs in the tenement houses and in them years weddings was in the house. The house would be all scrubbed for the wedding, like Christmas, and the place was shining. Where I lived they helped each other. Neighbours would scrub down each landing, scrub down all the house. And there'd be dancing and singing in the house, a melodion and a tin whistle, or a mouth organ. And they'd be out in the road and everyone then would join in outside. But back then if a young one, a woman, had a child and she wasn't married, oh, God help her. She'd be the *talk of the nation*! And then afterwards when the child was growed up they'd say, 'Oh, that's such a body's young one . . . sure, she had her before she was married.' Oh, they were looked down on, definitely. But when you got married it kind of took the harm out of the thing.

"Children was mostly born in the home then. But when I was a child you really didn't kind of know your mother was expecting. Like we were fooled, really, when you look back on it. You went to bed and got up the next morning and there was another child! I can't know up to this day how it was done . . . how we didn't hear me mother making sounds or roaring out or anything. Sometimes you'd know that something was going on and it would click with you because your mother would be saving up all these newspapers. That's the way I had me children meself, with newspapers all spreaded out on the bed. And then they were just rolled and taken out and they were all burned. When your mother went into labour the handywoman, like Mrs Dunleavy, would get everything prepared. She brought us home for my mother. And I was blessed with twenty-one children meself and I'd every one of them at home. I had twenty-one births and I've fourteen living. One died when he was eight months and another died when she was four years. The others were stillborn . . . only lived a few minutes, enough to hear them crying and that was the end.

"Most of the handywomen all had big families theirselves. They lit the fire and put on the pots of water, they tidied over and settled the bed and the newspapers. But the pain, you had to suffer it. You had *nothing* at all. Had to put up with it no matter how bad it was. Just hold on to the brass bed and the handywomen'd tell you what to do. She'd say to push or not to push. And then the handywoman would wash the baby with lukewarm water, no soap or anything, just to wash the mucus off it. You just wrapped it in a towel or piece of cloth that was clean. And we had no cradles then— our arms was our cradle. I reared mine in a shawl. All the neighbours would be coming in to visit you and your bed would be made up with the honeycomb quilt and you had a special little pillow and you put the baby on it and a little rug over it. And most of my children were christened the next day. We used to have an old saying, 'It strengthens them.'

"And a handywoman, she'd wake the dead, washed the dead and laid them out. A family'd always get the handywoman cause if you done anything for your own (deceased) it was kind of unlucky, it wasn't right. You *had* to get someone. Now Mattie Humphrey, she was a very old neighbour and came from Gardiner Street and she used to bring home a lot of children and she washed a lot of dead. Handywomen'd wash the body and shave the man and if the eyes was still a bit open you'd put pennies on their eyes to keep their eyes closed, just for a few hours. We used to do it just for the weight, to keep their eyes closed. Now the Jews, they'd say, 'That's their entrance fee!'—wherever they were going, across the Jordan. And you tied the mouth up if it was gaping. You tied it with a cloth or put a prayer book under the chin on the chest during the wake.

"So Mattie'd lay them out and put the shroud on them and then the honeycomb quilt. The dead was always laid out in a corner and there was a sheet put on the wall there and another sheet on the wall there (beside). And there'd be sheets there (on ceiling) like a canopy, put on with pins or tacks. And they got this black crepe paper for adults and red for a baby boy and blue for a baby girl. It was sold in folds and that'd be put all across the ceiling and all the way down, all pinned. And in the middle there'd be a cross made out of the crepe paper. And most people would go to the trouble to make little roses with the black crepe paper and we'd put them on the four corners of the cross, to make it nice. You got four candles laying out the dead, they had to be white. There was a table at the side of the bed and a white cloth on it and holy water and a feather to dip in the water for to shake on them, 'The Father, The Son, The Holy Ghost', on the body. And there was also the snuff, for anyone that wanted it.

"For a wake people weren't invited. See, the door was open and *anyone* could go up. They'd go to wakes like they're going to dances now. They might not even *know* the person. Everyone would go in and they'd sit around. You'd take out the furniture—well, there wasn't 'furniture', there was maybe only a dresser—and there'd be a big stool, maybe from one of the fellas' football club. They'd lend you a long stool, about four to six feet long, and that was put along one side of the room. And when you'd go in there'd be three or four people sitting there and you'd get a glass of porter and they'd make sandwiches. I used to love to hear that someone's dead cause you'd go to the wakes and they had the melodion and they were all singing and that went on *all night*. See, you had to do something to keep the long night going, like you couldn't shut that door and leave the dead person there on their own. This would go on till five or six in the morning and you'd look around and half of them would be asleep. Eventually you rambled off home about nine or ten in the morning and there'd be one or two would be after sleeping all night and, well, they'd go in and swill their face and go down to the pub then for a drink.

"And they played games to pass the time all night. Oh, they used to play 'Who has the button?' Everyone sat around and your man would have the button in his hand and he'd go along (and put the button in someone's closed hands) and no one knew who had the button. And then he'd say, 'Who has the button?' And you'd say, 'He has'—but he mightn't. So he'd say, 'Put out your hand' and you'd get a slap. It was like torture getting slapped. Another game we played was 'forfeits'. You'd be asked to do something, like go down to Nelson's Pillar and get a tram ticket with '608' on it. A whole bundle of them would go, be all on their knees looking. You'd be all over O'Connell Street and in the traffic looking for a tram ticket! And there'd be millions of tram tickets. No one would ever find it with the '608' and so you'd have to give them up your shoe or stockings, or give them your jumper or something. And then they'd say, 'Do you want your clothes? Well, here, go and get them' and they'd throw them out (window). And you'd be afraid for your life going out because it was pitch dark and maybe it'd be winter. Maybe some of the fellas would go and bring them up to you. But you never stripped really, like what they call it now—'nude'. No, you never done that. But you'd be stripped off into your petticoat and they'd be saying, 'Ah, that's enough now.' You know, the people were so old-fashioned.

"And there was another game, going knocking on people's doors. Now there was a man, 'Bollard' Browne, a huge big man. He worked on the quay. Oh, very gruff. Oh, a big double chin and he only had to look at you! You'd be even afraid walking by his door and if he ever looked at you you'd gallop. So they'd say, 'You go down and knock three times on Bollard Browne's door.' And Bollard would come out and he'd be *roaring* out. And you'd gallop! And he'd come into the wake . . . 'You'se are the ones doing this . . . what a gouger . . . I've got to be up for work in the morning, I can't sleep all day.' There'd be murder. So we'd say, 'alright, Bollard, we won't.' But we'd go off again and then it was, '*You* go down now and knock three times again on Bollard's!'

"The only ones that'd be kept out of a wake would be small kids cause they'd be afraid. See, as children you'd always hear about the banshee. Everyone knew what she looked like. She had long grey hair, not washed or combed, kind of dirty grey . . . wild. And she had a wrinkled face and a big hook nose like a dirty witch, always filthy and these long old clothes on her. Now this is the *truth*. I heard the banshee before he (husband) died. Oh, I did! It's a warning that someone was going to die. I heard it out here in the back. It was coming on to two in the morning and I woke up. About two or three days before he died—and, mind you, he wasn't sick. Ah, he was as well as me and you. This is as true as God. And it *wasn't a cat* because I know the cats out there and I know their cry. And the minute you open the window they clear. But he opened the window and that thing kept . . . it wasn't crying . . . it was *wailing*. And it went on and on and on. And the next morning I said to him, 'Did you hear that last night?' 'That wasn't a cat,' says he, 'that was the banshee. She was on her rounds last night, there's somebody going.' 'Ah', he says, 'in the next few days you'll hear of someone going, I'm telling you.' And it was himself!

"I don't feel any shame in coming from the Monto. The reputation was there cause of the girls. In them years they was called 'the girls' and in later years they'd say they were 'unfortunate girls', but never 'prostitutes'. We never heard the word 'whores', never heard 'prostitute'. You heard your mother say, 'Oh, the girls are down there,' around the gas lamp at Jack Maher's pub. His pub there on the corner of Corporation Street was a kind of figure-head going into the Monto. Oh, the girls used to drink there. And the girls hung around on the streets and the men used to come mostly off the boats. Most of the girls now that I can remember was from the country. It was for the money, just to keep theirselves going. And there was a lot of them that turned real religious. Looking back on it you can never say whether they were young or old cause of the way they dressed. The usual thing was a big white apron and a skirt underneath it and a shawl. The white apron was clean looking and it drew the attention. Oh, they were always clean. There's one woman I remember and I can picture her as if it was only yesterday standing at the lamp-post at Jack Maher's and she didn't wear a black shawl, she wore one of the big coloured Galway shawls, grey and fawn and all the flowers on it and all the big long fringe. It used to be beautiful. I couldn't afford one . . . we wore black shawls.

"The girls were good, and generous. If you went for a message for them you'd get thruppence or sixpence. And if they seen a kid running in his bare feet they'd bring him into Brett's and buy him a pair of runners to cover their feet. And if there was a row with men on the street they'd bring the children away when bad language would be getting used and give you a penny or a ha'penny and say, 'Now you're not going to go down there.' That happened to meself. Oh, they were very kind-hearted. Indeed, they were. Now when I got married I was only fifteen and we lived in Summerhill and there was an operation (brothel) there in the back yard and in fine weather the 'girls' used to be out there in the sun. It was a Mrs Smythe that had the house and I thought they were her daughters. There was about five or six of them. Ah, they were lovely looking girls, beautiful hair and lovely looking clothes. Now they were fond of kids, very, very kind, and I used to love going down for the water because they were most generous. I was only fifteen and I used to feel like a child the way they used to treat me. They'd be saying, 'She's only a child' and be giving me an apple and fruit. And one time they gave me a lovely box of chocolates. I was afraid to even open it it looked so lovely. And me husband went to kill me . . . 'You don't be taking nothing off of them, they're all bad women.' When he found out about it I got it!

"The girls had madams. I knew the women by name. One of them was our landlord's mother. She had a big house on Railway Street and the girls used to go in there. Me mother used to work in it, used to scrub for her. The madams were from around here and their families are still living up there . . . I wouldn't like to mention names cause there is families that's still alive. Now we didn't call them 'madams', the outsiders called them madams. We called them 'kip-keepers'. See, a 'kip' meant going for a sleep or a rest. The houses that they lived in were called kips. Like my mother used to say, 'Oh, she's a kip-keeper' and that was an awful thing. Very rarely you'd hear of a 'brothel', it was a 'kip'. The girls were very generous but the madams took *all* (their money) and very rarely would you hear of them being generous. But one family (kip-keepers) lived down there and in latter years they started giving money to the Church and there was one priest refused to take the money because he knew where it came from. That was the only priest I ever heard of refusing money!"

May Hanaphy—Age 85

Her long life has nearly spanned the twentieth century. Born in Golden Lane, her father died three months before her birth and her mother was left destitute with nine children. Well-meaning Protestants tried to persuade her mother to relinquish the children to their care, but she defiantly pronounced that she would go to work to keep the family together. This meant placing tiny and delicate May in the Poor Crèche on Meath Street for the first four years of her life. Her mother managed to hold on to all her children but several died of diphtheria. "If there are uncrowned saints in Heaven my mother's one," confides May.

As a young girl she relished the colourful street life just outside her tenement half door. She was confronted by the Black and Tans and when the Rebellion erupted watched from her safe window perch as neighbours looted shops. Back then Golden Lane was known as the "four corners of hell" for its drink and brawling. The best free show was the weekly family feud between two street trading families. It was pure bloody bedlam in the open street with knives, chains and hatchets. At the first cry of "ruggy-up" tenement dwellers would scurry out to watch at a discreet distance.

At age fourteen she got a job at Jacob's biscuit factory and was delighted to bring home a few shillings to her mother at week's end. It was also around this time that she began to understand the sad conditions which drove young girls into prostitution on the streets. Life, she learned, could be very cruel. The saddest day of her life was dashing home from the biscuit factory in a snowstorm to her mother's deathbed. Today she lives in a small but comfortable newly-built flat on Lord Edward Street. When comparing her childhood in the tenement slums with modern life in Dublin she says simply, "I'm just living on a new planet now."

"I remember life in Golden Lane as a lovely life . . . but poor. It was very old tenements and we were very poor growing up, but we accepted it as our lot. Now Golden Lane, how it got its name was years and years ago gold was supposed to be manufactured in the lane. See, there was Golden Lane, Copper Alley, Silver Street—queer names. When I was small everywhere was a lane. Golden Lane was very narrow—you could shake hands with the person across the street! It really was *old* Dublin, and all cobblestones for the horses. At that time the lane was full of half doors on the tenement houses and you'd lean over the half doors like that. And there was a place called Oliver's Alley that was supposed to be haunted when we were children. We were told there was a man murdered there for twopence in his pocket and that afterwards he was seen always sitting in the middle of the lane, a long, long lane.

"My father was only thirty-nine when he died. He died in October and I was born in January. My mother was thirty-seven at that time and there were nine of us children. We were just real poor, *very* poor. My mother had to go out to work for us. She had to wash up after painters, scrub down the floors after the painters in the big houses that the proper caste lived in at that time, the old Georgian and Victorian houses. Had to use a steel scrubbing brush to get all the stuff (paint) off the floor. We didn't know the hard things Mammy was doing for us, out working all day. See, the Protestants would come around and say, 'Mrs Hanaphy, you're not able (to care) for the children now, we'll take them for you.' Not forcibly—it was called 'Protestantising'. Like they would take you and send you to school and put you into a home and look after you. Of course, we'd have to adopt their religion, you know. They only went to mothers that had no father (husband). And my mother said, 'No, I'm not giving them up at all. I'm going to work,' says she. And she worked *very hard* for us and we were only babies. When she was young she was very pretty and we loved her because she was so dainty and we used to call her the 'little general' because her word was *law*. She was *marvellous*. She just *slaved* for us. She died in the last world war. And it broke our hearts. We often say, 'If there's uncrowned saints in Heaven my mother's one.'

"Now after I was born my mother had to bring me wrapped up to the Poor Crèche on Meath Street. That was a crèche for the poor babies, for the underprivileged. For the poor people who couldn't mind their babies when their husbands was dead and the mothers had to go out to work. It was free. See, under the British regime it was all fostered by the Government. You put your baby into the crèche during the day and collected your baby. My sister was only seven and she had to carry me to the crèche from Golden Lane up to Meath Street. Mother Scott was the matron of the crèche. Now she wasn't a nun, just a matron. And I remember singing, 'Mother Scott, I love you, Mother Scott, we do, there's not another mother in the world like you.' I just remember sitting on the floor and singing that song. You sat on the floor and played with bits of paper. That's all I really remember. Oh, I spent about four years in the crèche. I should have been only about twelve months in—you were only allowed twelve months—but Mother Scott was (feeling) so pitiful for my mother's plight, you see, and because I was very young and very delicate.

"We had a very hard struggle in the tenements. My mother's wages then was only nine shillings a week and our rent was one and six. Our room wasn't any bigger than this (12 by 15 feet) and we hadn't got the necessities, that was the sad part of it. One toilet in the yard for everyone. That was the hardest part. Oh, no locks, a swinging door and the door would be wide open. And then the children would soil the floor, you know. It wasn't nice. Mammy had a very hard life but she used to make a stew at night-time for us, maybe a rabbit stew, and a sheep's head for Sunday dinner. An ordinary sheep's head and it used to be hung on hooks outside the butcher's and the butcher would always split it down the centre and you could get a half or a whole one. And she'd go down to the yard and give it a thorough washing. There was hardly any meat on it. Oh, but the flavour! And you could get all pot herbs for a penny, a great big paper full of carrot, thyme, parsley and that'd be put in with the sheep's head . . . really beautiful. Mammy always cooked on a coal fire with an open grate and always a huge kettle on the hob. She was a great cook, a beautiful cook, and she never wasted a fire. And she'd bring us up to the Iveagh Market to get clothes. You could get a nice dress for four or five shillings. Stacks of clothing and they'd hold them up and auction them off. Then they might get tired and say, 'Root there yourself and see what you want.' 'Root', that was a great word here. My Confirmation dress was bought in the Iveagh Market.

"Ah, there was everything in the tenements . . . cats and rats. The rats would say 'good morning' to you at our house at the back. And you'd say, 'Ma, there's two rats down there' and she'd say, 'They won't touch you if you don't touch them.' Oh, and people always had birds in the windows all around the tenements. Everybody had a bird hanging up there outside the window. It was to add a bit of cheer. Oh, yes, they were always chirping. I had a budgie. They *talked* to you. Oh, my sister's bird fell *out* the window, a goldfinch. The rain must have loosened the nail and it fell down in the street. He wasn't hurt but the cage was smashed. And cattle was brought up from all parts of the country at four and five in the morning and they'd walk with the cattle drover and they'd soil the place, naturally. Cattle and horses soiling the streets so there was always manure around the place and the bluebottles were as big as the doorknob there. And *millions* of them! They were so numerous, the flies, that we would catch them and put them in the old tins we'd find on the street and say, 'How many have you got?' There was no hygiene then. The bluebottles would bring disease, that's why there was so much disease around the place, so much loss of life.

"There were a lot of deaths at that time. My mother lost two boys and a girl to diphtheria. At that time nearly every family lost children at six or seven years old . . . everybody lost children. If a little girl died we didn't understand *why*, *how* they died, or what happened to them. We just knew, 'Oh, so-and-so is dead, and she's twelve.' Then we'd always go around, ten or twelve of us children, with a little tin or a cardboard box and we'd collect pennies or ha'pennies from everybody for to buy a small wreath of flowers. We had a lady opposite us by the name of McGrail and she'd a big family and had a hard time rearing them up and she was a beautiful flower maker. She'd know of a death and buy fresh flowers in the market and make beautiful wreaths and bouquets out of them for a wake. She'd charge you maybe two shillings and then sixpence went on ribbon to bind it up. So the child was waked at home and you went up and put your bouquet on the end of the little coffin. The neighbours always prepared the corpse. That was the custom here. It was done in such a homely, warm atmosphere, a *loving* atmosphere, that you didn't cry or didn't weep. And when the corpse was on the bed we handed tea around and sandwiches and prayers was said and the rosary. Then they'd be buried. At that time it was horses for the hearse and it was 'trot, trot, trot' and crowds standing all along. At that period all the horse cabs stopped and drew up at the public houses and everyone would get their beer and came home *mouldy, maggoty drunk!*

"But we'd a wonderful childhood, Kevin. There were so many tenement houses around when we were young and you kept to your quarter and we were always in the streets. We used to skip on the road and play 'cat and stick' and we'd play marbles. And we had very long summer nights here when we were young. I remember being out till eleven and it'd be daylight. Girls would bring down skipping ropes and the boys would turn the ropes for them in the lane. Even the big married women would skip and their husbands would turn the rope for them. And I used to play a little melodion and I'd bring it down to the hall door and played that and we'd all dance until about half past ten that night. And you know George's Street? Well, George's Street was a second Moore Street at that period, packed with stalls and they were traders and they dealt in fruit. Women in those days . . . *really Dublin* and down-to-earth women. You'd love them, you'd *love* them now, honestly. They'd wear shawls and they liked taking their beer. Went down with their jugs for a gill of beer, or a half gill. God, there was great chat then . . . it was a great old life.

"Oh, and lots of characters around, Kevin. Lots of characters that had a tough life with kids. It was that innocent kind of jeering. There was Soodlum, he was a character that'd walk around with big things on his back, cans and bottles and strings and all that. His mind wasn't so good, the poor man. And we'd say, 'Here's Soodlum, *run!*' Or, 'Here's Johnny-Forty-Coats, *run!*' We'd run and jeer them. We were *bold*. And the lavender man would go around with a tray in front of him and a big string, a wooden tray like a bread board. And lovely sachets of lavender. Now we wouldn't have the money for the lavender. My mother used to have the wretched camphor balls to keep moths out, from biting your clothes. Oh, the *smell* of them was wicked and it never left your clothes. But we'd love to smell the lavender on his tray . . . and there were no handouts. But then we might bump into him purposely and upset all his lavenders on the little tray, give him a push if we wanted a chase. We were bold, all right. God love him, he was only trying to make a living too. Oh, the pranks years ago, there was millions of them.

"And the organ-grinders had their trade. During the First World War the Italians were poor too and they emigrated from Italy and came to Ireland for a living and they had the grinding organs in Chancery Lane and they went out and made money out of it on O'Connell Street and all, grinding organs with the monkeys on their back. If you had a penny they'd play the organ for you. Oh, I remember dancing around the organ and we'd be *delighted*. Lovely tunes they were. Some of them had little monkeys sitting on the top and he'd pull out your fortune. A small blue or pink envelope he'd pull out and your fortune was on it. And the monkey would wear maybe a little hat on him or maybe a little scarf or a little coat, or maybe nothing at all. But he always had a little hat on him. Then there was the ice cream makers. They'd come with the ice cream carts, push carts, and they'd scoop the ice cream out on to a wafer. They had ice. At that time ice was plentiful. People bought ice for the fish, the shops. As a child I can remember the ice carts going down the lane and often the ice falling off and we'd all grab for the ice.

"Now there was a chandler in Golden Lane, an old man with a beard, and he was called 'Johnny One Match'. Chandlers would sell candles, coal, turf, oils, sticks, matches, anything to do with lamps, with fires. You had an oil can and you'd get a pint of oil for a farthing or a ha'penny. Now, see, years ago we were all looking for matches and if you went into him for a match he'd give you *one*, that's all. If he was in *good humour* he'd give you one. So he was christened 'Johnny One Match'. Now Johnny One Match died and the Sineys took over the premises. They owned two houses along with their two shops. Oh, they were very comfortable, they were called the elite of the street. Oh, we classed them as rich. They had a *beautiful* drawing room and they had a piano, which was wonderful. And they had a little trap with a pony and a surrey on top. That was *great* then. They didn't mix with very many people. The whole family and the girls lived over on that side of the lane and they weren't allowed to play with us. But they'd go up to the far side of the lane and then call us over and then we'd play that way. I became very good friends with the girls and I got really pally with May and I'd go over to Siney's for Sunday tea. And me Ma'd say, 'If you get any chicken or jelly, eat it, eat all you're getting.' Cause we'd no chicken or jellies.

"There was money-lenders everywhere and they had the place skinned. Yes, 'skinned'. There was a lady in the lane and she was a fishmonger and, well, it was a custom that if you were short of money—which your mother always was—you went up to this lady. Her name was McEvoy. Now you could *not* get a loan off that woman except if you bought the fish off her. And those fish would be *old* . . . hopeless. She'd get the load of fish for nothing in the market, maybe fish that wasn't fit for consumption in the hot weather. You couldn't eat them. Oh, you'd have to throw them out! But that was the only way you'd get a loan. Now that was a very, very old Dublin custom and the more you bought the more loans she gave you. And, oh, she wouldn't give it to you except she knew you and you were a good pay. So she got the name of 'Payo' McEvoy—'Pay or you get no more!' Payo McEvoy lived in a magnificent home. Oh, yes. Ah, me mother would always hate going up and she'd say to us, 'Go on up and get a loan of four shillings.' Four shillings would go a long way then to feed you. It could feed a family for a day or two days. And you had to pay her back the following week. If you didn't pay and she got a few beers on her you *heard* it. Yeah, she was a very good beer sharker . . . all the *lane* heard it!

"And *everyone* had a Jewman. Mother had a little Jewman, Mr Bookman was his name, and he was very nice and kind. He knew my mother's circumstances and he never pressurised her. My mother'd often buy the sheets off the Jewman, bedclothes and table cloths, and pay them off by the week. But she never got into money-lending or heavy debt. Now a relation of ours over on the northside, she'd get £20 off her Jewman. That's a lot of money. But she was a devil for the beer. And then she'd *move*! See, it was easier to move then than pay the rent because Dublin at that time was a *hive* of tenement lanes. Sure, everywhere you went you saw 'rooms to let'. Oh, yes, much easier to move than to pay the Jewman or to pay the rent. My relative actually moved to England to escape the last loan. She was a devil.

"I remember the Black and Tans. We were born under the British regime and it was kind of accepted as a way of life. They would come in with a kind of black uniform and those tam o'shanters down sideways on their head. It wasn't (actually) a uniform but a kind of pouched blouse and black trousers, a pouched jacket and a belt . . . oh, an 'anything would do them' sort of thing. And revolvers. And they'd just come in and look around and see that there was only poor kids there and they'd say 'Any guns here?' And Charlie, my brother's friend, he was a rebel and he had a gun in me mother's drawer—but me mother never knew though. And me mother was afraid of her life that my brother might join the organisation. They were not called IRA then, they were called 'rebels', which was a nicer word. We didn't *hate* them (British and Black and Tans) or anything, isn't that funny? Cause we should have hated them. We were *so used* to the British regime and British soldiers on the street were nothing to us when we were young. It was just the army of occupation. Back then we didn't *realise* what the men were fighting for and we weren't for either side. We didn't realise how serious the situation was. When I got older . . . *now* I hate them.

"We lived in Golden Lane beside Ship Street barracks where the British soldiers were. My pals lived in Ship Street and we used to play there. And the British soldiers, if they were confined to barracks, like for being late, they'd call out of the windows to us in the street to buy them cigarettes. They'd throw the money out and you were to keep the change which, of course, was *great*. And we often had to push the little cigarettes one by one through the little wires. See, the wires were because anyone could throw a bomb in. And I remember the rebellion *so* well because there was a policeman down at the very end of Ship Street we used to call 'Daddy' and he was shot and we were *horrified*. See, there was a Protestant church just around the corner and it had this tower and snipers got into the tower and sniped right into the Castle. I believe that he was the first policeman to be shot during the Rebellion.

"Then the looting started. Now my Ma wouldn't allow us outside the street when the trouble started. But my brothers were older than us and they went with a crowd of fellas down Grafton Street and it was *terrible* they told my mother. People were getting trampled on when they were looting, taking things out of the shops. It was *shocking*. *Anyone* was doing it. See, we were curtailed for food during the Rebellion and there was nothing coming to anybody. They smashed everything in Grafton Street and they had all the best quality of stuff. Law and order had completely broken down. We had the front window now when the looting was going on and they were bringing up pianos on carts. 'Ma, Ma, come and look out, *quick!*' we'd say. 'Look, there's a piano coming up.' And we'd all rush to the window. Oh, yes, and chairs and anything they could get hold of they took. Beautiful chairs. People that lived all around us. Oh, the British went around afterwards when the Rebellion was quelled and *every* house was searched, every street was searched. And if they found anything then you got so many days imprisonment. Now didn't my brothers bring back a couple bottles of the choicest liqueurs. See, my brothers liked drink and they were very young when they drank. And my mother wanted to *kill* them. My mother said, 'We want food but we don't want that'—and Mammy got it and poured it down the pipe into the yard.

"Years ago people tried to make money in any way they could. The men were very fond of boxing and they'd box for money in the streets. There'd be a ring made around by the Patrick Street area. And there was the 'tossing school', only lads and men, and they flipped two coins up and if you backed heads and heads came up you'd win. No big stakes. It was an entertainment. But drink was cheap and that's how rows would start then. Drink was terribly cheap, tuppence a pint and maybe three pence for a glass of whiskey. So they made hay! And the poor wives never got much money and the husband would come home drunk. There was a word then—it's not used now—if your husband was out beering on you and didn't care about you and you wanted somebody else, well, it'd be called a 'fancy man'. They said, 'Oh, she has a fancy man.' Or he might have a fancy woman. That's how rows would start and, well, then the wife was beat up. Ah, you'd see black eyes every day of the week. And you knew very well . . . but that sort of thing, you never spoke about it. We wouldn't ask any questions. We'd just say, 'Oh, mother, she's got a terrible black eye' and she'd say, 'She was beaten up by her husband over going out with a fancy man.' That's the way it came down to us.

"And through drink there was rows in the street. Maybe a family feud between one another. There'd be nothing till they'd go into the pub. Our lane was called the 'four corners of hell'. There was a pub up that side, a pub on that corner, a pub that corner and down the lane there was a pub. It got the name 'four corners of hell' because the drink was so terrible. Now a family feud, there were the Connorses and the Ellises and they were dealers and they dealt in fruit and they were related, say first cousins. Anyway, when I'd be about fourteen my mother'd say, 'There's going to be a ruggy-up tonight, there's going to be murder tonight between the Connorses and the Ellises. On a Sunday or Saturday. Particularly on Saturday night and it'd be murder. *Murder!* Hatchets and big sticks. Oh, yes, especially hatchets. In each family there was about seven or eight. Well, they'd fall out and drink in the Circle

Pub over there and then the row would start. They'd come out in the street and they'd fight there and the hatchets and all would come out. Men and women both. Women in *particular* now would have it in for the other person, the other person's wife. Had big hatchets and hammers or whatever and they'd *kill* each other. And there'd be hair pulling, women's style. Oh, there'd be a good few casualties and some would have to go to the hospital. But there'd be no deaths, funny enough. That was nearly every Saturday and Sunday. And they never made it up, the Connorses and the Ellises, until they got older and it all kind of died down. And there were other families, like the Greene family, and they'd have their fights and you'd run around saying, 'Ruggy-up, ruggy-up . . . quick, quick, ruggy-up' and we'd all gather around. But you wouldn't interfere cause it was all family.

"Oh, there was always fighting, always fighting . . . it was a *wonderful* life, it was great. Then they'd say, 'Ruggy-up, here's the police' and the police had whistles and, oh, once you heard the whistle blew you blew too! See, if there was a row somebody'd send for the police if the row got hot. Now I remember at that time the DMP—that's the British police—were very hard on the men. Now I'm not speaking of the British as tyrants—but we know they kind of were in a way—but our *own* Irish men who joined the DMP were as bad. Oh, some were worse. I saw it myself because we were always looking out the window as kids. We had two tenement windows, one wouldn't open and everyone went for the other one. Now I remember this as a child and this is no fantasy, it was the real thing. When they'd get anyone (who was) drunk and helpless they were frog-marched into the old police station in Chancery Lane. They would make them walk on their hands and they'd be holding up their feet and frog-march them. Very painful. Saw them myself passing our window. I'd say now it'd be a form of cruelty.

"When I was fourteen I started at Jacob's (biscuit factory). They always took on girls at fourteen and we were known as 'Jacob's mice'. Now the first morning I started my mother had a lovely little red blouse on me and skirt and dressed up lovely. All polished up. And two little ribbons in my hair, two little plaits, up like two little drumsticks. Your hair was divided in the back and combed and you were plaited with a big ribbon at the end. I started out at eleven and six. Oh, I was *delighted*! I went home and said, 'Oh, Ma, look!' Gave it all to Mammy. *Every* penny. And she'd give you back sixpence or a shilling. We were delighted to give it to her. You know, Kevin, we didn't really know the value of money. We didn't want money . . . we didn't need money. We only wanted it for our parents because we played in the streets all day and we didn't buy anything. I *loved* the factory, loved my work, and I was never late.

"At that time the girls and boys growing up was really innocent. Oh, definitely . . . their little innocent way of skipping and everything. All we ever done to get a fella when we were young was rob their caps. If you fancied a fella you robbed his cap and you ran and he ran after you. There was an awful lot of chasing done. And we'd go 'clicking'. They don't use that term now—'Are you going out clicking tonight?' You'd be dressed up and all in a nice blouse and skirt and coat and hat. Oh, clicking was very popular then. That's how many a girl got a husband, going out at night-time. Oh, you'd go out for that purpose in that time. That's the way flirting went on. Now how you clicked was this—they'd (girls) go off along around the down-town, mostly O'Connell Street or maybe down Henry Street, strolling arm in arm, you know, slow walking. And two lads would come toward you and you'd get the eye and the two fellas would say, 'There's two mots.' We were called 'mots' then, the girls were. Those were some of the great old Dublin words. And you'd say to whoever you'd be with, 'Did you like them?' And if she said, 'Ah, yes,' well, then you'd look back and they'd look back. And then you'd walk on, walk slow . . . walk slow . . . 'Are they following us?' . . . 'I think so.' and then you'd stand at a window looking at clothes or shoes, but you'd make sure it wasn't any delicate garments. And next there'd be shadows behind us. And they'd just be standing there and they'd say, 'That's very nice, that looks nice doesn't it?' This was clicking. Now I done it myself. And the man would go for the small girl if he was small and the tall lad would go for the tall girl. It was done according to sizes and then a date was made.

"So you made a date then and the first times would be just walking and talking. And you walked back home, you didn't tell him where you lived. No, not on the first or second time. Then maybe the third night you might make a date for the pictures, if they were beginning to like you. Now you'd go to the pictures and your fella would naturally hold your hand. And if you didn't like him you'd be just squirming. You'd just put up with it for the night. Now say he got fresh with you and put his arm around you and say tried to kiss you or make some other advance . . . you'd be *squirming*. But you might get a nice fella.

"There was innocence then and girls were afraid too. There was fear as well as innocence. See, unfortunately the mothers told the girls nothing. *Nothing.* You had to learn yourself, learn it when you were fourteen, fifteen and sixteen . . . you know, when you had your period and that. You *had* to learn then. But you'd be afraid to ask your mother, or ashamed. You'd talk to an older friend about that, like my sister. But my mother'd say to us, 'If a man insults you take up your hand and slap him across the face.' She used to say that to us. But she never told us *how* we were insulted! We didn't know. And girls *did* become pregnant. Oh, yes. And it created fear and girls being put out of their homes. Oh, you were never kept once you became pregnant. A woman often went on the streets if the fella didn't want you, that was a cause of many people going on the streets. Some of them went into prostitution. And some drowned themselves. Out of despair. And the Church had no sympathy in those days. Like when you went to Confession . . . very tough on you. Often you were just afraid to go to Confession. Many a girl went on the street and many a girl was lost. Oh, *many* a girl took her own life. Oh, the Church, she's a good mother, but she's a *hard* mother.

"There was prostitution then and they had what were called 'bad houses' at that time in Whitefriar Street. Now actually the girls didn't go there for to commit any crimes but they just *slept* there to be off the streets. The girls would come and go. They went out and had their own standings, their own places, along Stephen's Green, Harcourt Street. These young girls would come up from the country and there was no work for them, only domestic service. And these old English quality style (families), the people who had the money and the big houses, well, they'd employ maids. And the girls from the country were paid very little money. And sometimes the bosses (husbands) and sons of the place would get those girls into trouble. So the country girls would come up, God love them, and they'd go into service and it (pregnancy) happened in their service and then the wife would put them out and they'd nowhere to go. They had to pay for their lodging and they had no other way of living—and they daren't go back to the country. So poverty would start prostitution.

"It wasn't called prostitution then but it did originate from that kind of life. Younger girls of that period were really slaves at that time. They were very vulnerable the young girls then. And if young country girls had babies at that time they'd need houses and there were no homes here for them and they couldn't go anywhere. A young girl who was pregnant had nowhere to go then. They were caught! There was a famous place in Whitefriar Street where this German family owned the tenement houses where the girls stayed. See, we had poor Italians and poor Germans around our place, very poor like ourselves, and they made their money in their own way. They had a place for these girls. Now I don't know if you ever heard of Frank Duff. He used to walk up and down Whitefriar Street in front of these houses and he'd be proselytising and just saying the rosary all the time. Mr Duff tried to take the girls from these houses and he'd walk up and down all day praying and saying the rosary. But he never interfered with them. Frank was a very, very nice young man—he'll be beatified sometime.

"My Mammy died when she was forty, died on a Friday at three o'clock. I was working in Jacob's at the time. And it was snowing and it was January. The sixteenth. And I went out in my overalls and I remember it being cold and snowing. And I ran out. And when I got home Mammy was just going. It was a hazy dream, something you couldn't realise . . . she was so good. She had a stroke and she was gone . . . to Heaven. The neighbours laid her out and done everything for her. I did the rosary myself, I was old enough. And the room was so small that the neighbours, they kneeled on the dark landing cause there was no space, you see, in the tenements. We didn't complain, we knelt on the stairs on the landing. And wreaths and all fresh flowers was put on Mammy's coffin. Now we didn't know (at the time) but mother was a silent, charitable giver. Molly (neighbour) came over and had a little boy with her by her hand and she had no father for the boy and mother always gave her money every week, a few pence, to keep them alive. And when she came over to kiss my mother goodbye she said, 'I've lost my best friend.' And we *never knew.* The funeral was on Monday morning and the horses drew up outside the door in Golden Lane. She had the black plumes on the horses and we were all in the cab and it was shaking like hell. And she was buried.

"Mother died up to the last minute working . . . she died in harness. That's another phrase for you, Kevin, that the people had . . . 'she died in harness.' Then we just grew up like that. I think when that happens, when your mother dies, you just grow up overnight."

Notes

INTRODUCTION (pp 1–5)

1. Reverend James Whitelaw, *An Essay on the Population of Dublin*, (Dublin: Graisberry and Campbell, 1805), p. 50.
2. 'War on the Slums', *Irish Press*, 1 October 1936, p. 9.
3. 'Religious Leaders Attack in Slum War', *Irish Press*, 9 October 1936, p. 9.
4. F. H. A. Aalen, 'The Working-Class Housing Movement in Dublin, 1850–1920', in Michael J. Bannon (editor), *The Emergence of Irish Planning, 1880–1920*, (Dublin: Turoe Press, 1985), p. 136.
5. 'Take Us Out of This Horrible Place', *Irish Press*, 2 October 1936, p. 9.
6. *Report of Inquiry Into the Housing of the Working Classes of Dublin, 1939/ 1943*, (Dublin: Government Publications Office, 1943), p. 17.
7. 'The Slum Peril', *The Daily Nation*, 8 September 1898, p. 5.
8. 'The Slum Question', *The Daily Nation*, 9 September 1898, p. 5.
9. Charles A. Cameron, *How the Poor Live*, (Dublin: private printing in 1904 and copy presented to the National Library of Ireland, 8 May 1905), p. 12.
10. Aalen, *op. cit.*, note 4, p. 136.
11. Lambert McKenna, 'The Housing Problem in Dublin', *Studies*, Vol. VIII, 1919, p. 280.
12. Joseph V. O'Brien, *'Dear, Dirty Dublin'*, (Berkeley: University of California Press, 1982), p. 136.
13. *Ibid.*, p. 136.
14. *Ibid.*, p. xi.
15. Aalen, *op. cit.*, note 4, p. 131.
16. Betty Messenger, *Picking Up The Linen Threads*, (Belfast: Blackstaff Press, 1988), p. xvi.
17. Bill Kelly, *Me Darlin' Dublin's Dead & Gone*, (Dublin: Ward River Press, 1983), p. 2.
18. Paul Thompson, 'History and the Community', in Willa K. Baum and David K. Dunaway (editors), *Oral History: An Interdisciplinary Anthology*, (Nashville, Tennessee: American Association for State and Local History, 1984), p. 41.

19. Fred Johnston, *Books Ireland,* (Dublin), April 1991, p. 80.
20. 'Voice of the People', *Irish Press,* 17 October 1936, p. 9.
21. Sidney Davies, *Dublin Types*, (Dublin: The Talbot Press Ltd, 1918), p. xviii.

CHAPTER 1. *HISTORY AND EVOLUTION OF THE TENEMENT SLUM PROBLEM* (pp 6–24)
 1. Sir John T. Gilbert, *Calendar of Ancient Records of Dublin*, (Dublin: Minutes of the Dublin Corporation, Vol. I, 1889), p. 459.
 2. Reverend James Whitelaw, *An Essay on the Population of Dublin*, (Dublin: Graisberry and Campbell, 1805), p. 50.
 3. For an historical account of the evolution and decline of Georgian Dublin, refer to: Kevin C. Kearns, *Georgian Dublin: Ireland's Imperilled Architectural Heritage*, (London: David & Charles Ltd, 1983), 224 ff.
 4. *Ibid.*, p.41.
 5. *Report of Inquiry Into the Housing of the Working Classes of Dublin, 1939/1943*, (Dublin: Government Publications Office, 1943), p. 24.
 6. 'War on the Slums', *Irish Press*, 2 October 1936, p. 9.
 7. *Report of Inquiry Into the Housing of the Working Classes of Dublin, 1939/1943, op. cit.*, note 5, p. 24.
 8. F. H. A. Aalen, 'The Working-Class Housing Movement in Dublin, 1805–1920', in Michael J. Bannon (editor), *The Emergence of Irish Planning, 1880–1920*, (Dublin: Turoe Press, 1985), p. 136.
 9. Donal T. Flood, 'The Decay of Georgian Dublin', *Dublin Historical Record*, Vol. XXVII, No. 3, 1974, p. 98.
10. 'Tenement Houses in Dublin', *The Irish Builder*, Vol. XXXI, 15 December 1889, p. 301.
11. 'Our North Slums', *The Daily Nation*, 15 September 1898, p. 5.
12. *Report of Inquiry Into the Housing of the Working Classes of Dublin, 1939/1943, op. cit.*, note 5, p. 17.
13. Aalen, *op. cit.*, note 8, p. 136.
14. For an analysis of the decay of Georgian architecture, see: Flood, *op. cit.*, note 9, pp 78–100.
15. 'Tenement Fire Hazards', *Irish Press*, 7 October 1936, p. 9.
16. 'Sanitation By-Laws Are Dead Letters', *Irish Press*, 9 October 1936, p. 9.
17. 'Collapse of a House in Dublin', *The Irish Times*, 10 November 1902, p. 1.
18. 'Dublin's Slum Problem', *The Irish Times*, 17 September 1913, p. 1.
19. *Ibid.*, p. 1.
20. *The Irish Builder, op. cit.*, note 10, p. 301.
21. T. W. Dillon, 'Slum Clearance: Past and Future', *Studies*, March 1945, p. 17.
22. *Ibid.*, p. 17.
23. Whitelaw, *op. cit.*, note 2, p. 56.
24. 'Tenement Houses in the City', *The Irish Builder*, Vol. XL, 15 September 1898, p. 141.

25. 'The Tenement System in Dublin', *The Irish Builder*, Vol. XLIII, 1901, p. 678.

26. Joseph V. O'Brien, *'Dear, Dirty Dublin'*, (Berkeley: University of California Press, 1982), p. 152.

27. *Irish Press, op. cit.*, note 16, p. 9.

28. 'Abolish the Slums', *Irish Press*, 9 October 1936, p. 16.

29. 'How the Poor are Housed in Dublin', *The Irish Builder*, Vol. XLI, 1 February 1899, p. 16.

30. 'Voice of the People from and on Slums', *Irish Press*, 12 October 1936, p. 9.

31. *Dublin Civic Survey Report*, (Dublin: Browne and Nolan, 1925), p. 42.

32. 'Overcrowding Worse Even in Dublin Slums', *Irish Press*, 22 October 1936, p. 9.

33. Miss Roney, 'Some Remedies For Overcrowded City Districts', *Journal of Social and Statistical Inquiry Society of Ireland*, Vol. XII, 1907, pp 52–61.

34. *Irish Press, op. cit.*, note 6, p. 9.

35. *Irish Press, op. cit.*, note 16, p. 9.

36. 'The Slum Evil', *The Daily Nation*, 10 September 1898, p. 5.

37. 'Rotarians Accept Doctor's Slum Tour Challenge', *Irish Press*, 13 October 1936, p. 9.

38. 'The Slum Evil', *The Daily Nation*, 3 September 1898, p. 5.

39. Charles A. Cameron, *Reminiscences of Sir Charles A. Cameron*, (Dublin: Hodges, Figgis, Ltd, 1913), p. 169.

40. 'War on the Slums', *Irish Press*, 6 October 1936, p. 14.

41. *Dublin Civic Survey Report, op. cit.*, note 31, p. 43.

42. *Irish Press, op. cit.*, note 40, p. 14.

43. 'Desperate Mother Tells Tragic Story: Doctors Call Help', *Irish Press*, 19 October 1936, p. 9.

44. *Ibid.*, p. 9.

45. Whitelaw, *op. cit.*, note 2, p. 54.

46. Miss Roney, *op cit.*, note 33, p. 52.

47. *Report on Slum Clearance in Dublin—1938*, (Dublin: Citizens' Housing Council, 1938), p. 30.

48. 'Shilling Playground Fund', *Irish Press*, 19 October 1936, p. 9.

49. 'The Dublin Slums', *The Daily Nation*, 13 September 1898, p. 5.

50. Anne V. O'Connor and Susan M. Parkes, *Gladly Learn and Gladly Teach*, (Dublin: Blackwater Press, 1938), p. 71.

51. Charles A. Cameron, *Autobiography of Sir Charles A. Cameron*, (Dublin: Hodges, Figgis & Co., circa 1925), pp 98–99.

52. *Ibid.*, pp 98–99.

53. 'Commissioner to Deal with Slum Problem', *Irish Press*, 13 October 1936, p. 9.

54. *The Daily Nation, op. cit.*, note 11, p. 5.

55. 'The Slum Evil', *The Daily Nation*, 7 September 1898, p. 5.

56. O'Brien, *op. cit.*, note 26, p. 162.

57. *The Daily Nation, op. cit.*, note 38, p. 5.

58. P. L. Dickinson, *The Dublin of Yesterday*, (London: Methuen & Co. Ltd, 1929), p. 175.
59. *Report of Inquiry Into the Housing of the Working Classes of Dublin, op. cit.*, note 7, p. 15.
60. *Irish Press, op. cit.*, note 6, p. 9.
61. 'The Slum Peril', *The Daily Nation*, 8 September 1898, p. 5.
62. Lambert McKenna, 'The Housing Problem in Dublin', *Studies*, Vol. VIII, 1919, p. 279.
63. 'Take Us Out of This Horrible Place', *Irish Press*, 2 October 1936, p. 9.
64. 'Famous Priest Calls for Full Government Powers in Slum Crux', *Irish Press*, 10 October 1936, p. 9.
65. 'Front Line Trenches of the Slums', *Irish Press*, 3 October 1936, p. 9.
66. *Irish Press, op. cit.*, note 30, p. 9.
67. 'Abolish the Slums', *Irish Press*, 10 October 1936, p. 11.
68. 'Slum Conditions Are More Miserable Now Than Three Generations Ago', *Irish Press*, 12 October 1936, p. 9.
69. 'Religious Leaders Attack in Slum War', *Irish Press*, 9 October 1936, p. 9.
70. 'Slums Are Going', *Irish Press*, 5 June 1936, p. 3.
71. *Irish Press, op. cit.*, note 64, p. 9.
72. *Report on Slum Clearance in Dublin—1938, op. cit.*, note 47, pp 3–4.
73. Mary E. Daly, 'Housing Conditions and the Genesis of Housing Reform in Dublin, 1880–1920', in Michael J. Bannon (editor), *The Emergence of Irish Planning, 1880–1920*, (Dublin: Turoe Press, 1985), p. 122.
74. Kearns, *op. cit.*, note 3, p. 25.
75. 'Dublin Artisans' Dwellings', *The Irish Builder*, Vol. XL, 1 February 1898, p. 18.
76. John D. Brewer, *The Royal Irish Constabulary: An Oral History*, (Belfast: Institute of Irish Studies, Queen's University, 1990), p. 14.
77. *Ibid.*, p. 18.
78. Paul Thompson, 'History and the Community', in Willa K. Baum and David K. Dunaway (editors), *Oral History: An Interdisciplinary Anthology*, (Nashville, Tennessee: American Association for State and Local History, 1984), p. xxi.
80. Eilis Brady, *All In! All In!*, (Dublin: Comhairle Bhéaloideas Éireann, University College Dublin, Belfield, 1984), Frontispiece.
81. Mary Maloney, 'Dublin—Before All is Lost', *Evening Press*, 17 May 1980, p. 9.
82. Ronan Sheehan and Brendan Walsh, *The Heart of the City*, (Dingle: Brandon Press, 1988), 186 ff.
83. Thompson, *op. cit.*, note 78, p. 42.
84. Maloney, *op. cit.*, note 81, p. 9.
85. Sherna Gluck, 'What's So Special About Women? Women's Oral History', in Willa K. Baum and David K. Dunaway (editors), *Oral History: An Interdisciplinary Anthology*, (Nashville, Tennessee: American Association for State and Local History, 1984), p. 222.
86. Thompson, *op. cit.*, note 78, p. 40.

CHAPTER 2. *SOCIAL LIFE IN THE TENEMENT COMMUNITIES* (pp 25–60)

1. Martin Dalton, 'Monday is Pawnday', *The Bell*, Vol. XIV, no. 5, 1947, p. 49.
2. Sidney Davies, *Dublin Types*, (Dublin: The Talbot Press Ltd, 1918), p. xviii.
3. Joseph V. O'Brien, *'Dear, Dirty Dublin'*, (Berkeley: University of California Press, 1982), p. 133.
4. 'Baby Hospital Joins Slum War', *Irish Press*, 12 October 1936, p. 9.
5. O'Brien, *op. cit.*, note 3, p. 136.
6. 'Tenement Houses in Dublin', *The Irish Builder*, Vol. XXXI, 15 December 1889, p. 301.
7. O'Brien, *op. cit.*, note 3, p. 136.
8. Raymond James Raymond, 'Pawnbrokers and Pawnbroking in Dublin: 1830–1870', *Dublin Historical Record*, January 1977, p. 15.
9. Charles A. Cameron, *Reminiscences of Sir Charles A. Cameron*, (Dublin: Hodges, Figgis Ltd, 1913), p. 167.
10. Charles A. Cameron, *How the Poor Live*, (Dublin: private printing in 1904 and copy presented to the National Library of Ireland on 8 May 1905), p. 10.
11. Mary E. Daly, *Dublin—The Deposed Capital*, (Cork: The Cork University Press, 1984), p. 266.
12. *Irish Press*, *op. cit.*, note 4, p. 9.
13. 'War on the Slums', *Irish Press*, 6 October 1936, p. 14.
14. *Dublin Explorations and Reflections*, written by an anonymous Englishman, (Dublin: Maunsel & Co. Ltd, 1917), p. 29.
15. Davies, *op. cit.*, note 2, p. xxv.
16. K. F. Purdon, *Dinny on the Doorstep*, (Dublin: Talbot Press, circa 1920), p. 22.
17. Bill Kelly, *Me Darlin' Dublin's Dead & Gone*, (Dublin: Ward River Press, 1983), p. 2.
18. 'Christian Front Advance on Slums', *Irish Press*, 16 October 1936, p. 36.
19. 'Christian Front Leader Enters Slum War', *Irish Press*, 15 October 1936, p. 9.
20. Purdon, *op. cit.*, note 16, p. 23.
21. James Stephens, *The Charwoman's Daughter*, (London: Macmillan and Co. Ltd, 1930).
22. *Fourth Report from the Select Committee of the House of Lords on Intemperance*, Vol. XIV, (London: House of Commons, 1878), p. 332.
23. *Report from the Select Committee on Sale of Intoxicating Liquors on Sunday (Ireland) Bill, 1877*, Vol. XVI, (London: House of Commons, 1877), p. 122.
24. Cameron, *op. cit.*, note 10, p. 14.
25. Cameron, *op. cit.*, note 10, p. 10.
26. *Report from the Select Committee*, *op. cit.*, note 23, p. 73.
27. *Dublin 1913: A Divided City*, (Dublin: The O'Brien Press, 1978), p. 50.
28. T. W. Dillon, 'Slum Clearance: Past and Future', *Studies*, March 1945, p. 13.

Bibliography

Aalen, F. H. A., 'The Working-Class Housing Movement in Dublin, 1850–1920', in Michael J. Bannon (editor), *The Emergence of Irish Planning, 1850–1920*, (Dublin: Turoe Press, 1985), pp 131–153.

Abercrombie, Patrick, Kelly, Sydney and Kelly, Arthur, *Dublin of the Future*, (Dublin: Hodder & Stoughton, 1922).

'Abolish the Slums', *Irish Press*, 9 October 1936, p. 16.

'All Nine Sleep in One Bed', *Irish Press*, 17 October 1936, p. 9.

'The Artisans' Dwelling Act', *The Irish Builder*, Vol. XXII, 15 June 1880, p. 171.

Ashe, F. A., 'Mountjoy Square', *Dublin Historical Record*, III, (1940–41), pp 98–115.

'Baby Hospital Joins Slum War', *Irish Press*, 12 October 1936, p. 9.

Barrington, Sir Jonah, *Historical Memoirs of Ireland*, (Dublin: Henry Colburn, 1833, two volumes).

Baum, Willa K. and Dunaway, David K. (editors), *Oral History: An Interdisciplinary Anthology*, (Nashville, Tennessee: American Association for State and Local History, 1984)

Beckett, J. C., *The Anglo-Irish Tradition*, (London: Faber & Faber, 1976).

'Behind the Rotten Facades in Mountjoy Square', *Hibernia*, 2 October 1980, p. 9.

Boydell, Barra, 'Impressions of Dublin—1934', *Dublin Historical Record*, Vol. XXXVIII, No. 3, 1984, pp 88–103.

Brady, Eilis, *All In! All In!*, (Dublin: Comhairle Bhéaoloideas Éireann, University College, Belfield, 1984).

Brewer, John D., *The Royal Irish Constabulary: An Oral History*, (Belfast: Institute of Irish Studies, Queen's University, 1990).

Butler, R. M., 'Dublin: Past and Present', *Dublin Civic Week Official Handbook*, (Dublin: Civic Week Council, 1927), pp 27–46.

Cameron, Charles A., *Autobiography of Sir Charles A. Cameron*, (Dublin: Hodges, Figgis & Co., circa 1925).

Cameron, Charles A., *How the Poor Live*, (Dublin: private printing in 1904 and copy presented to the National Library of Ireland on 8 May 1905).

Cameron, Charles A., *Reminiscences of Sir Charles A. Cameron*, (Dublin: Hodges, Figgis Ltd, 1913).

Carmichael, Rev. Cannon F. F., *Dublin—A Lecture*, (Dublin: Hodges, Figgis and Company, 1907).

Chesney, Kellow, *The Victorian Underworld*, (London: Temple, Smith Ltd, 1970).

Clarke, Desmond, *Dublin*, (London: B. T. Batsford, 1977).

'Collapse of a House in Dublin', *The Irish Times*, 10 November 1902, p. 1.

Collins, James, *Life in Old Dublin*, (Cork: Tower Books, 1978), reprint of original 1913 edition.

'Commissioner to Deal with Slum Problem', *Irish Press*, 13 October 1936, p. 9.

'The Corporation and Projections in the Streets', *The Irish Builder*, Vol. VI, No. 117, 1864.

Cosgrove, Dillon, *North Dublin City and Environs*, (Dublin: M. H. Gill and Sons Ltd, 1909).

Cowan, P., *Report on Dublin Housing*, (Dublin: Cahill and Co., 1918).

Craig, Maurice, *Dublin 1660–1860*, (Dublin: Allen Figgis Ltd, 1980).

Crosbie, Paddy, *Your Dinner's Poured Out*, (Dublin: O'Brien Press, 1982).

Crudden, Maime, 'Trades and Customs Long Ago', *Ireland's Own*, No. 5, April 1941, p. 6.

Daly, Mary, 'A Tale of Two Cities: 1860–1920', in Art Cosgrove (editor), *Dublin Through the Ages*, (Dublin: College Press, 1988), pp 113–132.

Daly, Mary, *Dublin—The Deposed Capital*, (Cork: Cork University Press, 1984).

Daly, Mary, 'Housing Conditions and the Genesis of Housing Reform in Dublin, 1880–1920', in Michael J. Bannon (editor), *The Emergence of Irish Planning, 1880–1920*, (Dublin: Turoe Press, 1985).

Davies, Sidney, *Dublin Types*, (Dublin: The Talbot Press, 1918).

De Burca, Seamus, 'Growing Up in Dublin', *Dublin Historical Record*, Vol. XXIX, No. 3, 1976, pp 82–97.

'Dereliction Reigns Supreme in Mountjoy Square', *Hibernia*, 5 June 1980, p. 6.

'Desperate Mother Tells Tragic Story: Doctors Call Help', *Irish Press*, 19 October 1936, p. 9.

'Destroy Slums: Keep Your City', *Irish Press*, 15 October 1936, p. 9.

Dickinson, David (editor), *The Gorgeous Mask: Dublin 1700–1850*, (Dublin: Trinity College Workshop, 1987).

Dickinson, Page L., *The Dublin of Yesterday*, (London: Methuen & Co. Ltd, 1929).

Dillon, T. W., 'Slum Clearance: Past and Future', *Studies*, March 1945.

'Dr Harbison on Slum Evil', *Irish Press*, 6 October 1936, p. 14.

Dublin—1913, (Dublin: O'Brien Press—Curriculum Development Unit, no authors cited, 1982).

'Dublin Artisans' Dwellings', *The Irish Builder*, Vol. XL, 1 February 1898, p. 18.

'Dublin City's Falling Down', *City Views*, No. 12, 1980, p. 1.

The Dublin Civic Survey Report, (Dublin: The Dublin Civic Survey Committee, 1925).

Dublin Explorations and Reflections, written by an anonymous Englishman, (Dublin: Maunsel & Co. Ltd, 1917).

The Dublin Housing Inquiry, in Parliamentary Papers, (Dublin), 7 February 1914.

'The Dublin Slums', *The Daily Nation*, 13 September 1898, p. 5.

'Dublin's Slum Problem', *The Irish Times*, 17 September 1913, p. 1.

'The Dublin Sweating System', *The Irish Builder*, Vol. XVIII, No. 380, 1875.

Dunne, John J., *Streets Broad and Narrow*, (Dublin: Helicon Ltd, 1982).

'Dwellings for the Very Poor', *Irish Builder and Engineer*, Vol. XLIV, 1904.

Flood, Donal T., 'The Decay of Georgian Dublin', *Dublin Historical Record*, Vol. XXVII, No. 3, 1974, pp 78–100.

Flood, Donal T., 'Eighteenth Century Dublin', *Dublin Historical Record*, Vol. XXXIII, No. 3, 1980, pp 109–110.

Fourth Report from the Select Committee of the House of Lords on Intemperance, Vol. XIV, (London: House of Commons, 1878).

Gahan, Robert, 'Some Old Street Characters of Dublin', *Dublin Historical Record*, Vol. II, 1939, pp 98–105.

Geoghegan, Joseph A., 'Notes on 18th Century Houses', *Dublin Historical Record*, Vol. VII, No. 2, 1945, pp 41–53.

Gilbert, J. T., *A History of the City of Dublin*, (Dublin: James McGlashan, 1854 one volume and 1859 two volumes).

Gilbert, J. T., *Calendar of Ancient Records of Dublin*, (Dublin: Minutes of the Dublin Corporation, Volume I, 1889).

Gillespie, Elgy, *The Liberties of Dublin*, (Dublin: O'Brien Press, 1973).

Glassie, Henry, *Irish Folk History*, (Philadelphia: University of Pennsylvania Press, 1982).

Grehan, Una, 'Background to Poverty', *Work to Do*, (Dublin: The Mount Street Club, 1945), pp 65–66.

'Heartbreak City', *The Irish Times*, 17 November 1979, p. 13.

Henchy, Deirdre, 'Dublin 80 Years Ago', *Dublin Historical Record*, Vol. XXVI, No. 1, 1972, pp 18–34.

Hoffman, Alice, 'Reliability and Validity in Oral History', in Willa K. Baum and David K. Dunaway (editors), *Oral History: An Interdisciplinary Anthology*, (Nashville, Tennessee: Association for State and Local History, 1984), pp 67–73.

'How the Poor are Housed in Dublin', *The Irish Builder*, Vol. XLI, 1 February 1899, p. 16.

Johnston, Mairin, *Around the Banks of Pimlico*, (Dublin: The Attic Press, 1985).

Kearns, Kevin C., *Dublin Street Life and Lore: An Oral History*, (Dublin: Glendale Press, 1991).

Kearns, Kevin C., *Georgian Dublin: Ireland's Imperilled Architectural Heritage*, (London: David & Charles Ltd, 1983).

Kearns, Kevin C., *Dublin's Vanishing Craftsmen*, (Belfast: Appletree Press, 1986).

Kearns, Kevin C. *Stoneybatter: Dublin's Inner Urban Village*, (Dublin: Glendale Press, 1989).

Keatinge, Edgar F., 'Colourful, Tuneful Dublin', *Dublin Historical Record*, Vol. IX, No. 3, 1947, pp 78–83).

Kelly, Deirdre, *Hands Off Dublin*, (Dublin: O'Brien Press, 1976).

Kennedy, Thomas (editor), *Victorian Dublin*, (Dublin: Albertine Kennedy Publishers, 1980).

Kenny, Carlos, 'The Pawn Ticket Climbs Up the Social Ladder', *Evening Herald*, 28 October 1982, p. 19.

Keogh, Dermot, *The Rise of the Irish Working Class*, (Belfast: Appletree Press, 1982).

Kirwan, Stephen, 'No Mean City', *Work to Do*, (Dublin: The Mount Street Club, 1945), pp 105–106.

Lawson, William, 'Remedies for Overcrowding in the City of Dublin', *Journal of Social and Statistical Inquiry of Ireland*, Vol. XIII, 1909, pp 230–248.

'Let Us Destroy Them Now!', *Irish Press*, 3 October 1936, p. 9.

Little, F. J., 'A Glimpse of Victorian Dublin', *Dublin Historical Record*, Vol. VI, 1943, pp 8–24.

Longford, Christine, *A Biography of Dublin*, (London: Methuen & Co., 1936).

Lynch, Paula, 'A Dublin Street: North Great George's Street', *Dublin Historical Record*, Vol. XXXI, No. 1, 1977, pp 14–21.

Lysaght, Moira, 'A North City Childhood in the Early Century', *Dublin Historical Record*, Vol. XXXVIII, No. 2, 1985, pp 74–87.

Lysaght, Moira, 'My Dublin', *Dublin Historical Record*, Vol. XXX, No. 4, 1977, pp 122–135.

McCourt, Desmond, 'The Use of Oral Tradition in Irish Historical Geography', *Irish Geography*, Vol. VI, No. 4, 1972, pp 394–410.

MacGiolla Phadraig, Brian, 'Dublin One Hundred Years Ago', *Dublin Historical Record*, Vol. XXIII, Nos. 2–3, 1969.

McGovern, Sean, '18th Century and the Present', *The Irish Times*, 22 October 1976, p. 10.

McGrath, Fergal, 'Homes for the People', *Studies*, June 1932, pp 269–282.

McGrath, Raymond, 'Dublin Panorama', *The Bell*, Vol. 2, No. 5, 1942, pp 35–48.

McGregor, John J., *New Picture of Dublin*, (Dublin: A. M. Graham, 1821).

McKenna, Lambert, 'The Housing Problem in Dublin', *Studies*, Vol. VIII, 1919.

MacThomáis, Eamonn, *Gur Cakes and Coal Blocks*, (Dublin: O'Brien Press, 1976).

MacThomáis, Eamonn, *Me Jewel and Darlin' Dublin*, (Dublin: O'Brien Press, 1974).

Maloney, Mary, 'Dublin Before All is Lost', *Evening Press*, 17 May 1980, p. 9.

'Massacre of the Innocents', *Irish Press*, 6 October 1936, p. 9.

Maxwell, Constantia, *Dublin Under the Georges, 1714–1830*, (Dublin: Gill & Macmillan Ltd, 1979).

Messenger, Betty, *Picking Up the Linen Threads*, (Belfast: Blackstaff Press, 1988).

Munck, Ronnie and Rolston, Bill, *Belfast in the Thirties: An Oral History*, (Belfast: Blackstaff Press Ltd, 1987).

Murphy, Frank, 'Dublin Slums in the 1930s', *Dublin Historical Record*, Vol. XXXVII, No. 3, 1984, pp 104–111.

Neary, Bernard, *North of the Liffey*, (Dublin: Lenhar Publications, 1984).

O'Brien, Joseph V., *Dear, Dirty Dublin*, (California: University of California Press, 1982).

O'Donnell, Peadar, 'People and Pawnshops', *The Bell*, Vol. 5, No. 3, 1942, pp 206–208.

O'Rourke, Madeline, 'Urban Decay and Renewal', *Taisce Journal*, Vol. 4, No. 4, 1980, pp 4–5.

O'Suilleabhain, Sean, *A Handbook of Irish Folklore*, (Dublin: The Educational Company of Ireland, 1942).

'Our North Slums', *The Daily Nation*, 15 September 1898, p. 5.

'Overcrowding Worse Even in Dublin Slums', *Irish Press*, 22 October 1936, p. 9.

'Pawnbroking in Ireland', (no author), *Dublin University Magazine*, Vol. XIV, No. LXXXIV, 1839, pp 675–682.

Peter, A., *Dublin Fragments: Social and Historic*, (Dublin: Hodges, Figgis & Co., 1925).

Peter, A., *Sketches of Old Dublin*, (Dublin: Sealy, Bryers and Walker, 1907).

'Plan to Save North Great George's Street', *Evening Press*, 12 December 1980.

Power, Bairbre, 'Farewell to the "Diamond"—With Songs and Sorrow', *Sunday Independent*, 6 September 1981, p. 20.

Purdon, K. F., *Dinny of the Doorstep*, (Dublin: Talbot Press, circa 1920).

Raymond, J. R., 'Pawnbrokers and Pawnbroking in Ireland: 1830–1870', *Dublin Historical Record*, January 1977.

'Religious Leaders Attack in Slum War', *Irish Press*, 9 October 1936, p. 9.

Report of Inquiry Into the Housing of the Working Classes of Dublin, 1939/43, (Dublin: Government Publications Office, 1943).

Report from the Select Committee on Sale of Intoxicating Liquors on Sunday (Ireland) Bill, 1877, Vol. XVI, (London: House of Commons, 1877).

Report on Slum Clearance in Dublin—1938, (Dublin: Citizen's Housing Council, 1938).

Robertson, Manning, 'Old and Future Dublin', *Centenary Conference Handbook*, (Dublin: Royal Institute of Architects of Ireland, 1939), pp 27–46.

Robertson, Olivia, *Dublin Phoenix*, (London: Alden Press, 1957).

Roney, Miss, 'Some Remedies for Overcrowded City Districts', *Journal of Social and Statistical Inquiry Society of Ireland*, Vol. XII, 1907, pp 52–61.

'Rotarians Accept Doctor's Slum Tour Challenge', *Irish Press*, 13 October 1936, p. 9.

'Sanitation By-Laws are Dead Letters', *Irish Press*, 9 October 1936, p. 9.

Scully, Seamus, 'Around Dominick Street', *Dublin Historical Record*, Vol. XXXIII, No. 3, 1980, pp 82–92.

'Slum Conditions are More Miserable Now than Three Generations Ago', *Irish Press*, 12 October 1936, p. 9.

'The Slum Evil', *Irish Press*, 3 September 1898, p. 5.

'The Slum Evil', *The Daily Nation*, 7 September 1898, p. 5.

'Slum Landlordism Exacts A Huge Tax from Human Anguish', *Irish Press*, 8 October 1936, p. 9.

'The Slum Peril', *The Daily Nation*, 8 September 1898, p. 5.

'Slums are Going', *Irish Press*, 5 June 1936, p. 3.

Somerville-Large, Peter, *Dublin*, (London: Hamish Hamilton, 1979).

Stephens, James, *The Charwoman's Daughter*, (London: Macmillan & Co. Ltd, 1930).

St John, Pete, *Jaysus Wept!*, (Dublin: Temple Bar Studios, 1988).

'The Street Life of Old Dublin', *The Lady of the House*, Vol. XXIII, No. 248, 1909.

'Take Us Out of This Horrible Place', *Irish Press*, 2 October 1936, p. 9.

'Tenement Fire Hazards', *Irish Press*, 7 October 1936, p. 9.

'Tenement Houses in the City', *The Irish Builder*, Vol. XL, 15 September 1898, p. 141.

'Tenement Houses in Dublin', *The Irish Builder*, Vol. XLIII, 1901, p. 678.

Thompson, Paul, 'History and Community', in Willa K. Baum and David K. Dunaway (editors), *Oral History: An Interdisciplinary Anthology*, (Nashville, Tennessee: American Association for State and Local History, 1984).

Urbanisation: Problems of Growth and Decay in Dublin, (Dublin: National Economic and Social Council, 1982).

'Voice of the People', *Irish Press*, 17 October 1936, p. 9.

'Voice of the People From and On Slums', *Irish Press*, 12 October 1936, p. 9.

Warburton, J., Whitelaw, J. and Walsh, Robert, *History of the City of Dublin*, (Dublin: T. Cadell and W. Davies, 1818, two volumes).

'War on the Slums', *Irish Press*, 2 October 1936, p. 9.

'War on the Slums', *Irish Press*, 6 October 1936, p. 14.

'What England Left Behind', *The Irish Times*, 18 May 1978, page iv of Special Supplement.

Whitelaw, Rev. James, *An Essay on the Population of Dublin*, (Dublin: Graisberry and Campbell, 1805).

Index

Numbers in bold brackets refer to photograph caption numbers

Aalen, F. H. A., 3, 7
Abusive husbands, 50–51, 63–4, 83, 121–2, 141, 195, 216
Act of Union, 1, 6
Adelaide Hospital, 80, 94
Adultery, 44, 51
Air raid shelters, 110, 126
Alcoholism, 23, 44
Alexandra College, 15
Amiens Street, 72
Anglesea market, **(33)**
Anglo-Irish, **(2)**, 6, 20
Animal gangs, 4, 23, 42, 55–6, 66–8, 77–8, 110–11, 126, 152, 205
Arbour Hill, 112
Arklow, 47
Artane, 84, 129
Artisan's dwellings, 16, 20
Ash Street, **(38)**, 56, 77, 152
Atheism, 43
Aungier Place, **(15)**

Baldoyle, 56, 111
Balladeers, 26, 156
Ballyfermot, 21
Bang-Bang, 150, 156
Banshee, 57–8, 65, 72, 75, 82, 95, 208
Barber shops, 120
Barry, Kevin, 84
Bathing, 61, 138, 193, 203
Beer dealers, 52
Begging, 100
Belvedere Newsboys Club, 203
Benburb Street, 179
Beresford Street, 8
Bewley's, 127
Bicycles, 161

Bishop Street, 94
Black and Tans, **(11)**, 62, 79, 84, 87–8, 114, 145, 167
Blackouts, 126
Blackpitts, **(37)**, **(46)**
Blue Lion (pub), 176
Bolton Street, 54
Bombs, 126–7
Bouncers, 55
Boxing clubs, 100
Braithwaite Street, 6, 131
Brannigan, Jim "Lugs", 56, 101, 111, 124–5, 129, 153
Bread counter, **(54)**
Brides, 47
Bride Street, 123
Bridge Street, 96
British Isles, 38
British soldiers, **(52)**, 114–15, 168, 179, 215
Brothels, 54, 69–70, 85, 98, 130, 210
Browne, Noel, 194
Buckingham Street, 65
Bull Alley, **(20)**
Burials, 89, 102, 161, 183
Burial societies, 101
Butchers, 33, 80, 98, 161–3
Butler, Polly, 69
Byrne, Alfie, 83

Cabra, 21
Cafe Continental, 55, 198
Cameron, Sir Charles, 2, 13, 15, 31, 52
Carman's Hall, 60, 119, 137, 152
Catholic Church, 43, 46, 50
Catholic clergy, 20, 44, 137
Cattle market, 41

Chamber Street, 8, 48, 114
Chancery Lane, (4)
Charity, 30, 112
Charwomen, (25), 30, 49, 180
Chemists, 35–8, 101, 103–5, 136, 139–44, 176–8
Chilblains, 36, 105
Childbirth, 46, 91, 107, 115–16, 122, 206
Children's court, 40, 120
Chimney sweeps, 119
Christ Church Cathedral, 99, 195
Christian Brothers, 84, 89
Christian values, 20, 43, 143
Christmas, 24, 32, 87, 92, 113, 125, 139, 149, 195, 205–6
Churching, 48, 91, 190
Church Street, 8, 18, (18)
Cinemas, 41, 72–3, 80, 152
City quay, 59, 86
Civil War, 87
Clanbrassil Street, 103
Clay pipes, 93, 109, 184
Clicking, 46, 218
Clothing, 34–5, (39), (40), 124, 186
Coffin makers, 94
Cole's Lane, 8, 11, 34, (34), 86
Comhairle Bhéaloideas Éireann, 22
Communism, 43
Community life, 4–5, 24–6, 133–4, 143, 158, 166
Confession, 45, 62, 110, 175, 190
Cooking, 90
Cook Street, 93
Coombe, 19, 53, 116, 121, 131, 144
Cooper, Becky, 69, 78, 85
Cork Street, 8
Cork Street Hospital, 73
Corner men, 26, 41, 56, 204
Corporation Street, 8, 32, 55–6, 58, 64, 90
Courting, 46–9, 109, 129–30, 151, 206, 218
Cozy Kitchen, 55, 198
Croke Park, 145, 161
Cross-stick Alley, (10)
Crumlin, 19, 21
Cumberland Street, (3), 8, 21, 34, 58, (59), 181
Custom House, 79

Daisy market, 34, (61), (62), 63, 139
Daly, Mary, 35
Dance halls, 91
Davies, Sidney, 26, 39, 43

Death, 57–60, 76, 92, 97, 102, 212, 220
Death rates, 14, 35
Delivery boys, (13)
Denmark Street, 140
Dentists, 37, 136, 177, 187
Depression (Great), 43, 97
Devil, 57, 60, 82, 95, 137
Devilment, 39, 83, 99, 109, 149, 181, 201
"Didley clubs", 32, 139, 188
Diet, 13–14, 32, 53, 72, 140, 162, 164, 194, 212
Dillon, T. W., 55
Diphtheria, 35, 73, 212
Dockers, (16), (17), 30, 62, 66, 78, 86, 88, 118
Dockland, (16), 25, 41
Doctors, 36–7
Dolphin's Barn, 132
Domestic disputes, 50, 121, 157
Dominick Street, 7, 17, 35
Donnycarney, 21
Doyle, Jack, 148
Drinking, 42, 44, 51–3, 78, 96, 118, 120–21, 157
Drovers, 30, 39, 86
Drunkenness, 17, 39, 49, 52–3, 125, 132
Dublin Artisans' Dwellings Company, 20–21
Dublin Castle, 15
Dublin City map (1829), (1)
Dublin Corporation, 8, 11, 13, 18, 19, 34, 83, 174
Dublin Folklore Project, 22
Dublin Historical Record, 31
Dublin Housing Inquiry (1913), 11, 15, 18, 21
Dublin Housing Inquiry Report (1914), 21
Dublin Metropolitan Police, 217
Dublin North City Folklore Project, 22
Duff, Frank, 219
Duke of Clarence, 15

Earlsfort Mansions, 15
Earl Street, (7), 159
Economic struggle, 29–32, 44
Employment, (12), (13), 29–30, 75, 118, 129, 132, 165, 174
Engine Alley, (45), 104, 108, 152
Entertainment, 39–42, 150
Eucharistic Congress (1932), (56), 96, 160, 168
Evictions, 4, 29, 66–7, 83, 90, 179, 197

Exorcisms, 57, 137
Factories, 30, 49, 86, 88, 90–91, 168
Family disputes, 49
Family size, 27, 74, 91, 123, 140, 162, 175
"Fancy man", 44, 151, 216
"Fancy woman", 44, 151, 216
Fawcett, Dolly, 55, 158, 198
Fenian Street, 61
Fires, 119
Flower boxes, 80, 195
Foley Street, 55–6, 82
Folklore, 3, 4, 22–4, 57, 200
Folklore Council of Ireland, 22
Folkways, 22
Food preservation, 33, 138, 159
Fortune tellers, 204
Francis Street, 8, 32, 36, 47, 103, 110,
    119, 184
Funerals, 89, 97, 102, 118, 199, 212
Furniture, 27, (43), (44), 71, 88, 90

Gaeltacht, 22–3, 58
Gaiety Theatre, 143
Gambling, 41, (41), 44, 49, 53–4, 96,
    124–5, 150, 157
Gangrene, 177
Gardai/Guards, 40, 43, 51, 54, 55, 56,
    65, 68, 77, 122–6, 153, 154–9, 205
Garden Lane, 119, 135
Gardiner Street, 8, 17, 29, 36, 37, (54),
    56, 81
George's Quay, 90
Georgian Dublin, 1, 6, 21
Ghosts, 57–9, 72
Gin palaces, 53
Glasnevin, 21, 76, 102
Glencree, 84, 99
Glimmer man, 90
Gloucester Diamond, 23, 163
Gloucester Street, 35, 79, 81
Golden Lane, 16, 38, 42, 210
Grafton Street, (8), 41–2, 54, 168
Granby Place, 145
Greek Street, 21, 168
Green Man Pub, 68
Grenville Street, 17
"Grushie", 47
Guards, see Gardai
Guinness's, 30, 52, 85, 93
Gypsy Lee, 204

Hammond Lane, 167
Handywoman, 48, 58, 115, 206

Haunted houses, 57
Haymarket, 179
Healers, 130
Health officers, 13
Health problems, 2, 12–14, 35–9, (50),
    101, 140, 164, 175
Henrietta Place, (5)
Henrietta Street, 7, 158
Henry Street, 30, 41, 46, 218
Herald Boot Fund, 34, 108
Hippo Wine and Squills, 105
Holy hour, 125
Home cures, 37, 80, 203–4
Home life, 4, 27–9, 164
Honey Palace, 77
Hooleys, 4, 59, 66
Horseman's Row, (32)
Horse market, 41
Housing Act (1924), 21
Housing Act (1931), 21
Housing Act (1932), 21
Housing Reform, 20–21
Huckster shops, 29, 101, 138, 151
Hunger, 4, 86, 88, 156
Hungry Thirties, 32
Hygiene, 36

Ice cream vendors, 94, 214
Illnesses, 4, 13, 35–9, 140
Inchicore, 21
Infant mortality, 35, 107
Inns Quay, 12
Irish Christian Front, 43
Irish Republican Army, 84–5, 87, 115,
    197, 215
Italians, 213, 219
Iveagh market, 33, (58), 63, 120, 134,
    186, 212
Iveagh public baths, 28, 99, 101, 138

Jack Maher's Pub, 77
Jacob's Biscuit Factory, 30, 217
Jameson's Whiskey, 30
Jarvey's, 199
Jembo-no-toes, 150, 191
Jewmen, 31–2, 72, 88, 100, 136, 146–9,
    153, 189, 196, 205, 215
Jews, 103, 149
Jeyes Fluid, 156
Johnny-Forty-Coats, 156, 213
John's Lane, 120
Johnston, Mairin, 3

Joyce, James, 2
Kelleher, Archdeacon, 43
Keogh's sack factory, 90–91
Kevin Street, 8, 82, 123
King Street, 205
Kip houses, 54, 85, 210
Knackers, 124

Labour Exchange, 86, 110, 144
Lamplighters, 72, 134
Lamp posts, 81
Landlords, 1, 7, 10–11, 29, 65, 74, 90, 174
Lavender man, 134, 213
Liberties, 8, 23, 25, 28, 36, 40, 52, 54,
    67, 112, 121, 124, 139
Liffey River, 64, 73, 127
Locke Hospital, 86, 178
Lodging houses, 98
London, 68
Looting, 216

McCormack, John, 160
McCormack, Spike, 111
McEvoy, "Paya", 214
McGuinness's Court, (48)
Madams, 55, 69, 85–6, 209–10
Malaria, 104
Malnutrition, 36, 175, 177
Malton's Georgian Dublin, (2)
Mark's Alley, 60
Marlborough Place, 16, 31, 180
Marlborough Street, 52, 54
Marriage, 47–8, 51, 82–3
Marrowbone Lane, (30), 56, 100, 145, 153
Mason's market, (32)
Mater Hospital, 84
Mayro cinema, 72, 152, 181
Meath Street, 36, 111, 128–9, 211
Medicines, 104, 141–2
Men's role, 49–51, 122, 176
Mercer Street, 21
Midwives, 48, 76, 83, 91
Mistear's Medical Hall, 103
Mitching, 84, 115
Moira House, 112
Money-lenders, 31–2, 49, 56, 63, 100,
    136, 152, 189, 214
Money saving, 32, 73, 81, 100, 136, 139
Montgomery Street, 54, 68
Monto, 4, (24), 54–5, 68, 77, 85, 209
Mooney's sack factory, 88
Moore Street, 4, 171
Morals, 43–6

Morgan's Cottages, (28), (47)
Mothers' role, 47–9, 79, 165, 167,
    175–6, 187
Mountjoy prison, 76, 128
Mountjoy Square, 17, 81
Music, 133

Neighbouring custom, 79
Newfoundland Street, 71
New Row, (2)
Newspaper selling, (23), 65, 127–8, 159
New Year's Eve, 114, 186–7, 195
North Earl Street, 33
North Great George's Street, 21, (64),
    (65), (66)
North King Street, 38, 55, 155, 162
North Strand, 73, 126
Nuns, 85

Oblong, May, 69, 85
O'Brien, Joseph, 2, 26, 28
O'Casey, Sean, 2, 140, 143, 155, 176
O'Connell, Sir John, 19
O'Connell Street, (6), 16, 41, 46, 54
Oliver's Alley, 211
Oral historians, 22–3
Oral history, 3, 22–4, 28, 49, 54
Organ grinders, 93, 100, 109, 130,
    213–14
Orphans, 4, 70–71, 107
Outings, 40, 170

Paddy Clare's Pub, 78, 90, 204
Paraffin oil, 93
Parnell Square, 91
Parnell Street, 36, 50, 176
Patrick Street, (19), (36), 119–20
Pauper's grave, 102
Pawnbrokers, 172–3
Pawnshops, (27), 31, 49, 74–5, 83, 129,
    167, 172–3, 188, 196
Pearse Street, 108
Penny banks, 81, 100, 144
Penny dinners, 98
Philanthropic Reform Association, 15
Phoenix Park, 18, 40, 46, 129, 160, 179
Pigeon House, 73
Piggeries, 36
Pig's feet, 80, 90
Pimlico, 100, 149
Plunkett, James, 2
Pneumonia, 35

Poitín, 76
Police clothes, 34, 108, 164, 186
Poor Crèche, 119, 211
Population, 6, 7
Power's Court, **(14)**
Powers Whiskey, 48
Prams, 94, 168
Premarital pregnancy, 45
Press (newspaper), 17–20
Prince of Wales, 16
Prostitution, 4, 23, 51, 54–5, 69–70, 75,
    78, 85, 98, 109, 130, 158, 198,
    209, 218–19
Protestant Row, 137
Protestants, 99, 197, 211
Publicans, 53, 96, 116, 118, 125
Public Health Acts, 12
Pubs, 26, 29, 49–50, 52, 55,-66, 69, 103,
    117–18, 120, 132–3, 157
Pudding Street, 69
Punch Bowl (pub), 59, 89
Purdon, K. F., 25, 39

Quakers, 98
Queens Terrace, 61
Queen Street, 155

Rabbits, 90, 124
Railway Street, 69–70, 74–5
Rats, 80, 98, 109, 135–6, 185, 194
Rebellion, 215–16
Red Biddy, 121, 125
Relieving officer, 99
Religion, 41, 43–6, 143
Report on Slum Clearance (1938), 20
Rialto Hospital, 97
Ringsend, 79
Robbery, 43
Robin Hood, 57
Rooms, **(43)**, **(44)**
Rotunda cinema, 72
Rotunda ward, 12
Royal Barracks, 179
Royal Sanitary Commission (1880), 35
"Ruggy Up", 39, 42
Rutland Street School, 32, 75, 160, 163

St Augustine Street, 106
St Stephen's Green, 54, 140, 219
St Vincent de Paul Society, 30, 49, 62, 74,
    86, 107, 111, 161, 169–70, 182, 187
Sandymount, 40, 82, 170

Sanitation, 12–14, 36, 132, 164, 176
Sanitation Commission, 12
Sanitation officers, 11, 13
Sarsfield Quay, 178
Scabies, 101, 104, 140, 177
Scabs, 88–9
School, **(57)**, 62, 73, 75, 84, 132, 138–9,
    144, 160, 163–6
Scrap collecting, 146, 150
Scutting, 99, 124, 149, 181
Sean McDermott Street, 33, 163
Sexual crimes, 43
Sexual diseases, 86, 178
Sexual morality, 44–6, 107, 109, 188, 190
Shanahan, Phil, 85
Shawls, **(27)**, 80, 98, 119
Shebeens, 52
Shell cocoa, 74
Sheriff Street, 67, 77
Shops, **(9)**, **(26)**, 93, 103
Sick and Indigent Roomkeepers' Society,
    30
Sinn Féin, 83
Sisters of Charity, **(51)**, **(53)**
Sive, Harry, 146–9
"Slop" buckets, 12, 27, 61, 93, 124, 138
Slum clearance, 20–21
Smallpox, 35, 123
Smithfield, 135, 179
Snugs, 78
Social life, 25–60
Social reformers, 14
Social segregation, 16–18, 41, 132, 158,
    166, 181
Soodlum, 213
Soup kitchens, 33
South Dublin Union, 102
Speak-easies, 69
Spirit grocers, 52
Stafford Street, 77
Stealing, 71–2, 76, 84, 99
Stephens, James, 49
Stew kitchens, 33, 98, 175, 182, 186
Stirling Street, **(35)**, **(49)**
Stone bruises, 65, 203
Story-telling, 150–51
Street dealers, 4, 26, 30, 34, **(36)**, 42,
    (52), **(58)**, **(61)**, **(62)**, 117, 119,
    134, 142, 144–5, 170–71, 216–17
Street fighting, 4, 39, 42, 56, 66–7, 77,
    100, 111, 119, 126, 152, 197, 205,
    216–17

Street games, 39, **(48)**, **(49)**, 65, 72, 81, 83–4, 94–5, 109, 120, 124, 179
Street life, 26, 39–40, **(48)**
Street markets, **(32)**, 33, **(33)**, **(34)**
Street singers, **(22)**, 90, 100
Street sweepers, **(12)**
Suicide, 23, 45, 218
Summerhill, 37, 163
Superstitions, 57–60, 95
Swift's Alley, **(29)**
Swimming, 99, 120
Syphilis, 86

Talbot Street, 54, 70
Tara Street public baths, 28, 91, 99
Teachers, 163–6
Tenements, 6–9
    collapses, 18, 61, 192
    congestion, 2, 7, 12–14, 35
    dangers, 8, 140
    distempering, 80, 156
    numbers, 1, 8
    occupants, 2, **(4)**, 8, 10–11
    property values, 1, 7
    room rents, 27, 29, 100
    smells, 155, 164, 174
    structure, 6–8
    types, 131
Thomas Street, 28, 106, 128
Tinkers, 42, 111
Tivoli cinema, 110
Toilets, 2, 12, 61, 124, 186, 193
Toss schools, **(41)**, 53, 124–5, 179, 181, 216
Townsend Street, 8, 21, 67
Tradesmen, 66
Trams, 40, 128
"Trigging" halls, 40, 94, 150
Tuberculosis, 2, 13, 35, 38, 73–4, 91, 96–7, 101, 106, 162, 177
Tuggers, 26, 30, 34, **(60)**, 124, 146–7

Turf, 124, 135, 138, 156, 168
Typhoid, 35

Unemployment, 4, 38, 41, 96
Unwed mothers, 85–6, 107–8, 116, 188, 206, 219

Vandalism, 43
Vermin, 13, 36, 61, 64, 80, 101, 132, 156, 177
Vicar Street, 152
Victorian reformers, 52
Vigilantes, 56, 153
Vikings, 94

Wakes, 4, 58–9, 66, 76, 97, 191, 200–201, 207–8, 213
War veterans, 97, 99–100, 102, 104, 150
Washing day, 28, 79, 93, 106, 114, 121, 182, 193
Weapons, 56, 101, 110, 217
Weddings, 47, 108, 189
Werburgh Street, 110, 127
Westmoreland Street, 128
Whitefriar Street, 97, 99, 218
Whitelaw, Rev. James, 1, 6, 10, 15, 17, 49
Whooping cough, 35
Wicklow, 47
Wife abuse, 22
Wiltshire Regiment, 179
Window washing, 81
Winetavern Street, **(63)**
Wit, 4, 25, 143
Wolfe Tone Street, 72, 169
Women's role, 47–9, 64, 117, 133, 140–41, 170
Woodbines, 95
Wood Quay, 12
World War I, 21

Yeats, W. B., 2
York Street, 29, 53, 117